FEMINISM BESIDE ITSELF

edited by

Diane Elam

and

Robyn Wiegman

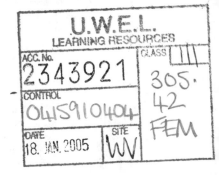
ROUTLEDGE | NEW YORK AND LONDON

Published in 1995 by
Routledge
29 West 35 Street
New York, NY 10001

Published in Great Britain in 1995 by
Routledge
11 New Fetter Lane
London EC4P 4EE

Printed in the United States of America.
Design: David Thorne

Library of Congress Cataloging-in-Publication Data

Feminism beside itself / edited by Diane Elam and Robyn Wiegman.
    p.   cm.
    Includes bibliographical references and index.
    ISBN 0-415-91040-4 (cloth) — ISBN 0-415-91041-2 (pbk.)
    1. Feminism. I. Elam, Diane, 1958– . II. Wiegman, Robyn.

HQ1154.F4435 1995   94-38174
305.42—dc20   CIP

FOR BILL READINGS

Bill Readings' death was in the future when *Feminism Beside Itself* was edited. And although his work does not appear as such here, thinking with Bill made this book possible. Originally, Bill's invisible presence had seemed too personal and too general to mention, but when that presence became a real absence, it could no longer go unremarked. We could have never understood in advance what it would mean for Bill to die in a plane crash on October 31, 1994. It seems all too evident now that responsibility and obligation come at times that can not necessarily be anticipated before an event. The radically contingent future, the future that is absolutely surprising as Levinas would say, includes the possibility of death—the possibility that marks, and remarks, a permanent obligation to the Other that we cannot calculate in advance. In the absence of calculation, what is to come is made possible by thinking together, by placing thought beside itself. And while we will never be able to think with Bill again, we can continue to think beside him, thinking together the futures of feminism.

CONTENTS |

III BESIDES...

ACKNOWLEDGMENTS

We express our appreciation to Marie Lessard who helped us prepare the manuscript. Her patience, expertise, and sense of humor were indispensable. This project would also not have been possible without the generous support and encouragement of Maureen MacGrogan at Routledge. The Society for the Study of Narrative first provided us with a forum in which to think about the issues that resulted in this collection, and we thank them for sharing their panel with us at the 1992 New York MLA meeting. Stephen Melville graciously allowed us to appropriate his title. Finally, the Social Sciences and Humanities Council of Canada (SSHRC) and the Québec Fonds pour la Formation de Chercheurs et l'Aide à la Recherche (FCAR) have provided the financial support that sustained this volume.

A version of Susan Gubar's "Feminist Misogyny: Mary Wollstonecraft and the Paradox of 'It Takes One to Know One,'" appeared in *Feminist Studies* 20, 3 (1994), pp. 453–73, and is reprinted by permission of the publisher. Grateful acknowledgment is made to the Yale Collection of American Literature, Beinecke Rare Book and Manuscript Library for permission to quote from Gertrude Stein's *The Making of Americans* notebooks; to Mountain Press for permission to quote from Irena Klepfisz's "Solitary Act," *A Few Words in the Mother Tongue* (Portland, Oregon: The Eight Mountain Press, 1990), p. 201, © 1982 Irena Klepfisz.

Bloomington and Montréal, 1994

CONTINGENCIES

Diane Elam

and

Robyn Wiegman

If introductory essays to anthologies on feminism carried a surgeon general's warning, this one would read: Subscribing to myths of collaborative editing may be hazardous to your intellectual health. The editors, we must warn you, are divided against themselves. As suggested by the essays gathered here, they find feminist gestures toward unity, collective and otherwise, more politically problematic than they often appear. But by foregrounding disagreement, they make no promise to agree to disagree. The editors want to resist even this attempt at wedded bliss.

Is this simply a reinstatement of radical individualism, a blithe compromise that differences are so difficult one can only stand in antithesis to "we," that utopian collective? After all, anyone struggling with feminism these days knows how inescapable is the need to hone our apprehension of differences, and the editors might speak here not simply of the expanding embrace of gender, race, and class but also of those political and psychic differences that cannot be explained by appealing to either bodies or their social locations. However, in resisting the shelter of "we" as the vehicle for a collective merger, the editors are not heralding a turn to "I." To speak for one's self, at least one of them has been known to say, is no less risky a political enterprise. It is similarly impossible to escape the representational and epistemological complexities of an individual claim to know.

What, then, could these editors do? Their influence on the conceptual and organizational shape of the volume cannot be disputed. They acquired the title *Feminism Beside Itself* to highlight how feminism had become increasingly anxious about itself. They were thinking of the outpouring of essays and books that proposed to assess feminism as a cultural presence in North America in the second half of the twentieth century—titles such as *Around 1981, Changing Subjects, Conflicts in Feminism, Feminism and Institutions, Feminist Theory in Practice and Process, Feminism Without Women, Gendered Domains, Theorizing Black Feminisms.*[1] They debated with one another why feminism's most elaborate and contentious conversation seemed now to be about its own political and philosophical assumptions, omissions, and oppressive complicities. What did it mean that feminism had become so self-referential? Their discussions turned often to historical explanations, to the way that feminism had become a regular feature of both popular and academic discourses. Perhaps it was precisely this public visibility, someone suggested, that undermined feminism's political identity by integrating into commodity culture the discourses of marginality and dissent that feminism had understood itself historically to be.

But how could you define with any kind of assurance what it is that "feminism had understood itself to be"? So much of the critical conversation being cited as symptomatic of the anthology's concern for the self-reflective gesture was a debate over this very question. As literary critics, the editors were quick to enfold this debate into those revolving around representation, which any writing of history necessarily engaged. They thus found themselves asking potential contributors to explore the history of feminism's identity along with the identity of its history. That none of these terms—feminism, history, or identity—existed apart from vigorous debates meant that their project would have to foreground its own participation in the anxieties that it hoped to discuss. For this reason, the editors began to consider not only the ways in which feminism had become self-reflective but also why it might want or need to be self-reflective in the first place. And on this, they initially went their separate ways.

She kept thinking about how feminism liked to imagine itself as the protagonist in an action adventure. Perhaps this was simply the influence of Hollywood movies in the 1980s—too many muscled men trying to reclaim their failed masculinity with slightly pumped up women at their

She kept thinking about what exactly it would mean for feminism to be self-reflective. It seemed to her that this was another way of talking about consciousness: putting feminism beside itself would gesture toward the possibility of a consciousness, a consciousness that could be historical. This may sides pretending to assert themselves. The feminist version has muscles too, of course, but here the heroine is trying to reclaim disciplinary knowledges for women, stalking the institution for the prisoners held hostage in this redundantly familiar, though still officially undeclared, war. Various methodological avenues of escape are tried and then, finally, the triumphant ending: feminism—you guessed it—gets to liberate women.

Can feminism afford to be skeptical toward such an ending? Or perhaps more pointedly, why is she? After all, in the academy generally, feminism has amassed a great deal of legitimacy. At various colleges and universities, for instance, Women's Studies has been transformed from a fledgling program to a tenure-lined department, and its emphasis on feminist knowledge has now extended into every discipline in the humanities and social sciences. In English, history, and sociology in particular, a familiarity with feminist scholarship is often an established part of doctoral competency, and courses at the undergraduate level now routinely take up issues raised by the study of women and gender. These institutional incursions, barely imaginable in the late sixties, place Women's Studies and feminist knowledge more generally at the center of interdisciplinary study and signify the pivotal nature of feminist intellectual work in the academy. From one perspective, such transformations indicate a femi-

echo the consciousness-raising politics that have been, and sometimes continue to be, of importance to feminism. But it also tries to go beyond that, holding open historical difference as constitutive of the possibility of thought. This is not a strictly Hegelian or Marxist claim. It means, more generally, that feminism cannot take itself to be one thing, if it is to be responsible *both* to its history and to its contemporary critical role.

Placing feminism beside itself, then, is a way of facing the challenge of what Michel Foucault called "critical ontology", a "permanent critique of our historical era."[2] In this sense, critique is a transgressive working at the frontiers of what appears to us as the very condition of our being; it is, in other terms, a "limit-attitude." Thus, to return to the volume's title once again, feminism's limit-attitude would be neither purely inside itself nor outside itself, but more properly beside itself. Neither fully of the past nor of the present, feminism's consciousness of itself would be contingent: It would be by no means clear what could be assumed in a discussion of the temporality or historicity of feminism.

For *Feminism Beside Itself* this also means, as Foucault would have it, that "the historical ontology of ourselves must turn away from all projects that claim to be global or radical."[3] So while the essays collected here are reflections on the consciousness of feminism and feminism's consciousness of itself, they in no way claim to

nism no longer locked in deadly battle with the institution. Territory, one
might say, has been conceded. And
yet, what action or adventure is there
beyond the end of such a story? If
feminism now makes its "home" in
the institution, can we continue to
claim its identity as bound to narratives that liberate women from the
academy's oppressive constraints? Or
has feminism now become in some
sense *other* to itself? Other, that is, to
this particularly powerful and propelling version of "its self"?

It's a rhetorical question, of course,
and the editor is using it to establish
some historical distinctions about the
way feminism has identified itself in
relation to the institution. For feminism can no longer simply posit itself
as the heroic interloper into the institution's patriarchal business as usual.
As an intellectual commodity, feminism demands her own institutional
wage. She—this is feminism now—
claims a reproductive legitimacy,
engaging in the practices of institutional generation, begetting scholars,
journals, book series, new curricula,
jobs, even job seekers. She takes her
seat at the table. In private, she wor-
ries over the ultimate price of this
meal. She is, let's say it, beside herself,
the watcher and the watched. She's
suspicious about her own institutional manners, her increasingly fine cut
cultivations. She fears that her political identity might be at stake.

But how? Has feminism now
become the tenured (re)productive

be entirely representative of that consciousness. In this regard, it seems
significant that many of the authors
whose work appears in this volume
now make their homes in North
American universities, often in literature departments. All of the essays
engage in one way or another with
Western feminisms, and English is the
prominent, although by no means
exclusive, language. These biases call
attention to the limitations imposed on
any collection of essays such as this
one. It should be said, then, that while
the essays in this collection all take
account of feminism's history, they do
not collectively constitute a history of
feminism. And likewise, while they are
all reflecting on feminism, they do not
supply feminism with either an authentic or complete consciousness of
itself.

More precisely, then, *Feminism
Beside Itself* does not constitute a
coherent project, and this introduction
should not be read as any kind of manifesto in the modernist sense of the
word—as signaling a break and a new
beginning grounded on abstract principles. Significantly, many of those dis-
enchanted with feminism tend, in fact,
to accept the description of it as an
Enlightenment project, which simply
takes its place alongside other
attempts to realize the potentiality
of mankind. Here feminism is
understood as a grand narrative of
liberation or emancipation, offering, as
it were, to release woman from the
bonds of her self-incurred immaturity.

wife, too caught up in institutional homesteading to reprise her renegade part? Or is she the institution's mistress, an increasingly well kept but finally excessive delight? Perhaps she is simply in feminine drag, performing her difference without succumbing to any romantic plot? Can she be *in* the institution but not *of* it—a member who subverts all the membership rules? Or does admission transform her too? These questions go to the heart, if you will, of feminism's political identity and identifications, demonstrating the anxieties about resistance and complicity, marginality and centrality, that compel her skepticism toward herself.

The contemporary currency of these questions arises not simply from the way feminism has reshaped institutional knowledges but from the impact that various critical discourses have had on feminism itself. As others before her have done, the editor organizes these discourses into two broad groups: postmodern conversations about power on the one hand, and feminist debates about differences among women on the other.[4] Linked together or cast at odds to one another, these conversations have challenged some of the most sacrosanct critical assumptions of contemporary feminism. Take, for instance, patriarchy as a critical concept. At one time, patriarchy was used rather unquestionably to describe the social totality of women's oppression, serving as the villain

Although feminism offers some critique of Enlightenment liberation—insofar as feminism cancels the Enlightenment's project of realizing universal *man* by refusing the elision of the specificity of woman that this universality implies—nonetheless, feminism can be understood to perform such a critique because feminism itself is a coherent project in the Enlightenment sense.

From this perspective, feminism may seem either to have been a bad project (the political Right) or to have been a project whose essential task has now been achieved and about which we no longer need to be preoccupied (the postfeminists). Taking its distance from either of these alternatives, one of the thoughts animating this anthology is that the strategic value of thinking of feminism solely in terms of a project is no longer self-evident and may even be damaging. It may be necessary to re-examine the terms in which we want to describe the work that feminism has to do, for while it is apparent that there is still a great deal of work to be done, it is by no means evident that the Enlightenment provides the only language in which that work can be discussed.

For this reason, the "historical-critical attitude" expressed in this volume is perhaps an experimental one, to borrow from Foucault once again.[5] The experiment here takes the form of an introduction that tries to do something other than summarize the volume's contents, editors who disin feminism's story of its necessary quest to liberate women. Under "patriarchy," women were categorical victims and men their undifferentiated coercive oppressors. But recent thinking on power and difference foreground both patriarchy's noncoercive forms and the importance of looking at other kinds of hierarchies (race, class, sexuality) to explain the complexities of women's social position. The category of "woman" has thus been differentiated from within feminism, and patriarchy as a concept has lost its totalizing edge.

For a feminism that has conceived of its political mission in the academy (and elsewhere) as a confrontation with "man," this reduction of patriarchy's explanatory function has seemed to threaten feminism's own political identity. More critical perhaps is the simultaneous demonstration that "women" as a category cannot be defined on the basis of shared political or social inferiorities. It is this threat—of a political identity no longer coterminous with the intellectual project of feminist knowledge—that compels this editor to ask various feminist scholars to put feminism beside itself in order to explore the shape and meaning of feminism's referential interest in itself.

agree with one another, and essays that likewise make incommensurate arguments so that their coming together takes on the quality of an experiment. As such, this anthology is open to criticism for lacking the kind of coherence and homogeneity characteristic of the proceedings of a Stalinist party congress. But the risk seems worth it—perhaps even necessary—if feminism is to keep its political force.

All of this is not to say, however, that this anthology has no structure whatsoever, even if it does suggest an awareness that the structure offered is arbitrary at best. The editors have organized the essays into three sections: *Beside Itself*; *Against Itself*; *Besides....* It would be misleading to assume, however, that the division into three sections suggests some kind of dialectical progression, in which the thesis of beside itself is negated by the antithesis of against, producing in the end a synthesis that is more than the sum of the parts. Instead, the point of the three sections is simply this: to call attention to a strong emphasis that runs throughout a particular set of essays and, at the same time, to make possible other, more thematic readings of the essays.

The first section, *Beside Itself*, introduces issues that re-surface throughout the volume, articulating feminism's historical concerns by asking questions about feminism as a history. How has this history been written? By and for whom? Under what assumptions about history, narrative, feminism, and political purpose? To raise such issues is in some sense to put feminism *Against Itself*. As a result, the second section explores more fully how feminism is in conflict with itself. These essays look at the terms by which feminism has constituted itself in order to define how these terms have often undermined feminism's most cherished political goals and beliefs. For instance, in viewing itself as an antagonist to patriarchy, feminism has often assumed that it could never participate in the oppression of women. However, to be "for women" can also mean being "against women," not only because the category of "women" is often cast in the specificities of race, class, and sexual privileges, but also because women are often themselves vigorous protectors of patriarchal power.

To differing degrees, the essays in the first two sections of the volume demonstrate that feminism actually never stands alone but is always *Besides...* something else. It stands with and in other(s), even when that other turns out to be within itself. Essays in the final section explore a few of the possibilities of what this something might be, turning in particular to issues of nationalism, personal narrative, and contemporary popular culture. By framing the question of feminism through a variety of disparate issues, the essays collected here do not move the volume toward any simple sense of closure. Rather, they demonstrate the impossibility of a comprehensive or completely representative feminism. As such, the editors offer a collection of essays that neither point in the same direction nor necessarily agree with one another. By questioning the unity and identity of feminism, we do not relinquish its political force but contingently agree that feminism's unknowability is its very strength.

NOTES |

1   Jane Gallop, *Around 1981* (New York and London: Routledge, 1992); *Changing Subjects*, ed. Gayle Green and Coppélia Kahn (London and New York: Routledge, 1993); *Conflicts in Feminism*, ed. Marianne Hirsch and Evelyn Fox Keller (New York and London: Routledge, 1990); *Feminism and Institutions*, ed. Linda Kauffman (Oxford: Blackwell, 1989); *Feminist Theory in Practice and Process*, ed. Micheline R. Malson, Jean F. O'Barr, Sarah Westphal Wihl and Mary Wyer (Chicago: University of Chicago Press, 1989); Tania Modleski, *Feminism Without Women* (New York and London: Routledge, 1991); *Gendered Domains*, ed. Dorothy O. Helly and Susan M. Reverby (Ithaca: Cornell University Press, 1992); and *Theorizing Black Feminisms*, ed. Stanlie M. James and Abena P. A. Busia (New York and London: Routledge, 1993). This list is only meant to give a brief sense of the proliferation of texts assessing feminism and should not be understood as a complete bibliographical survey.

2   Michel Foucault, "What Is Enlightenment?", tr. Catherine Porter, *The Foucault Reader*, ed. Paul Rabinow (New York: Pantheon Books, 1984), p. 42.

3   Foucault, "What Is Enlightenment?", p. 46.

4   See especially Jane Flax, "The End of Innocence," *Feminists Theorize the Political*, ed. Judith Butler and Joan Scott (New York and London: Routledge, 1992); Nancie Caraway, *Segregated Sisterhood* (Knoxville: University of Tennessee Press, 1991); and Linda J. Nicholson, "Introduction," *Feminism/Postmodernism*, ed. Linda J. Nicholson (New York and London: Routledge, 1990).

5   Foucault, "What Is Enlightenment?", p. 46.

I

BESIDE ITSELF

...women have always been making history, living it and shaping it.

—Gerda Lerner

The dream of a "total history" corroborating the historian's own desire for mastery of a documentary repertoire and furnishing the reader with a vicarious sense of—or perhaps a project for—control in a world out of joint has of course been a lodestar of historiography.

—Dominick LaCapra

With these stories of ours
      we can escape most anything,
with these stories we will survive.

—Leslie Marmon Silko

What has surfaced is something different from the unitary, closed, evolutionary narratives of historiography as we have traditionally known it:... we now get the histories (in the plural) of the losers as well as the winners, of the regional (and colonial) as well as the centrist, of the unsung many as well as the much sung few, and I might add, of women as well as men.

—Linda Hutcheon[1]

1

MAKING HISTORY

Reflections on Feminism, Narrative, and Desire

Susan Stanford Friedman

My reflections begin with the contradictory desires within contemporary American feminism revolving around the question of history, particularly what is involved when feminists write histories of feminism. On the one hand, a pressing urgency to reclaim and hold on to a newly reconstituted history of women has fueled the development of the field of women's history, as well as the archaeological, archival, and oral history activities of feminists in other areas of women's studies outside the discipline of history, inside and outside the academy. On the other hand, there has been a palpable anxiety within the feminist movement about the possibility that our activities as feminists—including the productions of our own history—run the risk of repeating the same patterns of thought and action that excluded, distorted, muted, or erased women from the master narratives of history in the first place. The first impulse is outer-directed; it has channeled phenomenal energy into the interrelated projects of the deformation of existing history and reformation of new histories of women, examining the place of gender in all cultural formations as they change over time. The second impulse is inner-directed and has applied the brakes to the new enthusiasms and in sober self-reflexivity insisted on problematizing the project of feminist history writing. With some exceptions, the reflexive impulse has found expression not so much in the field of women's history itself as in the discourses of feminist theory and activism. Feminism, particularly as it attempts to construct the stories of its own production, is caught between the desire to act and the resistance to action that threatens to reproduce what poststructuralists, like Luce Irigaray, call the economy of the same.

In this essay, I intend to explore the political necessity and creative possibilities of both the outer- and inner-directed activities. As well, I hope to show how the insight of one involves a blindness to the insight of the other, how ultimately both are necessary to the larger agenda of feminists "making history." I will first examine the underlying epistemological issues and then defend both the problematization of feminist history writing and the political necessity of this enterprise. Additionally, I will discuss how the competing needs to narrate and problematize the history of feminism reflect the desire for empowerment and fear of the will-to-power, the one affirming women's agency, the other muting it. Finally, I will suggest that feminists can be engaged in a dialogic, not monologic, project of writing feminist histories—in the plural—in which the politics of competing histories need not paralyze the need to tell stories about feminism.

FEMINIST EPISTEMOLOGIES AND MAKING HISTORY

The contradictory desires of feminists "making history" reflect the epistemological issues embedded in the double reference of the term *history* itself: first, to history as the past; and second, to history as the story of the past. The first meaning of history—what has happened—posits a base reality whose totality can never be fully reconstituted. The second meaning of history—the narrative of what has happened—foregrounds the role of the narrator of past events and consequently the nature of narrative as a mode of knowing that selects, organizes, orders, interprets, and allegorizes.[2] These two dimensions of *history*, in turn, reflect the double reference in my title, "making history." The feminist desire to "make history" entangles the desire to effect significant and lasting change with the desire to be the historian of change. As a heuristic activity, history writing orders the past in relation to the needs of the present and future. The narrative act of assigning meaning to the past potentially intervenes in the present and future construction of history. For feminists, this means that writing the history of feminism functions as an act in the present that can (depending on its influence) contribute to the shape of feminism's future.[3]

The heuristic and interventionist dimension of history writing—historiography as an act in the present on behalf of the future—raises the question of epistemology, central to understanding the inner-and outer-directed energies of feminist history writing, whether inside or outside the academy, whether within the field of women's history or more broadly within women's studies in general. For those working out of a positivist epistemology, the goal of history writing is to construct an objective account of the past based on thorough immersion in the empirical data and an unbiased assemblage of that data into an accurate sequence. The positivist belief in history writing as the production of objective truth may no longer be very prevalent in its purest form, although it once served as the philosophical bases for the formation of history as a discipline in the nineteenth and early twentieth centuries. However, the notion of history writing as the best possible reconstruction of the past—in a seamless narrative by an omniscient, invisible narrator—nonetheless continues to underwrite many projects, including feminist ones.[4] Within this framework, the heuristic and interventionist dimension of history writing tends to be unacknowledged or overtly denied, and thus covertly operative.

For those working out of a subjectivist epistemology, the Real of history is knowable only through its written or oral textualizations.[5] The past is therefore triply mediated—first, through the mediations of those texts, which are themselves reconstructions of what "really" happened; second, through the fragmentary and partial survival of those textualizations which are dependent upon the politics of documentation and the luck, skill, and persistence of the historian-as-detective who must locate them; and third, through the interpretive, meaning-making gaze of the historian. From this perspective, the excellence of history writing depends not upon the level of objectivity but rather upon the cogency of interpretation. And interpretation, as Hayden White and Dominick LaCapra preeminently theorize, introduces the mediations of language: the meaning-making of tropes, rhetoric, and narrative. Within the subjectivist epistemology, this dimension of historical discourse is often openly acknowledged as a source of speculation or even commitment.[6]

Both epistemologies have been at work in women's studies, as feminists from a variety of fields engage in "making history"—in the writing about feminism's past and the performance of feminism's present and future. Some feminists work within a positivist framework, emphasizing the "truth" of what has been recovered; others function within a subjectivist framework, foregrounding the interpretive dimension of their narratives; and still others combine aspects of each epistemology. This diversity of historiographic assumption reflects, I believe, the contradictions built into the foundations of women's studies itself, contradictions that continue to underlie and permeate most work in the field, whether acknowledged or not. On the one hand, women's studies developed out of the need to counter hegemonic discourses about women that ignored, distorted, or trivialized women's history, experience, and potential. Women's studies consequently formulated compensatory and oppositional histories that told the "truth" about women—whether it was about women's status in the so-called Renaissance, the production of women's writing in the nineteenth century, or the sexual brutalization of black women slaves. This search to discover the "truth" of women's history that could shatter the "myths" and "lies" about women in the standard histories operates out of a positivist epistemology that assumes that the truth of history is objectively knowable.

On the other hand, the early insistence in women's studies that hegemonic knowledge was produced out of and in the service of androcentrism necessitated a subjectivist epistemology that insisted on all knowledge as value-based, emerging from a given perspective or standpoint. No knowledge is value-free, many feminists claimed, including feminist knowledge. Thomas Kuhn's *The Structure of Scientific Revolutions* (1962) was widely used to promote women's studies as a "paradigm shift" of dramatic and revolutionary proportions within the institutions of knowledge.[7] The goal of writing history within this epistemological framework was not to discover the true history, but rather to construct the story of women's experience out of a feminist paradigm. Feminist histories countered hegemonic histories not with the objective truth, but with stories produced from a feminist perspective.[8]

Both feminist epistemologies developed out of and have continued currency because of the urgently felt *political* agenda of women's studies: to engage in the deformation of phallocentric history and the reformation of histories that focus on or integrate women's experience and the issue of gender. Why political? Because what we know of the past shapes what becomes possible in the future. Because the repositories of human knowledge constitute the building blocks of the symbolic order. Because knowledge is power, ever more increasingly so in what is coming to be called the Information Age. As much as my own work and sympathies operate primarily out of the subjectivist epistemology, I believe that both epistemologies are necessary to the enterprise as moderating influences on the potential excesses of each. On the one hand, the positivist epistemology can lead toward fundamentalist assertions of truth that obscure the interpretive perspectives of historical narrative. On the other hand, the subjectivist epistemology can lead toward the paralysis of complete relativism in which the Real of history vanishes into the play of story and discourse.[9]

It would be easy, but misleading, to align the positivist epistemology with the outer-directed, action oriented desire to "make history" and the subjectivist epistemology with the inner-directed, self-reflexive problematizing of feminist history writing. Certainly, the anxiety about the potential for replicating the master narratives of hegemonic discourse assumes the subjectivist model and foregrounds the role of the narrator in an interpretive ordering of the past. But to associate feminist history writing (whether in women's history or other fields of women's studies) with positivism would obscure the diversity of epistemologies present in these histories—some of which are positivist, some subjectivist, and some a combination, with the contradictory presence of both epistemologies underlying the endeavor as a whole. Moreover, it would too simply replicate the dismissive gesture that consigns everything but the act of poststructuralist problematizing to a bankrupt and naive humanism.

Instead, the epistemologies underlying feminism should aim for a negotiation between objectivism and subjectivism, between the search for the Real and a recognition that all access to the Real is mediated through discourse. As LaCapra writes, "extreme documentary objectivism and relativistic subjectivism do not constitute genuine alternatives. They are mutually supportive parts of the same larger complex."[10] He insists that his critique of positivist historiography does not mean that he abandons the empirical. He argues instead for a "dialogic and mutually provocative" relation between the empirical and the rhetorical as equally necessary parts of history writing.[11]

This interplay encompasses the kind of dialogue Shoshana Felman and Dori Laub advocate in *Testimony: Crises of Witnessing in Literature, Psychoanalysis, and History*.[12] They use the Holocaust as touchstone for theorizing a kind of history writing that acknowledges history as a form of representation and a testimony to the Real. On the one hand, history writing bears witness to "the encounter with the real" (xvi). On the other hand, this Real is not transparently present, but is rather "reinscribed, translated, radically rethought and fundamentally worked over by the text" of history (xv). The "empirical context," they argue, "needs not just to be *known*, but to be *read*" (xv). The Real to which we have access only through texts of various kinds must be read with an eye to the processes of textualization and interpretation. If the Real of the past is always mediated, then history writing should not only "encounter the real" but also reflect upon those forms of mediation.

IN DEFENSE OF PROBLEMATIZING (FEMINIST) HISTORY

Recognizing the contradictory and mutually interdependent epistemologies underlying women's studies introduces the necessity of problematizing feminist history writing. But how does the need to problematize go beyond the issue of competing epistemologies and move towards the politics of writing feminist history, especially the history of feminism? And what models for problematization have been developing within feminism in the past twenty years?

To answer the first question, I want to move outside the discipline of women's history proper to an example of less rigorous feminist history writing published in *The New Republic* in October, 1992: "Sister Soldiers" by Christina Hoff Sommers, a professor of philosophy at Clark University and the author of the heavily marketed, sensationalist *Who Stole Feminism?*[13] Billed as "Live from a Women's Studies Conference," this article narrates a partial "history" of the 1992 National Women's Studies Association convention in Austin, Texas by way of introducing a brief history of academic feminism in the United States. Sommers writes overtly from the perspective of what she calls "an older 'First Wave' kind of feminism whose main goal is equity" (30). As a feminist, she engages in a historiographic project whose covert agenda is to attack what she calls the newer "'Second Wave' gynocentric feminism, which since the early '70s has taken center stage in the universities" (33). Most academic feminists would recognize her article—in spite of its self-identified feminism—as consistent with the phenomenon of current attacks on women's studies coming from such media heroes as Charles Sykes[14] and Dinesh D'Souza and organizations like the National Association of Scholars. Sommers uses historiographic discourse—first, of the NWSA convention, then of the development of women's studies—to condemn the project of contemporary academic feminism. Her stories of the past represent her attempt to intervene in the present—to halt the march of what she opposes within feminism.

Sommers' diachronic discourse is easily unveiled as synchronic discourse in drag. Her narratives of the NWSA convention and the development of women's studies collapse quickly into figural representations of a demonized feminism. She practices a kind of metonymic historiography in which the telling anecdote of feminist excess stands in for the multi-faceted phenomenon of academic feminism. Substituting a part for the whole, she characterizes all women's studies through narrative recitation of single incidents that determine guilt by association. This metonymic smear begins with the title, "Sister Soldiers," which foreshadows her attack in the article on "gynocentric feminism" by echoing the name of the Afrocentric rap singer Sister Soljah, from whom candidate Bill

Clinton distanced himself during his presidential campaign. The implication of this allusion is that just as the liberal Clinton was right to separate himself from black ethnocentrism, as liberal feminist she is correct to distance herself from a gynocentric feminism that promotes "sisterhood." Whatever one thinks of Sister Soljah, Sommers' analogic figuration of academic feminism as Afrocentrism parallels the evocation of racist paranoia in the Willie Horton ad during the Bush–Dukakis presidential race in 1988.[15]

Sommers establishes her authority as historian by amassing narrative detail about the conference for the first third of the article. She carefully sets the scene of the conference and narrates its opening events, detailing Eleanor Smeal's late arrival for the initial address and the panelists who filled in until she came: "To pass the time, we were introduced to an array of panelists.... Still no Smeal. A panelist named Angela took the floor.... A weary Eleanor Smeal finally arrived..." (30). This narrative detail functions to produce what Roland Barthes calls the "reality effect," that is, the effect of reality, of objective history achieved through the piling up of "facts."[16] Detail establishes verisimilitude, which then lends credibility to her point of view, which seems to emerge objectively out of the data. She reports, for example, that "Louise and I were relieved when the proceedings were interrupted by a coffee break. Half-and-Half was available—though perhaps not for long. The eco-feminist caucus has been pushing to eliminate all meat, fish, eggs, and dairy products at NWSA events" (30). Sommers' manipulation of the reality effect in her narrative of the conference establishes her credibility for her accounts of feminist conferences and classrooms around the country. Metonymies of feminism appear throughout the rest of the article as characterizations of the norm: the women's studies program directors who joined hands in a "healing circle" and "assumed the posture of trees experiencing rootedness and tranquility"; the introductory women's studies course at Rutgers that requires students to perform "some 'outrageous' and 'liberating' act outside of class" and then share feelings about it in class; the "heady claim" by Elizabeth Minnich that "'What we are doing is comparable to Copernicus shattering our geo-centricity.... We are shattering andro-centricity'" (31–32). "Ouchings and mass therapy," she concludes, "are more the norm than the exception in academic feminism" (30).

Operating out of a positivist feminist epistemology, I could respond to Sommers' attack by saying that her history is "not true," that she is a "bad historian," and then I could offer counter-stories that are more accurate and have greater objective truth value. I could demonstrate that she exhibits no skill in handling her data, in assessing and demonstrating with evidence just how characteristic her anecdotes are of academic feminism in all its complexity and multiple formations. I might ask, for example, why she left out the massively influential presence of feminist scholars in professional associations and their conferences—such as the Modern Language Association, American Historical Association, American Psychological Association, American Political Science Association, and so forth. Shouldn't she have examined feminist activities at conferences within the traditional disciplines as well as at NWSA? It is not difficult to show, especially in the humanities, that academic feminism has permeated and altered (if not transformed) many traditional disciplines. But for historically specific reasons having to do with the formation of academic feminism in the United States, the place to see such change in process is not primarily NWSA conferences, but rather discipline-based feminist conferences, journals, and research, much of which is influenced by interdisciplinary feminist theory and knowledge, while at the same time retaining a methodological and substantive "home-base" in a pre-existing discipline.

From a subjectivist feminist standpoint, I might counter Sommers' history by critiquing the bias that shapes her narrative at every point—her claim to greater objectivity than the "Second Wave"; her metonymic substitutions of the part for the whole; her stagist designation of "First Wave" and "Second Wave" feminism, where the second is represented as a degeneration and betrayal of the first; her invocation not only of racial paranoia in the title but also more generally of conspiracy theories rooted historically in anti-Semitic discourse ("These women run the largest growth area in the academy..."; "They are disproportionately represented..."; "They are quietly engaged in hundreds of well-funded projects..." [30]). Indeed, the disdain she exhibits for academic feminism seems to operate on a binary of pure/impure in which she laments the contamination of reasonable feminism by the destructive distortions of irrational excess. Both positivist and subjectivist critiques of Sommers have merit: Sommers' history is both wildly inaccurate and anything but value-free.

Sommers' "Sister Soldiers" is easy to critique as historical discourse. However, her self-identification as feminist should warn us that the critical gaze, which we so willingly turn upon an attacker of academic feminism, we must also be ready to turn upon the historical discourse of its defenders. The danger of an exclusively positivist response to Sommers is that in posing a counter "truth," such a critique can easily remain blind to its own potential use of historiographic discourse as a power play in current feminist debates. The need for reflective problematizations suggests that we should be aware of the ways in which feminist histories can narrativize the past of feminism such that other feminist histories are discounted or discredited. Sommers' "history" of academic feminism does more than provide an occasion for epistemological analysis. It also reminds us that at any given moment in the history of feminism there are many feminists competing to tell the history of feminism and shaping their histories in relation to the politics of feminism's present and future. In general historiographic terms,

James C. Scott raises this question of the politics of competing histories in "History According to Winners and Losers," using the different histories that landed and landless peasants tell about the "facts" of Malaysia's "green revolution," the system of double cropping introduced in 1972.[17] He likens the histories of "winners" and "losers" in the green revolution to two groups of carpenters building competing edifices. Imagining them each to have comparable skills, training, and material, he notes that the houses they build "are, to mix metaphors, different stories told in the same language" (169). "Events," he writes, "are not self-explanatory… they do not speak for themselves" (167). The events are similar but the meaning given those events differs markedly. The narratives of those who benefited and those who lost out in the green revolution reflect their different class positions.

Jeannine DeLombard makes the same general point about feminist history in her review of Elizabeth Lapovsky Kennedy's *Boots of Leather, Slippers of Gold*[18]:

> History is written by the winners. If any winners have emerged from the lesbian community's internal struggle for self-representation, they are the predominantly white, well-educated lesbian feminists who have had access to the bullhorn and the media, including the publishing houses, since the late 1960s.
>
> Their depiction of 20th-century lesbian life before… 1969 as a gay Dark Ages is a familiar one in which lesbians eked out a dreary existence in seedy bars, their internalized homophobia and sexism betrayed by their heavy drinking, barroom brawls and butch-femme role playing.[19]

DeLombard praises *Boots of Leather, Slippers of Gold* for eluding that hegemonic lesbian narrative to construct a different history of Buffalo's lesbian community before the gay and lesbian rights movements of the 1970s.

Scott's and DeLombard's discussion of the competing histories of winners and losers raises a further question about the politics of representation. What access do winners and losers have to the construction of written histories that maintain visibility on the cultural terrain? Who controls the means for the production, reception, and dissemination of history? Scott and DeLombard both suggest that the history that gains currency in the economy of ideas belongs to the "winners." It's not that the "losers" don't create their own historical narratives, but rather that marginalized, "muted," or subaltern people often produce histories that are ephemeral—in oral form, undocumented, unpreserved, difficult to locate, or hard for an "outsider" to interpret.[20]

It has surely been a cornerstone of feminist critique that hegemonic histories tell the stories of "winners," namely, of powerful men and masculinist ideas. But shouldn't we also as feminists turn a self-reflective eye upon ourselves to recognize that feminist histories of feminism are not exempt from the politics of historiography? Feminism too has its "winners" and "losers," its stratifications and contested terrains. Whose story of feminism gains currency? What interests does it serve? Whose story is lost, marginalized? Why? The same questions feminists have asked of masculinist history about the erasure and distortion of women's lives must be put to feminist histories.

But *how* should such questions be framed? From what perspectives have such feminist problematizations been formulated? In the United States, the first feminists to ask such questions were those who felt marginalized within the feminist movement and women's studies by white, middle-class, heterosexual feminists. Women of color, lesbian women, and Jewish women in particular challenged the meaning of "woman" and assumptions about the unified subject of feminism. The emergence of Second Wave feminism beginning in the 1960s led, among academic feminists, to the early radical breakthrough of establishing the categories of "woman" and "women" as fully legitimate sites of intellectual inquiry. The initial emphasis of American feminism in the 1970s was on sexual difference—the different nature of women's experience, history, traditions, and culture from that of men. But if sexual difference dominated early feminist discourse, a groundswell of angry critique and institutional challenges from women marginalized by this hegemony within feminism led to a gradual change in emphasis.

By the late 1970s and through the 1980s, differences *among* women became increasingly a central focus of American women's studies and feminism more generally, due to the pioneering essays by writers like Alice Walker, Audre Lorde, Barbara Smith, Adrienne Rich, Johnnetta Cole, Bonnie Zimmerman, Rachel Blau DuPlessis, Gayatri Chakravorty Spivak, Cherríe Moraga, Gloria Anzaldúa, Alice Chai, and Chandra Talpade Mohanty[21]—to name a few—and edited collections such as *This Bridge Called My Back: Writings of Radical Women of Color* (Moraga and Anzaldúa); *But All the Women Are White, All the Men Are Black, and Some of Us Are Brave: Black Women's Studies* (Gloria T. Hull et al.); *Nice Jewish Girls: A Lesbian Anthology* (Evelyn Beck); *Lesbian Studies* (Margaret Cruikshank); and *Third World Women and the Politics of Feminism* (Mohanty).[22]

The impact of these challenges to feminism from within its boundaries was to problematize gender as *the* determining factor in women's lives.[23] Other forms of alterity and systems of stratification intersect with the gender system to disrupt analysis of women's lives solely in relation to gender. Discourses of multiple oppression, intersection, positionality, standpoint, and contradictory subject positions have, to a large extent, supplanted the monolithic category of "woman" in academic feminism in the United States.

Women's Words: The Feminist Practice of Oral History, edited by Sherna Berger

Gluck and Daphne Patai, brings this framework for problematization directly to bear on the methodology of feminist oral history.[24] Oral history, the editors explain, was quickly adopted by feminists in the 1970s as an ideal feminist methodology that could make available "in accessible forms the words of women who had previously been silenced or ignored" (2). Representing a range of disciplines using oral history, the feminists in *Women's Words* have discovered that doing women's oral history is "more problematic" than they "had imagined" and requires moving "beyond celebration of women's experience to a more nuanced understanding of the complexities of doing feminist oral history" (2, 3). Differences between the researcher and the researched as well as the power relations structuring the oral history exchange mediate between the reality of women's lives and the feminist history constructed by the research for dissemination in the academy or the media at large. The problematic of competing narrative authorities, for example, is the subject of essays by Katherine Borland and Sandra Hale.[25] Borland's feisty grandmother did not like the feminist interpretation Borland provided for her life, while Borland did not want to yield all her narrative authority to the woman whose life she retold. Hale, a white American anthropologist of working class background accorded the status of "honorary Sudanese," was frustrated in her attempt to get the life story of one of the Sudan's leading feminists, because this Third World woman, from a relatively elite family, wanted to use the researcher for her own political ends in the factional politics of her country. Patai and Gluck, in their own essays on their respective research in Brazil and the occupied West Bank, raise ethical and political questions about how national, ethnic, and class differences between researcher and researched inevitably problematize the processes and products of feminist oral history.[26]

The second major framework for problematization has come from poststructuralism. Beginning sporadically in the late 1970s, especially in French departments, and accelerating in the 1980s throughout the humanities, the arrival of European poststructuralist feminism, which emphasizes the theoretical and linguistic meanings of sexual difference, focused particularly on the role of language in the construction of femininity. Influenced by theorists like Jacques Lacan, Jacques Derrida, Roland Barthes, Julia Kristeva, Hélène Cixous, Luce Irigaray, Louis Althusser, and Michel Foucault, many feminists in the United States began to problematize feminism's essentializing or totalizing gestures and its roots in Enlightenment humanism.[27]

Although not all forms of problematization are poststructuralist, it is generally true that all poststructuralist theory aims to problematize. Echoing Jameson's command to "Always historicize!"[28], we might identify the poststructuralist imperative—if there is one—in a counter manifesto: "Always problematize!"

As R. Radhakrishnan writes, "post-structuralist thought" has an "indefatigable capacity for problematization and protocols of vigilance."[29] "Poststructuralism," Judith Butler writes, "is not strictly speaking, *a position*, but rather a critical interrogation of the exclusionary operations by which 'positions' [including feminist positions] are established."[30] In writing "against the grain of individualism, novelistic discourse, and personal testimony," Linda Kauffman asserts the foundation of poststructuralist critique: "I want continually to cast doubt on the status of knowledge—*even as we are in the process of constructing it*—a perpetual project."[31] And as Peggy Kamuf argues, the "erosion of the very ground on which to take a stand" is necessary for feminist critical practice.[32]

For many poststructuralist feminists, feminism is doomed to repeat the binarist structures of the phallogocentric symbolic order, if the most basic categories of feminism are not thrown open for question. *Woman, women, gender,* and *identity* are cultural constructs, the "effects," not the pre-existing causes, of discourse, especially for feminists influenced by the early work of Foucault. The formation of feminist positions and standpoints should not be exempt from metatheoretical interrogations just because it is feminist. We make a mistake, Butler warns in *Gender Trouble*, if we keep seeking what she calls "the subject of feminism."[33] As an expression of identity politics, the subject of feminism is just as much based on "foundationalist fictions" as the universal male subject of humanism (3). "Feminist critique," she writes, "ought to explore the totalizing claims of a masculinist signifying economy, but also remain self-critical with respect to the totalizing gestures of feminism" (13).[34] From this perspective, poststructuralist problematization of feminism itself is essential to avoid the erasure of heterogeneity and difference upon which the universal subject of humanism is based.

Historical narrative should itself be problematized, in the view of many poststructuralist feminists, because of what they see as its epistemological naiveté, its ideological formations, its association with the symbolic order, and its failure to acknowledge its allegorical and rhetorical foundations. In the field of women's history, Joan Scott is perhaps the foremost proponent of poststructuralist problematizations, of moving historical discourse away from the referential and toward the rhetorical (in de Manian terms), away from narratives of agency and toward the analysis of discursive effects (in Foucauldian terms). In *Gender and the Politics of History*, Scott advocates for feminist historians a "politics that are self-consciously critical of their own justifications and exclusions, and so refuse an absolutist or totalizing stance."[35] She promotes poststructuralist historiography as the only way to avoid a regressive objectivist epistemology that can do little more than reify the very notions of sexual difference that should be under question. "Women's history written from this [objectivist] position," she writes, "and the politics that follow from it, end up endorsing the ideas of unalterable sexual difference that are used to justify discrimination" (4). To avoid such repetitions, she advocates a "more radical feminist politics" based on the "more radical epistemology" of poststructuralism (4). Like Foucault, who warns in *The Archaeology of Knowledge* against "classical history" as a coercive discourse and promotes a "new history" that is synchronic rather than diachronic narrative,[36] Scott wants to shift feminist historiography away from a reconstruction of the past and toward an analysis of how meanings are constructed and function ideologically: "The story is no longer about the things that have happened to women and men and how they have reacted to them; instead it is about how the subjective and collective meanings of women and men as categories of identity have been constructed" (6).[37]

Poststructuralist feminist problematizations of historical narrative are situated within the larger field of historiographic debate represented particularly by the work of White and LaCapra. This debate in turn draws heavily on the more general (post)structuralist critique of narrative itself for what various theorists see as its dangerous alliance with mimesis and representationalism. Barthes, for example, in "The Discourse of History" attacks historical discourse as ideological narrative that obscures its own status as figuration behind the veil of representationalism. The discourse of history institutes "narration as a privileged signifier of the real."[38] The construction of the historian as "objective I" creates the illusion that history tells itself, that the Real speaks for itself (131–32). Historical discourse elides the distinctions between the signifier (the narrative), signified (the concept), and the referent (the "real" event). It does so by amassing facts that reproduce not reality, but "the reality effect" (139), a signifying practice he defines in more detail in "The Reality Effect." "History" and "narrative" serve ideological functions in part by veiling or naturalizing their own construction as an ordering discourse.[39] Introducing gender into this kind of critique of narrative and historical discourse, Julia Kristeva and Hélène Cixous variously associate narrative—particularly representational narrative—with an oedipal discourse that institutes and enforces the Law of the Father.[40] The poststructuralist critique of historical narrative begun in Barthes's structuralist work has extended into a widespread suspicion of narrative in all its forms as a discourse which is allied to the social order and serves an ideological, coercive, even authoritarian function.[41]

Other theorists are not so much hostile to narrative as they are suspicious of its tendency to obscure its own foundations in rhetoric. Paul de Man, for example, regards narrative—including historical narrative—as an allegory of temporality, a figuration of duration that is unaware of its own dependence on rhetoric. However much it presents itself as diachronic, narrative can be deconstructed to show its allegorical formation. "A rhetorical trope serves as the ground of a historical system," he writes in "Reading and History."[42] In relation to historical discourse in particular, de Man's approach suggests that chronological accounts may be governed less by the succession of events and more by such metaphoric structures as linear progress or regression, salvation or damnation, stagism, organicism, dualistic or even Manichaean conflict, the dialectic, the Weltanschauung, the war of the sexes or races, class struggle, sexual degeneracy, and so forth. Diachronicity potentially collapses into synchronicity, as Sommers' stagist historical narrative so clearly demonstrates.

Poststructuralist theory provides many important strategies for problematizations of feminism and feminist history writing, especially those that highlight linguistic effects and textual mediations. But poststructuralist problematizations should not be set up as the *only* route to the continual interrogation of the basic categories of feminist analysis and history making. Scott, for example, relies upon a reductionistic binary of objectivist and poststructuralist epistemologies, retaining for poststructuralism a unique radicalism that comes out of a distinctive "emphasis on its variability, its volatility, and the political nature of its construction" (5). She does not acknowledge the many feminisms before and parallel to poststructuralism that work out of subjectivist epistemologies which stress the constructedness of meaning and the politics of meaning-making. Like many poststructuralists, Scott accepts without question that feminists who are not poststructuralists remain caught within a "naive" humanism.

The other framework for problematizing that I have identified—the discourses of positionality and differences among women—is equally important, especially with its insistence on the multiple, interactive, and relational facets of identity. Moreover, these two frameworks are not in the least mutually exclusive. Their sites of "origin" are different—primarily European, particularly French philosophy and psychoanalysis versus primarily North American feminism. But the fertile mixing of these discourses, which began in a substantial way in the 1980s in the United States, has created an arena of overlap so that problematizations of linguistic mediation and positionality are often mutually reinforcing.

Whatever the framework for critique, the problematization of feminist history writing represents a thoughtful and necessary brake on the excesses of feminist "truth telling." We need to recognize the way in which any history represents *a* history, all the more dangerously if it assumes itself to be *the* history. If we can easily recognize that Sommers attempts to establish her own kind of feminism as *the* future of feminism, through her heuristic narrative of the NWSA conference and the spread of women's studies programs, then surely we must be ready to turn a critical eye inward to ask how our own histories of feminism might also engage in such play. Who are the winners and losers of our feminist histories of feminism?

IN DEFENSE OF FEMINIST NARRATIVE HISTORY

Interminable problematization of history writing poses a number of dangers that in themselves constitute a defense of feminist narratives of feminism. The first danger is the problem of paralysis, the kind of infinite regress and fetishization of indeterminacy that can develop out of constant navel-gazing. Perpetual self-reflexivity—particularly with its continual focus on linguistic construction—contains within it the potential of dangerous inaction or, to be more precise, action which in its constant inward turn inhibits an outer-directed energy for social change. As Daphne Patai writes in her problematization of feminist oral history across boundaries of difference: "It is a mistake to let ourselves be overwhelmed by these problems. The fact that doing research across race, class, and culture is a messy business is no reason to contemplate only our difficulties and ourselves struggling with them."[43] Indeed, to abandon the oral history of multiply oppressed women because of the researcher's mediating privilege would be to displace the women whose stories need to be told so as to focus attention all over again upon the problematic of the historian.[44]

This danger is more broadly endemic in poststructuralism itself and has been articulated by many within and outside the broad umbrella of poststructuralism.[45] In his efforts to define the limits of poststructuralist theory, Thomas Kavanagh argues that the banishing of language's mimetic function detaches literary studies from referentiality and delegitimates any concern for the "real" and "experience."[46] In his related critique of the political limits of Derridean deconstruction, Paul Smith argues that Derrida's continual effacement of subjectivity limits the possibility of agency "in such a way that it could not be adapted to *any* oppositional politics."[47] The "*desiring* subject/individual has no place in deconstruction," he writes, and thus "cannot take responsibility for its interpretations, much less for the history of the species" (50–51). Although their attempts from within a poststructuralist framework to return poststructuralist theory to history and politics are directed mainly at literary studies and theory, the implications of their argument for history writing are self-evident. Indifferent to the Real of women's lives, without intentional agency and political responsibility, feminist history writing potentially loses its subversive *raison d'être*, its oppositional bite.

Michèle Barrett brings this poststructuralist erasure of the Real and effacement of subjectivity to bear directly on poststructuralist feminism, here represented by the British journal *m/f*:

> The exclusive emphasis [in poststructuralist theory] placed on discursive practice....
> [is i]n some respects proper and valuable.... Yet the critique of feminist slogans elab-

orated in successive articles in *m/f* is surely politically inappropriate to the point of being destructive. One by one the campaigning slogans of women's liberation— 'The personal is political,' 'A woman's right to choose,' 'Control of our bodies'—is found to rest on errors of epistemology.... This critical exercise... fails to appreciate the grounding of such slogans in particular historical struggles. More importantly, perhaps, it leads us to ask what alternative political strategy is being offered.... Fundamentally, it is unclear that the project to deconstruct the category of woman could ever provide a basis for a feminist politics.[48]

Political struggle, Barrett suggests, depends upon establishing a historical ground from which to act.[49] The political problem with endless problematization of the ground on which we stand is the elimination of any position or standpoint from which to speak, organize for social change, or build coalitions based on common objectives. This applies as well to history writing as a form of feminist activism.

The second danger is also representative of a more general tendency within poststructuralism as it has been institutionalized in the academy. The constant undermining of feminism's discourse threatens to become its own hegemonic gesture, offering a totalizing dismissal of any activity not based in a critique of the grounds of discourse. Instead of opening up possibilities for feminist multivocalities, poststructuralist problematizations of feminism's so-called essentialism and humanism potentially constitute a new and exclusive orthodoxy, a new hierarchical power structure within academic feminism in which the theoretical problematizers often occupy the most prestigious and powerful positions. As Kavanagh writes, "What we had introduced as a discourse of the radically Other seems to have produced only the most resolute sameness and orthodoxy" (5). The hegemony of (poststructuralist) theory in the academy—not in any sense absolute but nonetheless influential—establishes theory as the "site of an unfettered *performance*," a "self-justifying performance," "freed from any referential function" (10). Rooted in a master-disciple system of theoretical proficiency and loyalty, poststructuralist theory can exhibit a politics of inclusion/exclusion based upon the binary of sophisticated/naive. "It is clearly a question of politics here," Kavanagh concludes, "a politics demanding the brutal disqualification of all who would remain outside or speak against the mutually sustaining dialogues of master and disciples" (12). Although Kavanagh doesn't specify further, the potentially gendered and racialized inflections of such binaries as master/disciple and theory/experience reinforce existing power structures in the academy.

From outside the poststructuralist umbrella, Barbara Christian's analysis parallels Kavanagh's. She writes that "it is difficult to ignore this new take-over [because] theory has become a commodity that helps determine whether we are hired or promoted in academic institutions.... Critics are no longer concerned with literature, but with other critics' texts, for the critic yearning for attention has displaced the writer and has conceived of himself as the center."[50] Her remarks about literary criticism can be adapted to history writing. The privileging of theory often rewards those who problematize feminism and focus their research not on what happened in the past but on other historians' texts. This power structure in the academy functions all the more insidiously because of the way poststructuralist theory potentially veils its own ideological power, obscures its own stoppage of the endless deferral of meaning by insisting on the "truth" of its own formulations and its dismissal of others deemed "humanist" or insufficiently unself-reflexive.[51] In relation to feminist history writing, this means that those engaged in continual problematization run the risk of establishing their critique—freed as Kavanagh says, from any concern for the referential—as hegemonic, as *the* meaning of feminism itself.

The third danger is implicit in the perpetual questioning of feminist history writing itself. This kind of critique covertly threatens, by extension, the whole multidisciplinary enterprise of writing women's history, of which writing the history of feminism is just one part. Writing women's history does not, of course, focus exclusively on women's experience. Rather, it begins with this compensatory center and then broadens its scope to question the formation and operation of the gender system as it intersects with other systems of social organization based on race, class, sexuality, religion, and national origin. Much of the work in women's history aims to recover and/or analyze anew lost, forgotten, never-examined, or phallocentrically understood aspects of women's experience and the gender system. Poststructuralist attempts to redirect women's history writing toward discourse analysis carry with them a dismissal of history writing as, in Joan Scott's words, the "story...about the things that have happened to women and men and how they have reacted to them."[52]

As Molly Hite writes in reference to literary studies as a form of history writing: "Being a feminist literary scholar seems more and more to be a matter of keeping abreast of the current repudiations. We're always killing off the Mother and riding sternly into the future on our newly phallicized hobbyhorses, call it modernity."[53] Gayle Greene reflects even more provocatively:

I sense a self-defeating tendency in all of this, a critical implosion that has the sound of a grinding halt. I wonder, also, if turning in on ourselves with this fierce self-scrutiny isn't a form of self-erasure, an analogue to our obsession with thinness, a way of assuring ourselves and others that we'll take up less space—a kind of professional/pedagogical anorexia.[54]

Deflecting the attention away from the Real of feminist history carries with it a broader displacement away from the Real of history itself, however mediated our knowledge of reality always is. The political consequences of this displacement threaten to return the dominant structures of history writing within the academy to what it was before the advent of women's studies. This danger brings us back to the political imperatives that underlay the founding of academic feminism in the 1960s and 1970s, however much later developments have altered, nuanced, and broadened those early manifestos for an activist feminist historiography. Writing about women's past represents a way to claim it, to assert the authority to interpret its meanings for the present and future. "What is new at this time," Gerda Lerner writes in *The Majority Finds Its Past*, "is that women are fully claiming their past and shaping the tools by means of which they can interpret it."[55] The premise behind such a statement is that making history in the present and future depends in part on the writing of women's past history.

What are the political consequences if the focus of feminist histories of feminism and women's history more broadly shifts entirely away from stories and analysis of (mediated) past realities and exclusively towards discourse analysis, constructivism, and critique of feminist historiography? Such an *exclusive* displacement would concede the arena of writing about historical *women* (as opposed to *woman* as a discursive effect) to non-feminists and anti-feminists. Like boycotting an election, an act designed to bring attention to the illegitimacy of the electoral process, such a withdrawal from writing about the "real" lives of women and historical configurations of gender leaves the field of narrative history entirely in the hands of the patriarchal mainstream. Yet just how much attention this withdrawal brings to the structure of the academy is not clear.

It is vitally important, I believe, for feminists to stake our claim, to insist on our presence within the academy as producers and teachers of new knowledges which should include new stories about how women and men lived, new interpretations as well of the events and meanings in the history of feminism. Do we want the Christina Hoff Sommers of the world to have free rein in constructing the stories of academic feminism? Certainly, it is a valid enterprise to critique the discourse of her history—indeed, much influenced by poststructuralist problematizations, that is just what I attempted to do. However, it is equally valid and important for alternative histories of academic feminism to be written, histories (however mediated) that attempt to get at the "real" events, ideas, and meanings of the formation, spread, and contradictions within women's studies. As Annette Kolodny writes, we must "take responsibility for recovering our history, lest others write it for us."[56]

The survival of feminism—of feminism as an ongoing history-in-process with a future—depends in part on our ability to reproduce ourselves in subsequent generations and to pass on what we have learned so that the wheel does not need to be reinvented by every generation. As Elaine Showalter writes, "each generation of women writers has found itself, in a sense, without a history, forced to rediscover the past anew, forging again and again the consciousness of their sex."[57] I am not suggesting that women's history and more specifically the history of feminism are fixed "truths" that must be handed down like precious heirlooms, or even that succeeding generations should be clones of their feminist foremothers (and occasional forefathers). Indeed, such action would induce needless stagnation and unnecessary rebellion. History, as a result of multiple interpretative acts, is necessarily fluid, ever-changing in relation to the heuristic needs of the present and the future. Moreover, in the family romance of political movements, new generations of feminists will inevitably resist as well as build upon the authority of the old in order to clear a space for new stories impelled by new historically specific conditions.[58] This fluidity and need for change, even conflictual change, should not obscure the politics of history writing as a form of memory. The loss of collective memories, of myriad stories about the past, has contributed greatly to the ongoing subordination of women. The unending, cumulative building of broadly defined histories of women, including histories of feminism, is a critical component of resistance and change. As Leslie Marmon Silko writes in *Storyteller*, "with these stories we will survive."[59]

I invoke Silko's celebration of the political imperative of storytelling on purpose. The final danger of perpetual problematization is its implicit attack on narrative in general and on history writing as a narrative act in particular. The poststructuralist critique of narrative as inherently authoritarian or totalizing implicitly condemns narrative history writing as part of the economy of the same, as the reproduction not the transgression of the symbolic order. However, the insistence of many minority women on the centrality of narrative to communal survival ought to call a halt to any wholesale condemnation of narrative as a reactionary or totalitarian epistemological mode. Louise Erdrich, for example, says in an interview, "I'm hooked on narrative.... Why is it that, as humans, we have to have narrative? I don't know, but we do.... The people in our families make everything into a story. They love to tell a good story. People just sit and the stories start coming, one after another."[60] Toni Morrison in some sense answers Erdrich's question: "Narrative is one of the ways in which knowledge is organized. I have always thought it was the most important way to transmit and receive knowledge. I am less certain of that now—but the craving for narrative has never lessened, and the hunger for it is as keen as it was on Mt. Sinai or Calvary or the middle of the fens."[61] In writing the history of her mother Rose Chernin, the well-known communist organizer, Kim Chernin recalls how "Very softly, whispering, I say to her, 'Mama, tell me a story'.... And yes, with all the skill available to me as a writer, I will take down her tales and tell her story."[62] Poet Irena Klepfisz in *Keeper of Accounts* faces the painful gaps in her memories of the Holocaust:

> So much of history   seems
> a gaping absence   at best a shadow
> longing   for some greater
> definition   which will never come
> for what is burned   becomes air
> and ashes   nothing more.[63]

And yet her long poem is a sustained effort in which lyric and narrative collaborate, however haltingly and inadequately, to testify to the history which has become "air," to recover the knowledge of what was lost as a precondition for living fully in the present and the future.[64] To forget the Holocaust is to risk its return.

The insistence on narrative as a mode of knowing, of remembering, essential for survival is not restricted to minority women whose cultural ties to the oral tradition remain strong. In her prose/poem/essay, "It Was a Dark and Stormy Night," for example, Ursula LeGuin argues that telling stories fulfills the needs of and for memory, testimony, and survival. Narrative staves off fear of the "dark and stormy night,"[65] of all the unnamed horrors of history, of death itself. "It remains true," writes Gayle Greene, "that stories, stories about the self, stories about women and about women's selves, had enormous power and continue to have power in the creation of feminist consciousness."[66] In *The Pleasures of Babel*, Jay Clayton sees the "turn to story" in American minority writers as the avant-garde of a return to narrative in many contemporary postmodern writers. The proliferation of what he calls, after Lyotard, multiple "local narrative communities" constitutes a kind of postmodern resistance to the "grand narratives" produced by the Enlightenment and its aftermath. Narrative serves in this regard as a localized site for the productions of multiple meanings. And although narrative can serve ideological and authoritarian ends, Clayton asserts, it can also function as a meaning-making discourse of resistance for many different kinds of communities, including feminist ones.[67]

Clayton's perspective on narrative provides the basis for a strong defense of narrative as an interpretive discourse that feminists can use for telling stories about the history of feminism itself. Narrative history is one of a number of transgressive strategies feminists can use to resist or subvert the stories of feminism told by various sectors of the dominant culture. To counter ideological narratives of feminism's alterity, feminists can tell counter-stories that chart their exclusions, affirm their agency (however circumscribed or complicit), and continually (re)construct their identities as feminists. Morrison's defense of narrative for African Americans can be adapted to the project of feminist history writing of feminism: "We are the subjects of our own narrative, witnesses to and participants in our own experience, and, in no way coincidentally, in the experience of those with whom we have come in contact. We are not, in fact, 'other.' We are choices."[68] Feminist history writing of feminism can be topical and spatial, as Giana Pomata has shown.[69] But narrative discourse can also represent the "choice" to formulate not *the* but many "subjects of feminism," many identities and stories, as the inscription of a desire to insist upon a feminist presence in the making of history.

THE QUESTION OF DESIRE IN AND FOR HISTORY

Thus far, my discussion of feminist history writing has put aside an important issue: desire. What does desire have to do with either the dangers or the necessities of feminists writing history, specifically histories of feminism? Theorists of narrative from Laura Mulvey to Teresa de Lauretis, Leo Bersani, Hayden White, Peter Brooks, and Jay Clayton have written positively and negatively about the entanglement of narrative and desire as a mode of knowing. Brooks in *Reading for the Plot*, for example, examines "the nature of narration as a form of human desire," one in which the "need to tell" functions as "a primary human drive that seeks to seduce and to subjugate the listener, to subjugate him in the thrust of a desire that never can quite speak its name."[70] Clayton in *The Pleasures of Babel*, on the other hand, refuses to see desire in narrative as a process of inevitable subjection. Rather, he regards the power of narrative desire as neither good nor bad, policing nor liberating, in and of itself. He argues for the historicization of narrative desire, for an analysis of how it works in given situations as a positive or negative force, whether as a disciplining structure or as a means of empowerment.[71]

To consider the implications of this linkage between narrative and desire for feminist historiography, let's take *desire* out of the realm of the purely erotic wherein it is mostly confined in theoretical discourse (Clayton is an important exception). "To know," in the biblical sense, means to encompass or possess sexually, a conflation of perception and sexuality that serves as a cornerstone of psychoanalytic configurations of Oedipal desire as a foundation of subjectivity, as Brooks' *Reading for the Plot* particularly illustrates. But recall that the appeal of knowledge in another, muted, biblical sense impels Eve's tasting of the apple from the Tree of Knowledge. Eve's desire for knowledge prefigures the drive for literacy, for access to books and education, that runs as a powerful current through the long history of intellectual women, as well as of women who struggle for the basics of literacy.[72] Harriet Jacobs powerfully configures another desire, the longing for freedom in *Incidents in the Life of a Slave Girl*,[73] while feminists like Sheila Rowbotham have articulated the desire of any oppressed group to "shatter the self-reflecting world which encircles it and, at the same time, project its own image onto history."[74]

The debates, divisions, and contradictions within feminism, as it projects its own image onto history, reflect different formulations of the politics of desire and its relation to historical narrative. On the one hand, the outer-directed, shattering, and projecting gaze of feminism embodies a will-to-empowerment, a desire to overturn patriarchal hegemonies and to make its mark on and in history. On the other hand, the critical inner gaze of feminism fears its own will-to-power, its capacity to repeat the power structures it sets out to transgress.[75] To put this opposition another way: The insistence on making history, on narrative as a potentially transformative mode of knowing, expresses the desire to transfer power to those who have not had it, while the problematizing of history making reflects the dangers of empowerment as a re-establishment of power over others. The one affirms the political importance and possibilities of agency and, by extension, the "subject of feminism." The other finds in the notion of agency a naive unawareness of how subjectivity is always already constructed within ideology, within the hegemonic discourses of the symbolic order.

These contradictory desires and differing notions of agency play themselves out in the debate between Linda Gordon and Joan Scott in an 1990 issue of *Signs* in which the two prominent feminist historians rather unfavorably review each other's books (*Heroes of Their Own Lives: The Politics and History of Family Violence* and *Gender and the Politics of History*) and then respond to each other's reviews.[76] Since the publication of *Woman's Body, Woman's Right: A Social History of Birth Control in America*,[77] Gordon has been widely known for her resistance to a "victim" paradigm of women's history and her advocacy of a complicated notion of social control that encourages the analysis of how women maneuver within the specific constrictions they face. In her response to Scott's attack, Gordon writes that she uses "gender to describe a power system in which women are subordinated through relations that are contradictory, ambiguous, and conflictual—a subordination maintained against resistance, in which women have by no means always defined themselves as other, in which women face and take choices and action despite constriction."[78] Scott, on the other hand, has been known for her advocacy of poststructuralism as a basis for writing history, particularly for Foucauldian concepts of coercive discursive systems and subjectivity as an effect, not a autonomous cause, of discourse. Scott argues for a "different conceptualization of agency," which "would see agency not as an attribute or trait inhering in the will of autonomous individual subjects, but as a discursive effect."[79]

Scott praises Gordon's *Heroes of Their Own Lives* for its account of an area of women's experience that has not been much explored: "she conjures up something of the experience of neglect, abuse, battering, and incest for those involved" (848). She is more enthusiastic about Gordon's analysis of how certain elements of this experience were constructed as "social problems" in the period from the 1880s through the 1960s, constructions that ironically "frequently contributed to the dissolution of the very households that, in principle, were supposed to be saved" by the social workers (849). But she faults what she sees as Gordon's "reading strategy," which she thinks "does not try to analyze closely the caseworkers' accounts" (850).

Moreover, Scott is not persuaded by what she sees as Gordon's secondary argument for the agency of these victimized women. Not the "will of autonomous individual subjects," this agency should be regarded, Scott believes, as a "discursive effect, in this case, the effect of social workers' constructions of families, gender, and family violence" (851). Although Gordon nowhere equates agency with autonomy, Scott identifies Gordon's book with a humanist feminism that regards women as autonomous subjects who resist the forces of social control. The "major achievement of the book," Scott believes, resides in its presentation of "the story of this process" that "constructs possibilities for and puts limits on specific actions undertaken by individuals and groups" (852). But she thinks the "book would have been even better…if it had explicitly articulated in a more sophisticated conceptual frame, one that refused the oppositional thinking of overly simple theories of social control (either domination or autonomous action) and thus moved beyond the individualistic notions of heroes and their agency implied by the title of the book" (852). Gordon's title, in Scott's view, marks the book as unsophisticated, caught up in "more [of] a wish than a historical reality, more [of] a politically correct formulation than anything that can be substantiated by the sources" (850).

Scott's lukewarm praise for and attack of Gordon's book, as well as her response to Gordon's review, recapitulates many of the conventional themes of poststructuralist problematizations of feminist history writing. There is the belittling of history which presents a *story* of women's experience, with its implicit attack on narrative itself as an inferior mode of historical writing. There is the insistence on problematizing everything, on linguistic and discursive analysis. There is the reduction of agency and subjectivity to *effects* of discourse, a Foucauldian emphasis on the construction of policing discursive formations, a dismissal of notions of empowerment, and a disregard for forms of opposition. There is the charge of naiveté and fear of reproducing the economy of the same.

Above all there is the privileging of poststructuralist theory as *the* radical ground of feminist activity. Echoing, perhaps unconsciously, the familiar and unanswerable defense of psychoanalysis (if you don't agree, it's because you are resisting), Scott concludes her response by reducing Gordon's statements to a resistance to poststructuralist theory:

> Where does this resistance to poststructuralist theory come from? Why is there such resistance at a moment in the history of feminism when—if we are to formulate new kinds of political strategies—we need to understand how, in all their complexity, collective and individual differences are constructed, how, that is, hierarchies and inequalities are produced?... Since it is the nature of feminism to disturb the ground it stands on, even its own ground, the resistance to theory is a resistance to the most radical effects of feminism itself.[80]

Whereas Scott's underlying agenda appears to be the promotion of poststructuralist feminist history, Gordon's review and response argue for the empowering effects of different theoretical perspectives and methodologies for feminism. She praises Scott's challenge to objectivism and demonstration that "studying language is vital" to the historical enterprise.[81] But she is not convinced by what she sees as the more ambitious aim of Scott's book: to establish "that language is and must be the only subject of history and that through linguistic analysis gender will be revealed" (854). She locates the strengths of the book in its essays on French history and its weaknesses in its critique of historiography which assumes a "'reality' 'behind' the language" (856–57). Ultimately, she remains unconvinced that poststructuralist theory is the *only* social theory that can write non-objectivist history sensitive to the linguistic structures of meaning. Gordon stresses the importance of a subjectivist epistemology, linguistic analysis, and the use of many kinds of social theory, including (but not exclusively) poststructuralist theory.

Instead of advocating a history that collapses into the metanarrative of how "hierarchies and inequalities are produced," Gordon argues for complicating the "top-down" model of social control with one that acknowledges societal constructions of power relations but does not reduce women to effects of discourse. Rather, she proposes a notion of agency that emphasizes women's negotiations within constriction—not a belief in women's always already autonomous empowerment, but instead a notion of women's struggle within the terms of a patriarchal system to survive as more than passive victim. In doing so, she theorizes a kind of history writing that acknowledges subjectivism and linguistic constructionism, while still embracing the power of narrative as a form of feminist activism and insisting that the Real not be reduced to language. She stands by her references to "'real' family violence" as something beyond the "competing understandings of those assaults."[82] "One of the things I like about writing history," Gordon concludes in her response, "is drawing meaning from stories, in the ambiguous, metaphorical, narrative language of daily life" (852).

WRITING FEMINIST HISTORIES: IN THE PLURAL

The *Signs* debate between Linda Gordon and Joan Scott demonstrates more than the oppositions between agency and its critique, between the will-to-empowerment and resistance to the will-to-power. It also acts out a contemporary struggle within feminism for the authority to "make history." *Who* will speak for feminism? In what way? Gordon makes no claim for exclusive authority. Her praise of Scott's book, so different from her own, invites the multiplication of feminist historiographic methodologies—what I am calling feminist histories *in the plural*. Scott, on the other hand, insists upon a singular methodology, her own poststructuralist one. Her denial of the subject of feminism, of agency, ultimately takes the form of a performative insistence on her own subjectivity and agency, one that dismisses other voices as naive, as poststructurally incorrect, and as insufficiently radical. Scott bases her defense of poststructuralist historiography in a critique of a feminist "politics that sets and enforces priorities, represses some subjects in the name of the greater importance of others, naturalizes certain categories, and disqualifies others."[83] Ironically, her attack on Gordon's non-poststructuralist historiography takes the form of enforcing a set of (poststructuralist) priorities and repressing other social theory in stressing the importance of poststructuralist theory. However much Scott warns against the politics of priority and dismissal, her own theorizing about historiography engages in a politics of dismissal and the suppression of heterogeneity.

Scott is not alone in this contradictory impulse to establish poststructuralism—which often promotes heterogeneity, multiplicity, difference, and open-ended *différance*—as the single pathway to revolutionary Truth. Other advocates of poststructuralism, particularly in literary studies, all too often perpetuate the binary of winners and losers in their attempt to shape the future of feminism. This performance of a poststructuralist will-to-power jars wildly against poststructuralist problematizations of hegemony. But poststructuralist feminists, of course, are not alone in the performance of monologic advocacy. In "The Race for Theory," Barbara Christian is as relentlessly dismissive of poststructuralist theory as Scott is for it. The promotion of feminist histories *in the plural* requires vigilance, not only openness to others but also self-reflective interrogation of one's own premises.

Feminist histories of the conflict between "French poststructuralism" and "American feminism" are a case in point for the tendency of history writing to fall unself-consciously into allegorical narratives of winners and losers, as well as for the urgency of problematizing such reductionisms. This conflict has achieved near-formulaic status in the scores of essays that address the meeting, opposition, and mingling of these different feminist traditions. The allegorical trope that governs these narratives is the agon, the dualistic struggle that is overdetermined by a (post)colonial discourse in intellectual history about the influence of continental theory on the naive, empirically oriented Americans.[84] By way of example, I want to focus on three such accounts, in all of which Kristeva figures curiously as invisible presence, as feminist hero or demon: Elaine Showalter's "Women's Time, Women's Space: Writing the History of Feminist Criticism" (1983/84); Toril Moi's *Sexual/Textual Politics: Feminist Literary Theory* (1985); and Gayatri Spivak's "French Feminism in an International Frame" (1981).[85]

Both Showalter's and Moi's accounts of the conflict use historical markers that create what we might call, after Barthes, a "history effect." Phrases in Showalter's essay like "in the second phase of this history," "in 1968," "since 1975," "since the late 1970s," and "within the past year or two" punctuate the loose narrative, creating a sensation of chronological progression and establishing an overall effect of historicization. Similarly, Moi's discussion of Anglo-American feminist criticism (chpt. 2–4) carefully follows the chronology of publication and passage through the decades from the late 1960s into the early 1980s, with the arrival of poststructuralist theory in the United States. Both writers borrow the generalizing discourse of periodization from history to characterize evolving phases in feminist criticism. Like historical periodization in general, these chronologies tend to erase the heterogeneity of feminist criticism at any given point in time. Moreover, their historical narratives dissolve into allegorical representations of their own theoretical positions within the field whose history they purport to tell. Consequently, the effect (although undoubtedly not the conscious intention) of the "history effect" in their narratives is to intervene in the debates of the present as a way of shaping the future of feminist criticism.

The allegorical foundation of Showalter's "Women's Time, Women's Space" begins in her unacknowledged displacement of Kristeva's "Women's Time," to which her title alludes. Showalter's chronology of stages covertly invokes and revokes Kristeva's dialectical progression of feminism in France, which she sees beginning in the humanist project of inserting women into the "men's time" of history, moving on to a terrorist assertion of feminine difference in "women's time," and heading in a utopian direction of individual mysticism beyond men's or women's time. Where Kristeva's "women's time" is a space outside history (which is constituted in and through the phallocentric symbolic order), Showalter's "women's time" is the separate *history* of women, which is distinct from the history of men but just as much a part of history as the story of men. Traditional periodizations of literary history do not work for women writers, Showalter asserts, because the patriarchal exclusions of women from the public sphere constituted historical conditions that made their writing different. Paralleling the critique of traditional periodization in the field of women's history,[86] gynocriticism develops a separate periodization based in "women's time." Showalter's title and its related argument thus function to assert her position within an unstated agon between herself and Kristeva, between an American feminist criticism and a French feminist theory.

Showalter does openly acknowledge, and even gesture generously towards, the importance of French feminist theory within the evolving history of American feminist criticism. Indeed, in narrating its arrival, she rejects the all-too-prevalent binarist accounts of French/American conflict: "In writing the history of feminist criticism, I want to avoid, however, such a hostile polarization of French and American feminist discourse, arid theory and crude empiricism, obscurantism or essentialism. In formulating or endorsing such hierarchical binary oppositions, we not only fall into the old dualistic traps, but genuinely misrepresent the much more complex and nuanced reality of feminist critical practice."[87] She argues instead for a historical narrative that recognizes how French and American feminist discourses in the United States have been "enriched by dialectical possibilities," mutually influencing each other as they established two modes of feminist critical discourse: gynocriticism (the historically oriented study of women writers) and gynesis (the theoretically oriented analysis of the feminine Other in discourse, especially in male texts).

In the final portion of her narrative, however, when she recounts how feminist criticism "since 1980" has in general "moved inexorably...back into standard critical time," Showalter's implicit privileging of gynocriticism becomes evident. By the end of the essay, "standard critical time," "men's time," and poststructuralist theory have been conflated into a single category, "modern criticism," to which she opposes "feminist criticism." "What is the relationship between feminist criticism and modern criticism?" she asks (41). Fear of and resistance to the feminine and feminism fueled the rise of "modern theory," which ironically has more recently become a fascination for feminist criticism itself, in its desire to feed off modern theory's energy and ability to lead the "way out of the labyrinth of indeterminacy, non-interference and self-referentiality post-structuralism has built for itself" (42). Her narrative concludes with a warning to feminists: "Insofar as the production of theory is now the business of modern criticism, there will be increased pressure on feminist criticism to accommodate itself more and more to prevailing terminologies and systems, abandoning in the process the political priorities and concerns for the personal that have made it effective in the past" (42).

What interests me here is not the accuracy or inaccuracy of Showalter's history, but how her own theoretical position within feminism heuristically governs the narrative. Her final opposition between feminist criticism and modern criticism subtly aligns feminist poststructural theory (gynesis) with "modern criticism" and thereby removes it from the category of "feminist criticism," which is implicitly represented by gynocriticism. The "dialectical enrichment," which she promoted earlier in the essay between gynocriticism and gynesis, recedes, displaced by the binaries of feminist criticism and modern theory, women's time and men's time, feminism and poststructuralism. History becomes synchrony, narrative becomes allegory in a chronological account of feminist criticism that overtly legitimates gynesis along with gynocriticism, but covertly promotes one kind of feminism over another.

Moi's openly polemical narrative of feminist criticism has none of the attempted pluralism of Showalter's narrative.[88] Like Joan Scott's, Moi's advocacy of poststructuralist heterogeneity inscribes a performance of singularity—her history as an erasure of any one else's. Moi's book opens with a feminist parable that demonstrates the need to "rescue" Virginia Woolf for feminism by reading her within a poststructuralist rather than a realist framework. This introduction openly allegorizes the agonistic binary of French and American feminisms in the form of an attack on Showalter's chapter on Woolf in *A Literature of Their Own* as a demonized metonymy of the reactionary humanism of American feminist criticism. Moi aligns what she sees as Showalter's preference for bourgeois realism over Woolf's modernism with "Lukács's Stalinist views of the 'reactionary' nature of modernist writing."[89] Showalter, and by extension the American feminist criticism she represents, is trapped in the "totalizing, humanist aesthetic" characteristic of realism, naively holding on to a belief in the unitary self and the referentiality of language. "What feminists such as Showalter and Holly fail to grasp," Moi writes, "is that the traditional humanism they represent is in effect part of patriarchal ideology" (8). Poststructuralism, represented especially by Kristeva, offers the only escape from this "crypto-Lukácsian perspective implicit in much contemporary feminist criticism" (8).

Moi's introduction thus announces in advance the teleological direction of the historical narrative which follows. Her diachronic narrative of the evolution of Anglo-American feminist criticism is heuristically governed by the allegory of progress. The Anglo-American feminists, caught in the economy of the same, repeating the patriarchal ideology of bourgeois humanism, await the revelations of poststructuralism, which starts coming across the Atlantic in the late 1970s. The four chapters on Anglo-American feminist criticism proceed chronologically, beginning with those who worked for social and political change in the 1960s, moving through the "images of women" criticism and gynocriticism of the 1970s, and ending with the inklings of "theoretical reflections" in the late 1970s, which paved the way for the introduction of poststructuralist feminist theory.

Moi doesn't actually narrate the influx of poststructuralist feminism into Anglo-American feminist criticism. Rather, the structure of the book itself suggests the book's promotion of poststructuralism. Part II, which consists of four chapters on Lacan, Cixous, Irigaray, and Kristeva, contains far fewer markers of historical discourse. Not a chronology, it is rather a presentation of theorists in ascending order of Moi's approval. Although she provides something of a materialist critique of Kristeva, Kristeva's work comes the closest to what Moi herself advocates and thus occupies the climactic position in Moi's teleological narrative governed by the allegory of progress. Part II of the book functions to rescue the Anglo-American feminism surveyed in Part I from its reactionary tendencies. "The central paradox of Anglo-American feminist criticism," she writes, "is thus that despite its often strong, explicit engagement, it is *in the end* not quite political enough... in the sense that its radical analysis of sexual politics still remains entangled with depoliticizing theoretical paradigms" (87). In Moi's agonistic narrative, French feminist theory carries not only the day in feminist criticism but also the torch of true feminist radicalism. Even more overtly than Showalter's account, Moi's history of feminist criticism collapses into allegories of struggle and progress in which poststructuralist feminism is the winner and what she calls bourgeois humanist feminism is the loser, a victory which her own historical narrative attempts to ensure.

Spivak's "French Feminism in an International Frame"—a set of theoretical reflections that makes no attempt at historical narrative—uses fragmentary stories as allegories that contain a critique of Western feminism, demanding a genuine discontinuity and heterogeneity. Stories of a Sudanese woman writing about clitoridectomy, of herself "choosing" English as a profession in Bengal, of the washerwomen on her grandfather's estate, of Kristeva traveling in China, serve as occasions that probe the relation between history and identity, between historically specific social orders and the destinies available to women within them. The allegorical function of these fragments is to disrupt the discourses of Western feminism, particularly the agon between French and Anglo-American feminist criticism. Within an international frame that includes the Third World, the great debates in Western feminism appear homogeneous, particularly in their inability to incorporate the "excess" of excluded Third World women.[90] This "inbuilt colonialism of the First World against the Third World" (152) is allegorically evident in Kristeva's *About Chinese Women*[91], a book based on a short trip to China in which she reports a millennia of Chinese history, with "sweeping historiographic scope," with "no encroachment of archival evidence," with "the most stupendous generalizations" and "no primary research" (137–38). Spivak's critique of Kristeva's primitivist Orientalism is scathing, all the more so because it uncovers how the poststructuralist unraveling of unitary identities that Kristeva directs at the West vanishes in the face of her desire for a totalized identity for Chinese women throughout the millennia. The very insight of French feminism in its critique of humanism—its insistence on discontinuity, heterogeneity, and excess—is lost when the First World faces the Third World.[92]

What Spivak's critique of Kristeva and Western feminism in general helps bring into view is how historical narratives about the clash between Anglo-American and French feminisms function covertly as theoretical arguments whose telos is to defeat other perspectives. Feminist histories of feminism can, in other words, all too easily become a narrative of winners and losers rather than a story of multiple, heterogeneous, voices. In the spirit of Spivak's critique of Western feminism, the reduction of feminisms to a single feminism in any historical account erases differences, obscures heterogeneity, and effectively denies voice to those who have less power.

Spivak's deconstruction of agonistic narratives of Western feminism, however, falls into the same trap she critiques by replacing the binary of Anglo-American and French feminisms with the binary of Western and Third World feminisms. Like the accounts of Showalter and Moi, Spivak ignores the many voices of American feminists—particularly those of women of color, lesbians, and Jewish women—who have since the 1970s been insisting on the multiple positionalities of women in relation to different systems of alterity. Showalter names such influential gynocritical feminists as Alice Walker, Barbara Smith, Audre Lorde, and Bonnie Zimmerman, but her history of feminist criticism does not acknowledge how these feminists launched a major problematization of gynocriticism for its homogenization of women. Moi justifies their absence from her account with a gesture of double dismissal: "Some feminists might wonder why I have said nothing about black or lesbian (or black-lesbian) feminist criticism in America in this survey. The answer is simple: this book purports to deal with the theoretical aspects of feminist criticism. So far, lesbian and/or black feminist criticism have presented exactly the same *methodological* and *theoretical* problems as the rest of Anglo-American feminist criticism" (86). And Spivak herself does not even mention the "Third World" and lesbian challenges *within* the West to feminist racism, classism, and heterosexism. Her (poststructuralist) refusal of narrative allows her to identify certain theoretical positions within Western feminism and drop out other voices whose existence would complicate her own allegorical binary of Western and Third World feminisms.

What lesson does the cluster of texts by Showalter, Moi, and Spivak hold for feminist historiography? It demonstrates the difficulty of and necessity for feminist histories *in the plural* instead of feminist history. Rather than seeking *the* definitive narrative of feminism, or of any given moment in feminism, we must acknowledge the potential for many localized narratives of feminism, none of which can claim to represent the totality of feminist history. This means that we need not only to foster the existence of many voices engaged in the dual tasks of making feminist history but also to acknowledge in our own histories the possibilities of other voices (re)telling the stories we have told. Linda Hutcheon argues for history *in the plural* in her notion of postmodern narrative history, which she sees located in the "paradox of the desire for and the suspicion of narrative mastery—and master narratives."[93] In postmodern history writing, "the narrativization of past events is not hidden; the events no longer seem to speak for themselves" (72), and the "seamlessness of the join between the natural and the cultural, the world and the text" is always open to interrogation (53). This awareness of the historian as narrator makes possible "the histories (in the plural) of the losers as well as the winners, of the regional (and colonial) as well as the centrist, of the unsung as well as the much sung few, and I might add, of women as well as men" (66).

Hutcheon's "histories (in the plural)" needs another turn of the screw, however, to avoid the construction of winners and losers. We need to extend the necessity of heterogeneity to histories written by the marginalized (whether postmodern or not). We need what Radhakrishnan calls a kind of "totality" based not on the narrative totalization of any given history but rather the totality of different narratives about that history:

> My objective here...is to suggest both that no one discourse or historiography has the ethicopolitical legitimacy to represent the totality, and that the concept of "totality" should be understood not as a pregiven horizon but as the necessary and inevitable "effect" or function of the many relational dialogues, contestations, and asymmetries among the many positions...that constitute the total field.[94]

For Radhakrishnan, such totality requires a negotiation between poststructuralist problematization and feminist praxis. Without poststructuralist theory, "feminist historiography...is in danger of turning into a superficial reversal of forces of power that would leave untouched certain general and underlying economies of meaning and history."[95] But feminist historiography also needs an "affirmative programmatic," a "determinate politics" based in "the intentional/agential production of meaning as change" (189, 203). Feminist historiography is different, he concludes, "precisely because it is still interested in creating and transforming history," with "making and doing history" (202–203).

The hegemonic posturing of some poststructuralist feminists, however, demonstrates that poststructuralist theory by itself is not sufficient protection against the production of histories of winners and losers in feminism, as the texts I have discussed by Joan Scott, Moi, and even Spivak illustrate. The "totality" of histories Radhakrishnan advocates requires not only the "affirmative program-matic" of feminists producing histories *in the plural* but also the widest possible range of self-reflective problematizations, which would certainly include, although not be limited to, poststructuralist interrogations.

The promotion of multiple feminist histories runs, of course, the risk of plu-ralism, of obscuring the structures of power within and outside the academy that constitute some histories as "more equal" than others in the brave new world of feminism. "Pluralism," Linda Gordon warns, "was never merely a recognition of variation but a masking of inequality."[96] The questions that need to be asked then, are: Which histories of feminism become canonical? Which fall into obscu-rity? Which stories do the media pick up and disseminate? Which do they ignore? Who tells the story and what is her/his position?

In spite of the risks of pluralism, however, I believe that negotiating the active and reflective modes of feminist historiography opens up the potential for femi-nists to engage in constructing histories *in the plural*, for recognizing that no single history can encounter the full dimensionality of the Real, and for reflect-ing upon our own processes of mediation. I have defended two positions that are all too often set up as mutually exclusive oppositions: the need to make history by writing history as a political act; and the need to problematize that activity so as to avoid the creation of grand narratives that reproduce the totalizing his-tories of winners in which the stories of losers are lost. Instead of either/or, I promote both/and, where the active and reflective supplement each other in creative negotiation. Feminist histories (in the plural) of feminism (in the plural) are essential for negotiating the interplay between action and reflection and between the Real and its textualizations.

NOTES |

I am indebted to Judith Walzer Leavitt and Diane Elam for criticisms of an earlier draft of this essay.

1 See Gerda Lerner, *The Majority Finds Its Past: Placing Women in History* (Oxford: Oxford University Press, 1979), p. 160; Dominick LaCapra, *History and Criticism* (Ithaca: Cornell University Press, 1985), p. 25; Leslie Marmon Silko, *Storyteller* (New York: Little Brown, 1981), p. 247; and Linda Hutcheon, *The Politics of Postmodernism* (London: Routledge, 1990), p. 66.

2 For discussions of Hegel's formulation of the double meaning of *history* see: Linda Orr, "The Revenge of Literature: A History of History," *New Literary History* 18 (Autumn 1986), p. 12 and Timothy Bahti, *Allegories of History: Literary Historiography after Hegel* (Baltimore: Johns Hopkins University Press, 1992), pp. 7–8.

3 For critiques of "presentism," see, for example, Herbert Butterfield, *The Whig Interpretation of History* (1959; rpt. New York: Norton, 1965) and George W. Stocking Jr., "On the Limits of 'Presentism' and 'Historicism' in the Historiography of the Behavioral Sciences," *Race, Culture, and Evolution: Essays in the History of Anthropology* (1968; revised edition Chicago: University of Chicago Press, 1982), pp. 1–12. Others, like LaCapra (*History*, pp. 43–44) and Orr ("The Revenge of Literature," *New Literary History*, pp. 15–16) see the teleological nature of history writing as inevitable.

4 Although few currently practicing historians operate out of a fully positivist frame-work, metahistorians continue to identify positivist historiography as worthy of critique. LaCapra (*History*, p. 136) claims that G. R. Elton's modified positivist assumptions in *The Practice of History* (New York: Crowell, 1967) still embody a consensus among many practicing historians. See also Bahti, *Allegories of History*; Hayden White, *The Content of the Form* (Baltimore: Johns Hopkins University Press, 1990), *Metahistory* (Baltimore: Johns Hopkins Univeristy Press, 1974) and "The Question of Narrative in Contemporary Historical Theory," *History and Theory* 23 (1984), pp. 1–33; David Harlan, "Intellectual History and the Return of Literature," *American Historical Review* 94 (June 1989), pp. 581–609; Orr, "The Revenge of Literature," *New Literary History*; LaCapra, *History*, especially pp. 15–44 and pp. 135–42, *Soundings in Critical Theory* (Ithaca: Cornell University Press, 1989), especially pp. 182–210, and "Intellectual History and Its Ways," *American History Review* 97 (April 1992), pp. 425–39; and finally, the advocacy of a historiography of pragmatics, based on a consensus-based theory of historical truth, in Joyce Appleby, Lynn Hunt, and Margaret Jacob, *Telling the Truth about History* (New York: Norton, 1994).

5 I capitalize the Real of history throughout as an adaptation of Jameson's reconfiguration of the Lacanian Real. Like Fredric Jameson and LaCapra, I object to the "fashionable conclusion that because history is a text, the 'referent' does not exist" (Jameson, *The Political Unconscious: Narrative as a Socially Symbolic Act* (Ithaca: Cornell University Press, 1981). Like Jameson, I believe that the Real of history "is *not* a text, not a narrative, master or otherwise, but that, as an absent cause, it is inaccessible to us except in textual form, and that our approach to it and to the Real itself necessarily passes through its prior textualization [and] its narrativization" (p. 35). See also LaCapra, *History*, p. 38 and "Intellectual History"; Lloyd S. Kramer, "Literature, Criticism, and Historical Imagination: The Literary Challenge of Hayden White and Dominick LaCapra," *The New Critical History*, ed. Lynn Hunt (Berkeley: University of California Press, 1989), especially pp. 122–28. Harlan,

White and Orr also explore these issues.

6 See Bahti; Orr; Gayatri Chakravorty Spivak, "A Literary Representation of the Subaltern: A Woman's Text from the Third World," *In Other Worlds: Essays in Cultural Politics* (London: Methuen, 1986), pp. 241–68; White "The Question of Narrative," *History and Theory*, pp. 1–3; and LaCapra's related discussion of the "documentary model" of history, which is aware of or denies the existence of rhetoric as part of the practice of history. White's "figural origins of historical knowledge," features a "dialogic" model in which the historian engages in a "dialogue with the dead who are reconstituted through their 'textualized' remainders" (*History and Theory*, p. 18, p. 21, p. 34 and p. 36). For overviews of White's and LaCapra's influential work, see Kramer, and Russell Jacoby, "A New Intellectual History?", *American Historical Review* 97 (April 1992), pp. 405–39.

7 For use of Kuhn's *The Structure of Scientific Revolutions* (1962; 2nd. ed. Chicago: University of Chicago Press, 1970), see, for example, Sandra Coyner's "Women's Studies as an Academic Discipline: Why and How to Do It," *Theories of Women's Studies*, ed. Gloria Bowles and Renata Duelli Klein (London: Routledge and Kegan Paul, 1983), a collection that contains the contradictory epistemologies that underlie women's studies as a field.

8 For developments in this kind of feminist epistemology, see standpoint theory in feminist philosophy, especially Nancy Hartsock, "The Feminist Standpoint: Developing the Ground for a Specifically Feminist Historical Materialism," *Discovering Reality: Feminist Perspectives on Epistemology, Metaphysics, Methodology, and Philosophy of Science*, ed. Sandra Harding and Merrill B. Hintikka (Boston: D. Reidel, 1983), pp. 283–310; and Donna Haraway, "Situated Knowledges: The Science Question in Feminism and the Privileges of Partial Perspective," *Feminist Studies* 14 (Fall 1988), pp. 575–99. See also theories of locational or positional knowledge in writers such as Adrienne Rich, "Notes toward a Politics of Location," *Blood, Bread, and Poetry: Selected Prose, 1979–1985* (1984; New York: Norton, 1986), pp. 210–232; Linda Alcoff, "Cultural Feminism versus Poststructuralism: The Identity Crisis in Feminist Theory," *Signs* 13 (Spring 1988), pp. 405–36; Paula Gunn Allen, "Kochinnenako in Academe: Three Approaches to Interpreting a Keres Indian Tale," *The Sacred Hoop: Recovering the Feminine in American Indian Traditions* (Boston: Beacon Press, 1986), pp. 222–44; Biddy Martin and Chandra Talpade Mohanty, "Feminist Politics: What's Home Got to Do With It?," *Feminist Studies/Critical Studies*, ed. Teresa de Lauretis (Bloomington: Indiana University Press, 1986); as well as Chandra Talpade Mohanty, "Cartographies of Struggle: Third World Women and the Politics of Feminism," *Third World Women and the Politics of Feminism*, ed. Mohanty (Bloomington: Indiana University Press, 1989), pp. 1–49; Deborah K. King, "Multiple Jeopardy, Multiple Consciousness: The Context of a Black Feminist Ideology," *Signs* 14 (Autumn 1988), pp. 42–72;

and Marion Smiley, "Feminist Theory and the Question of Identity," *Women and Politics* 13 (1993), pp. 91–122. Although the notion of the constructedness of all human discourse, including history, is often associated with poststructuralist theory, subjectivist epistemologies have been a part of women's studies since its origins in the late 1960s.

9 For other discussion of these epistemological issues in feminism, see Smiley; as well as *Feminism/Postmodernism*, ed. Linda J. Nicholson (London: Routledge, 1990), especially essays by Flax, Di Stefano, Harding, Benhabib, Harstock, and Bordo.

10 LaCapra, *History*, p. 137.

11 Harlan, "Intellectual History," *American Historical Review*, p. 433.

12 Shoshana Felman and Dori Laub, *Testimony: Crises of Witnessing in Literature, Psychoanalysis, and History* (London: Routledge, 1992). Henceforth, cited parenthetically in the text.

13 Christina Hoff Sommers, "Sister Soldiers," *The New Republic* (October 5, 1992). Henceforth, cited parenthetically in the text. And *Who Stole Feminism?: How Women Have Betrayed Women* (New York: Simon and Schuster, 1994). For a symposium on the book, see *Democratic Culture* 3, (Fall 1994).

14 Charles J. Sykes, *The Hollow Men: Politics and Corruption in Higher Education* (Washington, DC: Regnery Gateway, 1990).

15 The title may also echo the titles of widely disseminated feminist texts like Audre Lorde's *Sister Outsider: Essays and Speeches* (Trumansburg, NY: The Crossing Press, 1984); Robin Morgan's *Sisterhood Is Powerful* (New York: Random House, 1970); and *Sisterhood Is Global* (New York: Anchor Press/Doubleday, 1984). For another attack on women's studies from a self-identified feminist standpoint, see Karen Lehrman, "Off Course," *Mother Jones* (September/October 1993), pp. 45–51 and pp. 65–68.

16 See Roland Barthes, "The Reality Effect," *The Rustle of Language*, tr. Richard Howard (New York: Hill and Wang, 1986), pp. 141–48, and "The Discourse of History," *The Rustle of Language*, pp. 127–40, especially p. 140.

17 James C. Scott, "History According to Winners and Losers," *History and Peasant Consciousness in Southeast Asia*, ed. Andrew Tarton and Shigenharu Tanabe (Osaka: National Museum of Ethnology, 1984). Henceforth, cited parenthetically in the text.

18 Elizabeth Lapovsky Kennedy's *Boots of Leather, Slippers of Gold: The History of a Lesbian Community* (New York: Routledge, 1993).

19 Jeannine DeLombard, "Buffalo Gals," *New York Times Book Review* (October 24, 1993), p. 24.

20 See also James C. Scott's *Domination and the Arts of Resistance: Hidden Transcripts* (New Haven: Yale University Press, 1990), which argues that members of hegemonic and non-hegemonic groups are continually engaged in interpretive

storytelling in the form of public or hidden transcripts. A peasant, for example, might produce an acquiescent transcript in the presence of a landlord and a rebellious transcript for other peasants.

21 Among those, not cited elsewhere in this text are: Alice Walker, *In Search of Our Mothers' Gardens: Womanist Prose* (New York: Harcourt Brace Jovanovich, 1983), pp. 361–83; Barbara Smith, "Toward a Black Feminist Criticism," *The New Feminist Criticism: An Anthology*, ed. Elaine Showalter (New York: Pantheon, 1985), pp. 168–85; *All American Women: Lines That Divide, Ties That Bind*, ed. Johnnetta B. Cole (New York: The Free Press, 1986); Bonnie Zimmerman, "What Has Never Been: An Overview of Lesbian Feminist Criticism," *New Feminist Criticism*, pp. 200–224; Rachel Blau DuPlessis, "For the Etruscans," *New Feminist Criticism*, pp. 271–91; and Alice Yun Chai, "Toward a Holistic Paradigm for Asian American Women's Studies: A Synthesis of Feminist Scholarship and Women of Color's Feminist Politics," *Women's Studies International Forum* 8 (1985), pp. 59–66.

22 Among those, not cited elsewhere in this text are: *This Bridge Called My Back: Writings of Radical Women of Color*, ed. Cherríe Moraga and Gloria Anzaldúa (Watertown, MA: Persephone Press, 1981); *All the Woman Are White, All the Men Are Black, and Some of Us Are Brave*, ed. Gloria T. Hull, et al. (Old Westbury, NY: Feminist Press, 1982); Evelyn Torton Beck, *Nice Jewish Girls: A Lesbian Anthology* (Watertown, MA: Persephone Press, 1982); and *Lesbian Studies, Present and Future*, ed. Margaret Cruikshank (Old Westbury, NY: Feminist Press, 1982).

23 In *Feminists Theorize the Political*, ed. Judith Butler and Joan W. Scott (New York: Routledge, 1992), Butler and Scott misleadingly appropriate for post-structuralism the initial challenge to the category of "woman" (or "women") as an erasure of differences based on race, class, sexuality, religion, national origin.

24 *Women's Words: The Feminist Practice of Oral History*, ed. Sherna Berger Gluck and Daphne Patai (London: Routledge, 1991). Henceforth, cited parenthetically in the text.

25 Katherine Borland, "That's Not What I Said: Interpretive Conflict in Oral Narrative Research," *Women's Words*, pp. 63–76 and Sondra Hale, "Feminist Method, Process, and Self-Criticism: Interviewing Sudanese Women," *Women's Words*, pp. 121–36.

26 Sherna Berger Gluck, "Advocacy Oral History: Palestinian Women in Resistance," *Women's Words*, pp. 205–20. See also Julia Swindells who, in "Liberating the Subject? Autobiography and 'Women's History': A Reading of *The Diaries of Hannah Cullwick*," warns against reading texts such as *The Diaries of Hannah Cullwick* as the unmediated, authentic expression of a working class woman. Cullwick, a scrub woman in Victorian England, wrote the diaries at the command of her master, who was sexually aroused by her descriptions of drudgery (ed. Personal Narratives Group, *Interpreting Women's Lives: Feminist Theory and Personal Narratives*

[Bloomington: Indiana University Press, 1989], pp. 228–40).

27 For a sampling of poststructuralist feminist texts influential in the 1980s, see *New French Feminisms*, ed. Elaine Marks and Isabel de Courtivron (Amherst: University of Massachusetts Press, 1979); Jane Gallop, *The Daughter's Seduction: Feminism and Psychoanalysis* (Ithaca: Cornell University Press, 1982); Alice A. Jardine, *Gynesis: Configurations of Woman and Modernity* (Ithaca: Cornell University Press, 1985); Catherine Belsey, *Critical Practice* (London: Methuen, 1980); Chris Weedon, *Feminist Practice and Poststructuralist Theory* (Oxford: Basil Blackwell, 1987); and Toril Moi, *Sexual/Textual Politics: Feminist Literary Theory* (London: Methuen, 1985).

28 Jameson, *The Political Unconscious*, p. 9.

29 R. Radhakrishnan, "Feminist Historiography and Post-structuralist Thought," *The Difference Within: Feminism and Critical Theory* (Philadelphia: John Benjamins, 1989), p. 192.

30 *Feminists Theorize the Political*, ed. Butler and Scott, p. xiv.

31 Linda S. Kauffman, "The long goodbye: Against the Personal Testimony or, an Infant Grifter Grows Up," *Changing Subjects: The Making of Feminist Literary Criticism*, ed. Gayle Greene and Coppélia Kahn (London: Routledge, 1993), p. 129, p. 143.

32 Peggy Kamuf, "Replacing Feminist Criticism," *Diacritics* 12 (Summer 1982), p. 42.

33 Judith Butler, *Gender Trouble* (New York: Routledge, 1990), pp. 2–3. Henceforth, cited parenthetically in the text.

34 See Teresa de Lauretis' insistence on the necessity, however utopian, of seeking the "subject of feminism" (*Technologies of Gender: Essays on Theory, Film, and Fiction* (Bloomington: Indiana University Press, 1987). But where Butler means by the phrase the advocacy for women based on a common gender-identity, de Lauretis uses the phrase to indicate what she calls the "elsewhere" or "space-off" of a differently constituted feminist subjectivity. Like Kamuf ("Replacing Feminist Criticism") and Butler, de Lauretis returns centrally to Foucault, but her reliance on Foucauldian concepts of discursive practice is tempered by an insistence that feminists must recognize the limitations of his critiques of identity and experience.

35 Joan Wallach Scott, *Gender and the Politics of History* (New York: Columbia University Press, 1988), p. 9. Henceforth, cited parenthetically in the text.

36 Michel Foucault, *The Archaeology of Knowledge*, tr. A. M. Sheridan Smith (New York: Pantheon, 1972).

37 See also Swindells, "Liberating the Subject?"; Judith Stacey's call for poststructuralist historiography in "Can There Be a Feminist Ethnography?," *Women's Words*, pp. 111–20; and Gluck and Patai's brief acknowledgement of the importance of "contemporary literary theory" for an analysis of linguistic mediations in oral history in the introduction of *Women's Words*. At the 1993 Berkshire Conference for Women's Historians, poststructuralist theory was noticeably a more

significant presence than at the prior Berkshire conferences.

38 Barthes, "The Discourse of History," p. 140. Henceforth, cited parenthetically in the text.

39 See White's discussion of "The Discourse of History" and the general hostility of poststructuralism to historical narrative in "The Question of Narrative," *History and Theory*. See also Benjamin's critique of conventional narrative historicism and advocacy of a messianic, revolutionary "historical materialism" that juxtaposes constellations of time ("Theses on the Philosophy of History," *Illuminations: Essays and Reflections*, ed. Hannah Arendt [New York: Schocken Books, 1968], pp. 253–64).

40 See for example, Kristeva, *Revolution in Poetic Language*, tr. Margaret Waller (New York: Columbia University Press, 1984), especially pp. 58–59, p. 88 and p. 92, and "Women's Time," *Signs* 7 (1981), pp. 13–35; Hélène Cixous, "The Laugh of the Medusa," *New French Feminisms*, pp. 245–64, especially p. 250.

41 See for example Leo Bersani, *A Future for Astyanax: Character and Desire in Literature* (New York: Columbia University Press, 1984), especially pp. 3–16, pp. 51–88, pp. 189–316, who argues that narrative is inherently authoritarian, allied to the state through its connection to mimesis. See also Jay Clayton's critique of Bersani in *The Pleasures of Babel: Contemporary American Literature and Theory* (Oxford: Oxford University Press, 1993), pp. 71–82; and Teresa de Lauretis's *Alice Doesn't: Feminism, Semiotics, Cinema* (Bloomington: Indiana University Press, 1984), pp. 103–58, in which she finds narrative inseparable from an Oedipal configuration of desire in which subjectivity is constituted as masculine, a position she moves beyond in *Technologies of Gender*, in which she specifies "the modes of consciousness of a feminist subjectivity and its inscription" (p. xi). Peter Brooks, who values narrative as an important mode of knowing in *Reading for the Plot: Design and Intention in Narrative* (New York: Vintage, 1984), is a notable exception among poststructuralist theorists. A number of feminist critics find in women's writing a resistance to Oedipal narrative and a location of female subjectivity in pre-Oedipal narrative patterns. See for example DuPlessis, *Writing beyond the Ending: Narrative Strategies of Twentieth-Century Women Writers* (Bloomington: Indiana University Press, 1985); Margaret Homans, *Bearing the Word: Language and Female Experience in Nineteenth-Century Women's Writing* (Chicago: University of Chicago Press, 1986); Marianne Hirsch, *The Mother/Daughter Plot: Narrative, Psychoanalysis, Feminism* (Bloomington: Indiana University Press, 1989); Marilyn Sprengnether, *The Spectral Mother: Freud, Feminism, and Psychoanalysis* (Ithaca: Cornell University Press, 1990); and Elizabeth Abel, "Narrative Structure(s) and Female Development: The Case of *Mrs. Dalloway*," *The Voyage In: Fictions of Female Development*, ed. Elizabeth Abel et al. (Hanover, NH: University of New England Press, 1983), pp. 161–85. For an extended discussion, see Susan Stanford Friedman, "Craving Stories: Narrative and Lyric in Contemporary Theory and Women's Long Poems," *Feminist Measures: Soundings in*

Poetry and Theory (Ann Arbor: University of Michigan Press, 1994) and "Lyric Subversion of Narrative in Women's Writing: Virginia Woolf and the Tyranny of Plot," *Reading Narrative: Form, Ethics, Ideology*, ed. James Phelan (Columbus: Ohio State University Press, 1989), pp. 162–85.

42 Paul de Man, "Reading and History," *The Resistance to Theory* (Minneapolis: University of Minnesota Press, 1986), p. 67. See also de Man, *Blindness and Insight* (Minneapolis: University of Minnesota Press, 1983), especially pp. 142–66, pp. 187–228 and *Allegories of Reading* (New Haven: Yale University Press, 1979), in which he argues against the referential and for the figural function of narrative. See also Robert L. Caserio's discussion of de Man, "'A Pathos of Uncertain Agency': Paul de Man and Narrative," *Journal of Narrative Technique* 20 (Spring 1990), pp. 195–209; and Foucault's analysis of the relation between allegory and story in *The Order of Things* (New York: Vintage, 1970). For a variety of poststructuralist interrogations of history and historiography, see *Post-structructuralism and the Question of History*, ed. Derek Attridge, Geoff Bennington, and Robert Young (Cambridge: Cambridge University Press, 1987).

43 Daphne Patai, "U.S. Academics and Third World Women: Is Ethical Research Possible?," *Women's Words*, p. 150.

44 The other essays in Gluck and Patai's *Women's Words* also urge that the problems they reflect upon not lead to the abandonment of oral history methodologies. See also Marjorie Shostak, "'What the Wind Won't Take Away': The Genesis of *Nisa— The Life and Words of a !Kung Woman*," *Interpreting Women's Lives*, pp. 228–40, whose article on the production of *Nisa*, the personal narrative of a !Kung woman, on the one hand problematizes her own extensive mediation and on the other hand testifies to the urgency of (re)telling narratives of people whose way of life is under erasure.

45 I realize I risk here homogenizing the complex and different discourses of poststructuralism, but I do so strategically to emphasize what these various theories share in their common focus on constructivist discourse and their insistence on problematization, however much they might differ in other regards.

46 *The Limits of Theory*, ed. Thomas M. Kavanagh (Stanford: Stanford University Press, 1989), p. 10, p. 15 and p. 17. Henceforth, cited parenthetically in the text.

47 Paul Smith, *Discerning the Subject* (Minneapolis: University of Minnesota Press, 1988), pp. 50–51. Henceforth, cited parenthetically in the text.

48 Michèle Barrett, "Ideology and the Cultural Production of Gender," *Feminist Criticism and Social Change: Sex, Class and Race in Literature and Culture*, ed. Judith Newton and Deborah Rosenfelt (London: Methuen, 1985), p. 72.

49 For others who make variations on this point in relation to specific groups of women, see for example *Changing Our Own Words: Essays on Criticism, Theory, and Writing by Black Women*, ed. Cheryl A. Wall (New Brunswick: Rutgers University Press, 1989), especially p. 10; R. Radhakrishnan, "Ethnic Identity and Post-

Structuralist Différance," *Cultural Critique* 6 (Spring 1987), pp. 199–220; Teresa de Lauretis, "Feminist Studies/Critical Studies: Issues, Terms, and Contexts," *Feminist Studies/Critical Studies*; *Sexual Practice/Textual Theory: Lesbian Cultural Criticism*, ed. Susan J. Wolfe and Julia Penelope (Cambridge: Blackwell, 1993), pp. 1–24; Deborah McDowell, "Reading Family Matters," *Changing Our Own Words*, pp. 75–97; Chandra Talpade Mohanty's concept of "third world women" as an "imagined community" in "Cartographies of Struggle," *Third World Women*, pp. 1–49; and Eve Kosofsky Sedgwick's notion of the "minoritizing" discourse about gays and lesbians that must complement the universalizing discourse of queer theory in *Epistemology of the Closet* (Berkeley: University of California Press, 1990), especially pp. 40–41. See also *The Future of Literary Theory*, ed. Ralph Cohen (London: Routledge, 1989), especially pp. vii–xx.

50 Barbara Christian, "The Race for Theory," *Gender and Theory: Dialogues on Feminist Criticism*, ed. Linda Kauffman (Cambridge: Blackwell, 1989), p. 225.

51 See for example Paul Smith's chapter on feminism, in which he credits poststructuralist feminism with bringing poststructuralist theory in general back to historical and political questions but dismisses out of hand what he calls humanist feminism (*Discerning the Subject*, pp. 133–52). See my "Post/Poststructuralist Feminist Criticism: The Politics of Recuperation and Negotiation," *New Literary History* 22, 2 (Spring 1991), pp. 465–90 for extended discussion.

52 In Scott, *Gender and the Politics of History*, p. 6. Similarly, as an implicit dismissal of literary history, Butler explains that "the sudden intrusion, the unanticipated agency, of a female 'object' who inexplicably returns the [male] glance, reverses the [male] gaze, and contests the place and authority of the masculine position…couldn't quite hold my attention," (*Gender Trouble,* p. ix).

53 Molly Hite, "'Except Thou Ravish Me': Penetrations into the Life of the (Feminine) Mind," *Changing Subjects*, p. 125.

54 Gayle Greene, "Looking at History," *Changing Subjects*, pp. 16–17.

55 Lerner, *The Majority Finds Its Past*, p. 166.

56 Annette Kolodny, "Dancing Between Left and Right: Feminism and the Academic Minefield in the 1980s," *Feminist Studies* 14 (Fall 1988), p. 464.

57 Elaine Showalter, *A Literature of Their Own: British Women Novelists from Brontë to Lessing* (Princeton: Princeton University Press, 1977), p. 10.

58 It is beyond the scope of this essay to explore what I believe is an (not *the*) underlying cause of much conflict among academic feminists—namely, the generational issue. See for example Helena Michie, "Mother, Sister, Other: The 'Other' Woman in Feminist Theory," *Literature and Psychology* 32 (1986), pp. 1–10; Evelyn Fox Keller and Helen Moglen, "Competition and Feminism: Conflicts for Academic Women," *Signs* 12 (1987), pp. 493–511; and *Competition: A Feminist Taboo?*," ed. Valerie Miner and Helen E. Longino (New York: Feminist Press, 1987). An effort

to historicize the positions and perspectives of each generation could foster the multiplicity of generational voices rather than the silencing of one by another.

59 Silko, *Storyteller*, p. 247.

60 Michael Schumacher, "A Marriage of Minds: Louise Erdrich and Michael Dorris," *Writer's Digest* (June 1991), pp. 29–30.

61 Toni Morrison, "Memory, Creation, and Writing," *Thought* 59 (December 1984), pp. 385–90.

62 Kim Chernin, *In My Mother's House: A Daughter's Story* (New York: Harper and Row, 1983), p. 17.

63 Irena Klepfisz, "Solitary Acts," *A Few Words in the Mother Tongue* (Portland, Oregon: The Eight Mountain Press, 1990), p. 201.

64 For extended discussion, see my "Craving Stories."

65 Ursula K. LeGuin, "It Was a Dark and Stormy Night, or, Why Are We Huddling around the Campfire?," *On Narrative*, ed. W. J. T. Mitchell (Chicago: University of Chicago Press, 1981), pp. 187–96.

66 Greene, "Looking at History," *Changing Subjects*, p. 11.

67 See also Hite's discussion of the dual functions of narrative and its necessity for feminism ("'Except thou ravish me,'" *Changing Subjects*, especially p. 127).

68 Toni Morrison, "Unspeakable Things Unspoken: The Afro-American Presence in American Literature," *Michigan Quarterly Review* 28 (Winter 1989), p. 9.

69 Gianna Pomata's interesting historiographic essay, "History, Particular and Universal: On Reading Some Recent Women's History Textbooks," favors "particular" or local histories over any kind of generalizing histories and spatial/topical histories over chronological narratives (*Feminist Studies* 19, 1 [Spring 1993], pp. 7–50).

70 Brooks, *Reading for the Plot*, p. 61.

71 See Brooks, *Reading for the Plot*, especially pp. 37–61; Clayton, *The Pleasures of Babel*, especially pp. 3–31 and pp. 61–89; and Hutcheon, *The Politics of Postmodernism*, especially pp. 62–92.

72 Susan Stanford Friedman, "Forbidden Fruits of Knowledge: The Psychodynamics of the Education of Women and Women in Education," *The Annual of Psychoanalysis* 15 (1987), pp. 353–74.

73 Harriet A. Jacobs, *Incidents in the Life of a Slave Girl: written by herself*, ed. L. Maria Child and Jean Fagan Yellin (Cambridge, MA: Harvard University Press, 1987).

74 Sheila Rowbotham, *Women's Consciousness, Man's World* (Baltimore: Penguin, 1973), p. 27.

75 See Bahti's discussion of the will-to-power inherent in the "historicism in man," that is, the desire within man to make and write history (*Allegories of History*, pp. 5–6).

76 Linda Gordon, *Heroes of Their Own Lives: The Politics and History of Family Violence:*

Boston 1880–1960 (New York: Viking, 1988); and Scott, *Gender and the Politics of History*.

77 Linda Gordon, *Woman's Body, Woman's Right: A Social History of Birth Control in America* (New York: Grossman, 1976).

78 Linda Gordon, "Response to Scott," *Signs* 15 (Summer 1990), p. 852.

79 Joan Wallach Scott, "Review of *Heroes of Their Own Lives*, by Linda Gordon," *Signs* 15 (Summer 1990), p. 851. Henceforth, cited parenthetically in the text. Scott's approach to agency is based in the early work of Foucault, who by the late 1970s and early 1980s reintroduced concepts of the self and agency that his earlier work had discredited.

80 Joan Wallach Scott, "Response to Gordon," *Signs* 15 (Summer 1990), p. 859.

81 Linda Gordon, "Review of *Gender and the Politics of History,* by Joan Wallach Scott," *Signs* 15 (Summer 1990), pp. 854–55. Henceforth, cited parenthetically in the text.

82 Gordon, "Response to Scott," p. 853. Henceforth, cited parenthetically in the text.

83 Scott, *Gender and the Politics of History*, p. 9.

84 See my "Weavings: Intertextuality and the (Re)Birth of the Author," *Influence and Intertextuality in Literary History*, ed. Jay Clayton and Eric Rothstein (Madison: University of Wisconsin Press, 1991), pp. 146–80 for discussion of this (post)colonial dynamic.

85 See Elaine Showalter, "Women's Time, Women's Space: Writing the History of Feminist Criticism," *Feminist Issues in Literary Scholarship*, ed. Shari Benstock (Bloomington: Indiana University Press, 1987), pp. 30–44; Moi, *Sexual/Textual Politics*; and Spivak, "French Feminism in an International Frame," *In Other Worlds*, pp. 134–53.

86 See especially Joan Kelly, "Did Women Have a Renaissance?," *Women, History, and Theory: Essays of Joan Kelly* (Chicago: University of Chicago Press, 1984), pp. 19–50 and "The Social Relation of the Sexes: Methodological Implications of Women's History," *Signs* 1 (Summer 1976), pp. 809–23 for influential examples.

87 Showalter, "Women's Time," p. 36. Henceforth, cited parenthetically in the text.

88 However much Showalter can be criticized for her privileging of gynocriticism over gynesis in "Women's Time," "Feminist Criticism," or *The New Feminist Criticism*, it should be noted that she acknowledges the importance of poststructuralist feminist theory and criticism more thoroughly and respectfully than many feminist poststructuralists acknowledge the work of non-poststructuralist feminist critics.

89 Moi, *Sexual/Textual Politics*, p. 6. Henceforth, cited parenthetically in the text.

90 Spivak, "French Feminism in an International Frame," *In Other Worlds*, p. 141, p. 152. Henceforth, cited parenthetically in the text.

91 Julia Kristeva, *About Chinese Women*, tr. Anita Barrows (London: Marion Boyars, 1977).

92 See also Spivak's "Three Women's Texts and a Critique of Imperialism," *Feminisms: An Anthology of Literary Theory and Criticism*, ed. Robyn Warhol and Diane Price Herndl (New Brunswick: Rutgers University Press, 1991), pp. 798–814, in which she shows how Western feminist emphasis on narratives of individual female awakening obscures the colonial politics of novels such as *Jane Eyre*.

93 Hutcheon, *The Politics of Postmodernism*, p. 64. Henceforth, cited parenthetically in the text.

94 R. Radhakrishnan, "Nationalism, Gender, and the Narrative of Identity," *Nationalisms and Sexualities*, ed. Andrew Parker et al. (London: Routledge, 1992), p. 81. I am adapting Radhakrishnan's argument against the attempt by any single discourse of class, gender, nationality, sexuality (etc.) to subsume the others under its own hegemony.

95 Radhakrishnan, "Feminist Historiography," *The Difference Within*, p. 189. Henceforth, cited parenthetically in the text.

96 Gordon, "Review of *Gender and the Politics of History*, by Joan Wallach Scott," *Signs*, p. 858.

2

HOW TO SATISFY A WOMAN "EVERY TIME"...

Judith Roof

In 1993, an inspirational self-help sex manual reappeared in a massive promotion on the shelves of shopping mall book stores. Originally published in 1982, Naura Hayden's single-message missal *How To Satisfy a Woman "Every Time"...and have her beg for more!* enjoyed a fleeting second-life.[1] Promoting the simple precept that giving women sexual pleasure leads to lasting marriages, the garish red book's resurrection after eleven years not only suggests some odd parallels between early 1980s and early 1990s anxieties about the creeping empowerment of women, but it also offers the same miracle cure. Equating coital orgasm with emancipation and emancipation with domestic felicity, *How To Satisfy a Woman Every Time* makes sexual satisfaction the route to gender equality. While this orgasmic deliverance presumably makes everybody happy, it also essentially returns the imploring, but "liberated," sated woman to business as patriarchal usual, illustrating the staying power of that old disciplinary regimen, "one good fuck..." Hayden's thigh-squeeze formula for liberation provides a perverse, but not entirely perverted insight, into the narrative ideologies and metaphors that structure the self-perceptions of a women's movement whose historical destiny would be to produce, among other things, a book like Naura Hayden's.

It seems at best a stretch to link Naura Hayden to feminism, just as it seems almost criminal to count

Phyllis Schlafly as someone who represents women's interests. But both phenomena are integral effects of the ideologies of narrative that shape the histories that mainstream feminism writes for and about itself. These histories, including such early seventies' collections and manifesto analyses as Robin Morgan's *Sisterhood Is Powerful*, Adrienne Rich's *Of Woman Born*, and Ti-Grace Atkinson's *Amazon Odyssey*, establish the historical truth of gender oppression to argue for continuing feminist struggle.[2] All three influential feminist treatises employ historical narratives of gender oppression to explain and justify feminism's goals and modus operandi. In each, the notion that truth discovered through history will set women free is linked to narrative as a particular way of organizing knowledge, one that requires the coming together of opposites in a productive (or reproductive) joinder. This ideology of narrative is embodied and adapted in feminist accounts by two related structuring metaphors, sisterhood and maternity. Here, the coincidence of a belief in the power of historical truth, the hetero-ideology of the reproductive narrative, and a reliance on sororal and maternal paradigms determines the shape of cause/effect relations among eventsseen as propelling historical change. Thus, the very figuration of a feminist narrative of history demarcates not only what events are important and what issues might be considered, but it also determines how events and issues relate to one another and to the world.

SISTERHOOD IS POWERFUL

Commencing with the telling statement, "This book is an action," Robin Morgan's *Sisterhood Is Powerful: An Anthology of Writings from the Women's Liberation Movement* (1970) recalls a history of oppression in order to write a history of emancipation.[3] Compiling and arranging a series of analyses, testimonies, experiential witnessings, and histories into a narrative that establishes the truth of gender oppression, *Sisterhood* simultaneously presents the motive for feminist action and reports the exposure of oppression as feminism's happy result. The collection is organized into sections that, taken together, delineate the cause/effect trajectory of feminism's narrative of historical change. Proceeding from an introductory, historical overview, the book traces the liberating power of historical truth as such truth is reiterated in the individual chronicles of a somewhat diverse sample of women. The book's section titles—"The Oppressed Majority: The Way It Is," "The Invisible Woman: Psychological and Sexual Repression," "Go Tell It in the Valley: Changing Consciousness," "Up From Sexism; Emerging Ideologies," and "The Hand That Cradles the Rock: Protest and Revolt"—trace this telling of history as a moment of liberation. The collection's testimony is itself shaped as a narrative in which "the way it is" (the oppressive truth found through history) encourages a correspondent recognition of women's repression of their true selves (the truth brought to light in the present). In the collective telling of stories of oppression, in the production of an enlightened history, *Sisterhood Is Powerful* enacts its own narrative of social change, written now as the widespread consciousness of the truth of oppression. This new history, thus inscribed by the collection, represents the formulation of a narrative of revised or corrected knowledge that both prescribes and justifies further social action.

Integral to the collection's narrative of feminist history is the sisterhood paradigm, the first structuring metaphor to emerge in post-seventies' feminist accounts of itself. Appropriating the family narrative and valorizing the positions of least influence—sisters, mothers—Morgan's anthology appears to radicalize them into the sphere of most influence and most danger. Figured as an egalitarian variety within a still-hierarchical familial model, sisterhood cloaks the threatened sibling rivalry among the diverse positions and experiences of oppression presented in the book. While each sister—secretary, professional, high schooler, African-American, housewife, Chinese woman—can claim her own measure of sexist domination, the organizing paradigm of sisterhood appears to equalize the competing claims of these metaphorical sisters by emphasizing and empowering sisterly bonds within the larger, more hostile, cultural "family." Appealing to sisterhood's apparently egalitarian organization to defy the hierarchical, acquisitorial, and combative values of patriarchy, feminism's account of itself bravely substitutes a narrative of affiliation for filiation, sharing for debt, and generosity for generation. However, the unification of different women into a single sororal protagonist pitted against a figurative father not only tends to complete the erasure of positional differences among women (and all issues relating to position), but it also reinscribes a familial—even Oedipal—narrative as the pattern that defines the battle and the category sister in the first place. Sisterhood, thus, also invokes all of the power disparities of intra-familial squabbles whose resolution is usually a return to a status quo.

Sisterhood Is Powerful's sisterly familial narrative thus reflects both the effects of a powerfully insistent narrative hetero-ideology and an underlying belief in the power of the truth generated by a historical, but still reproductive, narrative. Morgan's "Introduction" to the collection is a radicalized telling of family history within an insistently-referenced reproductive frame. Linking the production of the book to histories of conception and birth—that of the book, her own contemporaneous experience of maternity, and issues about birth control, abortion, and child-care—Morgan's familial narrative defines feminism's primary conflict as a large-order marital spat on the level of social reality. Patriarchy, the system run by men, oppresses women in the name of gender ideology, and gender ideology is perpetuated by that oppression. Women's liberation in

Morgan's book is about recasting gender relations so that power is no longer gender-defined, thereby equalizing roles and making society functional for everyone. This victory narrative is a version of the heterologous (and overtly heterosexual) conflict/conjoinder pattern by which most modern narrative is already defined: it is a "marriage" plot where two "sides" of a binary opposition encounter conflicts and delays on their way to ultimate joinder and successful reproduction (of a child, of narrative, of satisfaction, of a less oppressive world). The narrative of women's liberation, then, tells the story of a hoped-for relationship where an ultimate rejoinder will guarantee the changes wrought by the conflict in getting there—actually much like good old Naura Hayden's recipe for satisfying sex.

Another clue to the centrality of this narrative hetero-ideology in Morgan's account is her constant references to familial and reproductive issues as defining both the stakes and the effects of the feminist battle. Repeated examples of the problems that make visible the need for change—child care, birth control, abortion, and the nuclear family, for instance—are the center of contention. This situates the entire historical narrative of feminist praxis within a very literal heterosexual, patriarchal, and specifically reproductive realm generated as much by the authority of experience as it is a product of the reproductive narrative from which it is derived. In so far as Morgan situates personal experience as the authority for a theory that rationalizes such narrative—"the theory, then, comes out of human feeling, not out of textbook rhetoric. *That's* truly revolutionary…"[4]—her emphasis on reproductive and family issues makes sense as constituting a large portion of women's experiential conflicts. The problem, however, comes in understanding the relation between the practical manifestation of sexual ideologies in experience and the way that same ideology already defines the terms and the dynamic of the history that is constructed. In other words, experience tends to reify the narrative that already founds the oppression and the choice of a reproductive *mise en scène* may be equally an effect of narrative ideology. Moreover, the reproductive narrative makes the consideration of issues other than those produced through this narrative difficult. These issues can only occupy the place of "difference," interference, blockage. This explains, for instance, Morgan's placing of racial issues as parallel to rather than as an integral part of women's liberation. Equally "other" to the reproductive narrative, but recognized as analogous to the spirit of emancipation, are such categories as "high school women" (too young to be married) and "female homosexuality," whose presence in the collection is a synecdoche for all differences among women. Even more other is pleasure without purpose, theorizations, analysis and interpretations that don't subscribe to the truth of history or to the narrative of eventual triumph and rejoinder such a feminist self-history inscribes.

On some level, however, Morgan is aware of the terms posed by the story itself. At the end of her narrative of feminist history, when she discusses the viability of the nuclear family, she asks what the alternatives to that social formation might be—the alternatives, in essence, to the narrative of conjoinder and reproduction. Her answers represent a range of possible joinders or rejections that, rather than displacing both the ending and its narrative, reaffirm it one more time. In suggesting celibacy, communes, separatist communities, extended families, even homosexuality as a "viable political alternative which straight women must begin to recognize as such," Morgan lists all of the possible endings to (and positions produced by) the hetero-narrative. But in wanting "a beautiful affirmation of human *sexuality*, without all these absurd prefixes," Morgan proceeds to write a narrative whose ideology already determines the choice of possible answers and the terms of the debate.[5] Sexuality (without those "absurd prefixes") becomes the revised model of an egalitarian joinder whose very freedom from prefixes both screens the disturbing differences those prefixes might import and cunningly returns a liberated, disavowed, but nonetheless still very heterosexual status quo. The result of all this is supposedly the possibility of ending in satisfaction.

Aligning literal reproduction with a conjunctive narrative model requires history, not only the specifically generational history of the nuclear family, but also history as the reproductive site of the truth that will produce a more egalitarian present. Telling history performs the adage that the truth will set you free, a narrative that both sustains a reproductive ideology (conjoinder provides a new truth) and is itself a version of it (liberating knowledge comes from conflict and is its answer). Within the aegis of very literal reproductive scenarios, Morgan's collection is preoccupied with narrating history both in its two inaugural essays and in the set of "Historical Documents" appended at the end. Consisting of a brief account of earlier feminist movements and a series of late-sixties manifestos, these framing histories situate feminism as an already historical narrative which in itself represents a political action. The volume's manifestoes, for example, represent the rebellious inscription of this revised feminist narrative of history. Including the NOW Bill of Rights, excerpts from the SCUM (Society for Cutting Up Men) Manifesto, Lilith's Manifesto, Redstockings Manifesto, and the WITCH Documents, the manifestoes in the collection embody the contradictory impetus of narrating history as praxis. Uncovering the truth of history and reinscribing it as action tends paradoxically to contain the change such truth might catalyze. Knowledge by itself is not enough to change the story. In fact, knowledge becomes the story's satisfaction.

Girded by histories understood to constitute action, *Sisterhood Is Powerful* suggests a historical recursivity. The repetition and reiteration of the same pattern (a narrative of history) within the very terms (narrating) already defined by the pattern (history) signals some anxiety about history and the narrating thereof, whose liberatory assumptions about the knowledge of oppression feminism had already accepted in order to define itself as feminism in the first place. By 1970, in other words, feminism was already a truth based on and derived from a history whose plot had consisted of narrating a true history, a history whose truth in the early seventies constituted the action the narrative required.

The overt feminist link between history, narrative, and liberation is already part of an ideology of history that does not escape either assumptions about the liberatory value of knowledge or the paradigm of conjoinder. Our idea of history, in large part, is shaped not by sets of pre-defined events but by our ways of selecting and organizing them. This is because history, as we understand it, is already narrative—a story with a beginning, middle, and projected end, with cause/effect relations, characters, and plot. And this narrative, as Hayden White suggests, is "a metacode, a human universal on the basis of which transcultural messages about the nature of a shared reality can be transmitted."[6] Implicit in White's observation is the idea that narrative is a form of knowledge, a way of organizing the known into a discourse. This "metacode" itself is not value free; rather, as Morgan's feminist history reveals, it is also constituted by meta-narratives that, in defining the possibilities for human knowledge and action, provide a legitimating frame for mapping human activity, especially including the writing of histories.

If, as Jean-François Lyotard contends, narratives legitimate certain ideologies of knowledge, then these meta-narratives of legitimation determine the understandings of knowledge that define the shape and assumptions of feminist accounts of events.[7] In this context, feminist narratives of the liberating truth of history would be close to what Lyotard identifies as narratives of the "self-grounding of freedom," where the "subject is concrete, or supposedly so. And its epic is the story of its emancipation from everything that prevents it from governing itself," is a narrative in which knowledge "is in the service of the subject; its only legitimacy…is the fact that it allows morality to become reality."[8] The idea that knowledge exists to inform the "practical subject about the reality within which" the subject can execute "prescriptive utterances pertaining to the truth" is the legitimating narrative of social movements, including feminism.[9]

This meta-narrative of knowledge and emancipation provides one of the underlying premises of feminist inscriptions of its own history: that knowledge of gender oppression prescribes and justifies the actions taken to emancipate female subjects from that oppression. Another related premise, Joan Scott points out, is that "history figures…as a participant in the production of knowledge about sexual difference."[10] Coming then from both directions, the link between history and knowledge permeates the 1970s feminist narratives of itself, produced by and producing knowledge about sexual difference and gender oppression. Early 1970s feminist anthologies, including Morgan's, are concerned with establishing a certain knowledge of sexual oppression. They situate themselves and their act of promulgating knowledge—a specifically historical knowledge—as the commencement of revolutionary action. This occurs despite the fact that adopting a concrete subject position (produced by the very system in which that subject was already oppressed) creates both political and narratological contradictions.

It is precisely the presence of this narrative ideology that makes Morgan's anthology both cogent and persuasive—already familiar and functioning within the larger meta-narrative that the collection serves. But narrative also defines which texts are seen as constituting the history that defines the movement. By collapsing experience into "theory," and by defining Women's Liberation as an emancipation *from* a hegemonic patriarchy whose scene of operations is the family, Morgan appears to define feminism in terms of patriarchy. At the same time, the coalescence of a reproductive narrative ideology with a meta-narrative of liberating knowledge produces this history, making the choice for her, requiring a patriarchal scenario, the valorization of history as action, and the equation of experience and theory. Those issues or questions that do not join reproduction, experience, and certain knowledge are situated as other to feminism and exist as side-bars: for instance, non-reproductive sexuality, pleasure, theory not tied to the language of experience, or speculation. Those positions unaccounted for within a heterosexual aegis become curiously aligned with the place of the "other," the excess variety that must be recognized, but which unless analogous, breaks up the unified subject of consciousness upon which this feminist narrative depends. Jill Johnston's contemporaneous *Lesbian Nation* is testimony to this split, as it recognizes and complains about the very heterosexual identification—even blindness—of early 1970s feminism.[11]

OF WOMAN BORN

While the sisterhood paradigm would seem to admit infinite variety, the other metaphor of feminist self-histories would appear to delimit feminist considerations to a fairly heterosexual, literally reproductive realm from the start. Expanding and theorizing maternity in the mid-1970s, Adrienne Rich draws out the potential power of the maternal as another governing figure of feminism's accounts of itself. Poised at the intersection of history and feminist consciousness, the essays collected in *Of Woman Born* not only investigate and critique the "institution" of mothering under patriarchy, but also posit the emancipatory possibilities of inscribing a more feminist history of mothering.

Proposing that the institution of mothering has been used as a pretext for the oppression of women while its positive powers, omitted in histories, serve as a potential source of feminist power and understanding, Rich simultaneously analyzes and inscribes a more liberating maternal history. As in Morgan's anthology, history itself is the legitimating locus of Rich's maternal theorizing as well as the liberatory narrative that itself constitutes feminist praxis.

Reclaiming maternity as neither necessarily patriarchal nor heterosexual, Rich writes a revised social history through which she tries "to distinguish between two meanings of motherhood, one superimposed upon the other: the *potential relationship* of any woman to her powers of reproduction and to children and the *institution*, which aims at ensuring that potential—and all women—shall remain under male control."[12] Imagined as a "relationship" hampered and suppressed by an institution other to it, maternity becomes the hidden truth that would set women free. Overtly situated as the flip-side of patriarchy, mothering becomes a model for woman-to-woman relationships as well as the paradigm for the narrative of female contribution, values, and validation. As in the sisterhood metaphor, the imagined quality of these relations embodies and enacts a different deployment of power whose more egalitarian and enlightened division might end gender oppression by providing a better pattern for human interaction. Like the sororal metaphor, maternity and its positive potentials emphasize values apposite to the institutional, proprietary, generational, patriarchal narrative of law and the perpetuation of property. For Rich, these maternal potentials are specifically rediscovered in a historical narrative written from the perspective of the already-suspected potentials of motherhood. Adopting Virginia Woolf's rationale for a woman-centered history, Rich's narrative of motherhood both begins with and proves the emancipatory narrative of maternity, creating a circle where the end is the beginning and where the history narrated is circumscribed by the terms it sets out to discover. In this sense Rich's history proves the thesis with which she begins: that motherhood is a powerful challenge to patriarchy. But it also shapes itself according to what Rich identifies as the two major manifestations of this oppressed maternal: "the biological potential or capacity to bear and nourish human life, and the magical power invested in women by men, whether in the form of Goddess-worship or the fear of being controlled and overwhelmed by women."[13]

The knowledge of maternal potential, as in sisterhood, defines the questions Rich's history may pose. As a model for human interaction, motherhood tends to limit the range of possible questions to those comprehended within the valorized, but primarily non-sexualized relations among women. Like Hélène Cixous who posits a gift economy as quintessentially feminine and liberating, Rich envisions nourishment as a metaphor of human relations that follow a female rather than a male model.[14] But this forecloses issues of class, non–reproductive sexuality and pleasure, theory, and analysis, making all creatures of a different, perhaps less nourishing economy. And while the positive potential of emphasizing life, nurturing, and giving may shift the emphasis of the familial narrative, it is still a creature of it; the danger is, as always, that valorizing the role to which one is already assigned merely perpetuates the system in which one is entrapped. Biology becomes theology or at least metaphysics.

Perhaps this unchanged familial location tempts Rich to bolster the potential power of the mother by summoning the more magical power mythically attributed to women, linked to goddess worship and to matriarchy even as this great mother is still all in the family. While the sisterhood narrative locates transformations, conflict, and production in a contemporaneous, familial frame, the great mother narrative evokes in a parallel, competing female form the intergenerational narrative patriarchy already works hard to sustain. This intergenerational narrative is a diachronic version of family conflict, whose transformations occur as a part of the process of history. Perhaps that is why maternity is so linked to the telling of history and why sisterhood must brace itself with a history it otherwise does not have except via a generational, historical model.

While the act of telling the revised histories of sisterhood and maternity appears to perform some political action, the reproductive narrative that defines them both tends to perpetuate a patriarchal status quo by preserving the narrative dynamic—the familial, heterosexual conjoinder—in the present and through history while seeming to allow specific elements to change. This narrative constant enables the orderly devolution of values and traits (tradition) while also appearing to account for progress and historical variation. Hence, motherhood's hidden values representing a sacred tradition can be rediscovered and can influence the present, even as successive daughters, at least in Julia Kristeva's account of "Women's Time," might change the scope and terms of the debate.[15] But this tradition is also highly conservative, reiterating—and in fact, amplifying—the narrative and ideological dynamic that is the problem in the first place.

In addition, the combination of the reproductive narrative and history (or history as a version of the reproductive narrative) imports a specific mechanism of inter-generational conflict that not only accounts for the limited kinds of change permissible between generations, but also delimits the kinds of relations—and hence questions—possible. At this point in time, this mechanism is a specifically oedipal rebellion, the challenge for power made by the younger generation to the previous in a specifically familial matrix. As the figure for transition and change through time, this oedipality paradoxically preserves the value of "originary" authority—the law of the father or the mother—by contesting position and historical priority. Sons fight fathers and daughters fight mothers to distinguish themselves from the past, inscribing a history whose model is precisely the alternation of potential (but institutionally repressed) difference and a return to an adjusted status quo, because the status quo of originary power is what is being fought for in the first place.

Sexually segregated, the oedipal conflict occurs between male and male or female and female; focusing attention on such conflict as the mechanism of change displaces even the question of gender relations to the margins. The competitive same-sex focus of the oedipal projects desire and resolution only within the heterosexual pattern of the family. It disallows almost any consideration of non-reproductive or extra-familial issues such as racial and class differences, and non-reproductive sexuality. It also prevents an analysis of the framing assumptions themselves unless such issues are understood within a familial metaphor. And racial issues and sexuality are generally transmuted into gendered, familial frames, but the answers, as might be anticipated, are the same answers the narrative supplies for the separate but unequal gender battle that plays through the family. The oedipal, of course, makes any analysis of framing assumptions itself an oedipal question, a challenge not of the idea of the family but of the law of the father that governs it.

Rich's evocation of matriarchy as a powerful, historically repressed, competing system superficially appears to upset this oedipal scheme by actively seeking to revive an originary maternal power instead of attempting to supplant and appropriate it. In Rich's model, knowledge of an origin—the great goddess—becomes the inspiration for change in the present. But in suspending inter-generational conflict in favor of the liberating character of a hidden tradition, Rich relocates the diachronic intergenerational oedipal battle back into contemporaneous conflict of competing modes of sibling power—matriarchy versus patriarchy. Situating the matriarchal values modelled on ideal mothering against patriarchal values constructs a conflict between supposed equals whose outcome might be victory for women or an egalitarian truce, but in any case a better family. The problem, of course, is in imagining that the values attributed to matriarchy overcome the generational and authoritarian structure in which they are embedded. Matriarchy is patriarchy with a different cast.

And maternity, while theoretically admitting all women, relies upon a quite literal heterosexually reproductive function (even in its extended metaphorical versions) and also tends to situate reproduction as a kind of female essence—something women do that men can't. As in the sisterhood model, this emphasis discourages the consideration of certain issues that do not fit easily into the hetero-reproductive structure and sidelines potential feminist positions other than those not comprehended even largely within a figurative maternal. Note, for example, how this generational maternal model works in Julia Kristeva's

"Women's Time" where the narrative of female oedipal progress through history quite literally disallows considerations of lesbian sexuality as a short-cir-
cuiting, short term resolution in a narrative bent on change as a function of
conjunction.

The maternal model, because of its diachronic cast, coalesces with history,
providing an automatic paradigm for feminist change through reference to an
unflagging but fearsome maternal alter ego whose emancipatory power lies in
the very fact of its existence, discovery, and evocation. Not only is this just like
the emancipatory quality of telling history in *Sisterhood Is Powerful*, but it also
constitutes a historical constant whose very power lies in its history and authenticity and in its value as an authentic authority for an alternative organization.
Maternity's fearsomeness, a quality Rich poses as natural, comes from its intrinsic challenge to patriarchy, but this fearsomeness also suppresses the quite literal
homosexuality the maternal construction would seem to require. And while
Rich is certainly not afraid of homosexuality, the maternal narrative disallows
it, displacing homosexuality in favor of a literal doubling or reproduction of
itself that appears in such forms as Nancy Chodorow's *Reproduction of Mothering*,
the idea of a female literary tradition, and in psychoanalytic theories of the female
as insufficiently differentiated.[16] And while we might understand those dis-
placements in accounts of female development and literary history as simply
homophobic, the maternal paradigm and its attachment to the reproductive narrative already disenables any consideration of lesbian sexuality and other
non-reproductive issues except as barriers to—as things that get in the way of—
the narrative of conjoinder and liberating knowledge.

THE OTHER SIDE OF WHAT CAN'T BE ASKED

The maternal metaphor does carry with it the fearsome spectre of the amazon,
the rebellious, independent woman as a metaphor for its challenge to patriarchy;
and this amazon figure, as Diane Griffin Crowder points out, evokes not only a
mythical history, but also the lesbian whose narrative of woman-to-women relations appears to provide a third alternative metaphor to shape feminist
self-histories.[17] But while Monique Wittig might try to mine the figure of the
lesbian for such a model, the lesbian as amazon is already subsumed within the
generational narrative, linked to halcyon matriarchy and delimited by a narrative
whose emancipatory compulsion rejects and contains as prehistorical and mythical both the independent woman and ideologically non-reproductive
positions.[18] Ti-Grace Atkinson sanitizes the amazon in her theories of feminist
revolution, making the figure curiously and insistently non-sexual (which means
again heterosexual). Atkinson's theory, contemporary to both Morgan's *Sisterhood*
and Rich's *Of Woman Born*, raises and openly rejects the questions that neither

Morgan's nor Rich's paradigms of narrative and history will allow to be raised. But Atkinson, who employs the same narratives, can pose these questions only for the purpose of denying their relevance, preserving the reproductive narrative despite herself, and playing out in a highly symptomatic form how the reproductive ideology of narrative disenables certain positions and considerations.

In *Amazon Odyssey*, Atkinson directly takes up the issues that the paradigms of sisterhood and maternity seem to omit, asking, for example, what the relation is between lesbianism and feminism, how gender oppression is related to class, and what shape is taken by the sexual presumptions of dominant culture. Atkinson seems to challenge directly the reproductive narrative; beginning her collection with a definition of the "reproductive function" as diachronic, "operational, or exist[ing] over time,"[19] Atkinson comprehends childbearing as "the function of *men* oppressing women."[20] Since, according to Atkinson, "the oppression of women by men is the source of all the corrupt values throughout the world" and since reproduction is the center of that oppression, Atkinson seems, at least on a literal level, to jettison the reproductive narrative for a class analysis. She also dismisses sexual intercourse in general by defining it as an oppressive institution that operates in the generational narrative. This would seem to inaugurate an inquiry into the nature of the way feminists think about the problems of family and reproduction as well as forge a direct challenge to reproductive ideology.

In appearing to reject the reproductive narrative, Atkinson seems to recapture the lesbian cast of the amazon by playing out more overtly and in a broadly historical discourse the validity of the lesbian position. But her class logic follows a covert but very conjunctive ideology of narrative, re-established through Atkinson's reliance on competing sibling realms: the political and the sexual. In their engendering, the sexual becomes the territory of patriarchy and the political the realm of feminism. This now gendered class analysis turns upon a literalized notion of sexual difference, not as a function, but as a concrete and fairly inflexible reality, dependent sometimes on the gender of the agent, sometimes on the agent's actions. Defining men and women as enemies in a class war, Atkinson employs what is essentially a narrative of sibling rivalry where contemporaries are locked in a battle for power whose result is the production of class consciousness (the liberating truth) and finally equality. By situating the class analysis within a conjunctive narrative, Atkinson returns issues of sexuality to the hetero-reproductive forum and at the same time reveals the mechanism for that return as the pressure of the hetero-ideology. This heterosexually recuperated class analysis allows Atkinson to dismiss spectacularly the lesbian by essentially categorizing her as sexual and patriarchal instead of political, declaring, for example, that "The *raison d'être* for feminism is the existence of class disparity between men and women. The *raison d'être* of lesbianism is sex, which is an apparent evasion of class disparity."[21] Such categorizing demonstrates how the very operation of the reproductive narrative requires not only gendered binaries, but an inevitable reduction and alternate positioning of any difference.

Because her class analysis is really a disguised hetero-narrative, Atkinson sees the only answer to the dilemma of class-gendered oppression as the elimination of sex altogether: the creation of what she calls "a sexless society, a society in which sex is pivotal neither personally, nor politically."[22] Linking sex to power and making intercourse the model for the deployment of such power limits all meaningful theory to the heterosexual. And seeing sex as the problem essentially prevents Atkinson from seeing how sex provides the paradigm and defines the problem as well as her approach, because centering sex as the cause inevitably imports the very narrative she is trying to avoid.

This early 1970s moment in feminist history, the history I tell in my peculiarly oedipal way, is conscious of history, but the narrative paradigm employed by all three texts limits their explorations to the familial, the heterosexual, the declarative, and the rigid purpose of reform. Because of their fix on a specifically conjunctive reproductive narrative, neither Atkinson nor Morgan nor Rich permit an exploration of sexuality, analysis, interpretation, or pleasure as these might be constituted away from the conjunctive, oedipal, reproductive narrative that comes to shape the "reality" of feminist action.

This is why feminist accounts of feminism lead to a Naura Hayden. Situating good sex as the end of liberation just as Atkinson situates sex as the enemy, Hayden simply tells the story again in overt, if simplistic terms, reiterating in a reduced almost caricatured 80s fashion the very terms of early 70s feminist debate. Hayden, too, has a hidden truth, one that history discovers and one that will set women free, make them equal to men, and make everyone happy. Hayden, too, relies on personal experience, on the discovery of a repressed potential whose visibility and recognition will set all women (and men) free. The difference between Hayden and the others is that she is naively, simplistically blatant about the terms of the discussion.

The pressure of this repro narrative also, however, leads to the more insidious result of Phyllis Schlafly and those like her who argue that women's liberation comes from cooperating with patriarchy. Schlafly, in fact, can be seen as a Naura Hayden who obligingly situates satisfaction as a product of patriarchy. Schlafly is the narrator of a story made whole and complete by its acquiescence to itself. Because the reproductive narrative inevitably returns to the family, and because the law of the father creates stability, security, and well-being despite its intrinsic lie, if women collude, all is well, complete, finishable, conjoined, settled. All we need, according to Schlafly, is to understand this arrangement as inherently equal and non-oppressive in the first place, as the right version of the right story that feminists, in their confusion, get all wrong by messing with its terms. And in a sense she is right. Feminists sometimes do mess with the terms without changing the story, managing only to change the view. Maybe that change is important, but it is not change enough.

The problem is that the feminist story of itself, which began in the 1970s, doesn't really change. In the 80s, the motherhood paradigm became dominant, underwriting such concepts as Showalter's gynocriticism and adopting the orphans of the 1970s—women of color and lesbians.[23] These newly-nourished children assuage the mother's guilt at having abandoned them both; and this guilt over a lapsed maternal metaphor partly explains why their belated inclusion is tied to feminist self-reform and reformulation. But the re-situation of racial and sexual issues within the maternal paradigm and its reproductive, emancipatory narrative also produces a continued feminist resistance to change, the constant reappropriation of those positions, and the insistent reproduction of the same old story. As in Atkinson, what appears at first to deny the story is really a part of the story, still umbilically linked to maternity as a governing epistemology.

So does this mean we should not write histories or tell narratives of feminism? Does this suggest that there is no escape from the hegemonic power of the reproductive ideology of narrative? I could at this moment retell the strategies for exploding narrative suggested by such insightful theorists as Teresa de Lauretis, Elaine Marks, or Roland Barthes, and suggest that we interrupt or play these narratives with a vengeance. But these solutions still rely on the form that is there, perhaps necessarily.[24] I suggest instead that we consciously detach history from narrative, that we look closely and ever-vigilantly at the stories *behind* the stories we tell, that we understand history as containing no truth, no knowledge, no enlightenment, that we narrate feminism not as a family affair or generational history, but as a partial story with no beginning and no end and no structuring binaries. If this sounds like extreme postmodernism or the end of the story itself, it is because *no* story is the point. After all, the issue is not how to satisfy a woman every time, which is what the story does, but how to time our satisfaction. Better yet, to know we can't get no satisfaction at all. There may be satisfaction in that.

NOTES |

1 Naura Hayden, *How To Satisfy a Woman Every Time...* (New York: Bibli O'Phile Publishing, 1982).

2 *Sisterhood Is Powerful: An Anthology of Writings from the Women's Liberation Movement*, ed. Robin Morgan (New York: Vintage, 1970); Adrienne Rich, *Of Woman Born: Motherhood as Experience and Institution* (New York: Norton, 1976); Ti-Grace

Atkinson, *Amazon Odyssey: The First Collection of Writings by the Political Pioneer of the Women's Movement* (New York: Links Books, 1974).

3 *Sisterhood Is Powerful*, p. xiii.

4 *Sisterhood Is Powerful*, p. xviii.

5 *Sisterhood Is Powerful*, p. xxxiii.

6 Hayden White, "The Value of Narrativity in the Representation of Reality," *On Narrative*, ed. W.J.T. Mitchell (Chicago: University of Chicago Press, 1981), pp. 1–23.

7 Jean-François Lyotard, *The Postmodern Condition: A Report on Knowledge*, tr. Geoff Bennington and Brian Massumi (Minneapolis: University of Minnesota Press, 1984).

8 Lyotard, *The Postmodern Condition*, pp. 35–36.

9 Lyotard, *The Postmodern Condition*, p. 36.

10 Joan Scott, *Gender and the Politics of History* (New York: Columbia University Press, 1988), p. 2.

11 Jill Johnston, *Lesbian Nation: The Feminist Solution* (New York: Simon and Schuster, 1973).

12 Adrienne Rich, *Of Woman Born*, p. 13.

13 Rich, *Of Woman Born*, p. 13.

14 Hélène Cixous, "Castration or Decapitation," tr. Annette Kuhn, *Signs* 7, 1 (1981), pp. 36–55.

15 Julia Kristeva, "Women's Time," tr. Alice Jardine and Harry Blake, *Signs* 7, 1 (1981).

16 Nancy Chodorow, *The Reproduction of Mothering: Psychoanalysis and the Sociology of Gender* (Berkeley: University of California Press, 1978).

17 Diane Griffin Crowder, "Amazons and Mothers: Monique Wittig, Hélène Cixous, and Theories of Women's Writing," *Contemporary Literature* 24 (1983), pp. 117–144.

18 See for example, Monique Wittig's *Lesbian Body*, tr. David Le Vay (New York: William Morrow and Co., 1975).

19 Ti-Grace Atkinson, *Amazon Odyssey*, p. 1.

20 Atkinson, *Amazon Odyssey*, p. 5.

21 Atkinson, *Amazon Odyssey*, p. 86.

22 Atkinson, *Amazon Odyssey*, p. 135.

23 As expounded in her "Toward a Feminist Poetics," *The New Feminist Criticism: Essays on Women, Literature and Theory* (New York: Pantheon Books, 1985), pp. 125–143.

24 See Teresa de Lauretis' idea of Oedipus with a vengeance in *Alice Doesn't: Feminism, Semiotics, Cinema* (Bloomington: Indiana University Press, 1984) as well as her summary of other techniques in "Sexual Indifference and Lesbian Representation" *Theatre Journal* 40, 2 (1988), pp. 155–177.

3

DOMESTICATION

Rachel Bowlby

In collections of essays on topics of current theoretical interest it's becoming quite common, if not yet a fully established part of the genre, to start off the piece with a little story about the final stages of its genesis. Such a story typically mentions the last-minute influence of a suggestion or critique by someone whose position, in terms of gender or race or sexual orientation, might give their opinion a legitimacy of a kind that the writer, by his or her own position, might be thought to lack. "I was discussing this article over breakfast with a lesbian friend, and she said...," writes someone who will thereby be identifying herself or himself as either a man, or straight, or both.

This type of gesture serves a number of functions. It seems to apologize for writers' disqualifications to speak about what they are going to speak about, marking an awareness that what they say will be open to modification. And it also does the opposite, making up for the disqualifications through the medium of the qualified friend who puts things right, and supplying the text with a provisional certificate of political, or even general, correctness: with an input from every possible position, the chances are that you can add up all the elements into a complete account.

A third element is the setting of the little story, which is regularly given a context of domestic intimacy: this is the sort of friend I have breakfast with. This aspect contributes to the legitimation effect ("some of my best friends…"), but it also provides a bit of human interest and narrative enigma, by hinting, through the provision of the homely detail, at the possibility of a personal story. In this instance, domestication functions in an odd kind of way: it supplements and disrupts the abstract theoretical scenario, taking us somewhere else. Yet it also harmonizes, calming down the possible disjunctions between the positions, theoretical and social, of the writer and his interrogator over the soothing influence of the shared bagels and cream cheese.

In these instances, an image of domestication serves as a hidden support to a theoretical argument which appears to be coming from somewhere else, from a would-be neutral, overview position which, for purposes of narrative and political plausibility, needs to be brought down to earth—into the kitchen. And this, it seems to me, is one of many diverse ways in which domestication, as a concept and as a theme, functions in relation to contemporary theoretical arguments, deconstructive and feminist in particular. In a minute, I will look at some of these, but first, let me just throw in one or two autobiographical nuggets of my own, which you can believe or not. They certainly have something to do with the writing of this paper, though I'm probably in no subject-position to say what.

In the summer of 1992, Gillian Beer asked me if I would like to give a lecture in a series that was being organized at Cambridge in the wake of a controversy over Derrida's election there to an honorary doctorate. I suggested the topic of domestication, and then noticed that this had happened in the week when I unexpectedly acquired a kitchen table, having always thought that the room wasn't big enough to take one. My pleasure at the transformation of this domestic space was both mitigated and reinforced by the events of the following two weeks, when I went to Paris—a place where I like to think I feel at home—and had my wallet snatched, twice within the space of one week. For the first time, I felt a strong sense of urban paranoia, if that's the phrase, huddling inside the cozy familiar interior of the place where I was staying, wondering how I was ever going to write this paper on, of all things, domestication.

The other story goes back a bit further, to earlier that year, when I woke up one morning to the sounds of two voices that turned out to be those of Gillian Beer and George Steiner, on the BBC Radio 4 *Today* programme, soundly and roundly in their different ways defending the importance of Derrida's work. As I drank my coffee and started to wake up, I reflected that, thanks to the Cambridge controversy, here was deconstruction apparently reaching, or being pushed, beyond the books and the seminar rooms, out onto the airwaves and the headlines and into the kitchens and bedrooms of the daily life of the supposed British nation. It was an ambivalent passage between hypothetical insides and outsides, crossing, erasing and reinforcing innumerable imaginary and symbolic borders. In some sense, it all seemed to suggest that Derrida was beginning to personify a particularly curious specimen of the proper noun: He was becoming what is called a "household" name.

It seemed to me that this process was at the very least a strange and unpredictable one, aligning Derrida with a hitherto unfamiliar and probably unwelcome peer-group. Not so much Heidegger, Kant, Descartes and the rest, or, in another connection, not so much Lacan and Kristeva and Foucault. Instead, this new grouping would include, I suppose—if you are British—the likes of Brian Redhead, Domestos, Bruce Forsyth, Boot's, Fergie, Chanel no. 5, and Jeffrey Archer. On the other side of the Atlantic, perhaps this near-meaningless anglo-domestic list should be rewritten to something like David Letterman, Mr. Clean, Hilary Clinton, Chanel no. 5, Tylenol and Judith Krantz. It can't be an easy or straightforward transition to find yourself sharing the household name status and facilities with such a heterogeneous community, one whose capacities for comfortable cohabitation, either with each other or with their new associate, might seem anything but assured.

And yet the notion of domestication is generally regarded as being the most obvious thing in the world—so obvious, in fact, that once someone or some idea is deemed to have been sent home in this public way, it is as if there is no more to be said. The front door closes definitively on a place removed and retired from the open air of its previous existence—and even though the movement implied is also one of extension, moving out. If a theory gets domesticated, that's the end of it. It becomes like everything else.

The term domestication is used in this way all the time in relation to deconstruction and to "theory" in general, including feminist theory. But it does not usually feature the specificity or concreteness of any recognizably domestic location, "Dunroamin" or wherever. Instead, "domestication" is used to signal something unproblematically negative that happens to a theory, when—what?— well, when it loses its radical edge, gets tamed, is co-opted or institutionalized (these last two words are often used virtually as synonyms of domestication). The "domestication" of deconstruction or other theories implies something that may include the kind of mediatization that occurred with the "Cambridge and Derrida" story, but refers generally to processes of simplification, assimilation and distortion—any or all of these—to which the theory in question falls victim or which it is powerless to resist. It will already be clear that domestication, in this sense, involves a very undeconstructive story—of a wild and natural identity, a full presence, subsequently, and only subsequently, succumbing to forces that deprive it of an original wholeness.

Here is one particularly clear example of how the term is invoked, from Judith

Butler's *Gender Trouble*, one of the most significant deployments of deconstruction in a feminist context:

> The complexity of gender requires an interdisciplinary and postdisciplinary set of
> discourses in order to resist the domestication of gender studies or women's studies
> within the academy and to radicalize the notion of feminist critique.

And later on, she says:

> Parody by itself is not subversive, and there must be a way to understand what
> makes certain kinds of parodic repetitions effectively disruptive, truly troubling, and
> which repetitions become domesticated and recirculated as instruments of cultural
> hegemony.[1]

What gets domesticated—in this case, a form of feminist theory—is something
defined as being subversive of what will thereby attempt to take it over, settle it
down, suppress its difference.

What interests me in this use of domestication in connection with theory as
something radical and subversive is the way in which the word itself, and the
implied narrative that it brings with it, can go unexamined within an argument
that is deconstructively on the look-out all the time for the subtle simplifica-
tions and assumptions that discourses of every kind install and seek to maintain.
In the opposition played out between radical critique and domesticating cultural hegemony, the qualifications of the two forces are not at issue: the first gets its
value from the very fact that it is a challenge to the second, which is identified
largely in terms of its superior force. In an inevitable movement, the latter then
brings the former under its sway.

Butler's argument does not attribute anything inherently good or natural to
the radical theory that succumbs to domestication: this is not a case of a hypothetical full presence or genuine content then becoming contaminated by
something else. Rather, the narrative proceeds in terms of power, with the oppositional, positive force inevitably succumbing to the stronger, negative one that
prompted its protesting existence in the first place. Implicitly, then, there are
three stages to the story: initial homogeneity or harmony of the hegemonizing
force, then the breakaway of the wild radical critique, to be followed by its rein-
tegration or re-assimilation into the dominant culture, accompanied by the loss
of its critical impetus.

At this point, we might take a first step back indoors to look at one of the stories implied by the word domestication in its more homely, extra-theoretical,
everyday existence. Within the word itself, home does not appear as the first

place or the natural place: It is a secondary development, *becoming* domestic. In one French usage, *domestiquer* means quite simply the subjugation of a tribe to a colonizing power. To "domesticate" is to bring the foreign or primitive or alien into line with the "domestic" civilization and power, just as a "domesticated" animal is one that has been tamed into home life. Something wild, pre-civilized, and verging on the non-human gets brought into line with an existing order represented in this case as more complex and sophisticated, but also as less natural.

In anthropology, too, the concept of domestication has had an unexpectedly dynamic, if less imperialistic, existence. The word is used to mark a turning point that is supposed to represent not so much a takeover, a "home" civilization taking in and thereby abolishing the difference of one that lies outside its domain, as a transition from what are thereby recognizable as two distinct states of culture. "The domestication of the savage mind," in Jack Goody's recapitulation of a categorization adopted by Lévi-Strauss in *The Savage Mind*, links together a whole series of two-term oppositions that are deployed in accounts of the history of humanity in general, and also in relation to the changes affecting what are now called "developing" countries in this century. Domestication in these connections is associated with a move from oral to literate culture; from collective life to individualism and private families; from myth to history; and from concrete to abstract thinking.[2]

The reliance on the two-term division and the set order of events—or rather the set position of the one event, which can somehow only be pointed to retrospectively as a boundary that a collectivity is seen to have passed—is of a type that deconstruction, even garden-variety or kitchen-variety deconstruction, would be quick to point out. Goody implicitly answers in another way: Yes, there are narratable changes, but historically and culturally they by no means fall into these easily superimposable parallels. This line is different from, but not I think necessarily incompatible with deconstruction, despite what kitsch deconstruction might think or be thought to think. To say that this is a pre-deconstructive mode of argument would be to restore just that narrative logic of identifiable progressions and demarcations that deconstruction seeks to make problematic: to operate, in fact, with an already "domesticated" version of deconstruction that would assert its own logics as superior to and clearly distinguishable from the others.

But there is still a further layer to this, which is indicated by the concentration on domestication as a process of civilization or taming. For insofar as domestication has to do with home, it would seem to elide the starting point. Home is the place of origin, the place that has always been left; domestication, then, would be a return to or reinvention of the home that you left or lost. This three-part story has its standard modern forms in relation both to daily life—wake up, go to work, return—and to the process of growing up: from home, out into the world, and then on or back to some form of domestic "settling down." In this narrative of nostalgia, home is imagined as a place of peace, stability and satisfaction that has subsequently ceased to be; but also as a withdrawal or seclusion from a "real" world envisaged as a source of the energy or the troubles or the mobility that are absent from the home.

It is in the context of this other kind of story that domesticity is imagined as a first place of wholeness and rest, but a place from which—and in order for it to be retrospectively seen as such—a separation has always taken place. Two books from the late fifties, one English, one French, illustrate this in very different ways. Richard Hoggart's *The Uses of Literacy* gives a nostalgic portrait of a working-class culture described in terms of concreteness, locality, and oral expression, and in the process of being subsumed by a materialistic American print culture.[3] In numerous vignettes, the home is represented as the focus and epitome of this all-but-lost world, which is seen as at once authentic and claustrophobic: It is not so much that it should not give way or give place to some other mode, but that it is being taken over by the wrong kinds of force. In place of the false commercial culture, endlessly secondarized through images of superficiality—tinsel, glitter, tawdriness, show—Hoggart would substitute something else, the abstract and general thinking of which his own argument, by implication, is meant to serve as an example. So the sequence here is not unlike the anthropological schema deployed by Goody, from oral to intellectual and from local to generalized; but here the terms are reversed, so that the domestic figures are the first, and in this case limited, devalorized state, prior and vulnerable to a mutation that may be negatively or positively viewed, in the direction of commercial fake, or in the direction of intellectual generality.

In a different genre, Gaston Bachelard's *The Poetics of Space* lyrically evokes the peace and dreaminess of the home as a place of corners and nests, with its secret and private spaces. Houses are associated with primitiveness and childhood, and thence with a capacity for maintaining throughout life the qualities of stability, habit and restfulness in which it begins. There is a lovely section on chests of drawers, which Bachelard sees as full of imaginative possibilities of a kind that are lost when philosophers like Bergson use them as no more than a polemical metaphor against tidy separation or compartmentalization of concepts, as though into drawers. Bachelard, for his part, wants to bring out the full poetic suggestiveness of such seemingly insignificant domestic things: "When Bergson speaks of a drawer, what disdain!"[4]

Nestlingly benign as Bachelard's enclosure is, it maintains itself nonetheless partly in its firm distance from two other, related schools or homes of thought.

First, there are the twentieth-century philosophers with their hyphen-crazy abstractions: a being-in-the-world that is always already split up. And second, there is the psychoanalysis of negativity, refusing a primary sense of oneness and always finding evidence of a threatening sexuality.[5]

Bachelard's distinction from Freudian psychoanalysis appears most clearly in his tranquil hymn to homeliness as a source of poetic inspiration:

> In its freshness, in its specific activity, the imagination makes of the familiar something strange [avec du familier fait de l'étrange]. With a poetic detail, the imagination places us before a new world.[6]

This version of strange or anxiety-provoking familiarity is a far cry from the covertly menacing reversibility of Freud's analysis of the uncanny, the homely *heimlich* which is also, within the same word, the unhomely, marking that unwelcome presence within what is most apparently reassuring in its familiarity and familiality. The house of Freudian psychoanalysis is irredeemably riven by the presence of ghosts, its comforting appearance of womblike unity doubled from the start by intruding forces, such that human life can never securely make a return to a place untroubled by the untimely and dislocating hauntings of other times and places, and other presences that interfere with the imagined separateness and identifiability of places and people who are known and loved.

I don't want to dwell—if that is the word—too long on Freud's uncanny.[7] But it is obvious that in psychoanalysis, the home is no place of harmony—and all the less for functioning so forcefully as the embodiment of a harmony that has always been lost. The home is where the muddle begins and continues; here domestication is not a smoothly operating process of adjustment or progress. And Freud, in fact, is rather specific about possible domestic disturbances, pointing out in *The Interpretation of Dreams* that "The ugliest as well as the most intimate details of sexual life may be thought and dreamt of in seemingly innocent allusions to activities in the kitchen."[8] This is, after all, the world of "kettle logic"; and along such murky paths of connection, we might reflect that if you hear, rather than write, the word "domestication"—if you return to that famous pre-civilized primitiveness of an oral culture—what you get, none too neatly tidied away into this capaciously polysyllabic word, is "mess" and "stickiness"— an Anglo-Saxon sprawl screeching for attention out of the nicely abstracted Latinate term. As every housewife knows.[9]

Which is perhaps the point at which to turn to look at the ways in which domestication has been treated as a theme in feminist writing. At first sight, the situation would seem to be quite straightforward, as with the deployment of the word in a figurative sense: just as feminists are sure that the "domestication" of feminist theories is to be regretted, so the rejection of domesticity has seemed a principal, if not *the* principal, tenet of feminist demands for freedom. The home figures as the place where the woman is confined, and from which she must be emancipated in order for her to gain access to a world outside that is masculine but only contingently so, and which offers possibilities of personal and social achievement that are not available within its limited sphere.

In various forms, this representation could be said to run right through the Western tradition of feminist writing from the past two hundred years—including in different ways Mary Wollstonecraft, Simone de Beauvoir, Betty Friedan, and at many points Virginia Woolf (the infamous "Angel in the House," derived from Coventry Patmore's best-selling nineteenth-century poem, whose Victorian domestic virtues must be violently abolished before the freer twentieth-century woman can emerge[10]). Before going into more detail about some of these versions, it's worth noticing some of the strong common denominators.

These representations literalize the imagery of inside and outside, in such a way that the home is figured as something close to a prison, walled off against a "real" world of events that is elsewhere. The condition of femininity, inseparable from women's domestication, is artificially imposed by social and/or masculine forces that women have been powerless or unwilling to resist, or have not recognized as limitations at all. True selfhood is attainable only by moving beyond the domestic, local, private boundaries. Though presently allowed chiefly or only to men, it is not inherently gendered: it is rather a right, or a nature, of which the present organization of things has unjustly deprived women.

In the second volume of *The Second Sex*, Beauvoir's chapter on marriage delivers a resounding critique of that state or estate's effect on the woman insofar as it "confines her to immanence."[11] As so often, the metaphor of confinement is given a naturalized foundation, a home base, in that it turns out to refer to a life contained within the domestic space. Beauvoir does begin by quoting some passages—from none other than Bachelard and Woolf's *The Waves*—on the positive symbolic associations of the *foyer*, of being inside and sheltered. But the critique is for the most part relentless: the housewife with her "days leading nowhere"[12] is deprived of the capacity to form and carry out projects; her work is mere repetition with no product at the end or in the future, and this automatically casts it into a secondary, devalorized mode:

> She simply perpetuates the present; she does not have the impression of conquering a positive Good but of struggling indefinitely against Evil. It is a struggle renewed every day…. Eating, sleeping, cleaning…, the years no longer mount upwards to the sky, they stretch out identical and grey in a horizontal sheet; every day imitates the one that preceded it; it is an eternal present, useless and without hope.[13]

There is a combination of temporal and spatial stasis—no progression as no movement outwards, outdoors, and of no building up towards the accomplishment of a lasting work. But this stasis is sustained by the need for it to be constantly, daily, reproduced—by the routine that is deplored for being always identical, and by the endless cleaning and cooking for an immediate consumption that leaves neither record nor surplus.

A woman's work, proverbially, is never done, to the point that this never-doneness can come to define it: an interminable task with no lasting result or addition. Beauvoir's account in some ways resembles the Marxist theory of the home as the site of the reproduction of labor power: no surplus value is produced in the home; instead, its "reproductive" function is one of the essential conditions for the production of surplus value to take place elsewhere. "Reproduction" operates here in a curiously devious way. On the one hand, it is the day-to-day servicing of the workers as one of the elements of production, needing to be fed, cleaned, and rested in order for them to be physically capable of going out again and doing the next day's work. On the other hand, it is the reproduction of lives, so that there will be more workers to man the factories. In this second implication, the term moves covertly from the biological to the economic, as the teleology of embryo development in the first of these discourses latches or hatches itself onto the parallel but quite different teleology of the needs of capitalism (workers as a supply to be kept up).

In Marxist theory, then, "reproduction" evidently does a lot of work for all its apparently secondary status. As in Beauvoir's version, the domestic sphere figures as the place which both makes possible and reinforces a difference attributed to the sphere of real projects or production. This difference is represented both spatially—in the respective "spheres" or sites—and temporally, in the demarcation of the linear, cumulative time of production and projects from the repetitive, cyclical time of reproduction and housework.

Engels's *The Origin of the Family, Private Property, and the State* (1884), an anthropological narrative of the development of human societies to their modern capitalist forms of organization, draws out the interdependence of the terms of this division in an especially sharp form. Engels's story is derived from the latest anthropological researches of the time, in particular the hypothesis that the present patrilineal, patriarchal order of things is not universal, but was preceded by forms of matrilineal (though not matri*archal*) organization called "mother right." The changeover from one to the other is glossed in unequivocally dramatic terms:

> The overthrow of mother right was the *world-historical defeat of the female sex*. The
> man seized the reins in the house also; the woman was degraded, enthralled, the

slave of man's lust, a mere instrument for breeding children. This lowered position of women, especially manifest among the Greeks of the Heroic and still more of the Classical Age, has become gradually embellished and dissembled, and, in part, clothed in a milder form, but by no means abolished.[14]

But the precipitating circumstances of the change are nothing other than the process of domestication itself. Previously, according to Engels's anthropological sources, societies were more or less polygamous, and they were communal: there was no private property, and extended households were not based on the nucleus of a single set of parents. The transition to patriarchy accompanies a whole series of other changes: the beginnings of monogamy, the one-couple family, the private home, privately owned property, competitiveness between men, surplus value in production, and the strict demarcation of male from female labor as between the household and what then became a separate site of work accorded a superior value.

At one fell swoop, one irrevocable crash and fall, this mythical moment resumes all the standard demarcations that separate the domestic from its outside, or that mark off the domestic as an enclave or "separate" sphere within the generalized norm of a world ordered according to a logic that excludes it but which depends absolutely upon it. Crucially, domestication marks the definitive division of masculine and feminine as operating in and governed according to spaces and times that are irreducible to one another but mutually dependent. Engels, bless his nineteenth-century feminist heart, is unequivocal about the specific implications of all this:

> The woman's housework lost its significance compared with the man's work in obtaining a livelihood; the latter was everything, the former an insignificant contribution. Here we see already that the emancipation of women and their equality with men are impossible and must remain so as long as women are excluded from socially productive work and restricted to housework, which is private. The emancipation of women becomes possible only when women are enabled to take part in production on a large, social scale, and when domestic duties require their attention only to a minor degree.[15]

It's worth noting in passing that Engels's emancipatory vision doesn't run or leap to the possibility that it might not have to be only women's attention directed towards "domestic duties"; and in a similar fashion, he consistently assumes in his discussions of marriage and sexuality that there is a natural desire for monogamy or "individual sex-love" on the part of women, and an equally natural desire for promiscuity on the part of men.

In Engels's myth of origins, the overthrow of mother right brings in its train not only the three estates designated by his book's title, but also, implicitly, the beginnings of various temporal lines—of history, of accumulation, of production (it is a classic instance of domestication in the sense described by Goody). Not only is the time before patriarchy thenceforth a kind of pre-time or non-time in relation to the forward directions that are now installed, but the private household comes to represent a kind of residue or throwback in the midst of the modern world.

It is in this sense that it can figure too as a refuge from the batterings and struggles of the world variously described as the "real" world or the "outside" world. Not long before Engels's manifesto in a very different mode, John Ruskin's lecture, "Of Queens' Gardens," from *Sesame and Lilies* (1865), sets in place an extraordinary celebration-cum-damnation of the domestic sphere, which Ruskin sees as the site on which to fight out and lay claim to a proper division of the sexes in terms of their respective natures which he takes to be at once different and complementary.

Ostensibly, the argument is asserting all the well-known virtues of a peaceful, innocent Victorian womanhood—unencumbered by work, and simply blossoming forth with a natural spontaneity that balances the rather more turbulent nature of the man. But the context for the assertion of what he calls the "harmonious idea"—glossed somewhat insecurely as "it must be harmonious if it is true"[16]—is the opposite, a situation of antagonism. Ruskin has opened his question as having to do with what he calls women's "queenly power," their "royal or gracious influence," which should be exercised "not in their households merely, but over all within their sphere." The domestic space moves out effortlessly to comprise a set of individual "territories": to each woman her own private colony for domestication.[17] At the same time, there is a specific contemporary background of disorder, which Ruskin explains in this way:

> There never was a time when wilder words were spoken, or more vain imagination permitted, respecting this question—quite vital to all social happiness. The relations of the womanly to the manly nature, their different capacities of intellect or of virtue, seem never to have been yet measured with entire consent. We hear of the mission and of the rights of Woman, as if these could ever be separate from the mission and the rights of Man—as if she and her lord were creatures of independent kind and of irreconcileable claim.[18]

It is a verbal unruliness—wild words—that needs to be tamed, civilized, constituted into its prescribed place. Unlike his contemporary Mill, Ruskin's starting point has to do with a difference, not a relative sameness, between the sexes.

Ruskin both acknowledges that this difference is somehow a tense one, productive of dissent and disturbance, and at the same time asserts almost by fiat that to that very extent—because it is not harmonious—it must be deemed and made so. "Vain imagination" has been reprehensibly "permitted": the issue is one of legislation, such that a disruptive or distracting element must be arbitrarily forbidden and/or put out of the way.

Ruskin then sets up his ideal social arrangements on the basis of a clearly distinguished difference of sexual natures:

> Now their separate characters are briefly these. The man's power is active, progressive, defensive. He is eminently the doer, the creator, the discoverer, the defender. His intellect is for speculation and invention; his energy for adventure, for war, and for conquest, wherever war is just, wherever conquest is necessary. But the woman's power is for rule, not battle—and her intellect is not for invention or creation, but for sweet ordering, arrangement, and decision. She sees the qualities of things, their claims, and their places.[19]

Wars and strife are taken to be inevitable, though not valued in themselves: they are subject to considerations of justice and necessity. And it is worth noticing too that in attempting to harmonize—to sweetly reorder, arrange and adjudicate the dissensions between the sexes—Ruskin himself is "eminently" less "a doer" than a woman.

The full expansion of this social arrangement then takes us swiftly away from all the worldly strife to the place of feminine security:

> This is the true nature of home—it is the place of Peace; the shelter, not only from all injury, but from all terror, doubt, and division. In so far as it is not this, it is not home; so far as the anxieties of the outer life penetrate into it, and the inconsistently-minded, unknown, unloved, or hostile society of the outer world is allowed by either husband or wife to cross the threshold, it ceases to be home; it is then only a part of that outer world which you have roofed over, and lighted fire in. But so far as it is a sacred place, a vestal temple, a temple of the hearth watched over by Household Gods...so far it vindicates the name, and fulfils the praise, of Home.[20]

Home must thus be constructed against, not in continuity with, the "outer life" of "anxieties" which must at all odds be kept out; it is defined not so much by its capacity to provide the basic needs of shelter and warmth, but by its exclusion of the outer, its standing against what is always trying to force or "penetrate" its way in. Consecrated against the secular troubles of the outside, home has become the haven in an aggressive world; it is where the heart is, but a heart constructed desperately as a defense against an intolerable and ineradicable pressure from what is thereby rejected to an indefinite external source of disturbance.

Here, domestication runs its complete course. Home is set up as a response to and bulwark against something perceived as a threat; it makes an interior separate from and set off against the dangers or anxieties that can then be safely thrown out onto an outside, an *out there*, whose differentiation has to be constantly re-established with the risk of every questionable foot across the threshold. But despite this order of things, home is also represented as the place that has always been there, the original temple of the Household Gods, something that pre-dates and will by implication outlive the incursions from the outside which in this light appear as no more than contingent and ephemeral.

Just a little excursion at this point—though we won't stray too far from the front door—on the history of home. Witold Rybczynski's charming book called *Home: A Short History of an Idea* documents this in loving detail, through developments in bourgeois forms of living accommodation and their accompanying notions of family intimacy and comfort. It is a reassuringly evolutionary history: the home and its pleasures were just waiting placidly to be found, at the end of a smooth historical path leading straight to the modern armchair and all the rest—all the rest you could ever want. So Rybczynski begins one of his central chapters like this:

> Privacy and domesticity, the two great discoveries of the Bourgeois Age, appeared, naturally enough, in the bourgeois Netherlands. By the eighteenth century they had spread to the rest of northern Europe—England, France, and the German states.... The house was no longer only a shelter against the elements, a protection against the intruder—although these remained important functions—it had become the setting for a new, compact social unit: the family. With the family came isolation, but also family life and domesticity. The house was becoming a home, and following privacy and domesticity the stage was set for the third discovery: the idea of comfort.[21]

Slowly and surely, in Rybczynski's story, things have been getting cozier and cozier: domestication is certainly a lengthy process (it took a while for people to discover how nice it is) but it is one that does no more and no less than fulfil wishes that are natural: "Domestic well-being is a fundamental human need that is deeply rooted in us, and that must be satisfied."[22]

There can be difficulties in the way of its attainment in particular periods, as with the mistaken austerity of modernist functionalism, or the contemporary postmodern bric-à-brac of decors vaguely alluding to heterogeneous styles from the past. Rybczynski is clear that this is a mistake:

It is not watered-down historical references that are missing from people's homes. What is needed is a sense of domesticity, not more dadoes; a feeling of privacy, not neo-Palladian windows; an atmosphere of coziness, not plaster capitals.[23]

The book ends with an argument that simply sets the natural home in relation to, and usually against, the machine, in the form of either outside experts imposing their views of what it should be, or mistaken and artificial contrivances, whether decorative or labor-saving. Rybczynski is not straightforwardly opposed to the presence or use of machines in the home, but they must be kept in their subordinate place to a natural form of domestic life that is clearly separable as such: "We must rediscover for ourselves the mystery of comfort, for without it, our dwellings will indeed be machines instead of homes."[24] As with Ruskin, nature has mysteriously metamorphosed into an injunction—"We must"—that needs to be constantly re-legislated.

Rybczynski has taken us calmly to a world where the incursions from outside are not as formidable in their home-breaking potential as Ruskin's, but are nonetheless there as a permanent threat that is also a permanent bolster to the setting up of home as an ideal. In Ruskin, the most sinister aspect of the territorial arrangements is the role ascribed to the woman. We have already come across her vaunted capacities for "sweet ordering"; more dangerously, she is responsible for all its disorders:

There is not a war in the world, no, nor an injustice, but you women are answerable for it; not in that you have provoked, but in that you have not hindered. Men, by their nature, are prone to fight.[25]

So the inside/outside opposition between home and world is now directly transposed onto the difference of male and female natures; and now the inside, previously secondary and reactive to the troubles of the world, is being allotted a dominant, controlling power whereby the healing sympathies of the feminine home are to spread their influence outwards, taking over the uncontrolled masculine spaces of strife. In this way Ruskin argues against the present situation in which:

You shut yourselves within your park walls and garden gates; and you are content to know that there is beyond them a whole world in wilderness—a world of secrets which you dare not penetrate; and of suffering which you dare not conceive.[26]

The movement of domestication thus ultimately reverses itself again, with a feminine force called upon to penetrate outwards to overcome the wilderness:

sweet ordering through the exertion of a counter-power that repeats in the other direction the invasion from the troubled outside.

Returning now briefly to Beauvoir, who has no doubt been resentfully and repetitively darning the Sartrean socks all this while, I would like to highlight one moment in her section on the domestic life of the married woman. For the most part, Beauvoir considers both oppression and emancipation from an individual perspective. It is an affliction of single and separate consciousnesses, not—as in Engels's analysis, for instance—an effect of a structure bearing upon women collectively as a sex.[27] But here in Beauvoir is a moment of break-out from the confinements of daily life—within the text, and for the woman it describes—and it is when the housewife goes shopping:

> While they are doing their shopping, women exchange remarks in the shops, on the street corners, through which they affirm "housewifely values," where each one derives a sense of her importance: they feel they are members of a community which—for a moment—opposes itself to the society of men as the essential to the inessential. But above all, buying is a profound pleasure: it is a discovery, almost an invention.... Between seller and buyer a relationship of tussling and ruses is set up: the point of the game for her is to procure herself the best buys at the lowest price; the great importance attached to the smallest of economies could not be explained merely by the concern to balance a difficult budget: the thing is to win a round. For the time she is suspiciously examining the stalls, the housewife is queen; the world is at her feet with its riches and its traps, for her to grab herself some loot. She tastes a fleeting triumph when she empties the bag of provisions onto her table.[28]

The shopping interlude is the one moment when domestication becomes something other than the stifling repetition of itself in solitude, as the housewives move outdoors to take a breath of collective fresh air and to enjoy what is practically the only pleasure that Beauvoir recognizes for them. Where Ruskin's woman is enjoined to be a perpetual moral "queen," Beauvoir's is granted it— "the housewife is queen"—as a momentary release and a "fleeting triumph."

It is interesting that this one interval of relative emancipation involves a collective experience founded in an affirmation of domestic values and a reversal of the normal hierarchy between the feminine-domestic and the masculine-worldly. A later French feminism would pause on this moment of reversal, and hold it out as a possibility of serious philosophical mutation. So Luce Irigaray, eminently Derridean in this strategy, would in effect pick up Beauvoir's denigration of the feminine condition in its absence of forward direction, its lack of an individual project, by classifying such values not as the neutral destination of the human individual, but as specifically masculine. The hitherto subordinated terms—repetition, non-unity, otherness—come forward in Irigaray's account to disrupt and break into what is thereby both identified and challenged as a monolithic, but potentially mutable, phallogocentric order.[29]

Though the argument and its implications are not the same, Julia Kristeva's essay "Women's Time" operates upon some comparable reversals. It identifies a quasi-tyrannical linear temporality—the time required for the teleologies of Western history and capitalist accumulation—with masculinity in the psychical sense and it suggests that other structures of time associated with femininity may now be coming to take a less subordinate place, alongside if not instead of the linearity which has dominated modern Western thinking and experience.[30]

None of the contemporary feminists, however, takes back the abstract temporal questions into the daily life of the kitchen which is where Beauvoir's disgruntlements begin. In fact, insofar as domestication gets a thematic mention in these more recent theories, it is to perpetuate the assumption that of course women would and should want to leave home and enter the workforce; or at least, not to be spending their days solely as housewives, a situation still implicitly marked by the imagery of confinement within a space that excludes participation in a real world elsewhere.

But in the age of postmodern technology, such straighforward separations are perhaps open to rethinking in a way that they never were before. All sorts of technical innovations—faxes, computer networks, and so on—have altered the terms on which one hypothetically private space is related to another. Telephones and radios can now be seen as historically first in this series of instruments that abolish the communicational boundaries of interior spaces from each other, or from the "world outside" in general. They have made possible, for better or for worse, a sharing of space between home and work, the reproductive and the productive spheres, in a way that has been excluded since the industrial revolution definitively divided the two, for all but a few eccentric professions. But this puts it too simply. For the new potential for blurring and overlap could also be said to show up the way in which the division of the domestic from its outside was previously sustained only through a literalization of the figure of the house within and separate from a surrounding world. Its four walls marked off a boundary that was supposed to keep clearly apart each of the two sides, the domestic and its other, whether defined as the real world or the outside world or the productive sphere.

One last trip to the shops before we finally come back home. For almost as long as the middle-class ideology of domesticity has existed, consumerism has provided a bridge, or at least a very brisk walk, between the home and the outside world. From nineteenth-century department stores to twentieth-century supermarkets, via the development at the turn of the century of brand-name goods and the vast expansion of advertising in all the media which enter the home—newspapers and magazines and later radio and television—consumption has been intimately bound up with the changing forms of domestication. So much so, that it has at various times been identified as the key to a female oppression now associated with a false, commodified form of home life, implicitly differentiated from something more authentic that either preceded the present situation or might be available in the future, if women could rid themselves of their subjection to the lures of commodities.

Betty Friedan's *The Feminine Mystique* (1963), the book that was so influential for the "second wave" of feminism on both sides of the Atlantic, is probably the best, as well as the first, example of this type of argument. It is also one of the quirkiest. For Friedan in effect claims that women won their emancipation—votes, professional rights—and then let it go, foolishly seduced by the determined operations of the men of Madison Avenue and their avatars in other areas of life who wanted to ensure their return to that homely place which Friedan uncomfortably names "the comfortable concentration camp." Here, consumption figures not as momentary freedom, but as a forceful social pressure driving women, against what are nonetheless their potentially better judgments, back to the "feminine" home.[31]

But the deeper accusation of Friedan's polemic is the fear that this creeping and artificial domestication is affecting men as well, who are sinking and sudsing into the ghastly "togetherness" of conjugally shared household activities—and the pattern is in danger of becoming perpetuated through a lack of paternal discipline and an excess of mother-love. The renunciation on women's part of real-world achievement values—"human" values, in Friedan's terms—in favour of the circumscribed and secondary values of the home seems to be leading inexorably to a corresponding domestication of the men, who are going soft in the head, as well as soft in the suds. Domestication implies for both sexes an alienation from a true, whole self whose field of operation is out there, somewhere else.

It will be clear that there are common elements between this argument and Beauvoir's. In both cases, domestication represents a deprivation of full human potential, and domestication is associated with a false version of femininity. Women should be allowed access—out of the home, into the wide world—to the prospects and projects of an authentic subjectivity which is not in itself gendered. The feminine exclusion is contingent, not structural, and identity is in fact diminished to the extent that it is bound to sex (women's lot as feminine, kept in their secluded place, rather than fully human). Because of their individualistic frameworks, both Friedan and Beauvoir see women's liberation as their own responsibility: resistance is up to each one on her own.

We have come full circle several times, repetitively but also with some differences, looking at various constructions of domestication in relation to its outsides, seen diversely as either a wilderness waiting to be tamed, or a neutral space of social reality and opportunity. The home itself functions as either a residual sanctuary for and source of moral values seen to be absent from the outside world, or (and the two are not mutually exclusive) as a place of rest, its dailyness and removal from the progressive, linear time operating elsewhere seen as complementary to, rather than subversive of, the dominant external order. In feminist versions, this becomes a stagnantly artificial prison or cage for a woman whose fulfillment can only be "outside."

How then might we think of the domestication of deconstruction or the domestication of feminism?

As for deconstruction—well, in one sense, of course, deconstruction is always already domesticated, or never not yet domesticated, to the extent that it does not pretend to set itself up as something outside, radically separable from, the structures and logics it comes to analyze. There is no such thing as a pure deconstruction; instead, it can only be seen insofar as it works in and through particular texts or structures. However, this is not much use in thinking about the more dismissive use of domestication that I began with: always-already structures tend all too easily to slip into "it's-all-the-same" structures, as though there were then no distinctions to be made between uses or adaptations of deconstructive methods. Such homogenisation is in turn related to one of the processes which gets damned as domestication: the transmission or presentation of deconstructive ideas.

The metaphor of accessibility is regularly used in this context, with a connotation of diminishment and simplification: insofar as you make the theory accessible, you automatically simplify it, abolishing a complexity that is seen as the virtue of the original. This characterization operates with particular force in conjunction with the idea of translation and importation, in a weakening and simplification that is assumed to occur in the movement from French to English. Associated with this is an implicit devaluation of English as the language of common sense, and behind this again lies the whole history of the development of theory in Britain and other English-speaking countries, where it has been valorized for qualities of Frenchness, complexity and difficulty seen to be absent from domestically English or Anglo-American traditions of thinking. In this context, inaccessibility and obscurity of presentation come to be linked as positive and indissociable terms.

Yet there is nothing inevitable about this state of affairs, no reason to assume that complexity has to go with obscurity, or accessibility with simplification.

Deconstruction is assuredly finding some homes in English-speaking intellectual culture, but such domestications need not be considered as necessarily
following a pattern of decline and distortion. There are doubtless more domestications, there and elsewhere, than are dreamed of in any common or kitchen
philosophy of domestication as the moment that marks the end of the interesting
story.

A different, though related argument applies in the case of feminist domestication (though I don't mean to imply a necessary separation of feminism and
deconstruction: there are many points of overlap between the two, in practice
and in theory; and most of those who bring them together would claim that
they are inseparable). The use of "domestication" as a straightforwardly negative metaphor, in need of no further analysis, implies simple binary oppositions
and two-stage stories, whereby something initially natural, spontaneous or subversive gets pushed into a conformity or homogeneity that deprives it of
whatever made it different. This much would apply to any deployment of
domestication; but in feminist contexts, there is an added irony because the
would-be abstract term is rich in thematic ambiguities and histories which, from
the point of view of feminist demands and aims, could hardly be closer to home.
Feminism cannot just get away from domestication, whether by sweeping it
under the carpet as a dusty old error, or by identifying it with an uncomplicated
and inevitable process of asssimilation.

Domestication, as the examples in this essay have demonstrated, is not such
a firmly fixed, univocal concept in the first place. And feminism, with its inherently undomesticated place—neither at home nor away from home—is uniquely
placed to engage in productive forms of domestic deconstruction. The results
will never be tidy, but they will always be different.

NOTES |

1   Judith Butler, *Gender Trouble: Feminism and the Subversion of Identity* (New York:
    Routledge, 1990), p. xiii, p. 139.

2   See Jack Goody, *The Domestication of the Savage Mind* (Cambridge: Cambridge
    University Press, 1977).

3   See Richard Hoggart, *The Uses of Literacy: Changing Patterns in English Mass Culture*
    (1957; rpt. Boston: Beacon Press, 1961).

4   Gaston Bachelard, *La poétique de l'espace* (1957; rpt. Paris: Presses Universitaires de
    France, Quadrige series, 1958), p. 79.

5   On hyphenating philosophy, see Bachelard, *La poétique de l'espace*, p. 128, p. 192; for
    the critique of a negative version of psychoanalysis, see e.g. pp. 112–13 and pp.
    155–7.

6 Bachelard, *La poétique de l'espace*, p. 129.

7 But I can't stop myself from adding a domestic detail from the last half hour: as I was typing this, to the reassuring dim backing of the radio, the voice of Dave Lee Travis—a household name on British radio until he faded ignominiously from the airwaves in the summer of 1993—filtered itself across asking some quiz question to some pub team somewhere in East Anglia about—as I subsequently reconstructed it—the total in tons of the quantity of cargo shifted through Heathrow Airport every year. A few moments later the reply came back, as it turned out just one or two off the correct answer, somewhere in the hundred thousands. With what sounded to me like genuine disturbance, DLT returns: "That's a little too close for comfort, that's a very uncanny guess." Well to me, about to start my paragraph on the uncanny, this too was a little too close for comfort, as if the radio, habitually used in some nebulous way to be alternately soothing and enlivening, or just *there* in an unremarkable domestically familiar way, had suddenly jumped out to take on a quite different role, utterly disturbing in its apparently benign reinforcement of the main direction of my attention.

8 Freud, *The Interpretation of Dreams* (1900), tr. James Strachey (Harmondsworth: Penguin, 1978), p. 463.

9 In which connection, there is the following searing passage from the end of Upton Sinclair's *The Jungle* (1906; rpt. Harmondswroth: Penguin, 1986), spoken by an advocate of cooperative communities:

> Surely it is moderate to say that the dish-washing for a family of five takes half an hour a day; with ten hours as a day's work, it takes, therefore, half a million able-bodied persons—mostly women—to do the dish-washing of the country. And note that this is most filthy and deadening and brutalizing work; that it is a cause of anaemia, nervousness, ugliness, and ill temper; of prostitution, suicide, and insanity; of drunken husbands and degenerate children.(p. 406)

> He goes on to imagine the hygienic twentieth-century wonders of a collectively owned "machine that would wash and dry the dishes, and do it, not merely to the eye and the touch, but scientifically—sterilizing them."(pp. 406–7).

10 See Virginia Woolf, "Professions for Women," *The Crowded Dance of Modern Life: Selected Essays*, Vol. 2, ed. Rachel Bowlby (Harmondsworth: Penguin, 1993).

11 Simone de Beauvoir, *Le deuxième sexe*, vol. II (1949; rpt. Paris: Gallimard, Folio essais series, 1986), p. 259.

12 Beauvoir, *Le deuxième sexe*, p. 259.

13 Beauvoir, *Le deuxième sexe*, p. 267.

14 Friedrich Engels, *The Origin of the Family, Private Property, and the State*, (1884; rpt. New York: Pathfinder Press, 1972), p. 68.

15 Engels, *The Origin of the Family*, p. 152.

16 John Ruskin, "Of Queens' Gardens," in *Sesame and Lilies* (1865; rpt. London: J.M. Dent, Everyman's Library, 1970), p. 50.

17 Ruskin, "Of Queens' Gardens," *Sesame and Lilies*, p. 49.

18 Ruskin, "Of Queens' Gardens," *Sesame and Lilies*, pp. 49–50.

19 Ruskin, "Of Queens' Gardens," *Sesame and Lilies*, p. 59.

20 Ruskin, "Of Queens' Gardens," *Sesame and Lilies*, p. 59.

21 Witold Rybczynski, *Home: A Short History of an Idea* (London: Heinemann, 1988), p. 77.

22 Rybczynski, *Home: A Short History of an Idea*, p. 217.

23 Rybczynski, *Home: A Short History of an Idea*, pp. 220–1.

24 Rybczynski, *Home: A Short History of an Idea*, p. 232.

25 Ruskin, "Of Queens' Garden," *Sesame and Lilies*, p. 75.

26 Ruskin, "Of Queens' Gardens," *Sesame and Lilies*, p. 75.

27 This is a point eloquently made by Michèle Le Doeuff in *L'étude et le rouet* (Paris: Seuil, 1989).

28 Beauvoir, *Le deuxième sexe*, p. 272.

29 See Luce Irigaray, *Speculum: de l'autre femme* (Paris: Seuil, 1974).

30 See Julia Kristeva, "Women's Time," *The Feminist Reader*, ed. Catherine Belsey and Jane Moore (London: Macmillan, 1989).

31 I discuss this in more detail in "The Problem With No Name: Rereading Friedan's *The Feminine Mystique*," *Still Crazy After All These Years* (London: Routledge, 1992).

The old patterns, no matter how cleverly
rearranged to imitate progress, still condemn us to cosmetically altered repetitions
of the same old exchanges.

—Audre Lorde
"Age, Race, Class, and Sex"

To exist historically is to perceive the
events one lives through as part of a story
later to be told.

—Arthur Danto
Narration and Knowledge[1]

4

TRANSFERENCES

Black Feminist Discourse: The "Practice" of "Theory"

Deborah McDowell

That remembering is political, and
inextricably bound to culturally contested issues, is now granted as freely
as is the understanding that "*why* we
remember and *what* we remember,
the motive and the content, are
inseparable."[2] To speak of "historical
knowledge" at all, and of feminist
critical theory most specifically, is
to stage or enter a vigorous debate
between those who see "history" and
"knowledge" as ontological givens
and those who don't. I identify with
those who don't, with those who
recognize that, despite its basis in the
concrete certainties of "then" and
"there," complete with recognizable
names and familiar faces, history is a
fantastical and slippery concept, a
making, a construction.[3] I side with
those who see history, to invoke the
current *lingua franca*, as a "contested
terrain" that often functions to
repress and contain the conflicts and
power asymmetries that mark the
sociopolitical field. That contempo-

rary students of culture and its institutions have, by and large, willingly adjusted their assumptions and altered their practices to fit these axioms is a salutary development. But we would do well to heed Renato Rosaldo's warning against the dangers of declaring historical knowledge constructed and simply ending the discussion there, for we must show in nuanced historical perspective, however difficult that is, "how it was constructed, by whom, and with what consequences."[4]

Here, I want to take some liberties with time and construe the present as the future's past in order to determine what "historical knowledge" of "contemporary feminist theory" we are constructing at this moment and with what consequences to which specific bodies. In other words, how are we telling the history or story of recent feminist theoretical developments? Who are the principals in that story? What are the strategies of its emplotment? How does it reconstitute timeworn structures and strategies of dominance? How does it produce imagined divisions of scholarly labor that recode familiar hierarchical relations? I ask these questions because I share with many others a keen interest in how race and gender figure into our scholarly pursuits, drives, and desires. And it seems to me that if we want an example of how contemporary theory gets historicized and of how social categories get woven into intellectual narratives, we need look no further than the representation of writings by African-American women in contemporary academe. The period since 1977 provides a convenient point of access.

I agree with Hortense Spillers that "in a very real sense, black American women are invisible to various public discourses, and the state of invisibility for them has its precedent in an analogy on any patriarchal symbolic mode that we might wish to name."[5] And while some have tried to restore black American women to discursive sight, their efforts have been often compromised by the compulsions of historical legacy and the imperatives of contemporary social design. Such compulsions and imperatives are especially evident in debates of the past several years about the supposed opposition between "theory" and "practice"[6] (sometimes appearing as "theory" and "politics"). These debates illuminate how often the divisions and cleavages of scholarly labor exist in masked relation to the divisions and cleavages of social life.[7] More specifically, the theory/practice opposition is often racialized and gendered, especially in discussions of black feminist thinking, which, with precious few exceptions, gets constructed as "practice" or "politics," the negative obverse of "theory." Although some black women have indeed helped to encourage this perception by viewing their writing as an enclosed and unified domain, fending off foreign intellectual invasion, they are neither the origins nor the primary agents of the theory/practice division that underwrites a familiar sociocultural contract.

What follows is not a singular narrative, but rather miscellaneous examples—call them "case studies"—about black feminist thinking that crop up in a variety of critical discussions. While I want to critique the tendency to construct "black feminist thinking" and "theory" as false unities, for purposes of easy reference I refer here to both in the singular, even as I am reminded that Hazel Carby's statements about black feminist criticism apply alike to "theory," that is, it must also be seen as a "locus of contradictions," a "sign that should be interrogated."[8] And although I select examples from a variety of critical denominations, I do so not to universalize or indict any whole, but rather to indicate the pervasiveness of the theory/practice division that has assumed a structural relevance and significance that can no longer be ignored.[9]

UNCOVERING TRUTH: COLORING "FEMINIST THEORY"

As we know, in the narrativization of any history, much depends on familiar vocabularies of reference, on the circulation of names, proper names—and some names are more proper than others.[10] I want to talk briefly about the circulation of one name—Sojourner Truth—and the "knowledge" that name helps to construct about black feminist thinking within the general parameters of feminist discourse.[11]

In the opening chapter of her study, *"Am I That Name?" Feminism and the Category of "Women" in History*, Denise Riley begins with a reference to Sojourner Truth and her famous and much quoted question, "Ain't I a Woman?", posed before the 1851 Women's Rights Convention in Akron, Ohio. Riley supposes that, in the current historical moment, Sojourner "might well—except for the catastrophic loss of grace in wording—issue another plea: 'Ain't I a Fluctuating Identity?'"[12] The temptation here is simply to find the humor in Riley's rewriting and move on, except that to do so is to miss the sociocultural assumptions that are attached to it, assumptions that escape the boundaries of Truth's time to project themselves boldly in our own.

Riley's move to appropriate Sojourner Truth introduces a subtle racial marker that distinguishes between Truth's original words and Riley's displacement. A familiar move in contemporary literary-critical discussion, Riley's "modernization" functions allegorically to make a common if subtle insinuation about black feminist thinking in general: it needs a new language. That language should serve a theory, preferably a poststructuralist theory, signaled in this context by the term *fluctuating identity*.

To trace the move from Sojourner Truth's "Ain't I a Woman" to Riley's "Ain't I a Fluctuating Identity" is to plot, in effect, two crucial stages in a historical narrative of academic feminism's coming of age. Following this evolutionary logic, academic feminist discourse can be said to have "grown out of" an attachment to what Riley terms that "blatant[ly] disgrace[ful]" and "transparently suspicious" category—"Woman."[13] That category happens to be personified by Sojourner's rhetorical and declarative question. Riley concedes that Sojourner represents one move in a necessary "double move" of feminist theory that recognizes that "both a concentration on and a refusal of the identity of 'woman' are essential to feminism."[14]

Constance Penley makes essentially the same point in *The Future of an Illusion*. Whereas in Riley's study Sojourner marks the point of departure, in Penley's she marks the point of closure. In the last two pages of the final chapter, she walks on to take a bow with Jacques Lacan. His "notorious bravura"—"the woman does not exist"—is counterposed to Sojourner Truth's "Ain't I a Woman?" Echoing Riley, Penley explains this counterposition as "two ideas or strategies...vitally important to feminism," though they might appear completely at odds.[15] Penley classifies the one strategy—represented by Lacan, Althusser, and Derrida—as "epistemological" and "metaphysical"; the other, represented by Sojourner Truth is "political." That Truth's declarative question—"Ain't I a Woman"—might be read as "political" *and* "epistemological" simultaneously seems not to have occurred to Penley, partly because she manipulates both these categories, consciously or not, to conform to an already polarized and preconceived understanding.

Is it purely accidental that, in these two essays, Sojourner Truth comes to represent the politics but not the poetics that feminism needs? Is hers a purely neutral exemplarity? Agreeing with Gayatri Spivak that "it is at those borders of discourse where metaphor and example seem arbitrarily *chosen* that ideology breaks through,"[16] I would argue that Sojourner is far from an arbitrary example. Possible intentions notwithstanding, Sojourner Truth as a metonym for "black woman" is useful in this context both to a singular idea of academic feminism in general and, in particular, to ongoing controversies within that discourse over the often uneasy relations between theory and politics.

The belief that feminism and whiteness form a homogeneous unity has long persisted, along with the equally persistent directive to feminist theorists to "account" for the experiences of women of color in their discourses. The unexamined assumption that white feminist discourse bears a special responsibility to women of color helps to maintain the perception that feminism equates with whiteness and relates maternalistically to women of color. Such assumptions are implied in the recently published *Feminist Theory in Practice and Process*. In "Naming the Politics of Theory," one section of the introduction, the editors challenge "feminist theory...to recognize the myriad forms of black women's race, gender, and class politics and to envision theories that encompass these lived realities and concrete practices."[17] Elizabeth Spelman's observation, from another context, is useful here: "It is not white middle-class women who are different from other women, but all other women who are different from them."[18]

That difference has become magnified and has assumed an even greater urgency since academic feminism, like all discursive communities on the contemporary scene, has accepted the constructive challenge to take its processes into self-conscious account. That is, difference has assumed this position since feminism has accepted the challenge to "theorize" about the work it does and the claims it makes. The strain to fulfill both requirements—to "theorize," on the one hand, and to recognize material "differences," on the other, has created a tension within academic feminist (read *white*) discourse. That tension is often formulated as a contrast, if not a contest, between "theory" and "practice/politics," respectively.

I must rush to add that race (here, read *black*) and gender (here, read *female*) are not the only stigmatized markers on the practice/politics side of the border, for they trade places in a fluid system of interchangeability with differences of nationality, sexuality, and class.[19] The now quiescent French/American feminist theory debate—illustrated most controversially in Toril Moi's *Sexual/Textual Politics*—provides one example of what I mean. Moi clumps Anglo-American, black, and lesbian women on the practice/politics/criticism side of the border; French women, on the theory side. After blasting the claims of Anglo-American feminist criticism, Moi then turns to answer those who "might wonder why [she has] said nothing about black or lesbian (or black lesbian) feminist criticism in America.... The answer is simple: this book purports to deal with the theoretical aspects of feminist criticism. So far, lesbian and/or black feminist criticism have presented exactly the same *methodological* and *theoretical* problems as the rest of Anglo-American feminist criticism."[20] Moi adds, "This is not to say that black and lesbian criticism have no...importance," but that importance is not to be "found at the level of *theory*...but the level of *politics*."[21]

In the context of these critical developments, the use of "Sojourner Truth" projects a myriad of meanings needed to perform the work of distinction and differentiation in the culture of academe. To begin with, as a metonym for "black woman," the name can be read as a mark of racial difference and distinction within "feminist theory," which points up its internal conflicts and ambivalence over the relative merits and value of "political" discourse. That markers of racial difference can be hidden in itineraries represented as "purely" (and thus neutrally?) epistemological, is evident in the following summary by Jane Flax:

Feminist theorists have tried to maintain two different epistemological positions.

The first is that the mind, the self, and knowledge are socially constituted, and what we can know depends on our social practices and contexts. The second is that feminist theorists can uncover truths about the whole as it "really is." Those who support the second position reject many postmodern ideas and must depend upon certain assumptions about truth and the knowing subject.[22]

The assumptions about Sojourner Truth examined so far—both explicit and implied—cast her categorically in that second position, despite the fact that the short text of the "Ain't I a Woman?" speech is a compressed but powerful analysis and critique of the social practices within the context of slavery that depend on biases of class and race to construct an idea of universal or True Womanhood. Truth challenged that dominant knowledge, offering and authorizing her experiences under slavery as proof of its underlying illogicality.

The truth that Truth knows, then, is not reducible to a mere statement turned slogan that acts as theory's *Other*, or theory's shadow side. The politics contained within *that* epistemology, within that way of knowing Truth, must be interrogated and the foundations on which it rests laid bare. Those foundations are sharply exposed when we remember the moment in Truth's career perhaps most frequently remarked: the degrading demand to bare her breasts.

After Truth delivered a speech in Silver Lake, Indiana, in 1851, a Dr. T. W. Strain alleged that Truth was a man. To prove that she wasn't, Truth bared her breasts.[23] The scene captures graphically Truth's fixity in the body and thus her distance from the "proper" white feminists enlisted to "verify" her sex. Her recuperation in these modern contexts forges a symbolic connection with that prior history, a conjunctive relationship to that past. It is precisely this earlier scene of verification that is being symbolically re-enacted today. The demand in this present context is not to bare the breasts to verify black womanhood, but to bare the evidence that proves positively the qualifications of black feminist discourse as "theory."

But the selection of Sojourner Truth as metonym raises still other problems that connect to the relation between the symbolic and the social, and the relation between the present and the past. The fact that Sojourner Truth was illiterate and that the words by which we know her were transcribed by stenographic reporters or admiring white friends has only begun to be interrogated with any complexity.[24]

The critical discourse tries to rematerialize its signs of omission around race. The utterance of "Sojourner Truth" (or any other metonym for black women) seems to perform for some an absolution of critical guilt, but the utterance is all there is. "Sojourner Truth"—or any other metonym for black women—is a name of which no more need be said. Truth's experiences beyond popularized cliches are not fully addressed.[25] She is useful simply as a name to drop in an era with at least nominal pretensions to interrogating race and the difference it makes in critical discussion.

But the repetition of Sojourner Truth's name makes no *real* difference. In dominant discourses it is a symbolic gesture masking the face of power and its operations in the present academic context. As a figure in remove, summoned from the seemingly safe and comfortable distance of a historical past, "Sojourner Truth" can thus act symbolically to absorb, defuse, and deflect a variety of conflicts and anxieties over race in present academic contexts. However, "Sojourner Truth" stirs up far more controversy than it settles, preventing any easy resolution of feminism's conflicts. Locked within that name is the timeless and unchanging knowledge (the very definition of "truth") of race and gender embedded in Western philosophy that now finds it way, like the return of the repressed, into the organization of knowledge in contemporary academe.

The repeated invocation of "Ain't I a Woman?"—detached from historical context—neither captures its immediacy for Truth's time nor re-activates it for our own. Put another way, the repeated invocation of "Sojourner Truth" functions not to document a moment in a developing discourse but to freeze that moment in time. Such a chronopolitics operates not so much as history but as an interruption of history, at least as black women might figure in it, a phenomenon recalling Hegel's description of Africa as outside the "real theatre of History" and of "no historical part of the World." "It has no movement or development to exhibit…. What we properly understand by Africa is the Unhistorical, Undeveloped Spirit, still involved in the conditions of mere nature, and which has to be presented…on the threshold of the World's history."[26]

The proposition that black feminist discourse is poised on the threshold of Theory's history has predictable consequences. Not least, this view helps to reconstitute the structures and strategies of dominance, even in work that strives zealously in an opposite and oppositional direction.

GENDERING AFRICAN-AMERICAN THEORY

We can observe such strategies of dominance in *Gender and Theory*, a recent anthology edited by Linda Kauffman. Kauffman tries studiously to prevent a reproduction of the simplistic divisions and antagonisms between black and white, male and female, "theory" and "politics." She explains in her introduction that while the title—*Gender and Theory*—posits a couple, the essays are arranged to permit men to respond to the essays by women and vice versa. That "structure is designed…to draw attention to such dichotomies in order to displace them by dissymmetry and dissonance."[27] Despite that goal, these very oppositions appear. In fact, we could argue that if theory is often to practice/politics what Europe is to America, what white is to black, what straight is to gay, in Kauffmann's anthology, theory is to practice what black male is to black female. This reductive accounting represents black women as categorically resistant to theory.

"Race" in Kauffman's anthology is constructed once again as synonymous with "blackness." Barbara Christian's "The Race for Theory" and Michael Awkward's response, "Appropriative Gestures: Theory and Afro-American Literary Criticism" are placed at the very end of the volume and thus apart from the preceding pairs of essays, none of which interrogates the racial inflections of "gender and theory." The racial opposition coordinates with oppositions of gender and genre, making theory male and practice female.

The question Kauffman poses in her introduction—"In what ways are Afro-American theory and Afro-American feminism complementary, and in what ways are they antagonistic?"—gets answered in the two concluding essays: "Afro-American theory" is gendered male and "Afro-American feminism" is gendered female.[28] And they function effectively as structural antagonists. Such a seemingly innocent juxtaposition has already quickly decided its conclusion: Michael Awkward's response to Barbara Christian calls for a "theory" to her "practice."[29]

One of the strengths of Awkward's response to Christian lies in its implicit recognition that poststructuralist theory cannot be homogenized, nor can it stand synecdochically for all theory. Although it is clear that he thinks Christian has missed the theoretical mark, he asserts that Barbara Smith's "Toward a Black Feminist Criticism" was "essentially a theoretical—if not [a] poststructuralist—discussion of critical practice and textual production."[30] Smith's essay, he goes on to say, "theorizes despite its lack of a clearly informed awareness of deconstruction, reader-response theory, [and] semiotics."[31]

Here, Awkward's vocabulary—"if not" and "lack of"—essentially negates whatever value he initially assigned Smith's essay, which is structured as the negative of the positive—an undifferentiated poststructuralism acting as the sole frame of reference. Making an uncritical link between black women as "writers" and black women as "critics" that holds the latter responsible for the survival of the former, Awkward offers a cautionary note: "But if the literature of black women is to continue to make inroads into the canon, if it is to gain the respect it doubtlessly deserves as an ideologically and aesthetically complex, analytically rich literary tradition within an increasingly theoretical academy, it will require that its critics continue to move beyond description and master the discourse of contemporary literary theory."[32]

If, as Awkward suggests, "black women's literature still does not assume the prominent place in courses and criticism that…it merits," I would ask whether that marginality can be explained exclusively by a lack of theorizing on the part of black women or rather whether that marginalization is often structured into the very theories that Awkward wants black women to master.[33] Again, my point should not be read as a simplistic rejection of "theory," even as it is narrowly associated in Awkward's essay with poststructuralist projects, but as a call for a more searching examination of the processes and procedures of marginalizing any historically subjugated knowledge.

Awkward's essay does more than close Kauffman's volume; it performs a kind of closure, or functions as a kind of "final word," that extends far beyond the boundaries of the collection, *Gender and Theory*. He leaves intact the cliched and unstudied distinctions between theory and practice represented by Paul de Man and Barbara Christian, respectively. It is paradoxical and ironic that an essay which privileges poststructuralist theory and extols de Man relies on an uncritical construction of theory as an autonomous entity with semantic stability and immanent properties that separate it from practice. It is all the more ironic that such a dichotomy should dominate in an essay that valorizes a body of theory identified most popularly with blurring such inherited and unmediated oppositions. But the dichotomies of Awkward's essay mark a difference and issue a set of limits—social limits—that extend beyond the academic realm. In identifying with Paul de Man, Awkward consolidates his own critical authority against Barbara Christian's, making theory a province shared between men.[34]

That theory is a province shared between men is nowhere more evident than in the wasteful *New Literary History* exchange, which brought to the boiling point one of the most controversial shifts in the history of African-American literary study: the "race" debate.[35] While this shift produced a schism among scholars in African-American literary study, that schism has been oversimplified and exaggerated and construed, all too often, as a gender war over the uses and abuses of "theory" for African-American literary study, a war with black men on the side of "theory" and black women against it.

Joyce Ann Joyce largely aided that perception with her much-discussed and critiqued essay "The Black Canon: Reconstructing Black American Literary Criticism." Recuperating the salient principles of the Black Aesthetic movement, Joyce argued for the responsibility of the black writer to his or her audience, for that writer's absolute and sovereign authority, for the use of the black literary text in fostering "Black pride and the dissolution of the double consciousness" and the inappropriateness of "white" critical theories to analyses of black literature.[36]

In their responses to Joyce's essay, both Henry Louis Gates and Houston Baker were warranted in questioning these aspects of her argument, although they were less so in dismissing as naive and anachronistic her questions about "the historical interrelationship between literature, class, values, and the literary canon."[37] Gates and Baker choose to evade these questions in order to focus on Joyce's stubborn resistance to reading "race" as a pure signifier or arbitrary function of language. In this debate, Joyce will not concede to her opponents that the complexities and irrationalities of social life in the United States are reducible to language games. And, even if they are, she comes just short of arguing, race still functions as a "transcendent signified" in the world.

Although he positions himself opposite Joyce in the *New Literary History* exchange, Houston Baker makes this same point eloquently in his essay, "Caliban's Triple Play," a critical response to "'Race,' Writing and Difference," the special issue that Gates edited for *Critical Inquiry*.[38] Baker persuasively notes the power and resilience of "racial enunciative statements" that assert themselves painfully at the level of felt and lived experience. His compelling arguments in this essay indicate a clear reluctance to hypertextualize race, a stance that would seem to connect him with Joyce, but such a connection must be sacrificed in order to forge and secure a greater bond between Gates and Baker, one that transcends and papers over their critical differences. The rhetoric of erotics that tinges Gates's response to Joyce clearly indicates that much more is at issue and at stake than Joyce's alleged unexamined resistance to theory.

Gates's decision to use Tina Turner's pop hit "What's Love Got to Do with It," which Joyce rightly if reactively perceives as glorifying the objectification of women, clearly sexualizes this exchange:

> it is an act of love of the tradition—by which I mean *our* tradition—to bring to bear upon it honesty, insight, and skepticism, as well as praise, enthusiasm, and dedication; all values fundamental to the blues and to signifying, those two canonical black discourses in which *Houston and I* locate the black critical difference. It is merely a mode of critical masturbation to praise a black text simply because it is…"black."[39]

In identifying *the* "two canonical black discourses," associated in their critical articulations with himself and Baker, Gates prepares the way for Baker to further consolidate a growing chain of male theoretical authority distinct from the dragrope of "black women critics" who constitute a "new black conservatism."[40] Although Baker argues that his critique is "directed against specific conservatisms, misjudgments, and errors," rather than "toward a group," it so happens that "black women" are linked to a widespread, if unspecified, group that shows "essential animosity toward recent modes of critical and theoretical discussion."[41] It is black women who fail to seize the abundant opportunities for the kinds of "theoretical daring and critical inventiveness" that mark the age and set the agenda for a transformative politics.[42] In Baker's view, that daring and inventiveness are seen mainly in the work of Derrida, Althusser, Lacan, and Baudrillard.

Curiously, in Baker's reasoning, all positions and/or questions not readily assimilable to their projects are conservative and atheoretical. Even more curious is the fact that the agenda for a transformative politics must repress gender, for those questions asked by the "conservative" black women, whom Baker chastises and corrects, are questions about the relations between gender and artistic production, questions that a good many people might regard as interventions in clear service of a transformative politics. Further, those in that service might challenge Baker to consider the various ways feminists have found his agents of change—Derrida, Althusser, Lacan, and Baudrillard—both useful to and limited for feminist projects. Indeed, to borrow Baker's words, if not his meaning, "the towers of an old *mastery* are reconstituted" in any implied suggestion that feminist critique works against, rather than in harmony with, other varieties of transformative politics and discursive priorities.[43]

NOTES TOWARD A COUNTER HISTORY

Where might we go from here? I would start with the forthright assertion that the challenge of any discourse identifying itself as black feminist is not necessarily or most immediately to vindicate itself as theory. Rather, its challenge is to resist the theory/practice dichotomy, which is too broad, abbreviated, and compromised by hedging definitions to capture the range and diversity of contemporary critical projects, including the range and diversity in the contributions of black women to that discourse. A far more valuable and necessary project would proceed from the commonplace assumption that no consideration of *any* intellectual project is complete without an understanding of the process of that project's formation. And thus any responsible accounting of the work of black women in literary studies would have to provide a history of its emergence and consider that emergence first on its own terms.

Of course, part of the historical accounting of recent critical production is underway, but unfortunately it leaves questions of the relations between race and critical discourse largely unexplored. A counter history, a more urgent history, would bring "theory" and "practice" into a productive tension that would force a re-evaluation of each side. But that history could not be written without considering the determining, should I say the *over*-determining, influences of institutional life out of which all critical utterances emerge.

It follows, then, that we have to scrutinize carefully the past two decades, which witnessed the uncanny convergence and confluence of significant historical moments, all contributing to the present shape and contours of literary studies. These are: the emergence of a second renaissance of black women writing to public acclaim; a demographic shift that brought the first generation of black intellectuals into the halls of predominantly white, male, and elitist institutions; the institutionalization and decline of African-American studies and women's studies; and the rising command in the U.S. academy of poststructuralism, regarded as a synonym for theory.

Our historical narrative would have to dramatize the process by which deconstruction came to stand synecdochically for poststructuralist theory, its dominion extending from the pages of arcane journals of critical theory, to the pages of such privileged arbiters of culture as the *New York Times Magazine* and *The New York Review of Books*, to the pages of *Time* and *Newsweek*.[44] The analysis would have to explore how deconstruction became associated as much with an ideological position as with a revitalizing and energetic intellectual project at roughly the same time that a few black women, following Barbara Smith's challenge, began to articulate a position identified as black feminist criticism. Smith focused on recuperating the writings of black women for critical examination and establishing reading strategies attentive to the intersections of gender, race, and class in their work.[45]

If we were to compare the salient terms of black feminist criticism and poststructuralist theory for this historical narrative, they might run as follows:

(1) While black feminist criticism was asserting the significance of black women's experience, poststructuralism was dismantling the authority of experience.

(2) While black feminist criticism was calling for nonhostile interpretations of black women's writings, poststructuralism was calling interpretation into question.

(3) While black feminist criticism required that these interpretations be grounded in historical context, deconstruction denied history any authoritative value or truth claims and read context as just another text.

(4) While the black woman as author was central to black feminist writers' efforts to construct a canon of new as well as unknown black women writers, poststructuralism had already rendered such efforts naive by asking, post-Foucault, "What Is an Author?" (1969) and trumpeting post-Barthes, "The Death of the Author" (1968).

(5) While black feminist critics and African-Americanists more generally were involved in recuperating a canon of writers and outlining the features of a literary tradition, a critical vocabulary emerged to question the very idea of canons and traditions.

But the salient terms of these admittedly tendentious synopses would also have to reveal some useful correspondences. Both black feminist criticism and deconstruction perceived the regulation and exclusion of the marginal as essential to maintaining hegemonic structures. Both described the structural and hierarchical relations between the margins and the center. Our narrative might then pause to ponder how these two reading strategies came to be perceived as antithetical, how their specific *units* of critical interest came to be polarized and assigned an order of intellectual value that drew on a racist and sexist schema with heavy implications and investments in the sociopolitical arrangements of our time.

CHOOSING SIDES

It is important that this shorthand history not be read to mean that poststructuralist theories and their practitioners constitute a reaction formation against the emergent noncanonical literatures, and thus black feminist thinking would do well without them. No, my aim is not to demonize poststructuralist theories or to see them as having invented the present hierarchies that pervade critical inquiry. The hierarchical arrangements of knowledge within which black feminist thinking is marginalized extend far beyond and are well anterior to these theories. Such arrangements are part and parcel of what has already been written about black intellectuals, male and female alike, part and parcel of a general and historical devaluation of black intellectual activity in whatever form it takes.

What viable position can then be taken in this context? We might begin to assert a provisional conclusion: When the writings of black women and other critics of color are excluded from the category of theory, it must be partly because theory has been reduced to a very particular practice. Because that reduction has been widely accepted, a great many ways of talking about literature have been excluded and a variety of discursive moves and strategies disqualified, in Terry Eagleton's words, as "invalid, illicit, noncritical."[46]

The value of Eagleton's discussion of literary theory lies mainly in its understanding of how critical discourse is institutionalized. In that process, the power arrogated to some to police language, to decide that "certain statements must be excluded because they do not conform to what is acceptably sayable" cannot be denied.[47] The critical language of black women is represented, with few exceptions, as outside the bounds of the acceptably sayable and is heard primarily as an illicit and non-critical variety of critical discourse defined in opposition to theory. Its definition and identity continue to be constructed in contemporary critical discourses, all of which must be recognized, distinguished, and divided from each other in the academy's hierarchical system of classifying and organizing knowledge. To be sure, the discourses that exist at any given historical juncture compete with each other for dominance and meaning, compete with each other for status as knowledge. But we must be constantly on guard for what Biodun Jeyifo is right to term a *misrecognition* of theory, a misrecognition that has "achieved the status of that naturalization and transparency to which all ideologies aspire and which only the most hegemonic achieve."[48]

Given this *misrecognition* of theory and the privileged status it enjoys, even in moments of embattlement, it is readily understandable why some black feminists and other women of color in the academy would argue for the rightful *recognition* of their work as "theory." bell hooks offers only one example.[49] In evaluating the position of black women in theory, hooks goes directly to the necessary site of any such evaluation: the micropolitics of the corporate university. In analyzing the production of feminist theory, she perceives "only one type of theory is seen as valuable" in the academy—"that which is Eurocentric, linguistically convoluted, and rooted in Western white male sexist and racially biased philosophical frameworks"—and hence other varieties get overlooked.[50]

Given hooks's astute understanding of the ways in which the parameters of "theory" have been constructed institutionally so as to eliminate the writings of black women, her observation that "little feminist theory is being written by black women and other women of color" runs oddly counter to her otherwise forceful critique.[51] For her assessment is accurate only if "theory" is very narrowly conceived to fit the very definition she decries. Moreover, her lament for the paucity of theory by black women seems dependent on a false distinction between "theory" and "creative writing."[52]

In describing the pedagogical imperatives of the feminist classroom, hooks observes that in the economy of the average feminist syllabus, the "imaginative works [of black women] serve purposes that should be addressed by feminist theory," a tendency that does a "disservice to black women writers and all women writers."[53] However useful novels and confessional writings are in the larger projects of feminist theory, hooks adds, "they cannot and do not take the place of theory."[54]

hooks's fears that the tendency in classes on feminist theory to identify "writing by working-class…and women of color as 'experiential' while the writings of white women represent 'theory'" reinforces racism and elitism.[55] Because of a long history that has constructed analytical thinking as the exclusive preserve of whites, hooks's concerns are fully understandable.[56] Although she is right to argue that "it does not serve the interests of feminist movement for feminist scholars to support this unnecessary and dangerous separation of 'theoretical' work and the work that focusses more on the experiential," her critique succeeds only if she preserves that very distinction, ironically valorizing "theory" in the process.[57]

While I would not presume to speak for or issue directives to "women of color," which would, in any case, assume a false and coherent totality, I openly share my growing skepticism about the tactical advantages of this position. I am far more interested, for the moment, in joining the growing number of critics—many of them "Third World"—who have begun to ask difficult questions about the material conditions of institutional life and have begun to view theory, in its narrow *usages* (rather than in any intrinsic properties to be assigned to it), as an ideological category associated with the politically dominant. It is important that such a statement *not* be read as a resistance to "theory" but as an insistence that we inquire into why that category is so reductively defined and why its common definitions exclude so many marginalized groups within the academy. Such is Barbara Christian's point in "The Race for Theory," although in their rush to condemn and contain her inquiry, critics missed that aspect of her critique.

The question that Christian raises about the theory/practice distinction and the racial assumptions that it encodes is echoed in the writings of a growing number of students of minority and postcolonial discourses. For example, Rey Chow addresses the problem of "the asymmetrical structure between the 'West' as dominating subject and the 'non-West' or 'Third World' as the oppressed 'other.'" She goes on to say, that "contrary to the absolute difference that is often claimed *for* the 'Third World'…the work of a twentieth-century Chinese intellectual foretells much that is happening in the contemporary 'Western' theoretical scene."[58] Chow's observations go far beyond and far deeper than a plea for a liberal, pluralist position here, beyond a plea for "equal time." Neither she nor the growing number of Third World intellectuals who have begun to interrogate the uses to which "theory" is being increasingly put is so naive as to suggest that the power of its gravitational field in academic discourse can be so simply and reactively resisted. Most of us know that the debate over the uses and abuses of theory, formulated as such, followed by a growing demand to choose sides, is a sterile and boring debate that diverts us from the more difficult pursuit of understanding how theory has been constructed as an exclusively Western phenomenon.

The view that theory cannot exist outside that narrow orbit is especially apparent in what Edward Said refers to as a "maddening new critical shorthand" that "makes us no less susceptible to the dangers of received authority from canonical works and authors than we ever were. We make lackluster references to Nietzsche, Freud, Lacan as if the name alone carried enough value to override any objection or to settle any quarrel."[59] Said's list of names requires its constructed others to embody the most popular terms of critical opprobrium. I am concerned to note that often these are the names of black American women who become fetishized, to quote Valerie Smith, and "employed, if not sacrificed, to humanize their white [and male] superordinates, to teach them something about the content of their own subject positions."[60] And nowhere is this more apparent than in a recent exchange with Jane Gallop, Marianne Hirsch, and Nancy K. Miller in *Conflicts in Feminism*, edited by Marianne Hirsch and Evelyn Fox Keller.

REMEMORIES

This was not a story to pass on.

—Toni Morrison, *Beloved*

In that exchange, Gallop describes the process of her coming to write the history-in-progress of feminist criticism through a reading of 1970s anthologies, a reading that would offer a more balanced version of the now largely disparaged seventies feminist criticism than recent years have generally seen. A part of the process of this project involved Gallop's own conversion to the idea of race. Asked by Hirsch how inclusive her history would be and whether she planned to include anthologies that foregrounded race, Gallop answered, and I quote in detail, perhaps in unseemly detail:

> I'm doing Pryse and Spillers's *Conjuring*. Race only posed itself as an urgent issue to me in the last couple of years. Obviously there has been a larger shift in the valent feminist discourses in which I participated. I didn't feel the necessity of discussing race until I had moved myself out of a French post-structural orbit and began talking about American feminist literary criticism....
>
> I was telling this guy in Syracuse that I thought in writing *Reading Lacan* I had worked through my transference both onto Lacan and onto things French in general. And he asked, "So who do you transfer onto now?" My first thought was to say, "no one." And then one of the things I thought of was a non-encounter with Deborah McDowell. I read work from my book last February at the University of Virginia. I had hoped Deborah McDowell would come to my talk: she was there, she was the one person in the audience that I was really hoping to please. Somebody in the audience asked me if I was writing about a black anthology. I answered no and tried to justify it, but my justification rang false in my ears. Some weeks later a friend of mine showed me a letter from McDowell which mentioned my talk and said that I was just doing the same old thing, citing that I was not talking about any books edited by black women. I obsessed over McDowell's comment until I decided to add a chapter on Pryse and Spillers's *Conjuring*. I had already vowed not to add any more chapters out of fear that I would never finish the book. As powerful as my fear of not finishing is, it was not as strong as my wish for McDowell's approval. *For McDowell, whom I do not know, read black feminist critic.* I realize that the set of feelings that I used to have about French men I now have about African-American women. Those are the people I feel inadequate in relation to and try to please in my writing. It strikes me that this is not just idiosyncratic. This shift, for me, passed through a short stage when I felt like what I was saying was OK. The way McDowell has come to occupy the place of Lacan in my psyche does seem to correspond to the way that emphasis on race has replaced for me

something like French vs. American feminism.[61]

It is important to note that Gallop sees her whole project as a "struggle over whose version of history is to be told to the next generation."[62] She continues, "Mainly I am saying that feminist criticism has not been well enough understood. I am writing a history of something that is too known in the sense that it is familiar, but that we don't really perceive anymore because we have our set notions and categories for what is going on."[63] Gallop's reference to our "set notions and categories" is far more suggestive and incisive than perhaps even she intends. And the philosophy of history that her reference encodes encourages me to assert my own, by way of looking back in time and simultaneously returning to Sojourner Truth.

In 1863 Harriet Beecher Stowe published "Sojourner Truth: The Libyan Sibyl" in *Atlantic Monthly*. It begins:

> Many years ago, the few readers of radical Abolitionist papers must often have seen the singular name of Sojourner Truth, announced as a frequent speaker at Anti-Slavery meetings, and as travelling on a sort of self-appointed agency through the country. *I had myself often remarked the name, but never met the individual.* On one occasion, when our house was filled with company, several eminent clergymen being our guests, notice was brought up to me that Sojourner Truth was below, and requested an interview. Knowing nothing of her but her singular name, I went down, prepared to make the interview short, as the pressure of many other engagements demanded.[64]

Stowe's "I had myself often remarked the name, but never met the individual" has a striking ring or at least a structural similarity to Gallop's "For McDowell, whom I do not know, read black feminist critic." Having risked the dangers of a typological philosophy of history, let me suggest that in these two narratives, removed from each other by a hundred and a quarter years, past and present become spectral adjacencies. While there are obvious risks in forging such a comparison, I do so out of understanding that intellectual inquiry is necessarily influenced and constrained by cultural traditions and social circumstances.

We might argue, then, that through the power of involuntary memory, the past is *transferred* to the present. While I obviously intend this play on words here, it is not idle play, for I want to capture that aspect of the transference that connotes a piece of repetition; the repetition is a transference of the forgotten past onto aspects of current situations. I want, moreover, to stress the rhetorical continuities between Stowe and Gallop in their own right as the legacy of a tradition of prefabricating blackness.

Both Stowe and Gallop commit what Ralph Ellison terms the "crime of reducing the humanity of others to that of a mere convenience, a counter in a banal game which involves no apparent risk to ourselves."[65] In "The Libyan Sibyl," Sojourner Truth is the counter to Stowe's conversion narrative, which assimilates Truth's complex life story to the civilizing rhetoric of Protestant evangelicism. In "Conflicts in Feminism," Deborah McDowell is the counter to an academic feminism now submitting to what Gallop calls the pressure of race.

But let me rush to insert here that my goal is neither to expose weaknesses in Jane Gallop's thinking nor to suggest that they are peculiar to her. In fact, in giving pause to her conversion narrative, I merely want to situate her within a general history. And Gallop would surely understand that, for as she prepares the reader for the delicate negotiations she must perform in the anthology study *Around 1981: Academic Feminist Literary Theory*, she takes care to note that:

> we are [all] stuck inasmuch as we speak from within history…. [We] can only know from within history, with at best partial ideological awareness, and in specific relation to institutionalized discourses and *group interests*.[66]

As Gallop recounts the process of her own conversion or coming to race in "Criticizing Feminist Criticism," she reveals again much more than she realizes. She confesses: "I can't discount being attacked in the name of Marxism or historicism or racial difference, things that I recognize as serious political, as opposed to what I think of as high theoretical."[67] Racial difference figures in her confession as a proper name, my name.

The assignment so far of black women to the "serious political" as opposed to the "high theoretical" is an oversimplified taxonomic distinction based primarily on the convenience of the privileged few, and thus it is perhaps fitting that Gallop's truncated account of her intellectual development turns, as her comments in "Criticizing Feminist Criticism" suggest, on references to class mobility:

> Around 1981, [I] experienced more anxiety about not being sophisticated enough whereas now my anxiety is about being bad, about having a white, middle-class outlook…. The anxiety about being a slob is an anxiety about not being high class enough, anxiety about being too low, whereas the other is anxiety about being too high. If you are looking up towards Derrida, Paris, sophistication, you feel like you're too low and you're anxious about not having something that comes from a higher class…. Now the situation is the opposite.[68]

Race, in this context, equals lower class equals black feminist, a multiplication of equations that helps to construct an identity, a subjectivity for black feminist thinking among the general critical discourses of our time. Although black feminist criticism can be marked at one point, as being on an yet unfinished trajectory, it is consigned to the status of the permanent underclass. In that sense, the identity of black feminist criticism has so far been anything but fluctuating. It has been solidly fixed to a reference schemata and a racial stigmata in a history we've read before.

NOTES |

This is a longer version of a talk presented at the Commonwealth Center for Literary and Cultural Change, University of Virginia, as part of a general symposium ("Is Knowledge Gendered?") and a specific panel on "Race and Gender in the Teaching of Historical Knowledge." I thank Susan Fraiman and Rick Livingston for helpful comments and suggestions.

1 Arthur C. Danto, *Narration and Knowledge* (New York: Columbia University Press, 1985), p. 343; Audre Lorde, "Age, Race, Class and Sex," *Sister Outsider: Essays and Speeches by Audre Lorde* (Trumansburg, New York: The Crossing Press, 1984), p. 123.

2 See Richard King, "Memory and Phantasy," *Modern Language Notes* 98 (December 1983), p. 1200. See also Pierra Nora, "Between Memory and History: *Les Lieux de Mémoire*," *Representations* 6 (Spring, 1989); and *The Invention of Tradition*, ed. Eric Hobsbawm and Terrence Ranger (New York: Cambridge University Press, 1983).

3 While certainly not peculiar to this tradition, this philosophy of history has long been prevalent in the writings of African Americans, especially in the historical or documentary fiction produced so insistently for the past twenty years. Random examples would include John A. Williams's two metahistorical novels *The Man Who Cried I Am* (New York: New American Library, 1967) and *Captain Blackman* (Garden City, New York: Doubleday, 1972). In both, history is a suspicious text constructed by paramilitary, conspiratorial agents. Other examples include Ishmael Reed's *Flight to Canada* (New York: Random House, 1976) and Sherley Anne Williams's *Dessa Rose* (New York: Williman Morrow, 1986), derived from her short story "Meditations on History." For a discussion of history and documentation in African American fiction see Barbara Foley, "The Afro-American Documentary Novel," *Telling the Truth: The Theory and Practice of Documentary Fiction* (Ithaca: Cornell University Press, l986). The now familiar argument that the generic conventions of narrative are evident in the construction of history has been articulated in works such as Hayden White's *Tropics of Discourse* (Baltimore: Johns Hopkins University Press, 1978); *The Content of the Form* (Baltimore: Johns Hopkins University Press, 1987), and *Metahistory* (Baltimore: Johns Hopkins

University Press, 1973).

4 Renato Rosaldo, "Others of Invention: Ethnicity and Its Discontents," *Voice Literary Supplement* (February 1990), p. 27.

5 Hortense Spillers, "Interstices: A Small Drama of Words," *Pleasure and Danger: Exploring Female Sexuality*, ed. Carole Vance (Boston and London: Routledge and Kegan Paul, 1984), p. 74.

6 Definitions are in order here, but they are difficult to pin down. Although the term "theory" operates much like a mantra in contemporary criticism, it is difficult to find anything but vague definitions of the term. Randomly chosen attempts at definition would include Jonathan Culler's, which defines theory as a "nickname" used "to designate works that succeed in challenging and reorienting thinking in fields other than those to which they ostensibly belong because their analyses of language, or mind, or history, or culture offer novel and persuasive accounts of signification." See *Framing the Sign: Criticism and Its Institutions* (Norman: University of Oklahoma Press, 1988), p. 15. In *Criticism in the University* (Evanston, Illinois: Northwestern University Press, 1985), Gerald Graff and Reginald Gibbons define theory as "simply a name for the questions which necessarily arise when principles and concepts once taken for granted become matters of controversy" (p. 9). Bruce Robbins uses theory to "refer to all those otherwise diverse conceptual innovations in the last twenty-five years or so which have combined to produce the single result of reshaping literary criticism." See "The Politics of Theory," *Social Text* 18 (1987), p. 5. What all these definitions lack, perhaps inevitably, is specificity and an awareness that "theory" is a term freighted with contemporary understandings and fraught with ambiguity.

7 For further discussion of this idea, see Pierre Bourdieu, *Distinction: A Social Critique of the Judgment of Taste* (Cambridge: Harvard University Press, 1984). In "The Self-Evaluations of Critical Theory," Evan Watkins notes similarly that "how we tell ourselves the history of recent theoretical developments…takes place in [that] shady zone between the boundaries of intellectual work and social situation" (*Boundary 2*, 12–13 (Spring/Fall 1984), pp. 359–78).

8 Hazel Carby, *Reconstructing Womanhood* (New York: Oxford University Press, 1987), p. 15.

9 One could raise at least two serious objections here. The first is that a focus on what has been written *about* black feminist thinking eclipses a more constructive, perhaps a more empowering, focus on what has been written *by* black feminists.

In her review of Patricia Hill Collins's *Black Feminist Thought*, for example, Farah Griffin commends Collins for moving black feminism "to a new level" by spending "little time castigating white feminists or black men for their failures in regard to black women." She praises Collins for focusing instead "on an exploration and analysis of thought produced by black women themselves. In so doing, she reinforces their status as subjects and agents of history." See *Women's Review of Books* 8 (February 1991), p. 14. While I would dispute Griffin's perception that the work of black feminists has been, to this point, simply other-directed, I regard her implied call for a necessary shift of focus and address *within* the work of black feminism absolutely essential. But such a shift alone is insufficient, for it ignores the often unequally positioned sites of knowledge production and their influence on how and if the work of black feminists is read, and on how and if it is read in a way that restructures, not simply annexes, knowledge in conditioned reflex acts.

One could raise a second objection: that my focus is too strictly and narrowly academicist, and curiously so if we consider that although its main address is now the UNIVERSITY, black feminist thinking does not stake its origins or find its shelter there, and even when academia is its central site, it strives to extend its borders. While the focus is narrow, its implications and imperatives for the organization and construction of "historical knowledge" are much broader.

10 For a discussion of the use of what Martin Jay terms "charismatic names" to legitimate critical arguments, see his "Name Dropping or Dropping Names?: Modes of Legitimation in the Humanities," *Theory Between the Disciplines: Authority/ Vision/Politics*, ed. Martin Kreiswirth and Mark A. Cheetham (Ann Arbor: University of Michigan Press, 1990), pp. 19–34.

11 For a discussion of Sojourner Truth as "standard exhibit in modern liberal historiography," see Phyllis Marynick Palmer, "White Women/Black Women: The Dualism of Female Identity and Experience in the United States," *Feminist Studies* 9 (Spring 1983), pp. 151-69.

12 Denise Riley, *"Am I That Name?": Feminism and the Category of 'Women' in History* (Minneapolis: University of Minnesota, 1988), p. 1.

13 Riley, *"Am I That Name?"*, p. 2.

14 Riley, *"Am I That Name?"*, p. 1. By her admission, Riley's "double move" is a concession to pragmatism. She maintains that "it is compatible to suggest that 'women' don't exist—while maintaining a politics of 'as if they existed'—since the world behaves as if they unambiguously did" (Riley, *"Am I That Name?"*, p. 112).

15 Constance Penley, *The Future of an Illusion: Film, Feminism, and Psychoanalysis* (Minneapolis: University of Minnesota Press, 1989), p. 179.

16 Gayatri Spivak, "The Politics of Interpretation," W. J. T. Mitchell, *The Politics of Interpretation* (Chicago: University of Chicago Press, 1982), p. 346.

17 *Feminist Theory in Practice and Process*, ed. Michelene Malson, Jean O'Barr, Sarah Westphal-Wihl, and Mary Wyer (Chicago: University of Chicago Press, 1989), p. 7.

18 Elizabeth Spelman, *Inessential Woman: Problems of Exclusion in Feminist Thought* (Boston: Beacon Press, 1988), p. 162.

19 In a very perceptive and persuasive essay, Judith Roof argues that "[w]hile the

materialist commitment to gender and the economic is a commitment to an "analysis," a racial or lesbian commitment is defined differently, as anachronistically political—'liberationists'—as activism instead of analysis." She asks, "Why for this moment are gender and class cerebral and race and sexual orientation experiential?" See "All Analogies Are Faulty: The Fear of Intimacy in Feminist Criticism," *A Lure of Knowledge: Lesbian Sexuality and Theory* (New York: Columbia University Press, 1992), p. 222.

20 Toril Moi, *Sexual/Textual Politics* (London and New York: Methuen, 1985), p. 86.

21 Moi, *Sexual/Textual Politics*, p. 87. Emphasis added.

22 Jane Flax, *Thinking Fragments: Psychoanalysis, Feminism, and Postmodernism in the Contemporary West* (Berkeley: University of California Press, 1990), p. 140.

23 For a brilliant discussion of this scene and of the materiality in which black women were embedded more generally, see Haryette Mullen, "'Indelicate Subjects': African-American Women's Subjectivity," *Subversions* (Winter 1991), pp. 1–7. See also Valerie Smith, "Black Feminist Theory and the Representation of the 'Other,'" *Changing Our Own Words: Essays on Criticism, Theory, and Writing by Black Women*, ed. Cheryl Wall (New Brunswick: Rutgers University Press, 1989), pp. 38–57.

24 Recent work by Nell Irvin Painter has begun to engage the nexus of paradoxes, ironies, and contradictions of these transcriptions and to inquire into why, until recently, Sojourner Truth, a "naive rather than an educated persona, seems to have better facilitated black women's entry into American memory" than any of her educated black female contemporaries. Painter's point is obviously not that only lettered or tutored black women should have facilitated that memory, but that Sojourner Truth as figure keeps alive the "disparities of power and distinctions between European and Euro-Americans and natives, domestic and foreign." See her "Sojourner Truth in Life and Memory: Writing the Biography of an American Exotic," *Gender and History* 2 (Spring 1990), pp. 3–16.

25 For example, it is seldom noted that during Reconstruction Truth assisted the resettlement of some blacks in the exodus to Kansas and worked on land reform.

26 Georg W. F. Hegel, "Geographical Basis of History," *The Philosophy of History*, tr. J. Sibree (New York: Colonial Press, 1991), p. 99.

27 *Gender and Theory*, ed. Linda Kauffman (New York: Basil Blackwell, 1989), p. 2.

28 *Gender and Theory*, ed. Linda Kauffman, p. 4.

29 Michael Awkward, "Appropriative Gestures: Theory and Afro-American Literary Criticism," *Gender and Theory*, ed. Linda Kauffman.

30 Awkward, "Appropriative Gestures," *Gender and Theory*, p. 240.

31 Awkward, "Appropriative Gestures," *Gender and Theory*, p. 242.

32 Awkward, "Appropriative Gestures," *Gender and Theory*, p. 243.

33 Awkward, "Appropriative Gestures," *Gender and Theory*, p. 239.

34 Here I make an obvious allusion to Eve Sedgwick's influential study, *Between Men:*

English Literature and Male Homosocial Desire (New York: Columbia University Press, 1985), which examines the "bonds that link males to males," through and over the bodies of women.

35 Valerie Smith's observations about the trajectory of African American literary studies is well taken in this context. In "Gender and Afro-Americanist Literary Theory and Criticism," *Speaking of Gender*, ed. Elaine Showalter (New York: Routledge, 1989), pp. 56–70, Smith argues that the dynamics of the male acquisition of power actually inform the critical positions of each generation. Referring specifically to "Discovering America: Generational Shifts, Afro-American Literary Criticism, and the Study of Expressive Culture," Smith notes that in the epigraph to his essay, Houston Baker "casts the connection of black expressive culture to literary criticism and theory in terms of the perennial battle between fathers and sons" (p. 67).

36 Joyce Ann Joyce, "The Black Canon: Reconstructing Black American Literary Criticism," *New Literary History* 18, 2 (Winter 1987), p. 341.

37 Joyce, "The Black Canon," *New Literary History*, p. 335. Questions concerning the literary canon and its historical shaping have received considerable attention in recent years. See, to name only a few examples, Jane Tompkins, *Sensational Designs: The Cultural Work of American Fiction, 1790–1860* (New York: Oxford University Press, 1985); Paul Lauter, *Canons and Contexts* (New York: Oxford University Press, 1991); John Guillory, "Canon," *Critical Terms for Literary Study*, ed. Frank Lentricchia and Thomas McLaughlin (Chicago: University of Chicago Press, 1990); and Richard Ohmann, "The Shaping of a Canon: U.S. Fiction, 1960–1975," *Politics of Letters* (Middletown: Wesleyan University Press, 1987).

38 The special issue and its responses are collected in '*Race,' Writing, and Difference* (Chicago: University of Chicago Press, 1986).

39 Henry Louis Gates, "'What's Love Got To Do With It?' Critical Theory, Integrity, and the Black Idiom," *New Literary History* 18, 2 (Winter 1987), p. 347. Emphasis added.

40 Houston Baker, "In Dubious Battle," *New Literary History* 18, 2 (Winter 1987), p. 367.

41 Baker, "In Dubious Battle," *New Literary History*, p. 363, p. 366.

42 Baker, "In Dubious Battle," *New Literary History*, p. 367. Diane Fuss makes essentially the same point in "'Race' Under Erasure? Poststructuralist Afro-American Literary Theory," *Essentially Speaking* (New York: Routledge, 1989), pp. 73–96. While she praises Gates, who has "perhaps done the most to open the floodgates for poststructuralist African American theory," and Baker, who "pioneers a fourth generational movement" (p. 81), Fuss, a white woman, asks, "What accounts…for the apparent resistance on the part of many minority women critics to what Barbara Christian has labeled 'the race for theory'?" (p. 95). In Fuss's analysis, "essentialism" is a kind of shorthand, catch-all term for all that is *not* poststructuralist theory,

a negation projected and branded onto black women. Interestingly, Fuss acknowledges that a form of essentialism inheres in the work of Gates and Baker, but she redeems their variety of essentialism, primarily because she views it as redemptive, having "saved" African American literary study from what she terms the "bedrock of essentialism" (p. 86).

43 Baker, "In Dubious Battle," *New Literary History*, p. 369.

44 Jonathan Arac, Wlad Godzich, and Wallace Martin described the spread of deconstruction in their preface to *The Yale Critics* (Minneapolis: University of Minnesota Press, 1987). Although not simply mimicking deconstruction, other critical discourses have attempted to establish grounds of compatibility with it. A random list might include Mary Poovey's "Feminism and Deconstruction," *Feminist Studies* 14, 1 (Spring 1988), which describes deconstruction as a discourse with vast enabling possibilities for feminism. Michael Ryan's *Marxism and Deconstruction* (Baltimore: Johns Hopkins Universisty Press, 1982) is an effort at what he calls a "critical articulation," which is not only a comparative reading of the two discourses, but also an "attempt to develop a new form of analysis which would be both marxism and deconstruction," an "alloy of the two" (p. xv, p. xiii). Similarly, in the introduction to his *Black Literature and Literary Theory* (New York: Methuen, 1984), Henry Louis Gates Jr. collects a group of essays that draws on various critical methodologies and reading strategies, but believes the signal challenge of black literary study is "to bring together, in a new fused form, the concepts of critical theory and the idiom of the Afro-American and African literary traditions" (p. 10). In the economy of the volume, however, the Yale School and its varieties of deconstruction predominate. Even though Gates's more recent essays call for black critics to "invent their own…black, text-specific theories," deriving from a "black formal cultural matrix," he also challenges them "not to shy away from white power— that is, literary theory," but to "translate it into the black idiom" (*Loose Canons: Notes on the Culture Wars* (New York: Oxford University Press, 1992), pp. 78–79). The hegemony of "theory" (or white power) in this proposed hybridization is clear.

45 Barbara Smith, "Toward a Black Feminist Criticism," *The New Feminist Criticism*, ed. Elaine Showalter (New York: Pantheon, 1985), pp. 168–185.

46 Terry Eagleton, *Literary Theory: An Introduction* (Minneapolis: University of Minnesota Press, 1983), p. 203.

47 Eagleton, *Literary Theory*, p. 203.

48 Biodun Jeyifo, "Literary Theory and Theories of Decolonization," unpublished manuscript. Also see his "On Eurocentric Critical Theory: Some Paradigms from the Texts and Sub-Texts of Post-Colonial Writing," *After Europe: Critical Theory and Post-Colonial Writing*, ed. Helen Tiffin and Stephen Slemon (Sydney: Dangaroo Press, 1989).

49 See especially bell hooks, "Feminist Theory: A Radical Agenda," *Talking Back: Thinking Feminist. Thinking Black* (Boston: South End Press, 1989), p. 36. See also Michele Wallace who articulates a similar position in two essays from her collection *Invisibility Blues: From Pop to Theory* (London: Verso, 1990). In "Variations on Negation and the Heresy of Black Feminist Criticism," Wallace registers her concern that "black women writers and academics seem disproportionately under-represented in the sphere of knowledge production, in which literary criticism is included" (p. 215). While, in this essay, she concludes that "nobody in particular and everybody in general seems responsible for this situation" (p. 214), in "Negative Images: Toward a Black Feminist Cultural Criticism," she suggests that black women are largely responsible for this vacuum. She chastises them for producing "an idealized and utopian black feminism, which…remains almost entirely unarticulated and untheorized" (p. 252). Echoing Michael Awkward, Wallace asserts, "I am firmly convinced that if black feminism, or the feminism of women of color, is going to thrive on any level as a cultural analysis, it cannot continue to ignore the way that Freud, Marx, Saussure, Nietzsche, Levi-Strauss, Lacan, Derrida and Foucault have forever altered the credibility of obvious truth, 'common sense' or any unitary conception of reality" (p. 248). The importance of the work in this heterogeneous list is more asserted than argued, and recalls again Martin Jay's point, in "Name Dropping or Dropping Names?", about the "charismatic names," the ritualized forms of citation used to legitimate critical arguments simply through the act of reference.

50 hooks, "feminist theory," *Talking Back*, p. 36.

51 hooks, "feminist theory," *Talking Back*, p. 38.

52 The familiar and assumed distinction between "literature" and "criticism" has been widely problematized in contemporary critical discussion, as literary critics have rejected the "secondary" roles of servants to the master, "primary" texts, and claimed for themselves a status equal to that of creative writers. As Barbara Hernsstein Smith puts it, "theory cannot be seen as distinct from and opposed to literary 'creation' but as a central and inevitable aspect of it." See her "Value/Evaluation," *Critical Terms for Literary Study*, ed. Frank Lentricchia and Thomas McLaughlin (Chicago: University of Chicago Press, 1990), p. 181. In the "Race for Theory," Barbara Christian wants Smith's refusal of the distinction between "theory" and "creative writing" to work in reverse (*Gender and Theory*, ed. Linda Kauffman, pp. 225–237). That is, she wants to blur the distinction between the two in order to argue that if "theory" can be "creative writing," creative writing can be theory. But in arguing that "people of color have always theorized…in narrative forms, in the stories [they] create, in riddles and proverbs" (p. 226), she falls into the same logic that traps bell hooks. In other words, to reverse the theory/creative binarism in order to claim for the literatures of "people of color" status

as "theory" is still to give primacy to "theory."

53 hooks, "feminist theory," *Talking Back*, p. 38.

54 hooks, "feminist theory," *Talking Back*, p. 38.

55 hooks, "feminist theory," *Talking Back*, p. 37.

56 Cornel West makes a similar argument in "The Dilemma of the Black Intellectual," *Cultural Critique* 1 (1985): "Charges of intellectual inferiority can never be met upon the opponent's terrain," he writes. Rather, "the terrain itself must be viewed as…unworthy of setting the terms of contemporary discourse" (p. 117). West goes on to discuss the "place" of black intellectuals in Marxist thought, noting, "the Marxist privileging of black intellectuals often reeks of condescension that confines" the roles of black intellectuals to "spokespersons and organizers; only rarely are they allowed to function as creative thinkers who warrant serious critical attention" (p. 118).

57 hooks, "feminist theory," *Talking Back*, p. 38.

58 Rey Chow, "'It's You, and Not Me': Domination and 'Othering' in Theorizing the 'Third World,'" *Coming to Terms: Feminism, Theory, Politics*, ed. Elizabeth Weed (New York: Routledge, 1989), p. 161.

59 Edward Said, *The World, the Text, and the Critic* (Cambridge, MA: Harvard University Press, 1983), p. 143.

60 Valerie Smith, "Black Feminist Theory and the Representation of the 'Other,'" *Changing Our Own Words: Essays on Criticism, Theory, and Writing by Black Women*, ed. Cheryl Wall (New Brunswick: Rutgers University Press, 1989), p. 46.

61 Jane Gallop, Marianne Hirsch, and Nancy K. Miller, "Criticizing Feminist Criticism," *Conflicts in Feminism*, ed. Marianne Hirsch and Evelyn Fox Keller (New York: Routledge, 1990), pp. 363–64. Emphasis added.

62 Gallop in "Criticizing Feminist Criticism," *Conflicts in Feminism*, p. 362.

63 Gallop in "Criticizing Feminist Criticism," *Conflicts in Feminism*, p. 363.

64 Harriet Beecher Stowe, "Sojourner Truth: The Libyan Sibyl," *The Atlantic Monthly* (1863), p. xxx. Emphasis added.

65 Ralph Ellison, "The World and the Jug," *Shadow and Act* (New York: Vintage/Random House, 1972), p. 124.

66 Jane Gallop, *Around 1981: Academic Feminist Literary Theory* (New York: Routledge, 1992), p. 9. Emphasis added.

67 Gallop, "Criticizing Feminist Criticism," *Conflicts in Feminism*, p. 352.

68 Gallop, "Criticizing Feminist Criticism," *Conflicts in Feminism*, p. 353.

5

IN THE NAME
OF FEMINISM

Valeria Wagner

The following passage is from an article written by a woman who signs simply "Claudia," in what could be considered a feminist gesture of refusal of the patriarchal family structure. But Claudia is no feminist:

> I am not so naive to believe that what I write can change anyone's views; I merely hope to encourage the more perceptive reader to cut through the hypocrisy of feminism and recognise the women's movement for what it is: middle-class aspirations and puritanism masquerading as rebellion.[1]

Is Claudia's provocative position just an expression of an anti-feminist backlash? It might be, although I am sure the reader will find it easy to imagine circumstances in which feminists behave as middle-class women upholding puritan values. The critiques of feminism that Claudia develops in the rest of the article have in fact become common currency in contemporary feminism: that feminism is still blind to the categories of race and class; that this blindness benefits women from a particular race and class; that this perpetuates a capitalist economy based on exploitation. True, Claudia expresses her point of view somewhat categorically—she argues, for example, that "the feminist demand, 'a woman's right to work', signifies nothing more than her own 'right' to exploit other women (and men) in the form of a career,"[2] and that the construct of 'patriarchy' gives theoretical justification to feminists' exploitation of other women, minimising as it does the importance of class differences between women. Thus working-class women have their existence theorized away.[3]

But we should remember that her critiques echo, or are echoed by, feminists such as Juliet Mitchell, who suggests that "by setting up the opposition of the sexes as dominant, we helped to produce the ideological notion of a 'classless' society."[4] For Mitchell,

Feminism does emanate from the bourgeoisie or the petite-bourgeoisie, the social class which, in capitalist society, where it is dominant, gives its values to the society as a whole. It represents its particular interest as universal interest, its women as 'woman.'[5]

Claudia and Juliet Mitchell part ways when the latter states that "to see this is not to turn aside from feminism, but to note that as yet it has not transcended the limitations of its origins."[6] For Claudia, instead, there is "as yet" no room for change in what she obviously perceives as a homogeneous feminist movement.

Of course, Claudia's negative image of feminism can be explained away by appealing to her particular experience of "the women's movement." It can be argued that she was unlucky, she encountered the "wrong" kind of feminists; that she was on the "wrong" continent; that this happened in the eighties, but the nineties are different, etc. In other words, it can be argued that although Claudia's critiques are valid as far as her own experience is concerned, they do not apply to feminism "in general." But the same argument would apply to Juliet Mitchell's more positive perception of feminism: she does not have a privileged knowledge of feminism "in general," her experiences of the movement must have been as particular as Claudia's. Thus the appeal to experience simply begs the question of the reasons that have led these two women to react so differently to feminism, on the grounds of otherwise largely coincident critiques of the movement. What allows Juliet Mitchell to retain her allegiance to feminism, and what makes it impossible for Claudia to imagine other forms of feminism and to identify with them?

Let me begin with Claudia once again. That it really is impossible for her to identify with feminism is apparent from the paragraph that precedes her strong identification *of* feminism:

As a result of the mutual rejection of the women's movement and myself I am outraged when people assume that if I am independent and unconventional I must be a feminist, and that I have feminism to thank for any self-confidence I may have gained over the years, I am deeply insulted by those men and women who presume to tell me what is and what is not oppressive to me.[7]

Claudia's categorical rejection of feminism here is linked to feminism's identification and appropriation of *her*. She objects, on the one hand, to the authority that feminism confers on those speaking in its name—the men and women who "presume" to know more about Claudia's condition than herself—and on the other hand to the recuperative power of feminism as a discourse. She is not, here, reacting against a specific bunch of women, but rather against an influential and growing discourse which, in her view, threatens to engulf and neutralize her own difference and claims. It is this capacity to integrate into itself different discourses that homogenizes the "women's movement" to the extent that it becomes, in Claudia's discourse, the establishment itself. Hence the impossibility of recuperating feminist discourses for her own purposes, or of claiming that the establishment-associated feminism is *not* feminism. Claudia's assumption is that to address feminism is useless; she will not be heard. The most she can do is to address "the more perceptive readers" to confirm the suspicions they must already foster about feminism.

At this point it may have become obvious why Juliet Mitchell can afford to identify with feminism, while leaving the question of the identification *of* feminism open. Juliet Mitchell is, in various ways, integrated into the establishment which Claudia criticizes and excludes herself from: she is, according to the contributors' notice in *What is Feminism?*, "a psychoanalyst who has lectured extensively throughout Europe and the English-speaking world," and who has published a number of books on women- and feminism-related subjects. While Claudia seems to have published her article on her own, as a pamphlet (that was only later partly reprinted in the anarchist journal where I happened to read it), Juliet Mitchell's *Reflections on Twenty Years of Feminism* was published by Basil Blackwell. In short, Juliet Mitchell is an authority on feminism—a feminist scholar as well as a scholar on feminism—and is not subject to the authority of feminism, as Claudia is. It is the two women's different positions—"outside" and "inside" institutional frames—that seem to me to be at the root of their divergent attitudes towards feminism, which determines their view of feminism as a closed and monolithic ideology, or as a changing and potentially varied movement.

I now argue that Claudia's view of feminism as a "unified front" is justified—not because there is, in fact, any such unified feminist movement—but because the institutionalization that feminism has both suffered and achieved allows differences to be expressed within feminism only to the extent that they can be made to appear as *more* feminism. By the institutionalization of feminism I mean its increasing representation within the establishment that it strives to change, its integration into the political landscape,[8] its considerable media-coverage (especially in England and the United States), and, most importantly, its constitution into a discipline of its own inside the academy (and this is beginning to happen in non-anglophone Europe too). I say most importantly because academic feminism is responsible for the "existence" of feminism "for itself," that is, a feminism that survives relatively independently from actual feminist movements, a feminism rallied around specific actions and claims. And needless to say, it is also through universities that many people, men and women alike, encounter feminism and are taught to think about it and in terms of it. I now turn to this exemplary form of institutionalized feminism to address the issue of the homogeneous appearance of feminism in spite of its factual heterogeneity.

It is now generally accepted that feminism never was, in spite of its white middle-class origins, a unified movement properly speaking. Nancy F. Cott for example observes, with regard to the highpoints of feminist movements in the United States, that

> If we look closely at even the extraordinary periods of 1912–19 and 1967–74, they exhibit not 'unity' but strategic coalition. Whether we see this as heroic, or lamentable, or merely human nature, it seems that mass movements of women have only been possible when women have instrumental or 'expedient' reasons for advancing gender interests—when, in other words, characteristics or aims besides gender grievances also motivate them. The vote, for instance, was pursued for different reasons by socialists and by members of the Daughters of the American Revolution, by black women and white racists; 'sexual politics' has been differently understood by, though equally central to, radical lesbians and middle-class wives.[9]

Consequently, it is not surprising that, in periods of political stagnation, or situations where there are no specific aims to rally women or partisans of feminism together, this lack of cohesion should be deeply felt.[10] It is not surprising either to find that in universities, where feminism has been "disciplined," the question of the nature of feminism, or its identity, or its unity, should become a major concern. As a discipline, feminism is necessarily schooled: taught to others and to itself. Hence the inevitable construction of an "it," and the ensuing questioning of it. And there is in fact much talk in universities, to use the terms of our editors, about feminism's loss of "its unique presence to itself," a uniqueness which, as it disappears from present and past alike, could threaten the possibility of a feminist presence at all.

But this isn't the case. It is true that feminism's "unique presence" has been and still is severely questioned and criticized. But now this questioning has turned into the acknowledgment and celebration of the differences and disagreements which, ten years or twenty years ago, feminists might have liked to cover up. Now it is common currency to assert that there are *many* feminisms, not just one: a statement that is meant to comprehend both the statement of fact that there are many feminist groups and associations (at least in Europe and North America) acting independently from each other; and the statement of "value" that feminism has now acknowledged certain of its former limitations— it now recognizes and problematizes the categories of race, class and gender that deconstruct the category of "woman" on which feminism was "first" grounded. Thus the multiplication of "feminisms" is now read more as a sign of the healthy progress that feminism is making rather than as a sign of unbridgeable disagreements. In other words, all critiques of feminism and revindications of different feminisms become feminism's self-critiques, where feminism, one suspects, still remains the copyright of a dominant group of people, however difficult they may be to define.

A good example of the unifying drive underlying the emphasis on difference in certain academic feminist discourses appears in Rosemarie Tong's *Feminist Thought*.[11] In the introduction, at the end of a quick review of the different trends in feminism that will be discussed throughout the book, the author presents postmodern feminism as the advocate of "difference," and then makes the following commentary:

> As attractive as the postmodern approach to feminism may be, some feminist theorists worry that an overemphasis on difference may lead to intellectual and political disintegration. If feminism is to be without any standpoint whatsoever, it becomes difficult to ground claims about what is good for women. It is a major challenge to contemporary feminism to reconcile the pressures for diversity and difference with those for integration and commonality. We need a home in which everyone has a room of her own, but one in which the walls are thin enough to permit a conversation, a community of friends in virtue, and partners in action. Only such a community can make feminist ethics and politics possible.[12]

The writer's position towards the multiplicity of feminism here is rather obvious: she believes difference and "variety" (the introduction bears the subtitle *The Varieties of Feminist Thought*) within feminist politics and thought are desirable, but only to the extent that they do not undermine the "integrity" of feminism. What such an integrated feminism might be like is unsurprisingly conveyed through the image of the *home*, a place of subdued disagreement in which differences would, in the author's imagination, be solved by the osmosis of discussion. Considering that the reference to Virginia Woolf,[13] one of the mainstays of the Anglo-American feminist literary tradition, is preceded by the intervention of the "many feminist theorists," it is difficult not to identify the university buildings as the author's model home. In the academy the cohabitation of feminist and antifeminist, racist and anti-racist, fascist and anti-fascist, etc, is not only enabled but enforced; here conversation may be hindered by differences, but we continue to be "partners in action"—an action from which the aims are generally left out of discussions.

But if conversation, understood as dialogue, may be understandably difficult in such an "ideal home" of feminism, it also fulfills a very important function: it ultimately keeps the sense of an "integrated" feminism alive through the discussion of the self-same differences that might otherwise lead to its "disintegration." Specifically, Tong's discussion of "pro-difference" feminists soon becomes a strategy to authorize more "moderate" feminists to reassemble diverging tendencies under an umbrella feminism. Postmodern feminists are presented as indulging in their emphasis on difference, unaware of the consequences of their inclinations: difference is "attractive," not something one decides or chooses to advocate with a complete rationale, but rather an experience that one—and there is the hint of individualism here—lets oneself plunge into, without justification. The imprudent unconcern of postmodern feminists justifies the concern of the "many" feminist theorists who can "see," from their theoretical standpoint, what is "really" happening. But are they really witnessing the "disintegration" of "any standpoint whatsoever"? The answer is no: an emphasis on difference should logically lead to the institution of *many* standpoints, and not to the abolishment of *all* standpoints. In other words, the concern over the lack of a feminist standpoint presupposes the necessity of a unique standpoint from which all the newly established standpoints can be observed. It is the possibility of such a unified view of feminism that "difference" undermines, leaving the "many theorists" standing on thin air.

The "many theorists" in this account are, of course, not worried about their own skin; they fear the consequences of the disintegration of the unique standpoint of theory, without which what is "good" and "for women" cannot be determined. In my opinion, this is a "good" thing, if only because neither "the good" nor "women" can be specified theoretically. It is also "good" in that it reveals the authoritative use of theory, here made to stand for the global perspective that can show feminism the way.[14] The "many feminist theorists" know what the others don't know, a knowledge that entitles them to become, in the next line, "contemporary feminism" itself, united in the challenge to reconcile the pressures for "diversity and difference" with "integration and commonality." But how can reconciliation take place if the pressure for "difference" is one of "difference" *from* feminism (a single feminism, or the dominant form of feminism, which obviously varies from context to context), and the pressure for "integration" is one for the integration *into* the self-same feminism? This predicament doesn't function as a problem in the discourse for the multiplicity of *feminisms*; rather, it constitutes, as long as it is maintained, an efficient solution to itself. The mere existence of unreconcilable differences feeds the belief in a reconciled feminism and provides the grounds on which strategies of self-authorization of a "united feminism," through the discrediting of the "internal opponents" of feminism, can be enacted.

The question that remains unasked is why feminism *should* be unified, integrated, coordinated, in agreement, etc. The answer, which the passage under consideration provides (that it is necessary to ground a point of view, and that this is in turn necessary to judge what is good for women), falls back on the universalist premisses which "pro-difference" arguments criticize. It also ultimately reduces political and ethical issues to the question of the identity of feminism. In other words, the author's concern over the making of feminist ethics and politics is preceded, and suspended, by the concern over the making of a community of feminists, and therefore, by the question of which feminism might reassemble such a community. In the process of this shift, the question of what identity is *for* is left out. In the words of Jenny Bourne, "the mistake is to view identity as an end rather than as a means."[15]

In the context of the transition of feminism from movement to discipline (and here "discipline" stands for institutionalization in its broadest sense), which more often than not divests feminists of the support of circumstance in exchange for a statutory authority, "mistake" might not be the right word to qualify the self-reflexive turn of feminism. Institutions confer *de facto* representational power on feminism in spite of most feminists' awareness of the limitations of this representation. This certainly doesn't mean that feminism should be given up altogether—I do not think that Claudia's rabid anti-feminism is the only possible alternative to counter the "united front" of feminism. But as feminism's unique presence to others, if not to itself, increases, it may be worth hesitating before speaking in its name. Whatever impetus different feminist movements have in common, they can converge under guises other than "feminism." In fact this "nomad" behavior—to take up the image of a sedentary feminism invoked by the use of the figure of the "home" *of* and *for* feminism—may well be the only way to impose the famous differences that different groups revindicate.

Let me conclude with an anecdote drawn from my early experiences of feminism in Geneva, and which, in fact, marks my conscious allegiance to (and identification of) the movement. At that time I played in a band (I was in my late teens), and we were asked to participate in a performance that was to commemorate the late access of Swiss women to vote (1971) as well as the even later inscription of an article stating the equal rights of men and women in the constitution (1981). As we were discussing the details of the performance, it dawned upon me that this was going to be a *feminist* act. I remember asking the others, who were "older women" to me, whether this was the case. I was told "Yes, why?," and I answered, rather stupidly, "I just wanted to know." Ultimately, what I gathered from their answer was that "feminism" is what you make of it in the company of others.

But what *did* we make of it? I remember the facts, of course. The performance took place at the *Parc des Bastions*, beneath a wall on which the statues of Calvin, Knox, De Bèze and Farel are sculptured, no doubt so as to suggest the comparison and the contrast between the two reforms. We lined up beneath the statues and accomplished, frenziedly, a series of household tasks—vacuuming, cleaning, ironing, washing, dusting, etc—one after the other. The tasks had an assigned place, so we moved from one to the other faster and faster until we all threw away and/or broke (preferably both) our household tools in revolt, and ran to our instruments to play a few noisy emancipatory tunes. The performance turned out to be fun, although of limited success (only about 50 spectators, mainly friends, and about 100 unwilling auditors). This was, one would like to think, as straightforward, innocent, and uncontroversial a feminist act as there could be: We were commemorating events that in principle affected all Swiss women. And we did this by staging the revolt of women against their traditional and silent role, followed by their forceful appropriation of the public scene and of their voices, or noises. As I give our little performance more thought, however, its feminist status becomes more problematic.

First of all, and leaving aside the ambiguity of the commemoration itself (it could be read as a celebration of the "emancipation of women" or of the Swiss government for having taken the necessary steps; as a critique of the belatedness of the events; a celebration of feminist achievements; as a statement on what still had to be accomplished…), the issue of women's right to vote, the cornerstone of feminist action, was at that time far from straightforward in Switzerland. In 1989 the men of the canton of Appenzell voted against it once again, and in 1990, following an appeal by a group of fifty-two women and a group of forty-eight men, the Swiss Federal Court finally ruled that it was unconstitutional to refuse the women of Appenzell the right to vote, imposing it accordingly.[16] This decision however was regreted by many other women, who not only resented the state's charity and righteousness but also feared for the equilibrium of their small society. For us, however, it was obvious that the right to vote was unconditionally good and desirable for all women, and our belief in all women's need to access political representation was conveyed in our performance in our insistence on women's representability. Not only were we all women, but we also pretended to be "women"—all women, women in general.[17]

But then, and here is probably the most interesting point of this anecdote, although our performance set up a representational frame, it also performed the collapse of this frame. Consider our choice of liberating or liberated activity that was to conclude the show. The reasons for the choice of an artistic activity as the reverse, or maybe the escape from, the oppressing activity are rather obvious—taking the place of men on the public scene, self-development and self-expression, group activity, etc. As for the choice falling on music, well, this was just one of the things we did at the time, being young and trendy. Grabbing the instruments could not be read, literally, as an injunction for all women to play music, although we may have been under the illusion that we were the most enlightened women around. What came through in the performance, I think, is that we were doing what we, not feminism, and not "we as feminists," did, preferred doing, enjoyed particularly, or even found the most fitting thing to do. In other words, in a sense the "feminist" performance stopped when the musical performance started—or maybe only began at that moment, but would not have answered to the name of "feminism."

Quite involuntarily, it seems to me that we managed to reverse the dangerous slippage from "us" to "feminists" to "feminism" that operated at the beginning of the performance, because we turned from a representational to a non-representational mode of performance. In the transition from denunciation to "action" (the concert), which could have indicated what "feminism" does ("this" is feminism), or what we "as" feminists are capacitated to do, there was just "us," playing.[18] At the moment a self-reflexive move was to be expected, or as a result of such a move, feminism disappeared from the scene. And I don't think this is a problem, as long as there is a scene where political acts can be played—this is what is really under threat.

It seems to me that the problem that not only feminism, but all political movements, have to face now is having to respond locally to the unlocalized (economic) forces that determine the political, and consequently finding a means and space of access to those forces. I have no solution to this "general" problem, indeed the problem still needs to be defined and understood. I can, however, anticipate that whatever new outlets the political can find or create, they will not themselves be enabled by any attempt to globalize (delocalize) political movements. On the contrary, such attempts would simply leave political movements without grounds on which to fight, and without political struggles to fight for—turning (as is the trend now in Europe and the USA) into mere movements, preoccupied with the mechanics of their moving. From this perspective, the preoccupation of (certain) academic feminism(s) with "itself" can be considered as the displacement of the problem of *political* disempowerment by that of the empowerment of identity.

The name of "feminism" does not, on its own, contribute to feminist aims— "feminism" is not the "open sesame" that opens the door to a treasure-house of political answers. In fact, quite the contrary seems to be true whenever a supposed fulfilment (unity, integration) of "feminism" is conflated with the fulfilment of feminist aims. It is now urgent to uncouple feminist *actions* from the globalizing discourse of a supposedly integrated feminist *movement*—to "do" feminism rather than act out the play of feminism.

In the course of this passage from movement to action feminism will inevitably become something else; it is bound to take forms unrecognizable to each other. And if feminism is considered *not* as an issue in itself but as an issue in political action and a creation of political spaces, then it better travel light and leave the burden of identity behind.

NOTES |

I am grateful to Saba Bahar, Diane Elam, and Christopher Mikton for their comments on this essay. I would also like to thank Leonardo Malfanti and Jamie McGowan.

1 From *I, Claudia, Feminism Unveiled*, rpt. excerpts in *Demolition Derby* 2, p. 14. The journal bears no date, but seems to be based in Montréal. As for the article, it seems to have been written in the early 80's.

2 *I, Claudia*, p. 16.

3 *I, Claudia*, p. 17.

4 Juliet Mitchell, "Reflections on Twenty Years of Feminism," *What is Feminism?*, ed. Juliet Mitchell and Ann Oakley (Oxford: Basil Blackwell, 1986), p. 45.

5 Mitchell, "Reflections," *What is Feminism?*, p. 47. Here Mitchell's statement leaves open the question of *what* feminism "emanates" from the petite-bourgeoisie: does the feminism embodied in the National Association of Colored Women's Clubs, for example, share the same origins as the feminism that Mitchell rightly criticizes? And if so, how can the "emanation" of the latter from the former be understood? For more on African-American women's movements, see Angela Davis, *Women, Culture & Politics* (New York: Vintage Books), 1990.

6 Mitchell, "Reflections," *What is Feminism?*, p. 47.

7 *I, Claudia*, p. 14.

8 In *Feminist Thought: A Comprehensive Introduction* (Boulder: Westview Press, 1989) for example, Rosemarie Tong tellingly organizes the "variety" of feminist thoughts under the following headings: liberal feminism, marxist feminism, radical feminism on reproduction and mothering, radical feminism on gender and sexuality, psychoanalytic feminism, socialist feminism, existentialist feminism, postmodern

feminism. This classification shows the "disintegration"—to take up a term she herself uses in the introduction—of feminism into multiple trends as well as its assimilation within existing trends, however corrective or critical this integration turns out to be. Only "radical feminism" escapes this double effect—it is defined in terms of the specific issues they discuss—because, I suppose, its "radicality" does not let itself be thought in terms of a movement by virtue of the centralization which the term may imply. What Tong significantly leaves out of the classification are the increasing number of "non-feminist feminists," or "independent feminists," who do not adhere or identify with any of the above trends, or who do not, at least, have an articulated discourse on feminism which would make them recognizable.

9 Nancy F. Cott, "Feminist Theory and Feminist Movements: the Past Before Us," *What is Feminism?*, p. 59.

10 There are, of course, mobilizing issues nowadays, such as the abortion controversy, women and AIDS, demand for equal wages between men and women, actions against the growing violence against women, etc. But these causes have hardly given rise to a feminist mass movement. In fact, issues such as the women's right to abortion divide feminists rather drastically. Needless to say, this division discredits neither the causes nor the women and men working on them, rather, it shows that "feminism" is not the rallying cry some would like it to be.

11 Although I have already refered to Tong's book, I do not want to insist too much on its particularity. Tong's views are obviously her own, but they are enabled, or encouraged, by the academic context in which they take place. I would therefore like to avoid the issue of the author's "responsibility" and consider her text instead as a result of the complex interaction between institutions and individuals.

12 Tong, *Feminist Thought*, p. 17.

13 Who also claimed, as we know, £500 a year—a condition bound to encourage leisured conversation and to provide the means and occasion to be virtuous.

14 I have all too often encountered the term "theory" serving the same function, especially with regard to feminism—once, for instance, in a philosophy seminar that was to focus on the concept of the feminine in philosophy. The professor introduced his seminar with the warning that he was not going to talk about feminism, and then precisely proceeded to talk about, or rather, criticize, feminism. He was particularly harsh on feminist activists. He thought that feminism was o.k., but it lacked theory. He thought that Derrida was the most appropriate thinker to fill this lack. I can only say to this that the *cliché* of the great thinker who single-handedly opens new paths for thought does not fit in any of the feminist discourses I have encountered and respected; that many feminist movements have remained outside the tradition of written texts to which the concept of theory belongs; that the activity of thinking, that I hope we all indulge in at times, need not be associated with

any such specific authorial traditions.

15 Jenny Bourne, "Jewish Feminism and Identity Politics," *Race and Class Pamphlet* 11, (London: The Institute of Race Relations, 1987), p. 22.

16 The Federal Court decided, basically, that article 4.2 of the Swiss constitution, stating the equality between men and women, overruled article 74.4, which stipulates the canton's right to decide over the right to vote on cantonal matters.

17 That we were acting *as* women was apparent in our choice of the womanly activity, housework, which I'm pretty sure none of us spent much time doing. Our use of the "symbol" of the housewife as the oppressed woman, or of housework as a symbol of the oppression of women and their exclusion from society, could also raise a few objections.

18 By "us" I do not mean our real, deep, true, selves. The "us" I am talking about is not more essential than feminism, or what lies, as it were, "beneath" a feminist. I am talking about the particular group of people who could be pointed at while the performance took place.

II

AGAINST ITSELF

6

FEMINIST MISOGYNY

Mary Wollstonecraft
and the Paradox of
"It Takes One to
Know One"

Susan Gubar

In a self-reflexive essay representative of current feminist thinking, Ann Snitow recalls a memory of the early seventies, a moment when a friend "sympathetic to the [woman's] movement but not active [in it] asked what motivated" Snitow's fervor:

> I tried to explain the excitement I felt at the idea that I didn't have to be a woman. She was shocked, confused. *This* was the motor of my activism? She asked, "How can someone who doesn't like being a woman be a feminist?" To which I could only answer, "Why would anyone who likes being a woman *need* to be a feminist?"
>
> Quite properly my colleague feared woman-hating…. Was this, as [she] thought, just a new kind of misogyny?

Though Snitow eventually finds "woman-hating—or loving— … beside the point," she admits that she "wouldn't dare say self-hatred played no part in what I wanted from feminism," a remark that takes on added resonance in terms of her first reaction to consciousness raising: "'Woman' is my slave name," she felt back then; "feminism will give me freedom to seek some other identity altogether."[1]

"'Woman' is my slave name; feminism will give me freedom to seek some other identity altogether": Snitow's formulation dramatizes a curious contradiction that feminism exhibits from its very inception to present times. The oxymoronic title of this essay—feminist misogyny—risks political incorrectness and implicitly asks us to pause, to consider the efficacy of the appellations "feminism" and "misogyny," not to derail our commitment to social justice but to make it more savvy, more supple. When put to the test in the "Can you really tell?" game, current conceptualizations may not always help us distinguish feminist from misogynist claims.

On the one hand, can you judge the sexual politics of the thinker who wrote the sentence "There is a pleasure, …an enjoyment of the body, which is…*beyond the phallus*?" What does it mean that this apparently liberated sentiment comes from Jacques Lacan (the same Lacan who boasted, "[women] don't know what they're saying, that's all the difference between them and me")?[2] On the other hand, can you surmise the ideology of the writer who declared that "woman is body more than man is" or of the theorist who stated that "*woman has sex organs more or less everywhere?*"[3] What does it mean that these two quotations, authored by feminist theorists Hélène Cixous and Luce Irigaray, eerily reiterate a proposition made by masculinist writers from Rousseau to Ambrose Bierce, so as to deny women equal educational opportunities, specifically the idea that "to men a man is but a mind…. But woman's body is the woman"?[4]

Pursuing the same inquiry, we might ask why Denise Riley recently chose the allusive title *"Am I That Name?"* (1988) for a book advocating a poststructural approach to feminism, when the line (originally spoken in the femicidal atmosphere of Shakespeare's *Othello*) conflates the "name" woman with the name-calling that demotes woman to whore?[5] Finally, who would guess that this critique of Adrienne Rich—"The feminist dream of a common language…is a totalizing and imperialist one"—issues not from Lacan or some modern-day Iago but from the women's studies scholar Donna Haraway?[6] If the histories of feminism and misogyny have been (sometimes shockingly) dialogic, as I will try to suggest, what impact should that have on the ways in which we understand the once and future state of feminist theory?

The subtitle of my meditation may seem just as incongruous as its title because we generally view Mary Wollstonecraft as a pioneer whose feminist efforts were tragically misunderstood by the misogynist society in which she lived. And, of course, as the aesthetic foremother of feminist expository prose, Wollstonecraft established a polemical tradition mined by such literary descendants as Olive Schreiner, Emma Goldman, and Virginia Woolf as well as by contemporary thinkers from Simone de Beauvoir to Kate Millett and, yes, Cixous and Riley. Indubitably, all of these theorists profited from and extended Wollstonecraft's insistence on righting the wrongs done to women. Paradoxically, however, they also inherited what I am calling her feminist misogyny. Indeed, the very troubling tenacity of this strain in feminist expository prose calls out for further thought.

That Wollstonecraft did, in fact, function as an effective advocate for women is probably self-evident, especially to anyone familiar with the political and literary culture into which she interjected her views. Though I will be examining a pervasive contradiction in her life and work, in no way do I mean to diminish or disparage her achievements. Quite rightly regarded as the founding feminist text in English, *A Vindication of the Rights of Woman* (1792) links the radical insurrection of the French revolution to the equally radical insubordination of the feminist project. Nor do I think we should judge Wollstonecraft by late twentieth-century definitions of feminism and find her wanting, "as if"—to quote Frances Ferguson—"Wollstonecraft would have turned out better work if she had had a word processor or a microwave oven."[7]

Although she has been faulted for adhering to a suspect faith in reason as an innate human characteristic,[8] Wollstonecraft exploited enlightenment language to claim that—at least theoretically—men and women were alike in being endowed with reason, a divine faculty that only needed to be cultivated so as to perfect the human species. Many of the thinkers of her time emphasized the differences between the sexes, with the influential Rousseau demanding that women's education "should be always relative to the men. To please, to be useful to [men,]... to advise, to console us, to render our lives easy and agreeable: these are the duties of women at all times."[9] But Wollstonecraft believed that because both sexes shared an equal capacity for reason, women—considered as *human*, not as sexual, beings—should benefit from the educational programs historically only afforded men. In addition, Wollstonecraft's commitment to rationality made her especially sensitive to representations of female irrationality that enslaved women's hearts and minds.

From her meditations on the Bible and Milton's *Paradise Lost* to her interpretations of Pope's, Dr. Gregory's, and Rousseau's treatises, Wollstonecraft's analyses of debilitating female images assume that we are what we read, and therefore these passages in *A Vindication of the Rights of Woman* constitute one of the earliest instances we have of feminist criticism. According to Wollstonecraft, female readers necessarily internalize male-authored and manifestly false impressions of who they are and what they should aspire to be, impressions that weaken rather than strengthen women's self-image. Confronting the socialization process effected by reading as well as by other childrearing practices, Wollstonecraft used her expository prose and her two novels to theorize about the psychological and cultural engendering of femininity. None of her contemporaries devised as sophisticated a model for understanding the social construction of womanhood, speculations that laid the groundwork for Simone de Beauvoir's famous claim that "one is not born a woman, but rather becomes one."[10] Yet it is in this area—Wollstonecraft's analysis of the feminine—that we will find most striking evidence of the contradiction in her thinking that I am terming "feminist misogyny."

What image of woman emerges from the pages of *A Vindication of the Rights of Woman*? Repeatedly and disconcertingly, Wollstonecraft associates the feminine with weakness, childishness, deceitfulness, cunning, superficiality, an overvaluation of love, frivolity, dilettantism, irrationality, flattery, servility, prostitution, coquetry, sentimentality, ignorance, indolence, intolerance, slavish conformity, fickle passion, despotism, bigotry, and a "spaniel-like affection."[11] The feminine principle, so defined, threatens—like a virus—to contaminate and destroy men and their culture. For, as Wollstonecraft explains, "Weak, artificial beings, raised above the common wants and affections of their race, in a premature unnatural manner, undermine the very foundation of virtue, and spread corruption through the whole mass of society."[12]

Here in *A Vindication*, as in the next sentences I quote, femininity feels like a malady:

> [Women's] senses are *inflamed*, and their understandings neglected, consequently they become the *prey* of their senses, delicately termed sensibility, and are *blown about* by every momentary *gust* of feeling. Civilized women are, therefore, …*weakened* by false refinement…. Ever *restless* and *anxious*, their *over exercised* sensibility not only renders them *uncomfortable* themselves, but *troublesome*…to others…. [T]heir conduct is *unstable*, and their opinions are *wavering*…. By *fits and starts* they are *warm* in many pursuits; yet this *warmth*, never concentrated into perseverance, soon *exhausts* itself…. *Miserable*, indeed, must be that being whose cultivation of mind has only tended to *inflame* its passions! (emphases mine)[13]

According to this passage, civilized women suffer from an illness, a veritable fever of femininity, that reduces them to "unstable" and "uncomfortable," "miserable," exhausted, invalids. Wollstonecraft's description of women's restlessness, of the "warm gusts" of inflammation they suffer, sounds like nothing less than contemporary complaints about hot flashes and menopausal mood swings, as if the long disease of femininity has itself become a critical "change of life." At the close of the paragraph in which these words appear, Wollstonecraft takes to its logical conclusion the implications of women's "fits and starts": when "passions" are "pampered, whilst the judgement is left unformed," she asks, "what can be expected to ensue?" and she promptly answers, "Undoubtedly, a mixture of madness and folly!"

Elsewhere in a related series of metaphors, women operate like "gangrene, which the vices engendered by oppression have produced," and the mortal damage they inflict "is not confined to the morbid part, but pervades society at large."[14] Even if she is not noxious, the female is obnoxious, a diminished thing that has dwindled, dehumanized, into something like a doll, providing merely an aimless leisure pastime for men: "She was created," Wollstonecraft claims, "to be the toy of man, his rattle, and it must jingle in his ears whenever, dismissing reason, he chooses to be amused."[15] Like a virus spreading corruption; like an illness condemning its victim to madness; like gangrene contaminating the healthy; like a jingling toy distracting irrational pleasure-seekers: because femininity figures as, at best, frivolity and, at worst, fatality, the principle character emerging from the pages of *The Vindication of the Rights of Woman* is the femme fatale.

Wollstonecraft's derogations of the feminine, to be sure, are framed in terms of her breakthrough analysis of the social construction of gender. The above quotations, for instance, insist that women's "senses are inflamed" because "their understandings [are] neglected"; that women are artificially "raised" above the race; that the gangrene of their vices is "engendered" by oppression; and that they are "created" to be toys. Thus, her thesis—that a false system of education has "rendered [women] weak and wretched"—emphasizes the powerful impact of culture on subjectivity, the capacity of the psyche to internalize societal norms.[16] Indeed, Wollstonecraft stands at an originatory point in feminist thought precisely because she envisioned a time when the female of the species could shed herself of an enfeebling acculturation or feminization. Yet although (or perhaps because) *A Vindication* sets out to liberate society from a hated subject constructed to be subservient and called "woman," it illuminates how such animosity can spill over into antipathy of those human beings most constrained by that construction.

Laying the groundwork for the first and second wave of the women's movement, *A Vindication of the Rights of Woman* implies that "'Woman' is my slave name; feminism will give me freedom to seek some other identity altogether." About the "few women [who] have emancipated themselves from the galling yoke of sovereign man," therefore, Wollstonecraft speculates that they are virtually transsexuals. Just as Newton "was probably a being of superior order accidentally caged in a human body," she imagines that "the few extraordinary women" in history "were *male* spirits, confined by mistake in female frames."[17] No wonder that, as Mary Poovey has pointed out, Wollstonecraft often speaks of herself "as a philosopher," "as a moralist," even "as [a] man with man," concluding her work with a plea to "ye men of understanding."[18] Rarely, in other words, does she present herself as a woman speaking to women.

Curiously, then, Wollstonecraft's radical stance nevertheless ends up aligning her with women's most fervent adversaries, as she herself admits: "after surveying the history of woman," she concedes, "I cannot help, agreeing with the severest satirist, considering the sex as the weakest as well as the most oppressed half of the species."[19] And several passages in A *Vindication* do seem to agree with "the severest satirist[s]" of women. While analyzing the "sexual weakness that makes woman depend upon man," for example, Wollstonecraft scorns "a kind of cattish affection which leads a wife to purr about her husband as she would about any man who fed and caressed her."[20] If the female looks subhuman in her cattiness here, elsewhere she appears sinful in her cunning trickery. To castigate those made "inferior by ignorance and low desires," Wollstonecraft describes "the serpentine wrigglings of cunning" that enable women to "mount the tree of knowledge, and only acquire sufficient to lead men astray."[21] Like their foremother, Eve, women bear the responsibility for the fall of man and they do so because of their misuse of knowledge. Predictably, one of Wollstonecraft's favorite Greek allusions is to Eve's prototype, Pandora.

And a number of other passages in A *Vindication of the Rights of Woman* concur with the severest satirists of the weaker sex, whom Wollstonecraft actually echoes. Take, for example, the following attack on the institution of marriage as a commodities market:

> It is acknowledged that [women] spend many of the first years of their lives in acquiring a smattering of accomplishments; meanwhile strength of body and mind are sacrificed to libertine notions of beauty, to the desire of establishing themselves—the only way women can rise in the world—by marriage. And this desire making mere animals of them, when they marry they act as such children may be expected to act—they dress; they paint, and nickname God's creatures—Surely these weak beings are only fit for a seraglio![22]

Not only does Wollstonecraft paraphrase Hamlet's angry speech to Ophelia— "You jig, you amble, and you lisp; you nickname God's creatures and make your wantonness your ignorance"; by relegating the feminine woman to a seraglio, she also glosses his refrain—"get thee to a nunnery": both nunnery and seraglio were common euphemisms for whorehouse. But the word "seraglio"—a Turkish or Eastern lodging for the secluded harem of Islamic noblemen—captures Wollstonecraft's disdain for a feminine lassitude so degenerate, so threatening to Western Civilization that it must be marked as what Edward Said would call a kind of "Orientalism."[23]

If we compare Wollstonecraft's portrait of the feminine here with the notoriously severe eighteenth-century satirists of the weaker sex, it becomes clear that she shares with them Hamlet's revulsion. Judge Wollstonecraft's emphasis on libertine notions of beauty, for example, in terms of Pope's famous lines in his

"Epistle to a Lady"—"ev'ry Woman is at heart a Rake" and "Most women have no characters at all"—as well as his insistence that the best woman is "a contradiction" in terms, "a softer man." Consider her picture of female animality and dilettantism in relation to Swift's monstrous Goddess of Criticism in *The Tale of the Tub*, a symbol of ignorance portrayed as part cat, part ass. Compare Wollstonecraft's vision of feminine hypocrisy and prostitution to Swift's attacks in his mock pastorals on dressing and painting, debased arts that conceal syphilitic whores; or place her indictment that unaccomplished women "nickname God's creatures" up against Dr. Johnson's comparison between a woman preaching and a dog dancing. Finally, examine Wollstonecraft's childish wives in terms of the Earl of Chesterfield's definition of women as "children of a larger growth."[24]

Why does Wollstonecraft's text so eerily echo those composed by masculinist satirists?[25] A number of critics have noted problems, tensions, and repressions in the *oeuvre* produced by Wollstonecraft.[26] In particular, these scholars claim that, by appropriating an enlightenment rhetoric of reason, Wollstonecraft alienated herself and other women from female sexual desire. While it is certainly the case that throughout *A Vindication of the Rights of Woman*, Wollstonecraft elevates friendship between the sexes over romantic and erotic entanglements (which she condemns as ephemeral or destructive), I would view this motif not merely as a repression of sexuality but more inclusively as a symptom of the paradoxical feminist misogyny that pervades her work, only one sign of the ways in which Wollstonecraft's feminism operates vis-à-vis feminization and by no means an eccentric fault of her philosophizing. For, as Cora Kaplan has insightfully remarked, "There is no feminism that can stand wholly outside femininity as it is posed in a given historical moment. All feminisms give some ideological hostage to femininities and are constructed through the gender sexuality of their day as well as standing in opposition to them."[27]

If feminist expository prose necessarily situates itself in opposition to self-demeaning modes of feminization even as it is shaped by them, what Moira Ferguson describes as Wollstonecraft's propensity "to find women culpable of their vanity, their acceptance of an inferior education, their emphasis on feeling," her tendency to "locate herself outside what she deem[ed] self-demeaning behavior," takes on not only personal but also political and philosophical import.[28] Indeed, the tensions at work in Wollstonecraft's text dramatize, on the one hand, the ways in which "feminisms give some ideological hostage to femininities," as Kaplan puts it, and on the other hand, the ironies embedded in the stage of patrilineal affiliation that Sandra Gilbert and I have examined in the aesthetic paradigm we call "the female affiliation complex."[29]

To take the first subject first, is it possible to view Wollstonecraft's description of the fever of femininity in *A Vindication of the Rights of Woman* as a portrait of any middle-class woman of her age, indeed as a *self*-portrait? Could the disgust at fallen, fated, or fatal females be *self*-disgust? In the words of Emma Goldman, the "sexually starved" Wollstonecraft was "doomed to become the prey of more than one infatuation" and her "insatiable hunger for love" led not only to a tragic desire for the married painter Fuseli but also to the two suicide attempts resulting from her tempestuous involvement with the philanderer Gilbert Imlay.[30] Wollstonecraft was so overcome by passion for Fusseli that she had suggested a *ménage à trois* to his shocked wife; after discovering Gilbert Imlay's actress-mistress, she soaked her skirts so as to sink into the water after she threw herself from Putney Bridge. Did anyone better understand slavish passions, the overvaluation of love, fickle irrationality, weak dependency, the sense of personal irrelevance, and anxiety about personal attractiveness than Wollstonecraft herself?

Thus, Virginia Woolf, considering the various ways in which Wollstonecraft "could not understand…her own feelings," believed that the eighteenth-century polemicist made theories every day, "theories by which life should be lived," but "Every day too—for she was no pedant, no cold-blooded theorist—something was born in her that thrust aside her theories and forced her to model them afresh."[31] From the perspective of Goldman's and Woolf's essays, therefore, the misogyny of *A Vindication* dramatizes the self-revulsion of a woman who knew *herself* to be constructed as feminine and thus it exhibits a kind of "anti-narcissism."[32] Indeed, what both Goldman and Woolf implicitly ask us to confront is the disparity between the feminist feats of *A Vindication of the Rights of Woman* and the gothic fates inflicted on Wollstonecraft's fictional heroines in *Mary, a Fiction* (1788) and *Maria* (1798).

Of course the subtitle of *Maria*—*The Wrongs of Woman*—establishes it as a counterpart or extension of *A Vindication of the Rights of Woman*, as does the gloomy insight of its heroine when she asks, "Was not the world a vast prison, and women born slaves?"[33] Curiously, however, both novels negate or traverse the argument of *A Vindication* which, after all, condemns precisely the conventions of sentimental fiction *Mary* and *Maria* exploit. For the enflamed, volatile emotions Wollstonecraft castigates as weakness, folly, and madness in *A Vindication* infuse, motivate, and elevate the heroines of both novels. After weeping, fainting, and bemoaning her love for a dead friend and a dead lover, the admirable paragon of sensibility who is the central character of *Mary* exclaims, "I cannot live without loving—and love leads to madness."[34] Just as rapturous and tearful, the heroine of *Maria* exhibits the passion denounced throughout *A Vindication* in a narrative that at moments seems not to caution against romance so much as to consecrate it: "So much of heaven" do the lovers of *Maria* enjoy together "that paradise bloomed around them…. Love, the grand enchanter, 'lapt them in Elysium,' and every sense was harmonized to joy and social extasy."[35]

But the startling slippages in Wollstonecraft's thinking about heterosexuality are accompanied by equally dramatic strains in her meditations on the bonds between women. Though historians of homosexuality have been led by Wollstonecraft's emotional relationships with Jane Arden and Fanny Blood to argue that the female intimacies celebrated in *Mary* should be situated on what Adrienne Rich calls a "lesbian continuum," several passages in *A Vindication of the Rights of Woman* inveigh against the "grossly familiar" relationships spawned in female communities.[36] Women "shut up together in nurseries, schools, or convents" engage in "nasty customs," share "secrets" (on subjects "where silence ought to reign"), and indulge in "jokes and hoiden tricks."[37] Wollstonecraft the novelist valorizes the nurturing comfort and intensity of female intimacies; however, Wollstonecraft the philosopher hints at the obscene debaucheries of such contacts.

The odd juxtapositions between the *Vindication* and the novels imply that the misogynist portrait of the feminine penned by the feminist may, in fact, represent Wollstonecraft's efforts to negotiate the distance between desire and dread, what she thought she should have been and what she feared herself to be. In other words, *A Vindication of the Rights of Woman* presents a narrative voice of the feminist-philosopher and a fictive profile of femininity that interact to illuminate a dialogue between self and soul, the culturally induced schizophrenia of an anti-narcissist. And in some part of herself, Wollstonecraft seemed to have understood this very well. In October 1791, after she had begun composing *A Vindication of the Rights of Woman* and while she was sitting for a portrait a friend had commissioned, she wrote that friend the following lines: "I do not imagine that [the painting] will be a very striking likeness; but, if you do not find me in it, I will send you a more faithful sketch—a book that I am now writing, in which I myself...shall certainly appear, head and heart."[38]

Just this dialectic—between head and heart, between a hortatory philosophic voice and a debased self-portrait of femininity—characterizes the feminist misogyny Wollstonecraft bequeathed to her literary descendants, including feminist polemicists writing today. Partially, it was informed by Wollstonecraft's inexorable entrapment inside a patrilineal literary inheritance. In *The War of the Words*, Sandra Gilbert and I argued that women writers before the late nineteenth century necessarily affiliated themselves with an alien and alienating aesthetic patrilineage. But this is even more true for the author of feminist expository prose than it is for the woman poet or novelist who, like Elizabeth Barrett Browning, "look[ed] everywhere for [literary] grandmothers and [found] none" because, instead of looking for aesthetic grandmothers, Wollstonecraft set out to debate the most powerfully paternal influences on her own culture: Moses and St. John, Milton and Rousseau, Pope and the authors of conduct and etiquette books.[39]

As a genre, feminist expository prose inevitably embeds itself in the misogynist tradition it seeks to address and redress. Representing the masculinist voice in order to controvert its messages, one chapter of *A Vindication*—brilliantly analyzed by Patricia Yaeger—proceeds by lengthily quoting Rousseau's portrait of womanhood "in his own words, interspersing [Wollstonecraft's] comments and reflections."[40] Thus, another dialectic emerges beyond the one between the individual author's head and heart, specifically in *A Vindication* the conversation between Wollstonecraft and Rousseau and more generally in the expository prose of her descendants the dialogic relationship between the histories of feminism and misogyny.

"It Takes One to Know One": the "One" in my subtitle is meant to indicate that it takes a feminist to know a misogynist, and vice versa. The terms of their engagement—as they bob and weave, feint and jab, thrust and parry in their philosophical fencing match or boxing ring—are particularly important to understand because, although feminism historically has not been the condition for misogyny's emergence, the pervasive threat of misogyny brought into being feminist discourse. To the extent that there can be (need be) no feminism without misogyny, the sparring of this odd couple—the feminist, the misogynist—takes on a ritualized, stylized quality as they stroll through the corridors of history, reflecting upon each other and upon their slam dancing. A full description of the choreography of their steps remains beyond the scope of this paper; however, a brief study of the eccentric dips and swirls executed by these curiously ambivalent partners at the beginning and end of this century can begin the task Judith Butler sets feminist critique, namely understanding "how the category of 'woman,' the subject of feminism, is produced and restrained by the very structures of power through which emancipation is sought."[41]

Like Mary Wollstonecraft's, Olive Schreiner's feminist prose stands in a vexed relationship to her fiction: specifically her polemical *Woman and Labour* (1911)—calling for "New Women" and "New Men" to enter "a new earth"—contrasts with a novel that obsesses over the self-pitying masochism of those who dream of altered sexual arrangements, just as it broods with nauseated fascination on the horrible tenacity of traditional women.[42] The would-be author of an introduction to *A Vindication*, Schreiner formulated her demands for female liberation as an attack not on men but on women, and specifically on what she called "the human female parasite—the most deadly microbe…on the surface of any social organism."[43] In *Woman and Labour*, which functioned as "the Bible" for first wave feminists, the idle, consuming "parasite woman on her couch" signals "the death-bed of human evolution."[44] Strangely, too, Schreiner seems to blame the limits of evolution on female anatomy when she speculates that the size of the human brain could only increase "if in the course of ages the *os cervix* of women should itself slowly expand."[45]

Just as discomforting as the thought of an os cervix having to extend so as to produce larger human heads may be the less biologistic but comparable woman-blaming in Schreiner's second-wave descendants. Perhaps Ann Douglas's *The Feminization of American Culture* (1977) furnishes the best case among the pioneers in women's studies. For here, nineteenth-century women's "debased religiosity, their sentimental peddling of Christian belief for its nostalgic value," and their "fakery" manage to "gut Calvinist orthodoxy" of its rigorous intellectual vitality.[46] So aware was Douglas herself about faulting women for the fall (the "feminization") of American culture that she used her introduction to defend herself against the charge that she had "Sid[ed] with the enemy." Though Douglas claimed to be motivated by a "respect" for "toughness," this (implicitly male) toughness seems entwined with self-hatred: "I expected to find my fathers and my mothers," she explains about her investigations into the past; "instead I discovered my fathers and my sisters" because "The problems of the women correspond to mine with a frightening accuracy that seems to set us outside the processes of history."[47]

About the immersion of Douglas's contemporaries in the literary history of the fathers, we might ask, what does it mean that a generation of readers was introduced to the works of Henry Miller and Norman Mailer through the long quotations that appeared in Kate Millett's important text, *Sexual Politics* (1969)? In this respect, her work typifies a paradox that persists in a branch of feminist criticism which, following in the wake of *A Vindication*, tackles the problematics of patriarchy by examining sexist authors (from Milton to Mailer) or by exploring male-dominated genres (pornography, the Western, adventure tales, men's magazines, film noir). No matter how radical the critique, it frequently falls into the representational quandary of *A Vindication of the Rights of Woman*: replication or even recuperation. Throughout the feminist expository prose of the 1970s, the predominant images of women constellate around the female victim: foot-binding and suttee, cliterodectomy and witch-burning appear with startling frequency; the characters of the madwoman, the hysteric, the abused whore, the freak, and the female eunuch abound.

From *The Troublesome Helpmate* (1966), Katharine Roger's ground-breaking history of misogyny in literature, to my own work with Sandra Gilbert, moreover, feminist literary criticism has demonstrated that the most deeply disturbing male-authored depictions of women reveal with exceptional clarity the cultural dynamics of gender asymmetries. Thus, although Sandra and I usually focus on the female tradition, it seems striking that our most extended meditations on male authors center on such infamous masculinists as Milton, Rider Haggard, Freud, D.H. Lawrence, and T.S. Eliot, rather than, say, John Stuart Mill, George Meredith, or George Bernard Shaw, all self-defined friends of the women's movement. When questioned about our reliance on Freud, Sandra and I tend to respond by emphasizing how we have sought to disentangle the *descriptive* powers of his insights into the sex/gender system from the *prescriptive* overlay contained in the values he assigns aspects or stages of that system.

Perhaps this speculation tells us as much about the masculinist tradition as it does about the intervention of feminism. Can we extend it by proposing that misogynist texts often elaborate upon feminist insights, but within structures of address or rhetorical frames that—in different ways, to different degrees—vilify, diminish, or dismiss them? To return to *Hamlet* or, for that matter, *Othello* and *King Lear*, can it be that Shakespeare's portraits of femicidal heroes lay bare the causes and dynamics of woman-hating, albeit in plots that equivocate about the value placed upon such an emotion? To return to Freud, didn't his description of psychosexual development in Western culture make possible the radical revisions of a host of feminist theorists, ranging from Joan Riviere and Karen Horney to Shulamith Firestone, Juliet Mitchell, Gayle Rubin, Nancy Chodorow, and Adrienne Rich? In other words, if Wollstonecraft's *Vindication* embeds within it a misogynist text, do Shakespeare's *Hamlet*, Milton's *Paradise Lost*, Rousseau's *Confessions*, and Freud's "Female Sexuality" contain antithetical feminist subscripts?[48]

The idea of feminist misogyny might thereby explain a host of critical controversies over the ideological designs of individual authors or texts. For at the current time probably every "major" writer in the canon, possibly every touchstone work, has been claimed by one scholar or another as prototypically feminist and quintessentially masculinist. Nor is this surprising, given that each individual's "language," according to the foremost theorist of this issue, "lies on the borderline between oneself and the other." As Bakhtin's most evocative description of the "overpopulation" of language explains,

> The word in language is half someone else's...it exists in other people's mouths, in other people's contexts, serving other people's intentions; it is from there that one must take the word, and make it one's own.[49]

"[E]xpropriating" language from the purposes or designs of others, "forcing it to submit to one's own intentions and accents": this is the "complicated process" in which feminists and misogynists necessarily engage so their discourses inevitably intersect in numerous ways, undercutting or supplementing each other over time, contesting what amounts to a complex nexus of ideas, values, perspectives, and norms, a cultural "heteroglossia" of gender ideologies and power asymmetries. Like the concept of black self-hatred and Jewish anti-Semitism, feminist misogyny might bring to critical attention the interlocutionary nature of representation; that is, the crucially different effects of the sentence "I am this" and "You are that."[50]

Inevitably, as the interaction between "I am this" and "You are that" implies, feminist consciousness today still bears the marks of its having come into being through interactions with a masculinism that has been shaped, in turn, by women's independence movements, a phenomenon that explains a number of anomalies: that Mary Daly, not Norman Mailer, entitled a volume *Pure Lust* (1984) and coined the phrase "fembot," for instance; that Norman Mailer, not Kate Millett, wrote *The Prisoner of Sex* (1971); that after Kate Millett's *Sexual Politics*—an analysis of masculine domination, feminine subordination—she published *The Basement* (1979), a gothic meditation on the sexual subordination and ultimate annihilation of a young girl by a power-crazed, sadistic *woman*.[51] Similarly, feminist misogyny amplifies the eerie reverberations set in motion by Germaine Greer's decision to follow *The Female Eunuch* (1970) with *Sex and Destiny* (1984). The former sprinkles quotations from *A Vindication* throughout a plea for a "revolution" in consciousness that requires that women refuse to bow down to "the Holy Family," reject the desexualization of their bodies, and protest against the manifold ways "our mothers blackmailed us with self-sacrifice."[52] However, the latter champions the family as the best social organization for women and children; touts chastity, coitus interruptus, and the rhythm method as optimal birth control methods; and nostalgically hymns the praises of the nurturance provided in so-called primitive cultures, specifically lauding "Mediterranean mothers [who] took their boy babies' penises in their mouths to stop their crying."[53]

Feminist misogyny in Mary Wollstonecraft's *oeuvre* may also help us understand why Andrea Dworkin has supplemented her anti-pornography expository prose with a gothic novel that could be said to be pornographic: *Ice and Fire* (1986) stands in as vexed a relation to *Intercourse* (1987) as *Mary* and *Maria* do to *A Vindication*. Dworkin the anti-pornography polemicist condemns sexual intercourse in our culture as "an act of invasion and ownership undertaken in a mode of predation: colonializing, forceful (manly) or nearly violent."[54] However, her novel *Ice and Fire* includes two types of sexually explicit scenes that contravene this definition, one in which "a girl James Dean" uses men to invade or colonize herself:

> When a man fucks me, she says, I am with him, fucking me. The men ride her like maniacs. Her eyes roll back but stay open and she grins. She is always them fucking

her, no matter how intensely they ride.

In the second, the female narrator takes on the office of instructing her male lover on how to invade or colonize her:

> I teach him disrespect, systematically. I teach him how to tie knots, how to use rope, scarves, how to bite breasts: I teach him not to be afraid: of causing pain.[55]

To be sure, when the masochistic speaker here explains about her abusive lover "Reader, I married him" and when "Reader, he got hard" metamorphoses into "he got hard: he beat me until I couldn't even crawl," we are meant to understand that Dworkin is returning to the romance tradition of Charlotte Brontë's *Jane Eyre* ("Reader, I married him") so as to uncover its abusive sexual politics.[56] Nevertheless, the question remains, if the anti-pornography ordinance Dworkin framed with Catherine McKinnon were deemed constitutional, would she be able to publish this kind of fiction? How can it be that her heroines resemble the actresses in the snuff films she seeks to outlaw, women bent on finding sexual fulfillment in their own destruction?

More generally, the feminist misogyny that pervades Dworkin's work typifies the uncanny mirror dancing that repeatedly links feminist polemicists to their rivals and antagonists. In 1975, the feminist-linguist Robin Lakoff published her ground-breaking *Language and Woman's Place*, a description of the genderlect she called "women's language": euphemism, modesty, hedging, polite forms of address, weak expletives, tag questions, empty adjectives and intensives, and hypercorrect grammar were said to characterize women's speech. Curiously, her findings accorded with those of Otto Jesperson, whose 1922 study *Language: Its Nature, Development and Origin* proved that women were timid, conservative, even prudish language-users and thus incapable of linguistic inventiveness. As I intimated earlier, another odd coupling could be said to exist between Jacques Lacan, who viewed women as inexorably exiled from culture, and the French feminists Luce Irigaray and Hélène Cixous, who valorize female fluidity, multiplicity, sensuality, and libidinal *jouissance*. Are all these feminists dancing with wolves?

"Feminism," Nancy Cott reminds us in much less heated or metaphorical terms, "is nothing if not paradoxical":

> It aims for individual freedoms by mobilizing sex solidarity. It acknowledges diversity among women while positing that women recognize their unity. It requires gender consciousness for its basis, yet calls for the elimination of prescribed gender roles.[57]

Just as aware of internal differences, Jane Gallop locates tensions within the psychology of feminism that explain the questions with which I began, the query of Ann Snitow's friend ("how can someone who doesn't like being a woman be a feminist?") as well as Snitow's response ("Why would anyone who likes being a woman need to be a feminist?"): "The feminist," according to Gallop, "identifies with other women but also struggles to rise above the lot of women. Feminism both desires superior women and celebrates the common woman."[58]

Over the past two decades, the stresses described by Cott and Gallop, along with professional competition inside the academy and social setbacks outside it, have given rise to internecine schisms in women's studies, divisions widened by feminists faulting other feminists as politically retrograde or even misogynist: activists and empiricists denounced theorists and vice versa; lesbian separatists castigated integrationists; "pro-sex" and anti-pornography advocates clashed; class and race divided feminists, as did competing methodologies based on sexual difference or sexual equality, as did contested definitions of womanhood arising from cultural or poststructuralist thinkers.[59] In-fighting reached a kind of apex in literary criticism as various histories began to appear, some featuring feminist critiques of feminism which served intentions not always hospitable to academic women. Here the Toril Moi of *Sexual/Textual Politics* (1985) can officiate over feminist woman-bashing: Moi dismisses American women's studies scholars as "patriarchal" because of their naive faith in the authority of the female subject and the unity of the work of art while she touts as her heroine Julia Kristeva, who "refuses to define 'woman'" and judges the belief that one "is a woman" to be "absurd."[60]

This atmosphere in which women need to beware women is probably what has led me to see feminist misogyny now and not, say, back in the seventies. As "constructionists" like Moi continue to vilify "essentialists," both groups segue into defensive and offensive steps that recall nothing so much as the rhythms of competing nationalities satirized in Sheldon Harnick's song "Merry Little Minuet":

> The whole world is festering with unhappy souls.
> The French hate the Germans, the Germans hate the Poles,
> Italians hate Yugoslavs, South Africans hate the Dutch,
> And I don't like anybody very much.[61]

Does the price of institutionalization—of women's studies' inclusion in the academy—consist of our reduction to a plethora of jostling fields or approaches in which unhappy souls war for precedence with even more ferocity than they do in longer established areas or departments?

Have we attained our maturity in an age of ethnic purges and nationalistic frays that in our own domain take the form of battle dances that cause us to lose sight of our common aim to expropriate not only language but also society of overpopulated intentions hostile to women's health and welfare? When strutting our stuff with each other, among ourselves (and who, after all, are "we," given our institutional, generational, ethnic, and methodological differences?), have we lost sight of the ways in which unsympathetic outsiders or hostile institutions can appropriate or co-opt our internal debates, transforming self-critiques into assaults against our larger project? The recent brouhaha over Katie Roiphe's book epitomizes such difficulties. When in *The Morning After: Sex, Fear, and Feminism on Campus* Roiphe—a self-defined feminist—attacked *Take Back the Night*, anti-pornography, and sexual harassment activists for re-enforcing Victorian stereotypes of predatory men and victimized women, it seemed eerily appropriate that she aligned herself with Ishmael Reed by entitling one of her chapters "Reckless Eyeballing": just as Reed's masculinist novel *Reckless Eyeballing* lambastes Alice Walker for promoting a knee-jerk, racist suspicion about the criminality of African-American men (and in the process illuminates the culturally diverse constructions of the feminist-misogynist dialogue), Roiphe's chapter presents contemporary feminists as retrograde zealot-puritans who would criminalize all men and indeed all forms of heterosexuality.[62]

Questioning another feminist critique of other feminists, namely constructionists' wholesale dismissal of essentialists, Diana Fuss has recently argued that "the political investments of the sign 'essence' are predicated on the subject's complex positioning in a particular social field, and...the appraisal of this investment depends not on any interior values intrinsic to the sign itself but rather on the shifting and determinative discursive relations which produced it."[63] Similarly, about feminist misogyny I think that—instead of furnishing us with yet another label to brand each other—it should make us sensitive to the proliferation of sexual ideologies, to the significance of who is deploying these ideologies and with what political effect, even as it breeds a healthy self-skepticism born of an awareness of our own inexorable embeddedness in history. Because we cannot escape how culture makes us know ourselves, we need to understand that even as our own theorizing engages with the social relations of femininity and masculinity, it is fashioned by them. Ultimately, then, the game of "Can you really tell?" reminds us that claims and counter-claims in the feminist-misogynist dialogue cannot be appraised without some consideration of the complex social identities, rhetorical frameworks, and historical contexts upon which they are predicated.

To adopt Gallop's words once again, "I am as desirous of resolving contradictions as the next girl, but I find myself drawing us back to them, refusing the separations that allow us to avoid but not resolve contradiction."[64] On the list of paradoxes she and other thinkers have enumerated, I would write the one so telling and compelling in the work of Mary Wollstonecraft. For the contradiction-in-terms that her life and letters dramatizes continues to fashion the discourses through which many have struggled to vindicate the rights of men and women. As I think this, I seem to see them lining up for a succession of *pas de deux*; or is it a Virginia Reel? a dos-e-doe? a last tango? a merry little minuet?—Rousseau and Wollstonecraft, Havelock Ellis and Olive Schreiner, Freud and Woolf, Sartre and Beauvoir, Mailer and Millett or Dworkin, Lacan and Irigaray or Cixous, Reed and Walker.

But out of whose mouth does a voice issue to save the waltz by declaring, "Your turn to curtsy, my turn to bow"? And who takes the lead, if (when?) we turn to tap-dance or shuffle along with one another?

NOTES |

Parts of this essay were presented at the University of Evansville, Indiana State University, Indiana University (Bloomington and South Bend), and Eastern Michigan State University. I am indebted to the reactions and suggestions I received, many of which found their way into the finished version, especially those furnished by Mary Favret, Sandra M. Gilbert, Don Gray, Karen Hanson, Andrew Miller, Jean Robinson, Mary Jo Weaver, and Robyn Wiegman.

1 Ann Snitow, "A Gender Diary," *Conflicts in Feminism*, ed. Marianne Hirsch and Evelyn Fox Keller (New York: Routledge, 1990), p. 33, p. 9.

2 Both Lacan passages are discussed by Jane Gallop, *The Daughter's Seduction: Feminism and Psychoanalysis* (Ithaca: Cornell University Press, 1983), p. 34, p. 45.

3 Hélène Cixous in Cixous and Catherine Clement, *The Newly Born Woman*, tr. Betsy Wing (Minneapolis: University of Minnesota Press, 1986), p. 95; Luce Irigaray, *This Sex Which Is Not One*, tr. Catherine Porter with Carolyn Burke (Ithaca: Cornell University Press, 1985), p. 28.

4 Ambrose Bierce, in "Know Your Enemy: A Sampling of Sexist Quotes," *Sisterhood Is Powerful; an anthology of writings from the women's liberation movement*, ed. Robin Morgan (New York: Random House, 1970), p. 34. Throughout this paragraph, I am grateful to Henry Louis Gates, Jr., who questions the efficacy of the "Can you really tell?" test with reference primarily to the ethnicity of the author in "'Authenticity,' or the Lesson of *Little Tree*," *New York Times Book Review* 24 (November 1991), p. 1.

5 Denise Riley, *"Am I That Name?": Feminism and the Category of 'Women' in History* (Minneapolis: University of Minnesota Press, 1988). Tania Modleski cogently

argues about this and other so-called "postfeminist" theorists that "for many 'women' the very term arouses a visceral, even phobic reaction" (*Feminism Without Women: Culture and Criticism in a 'Postfeminist' Age* [New York: Routledge, 1991], p. 16).

6 Donna Harraway, "A Manifesto for Cyborgs: Science, Technology and Socialist Feminism in the 1980s," *Socialist Review* 80, 15, 2, (March–April 1985), p. 92.

7 Frances Ferguson, "Wollstonecraft Our Contemporary," *Gender and Theory: Dialogues on Feminist Criticism*, ed. Linda Kauffman (Oxford: Basil Blackwell, 1989), pp. 60–61.

8 See Timothy J. Reiss, "Revolution in Bounds: Wollstonecraft, Women, and Reason," *Gender and Theory*, pp. 11–50.

9 Rousseau's infamous remark appears in Mary Wollstonecraft, *A Vindication of the Rights of Woman*, ed. Carol H. Poston (1792; rpt. New York: Norton Critical Edition, 1988), p. 79.

10 Sandra M. Gilbert and I have examined the seeming eccentricity of the literary women of Wollstonecraft's generation and the problem they pose to conventional definitions of the period in "'But Oh! That Deep Romantic Chasm: The Engendering of Periodization,'" *Kenyon Review* 13, 3 (1991), pp. 74–81. For an interesting discussion of Beauvoir's much quoted point, as well as Monique Wittig's revisionary response to it, see Judith Butler, *Gender Trouble: Feminism and the Subversion of Identity* (New York: Routledge, 1990), pp. 111–12.

11 Wollstonecraft, *Vindication*, p. 34.

12 Wollstonecraft, *Vindication*, p. 9.

13 Wollstonecraft, *Vindication*, pp. 60–61.

14 Wollstonecraft, *Vindication*, p. 178.

15 Wollstonecraft, *Vindication*, p. 34.

16 Wollstonecraft, *Vindication*, p. 7.

17 Wollstonecraft, *Vindication*, p. 35. Equally telling, as Elissa S. Guralnick points out, Wollstonecraft couples the term "woman" with bashaws, despots, kings, emperors, soldiers, and courtiers, all of whom exercize "illegitimate power" and thus "enjoy the degradation of the exalted": Wollstonecraft, *Vindication*, p. 21 and Guralnick, "Radical Politics in Mary Wollstonecraft's *A Vindication of the Rights of Woman*," Wollstonecraft, *Vindication*, pp. 308–16.

18 Mary Poovey, *The Proper Lady and the Woman Writer: Ideology as Style in the Works of Mary Wollstonecraft, Mary Shelley, and Jane Austen* (Chicago: University of Chicago Press, 1984), pp. 79–80. Along similar lines, Joan B. Landes argues that Wollstonecraft subscribes to an ideology of republican motherhood that views women's civic role as one performed inside the home, ascribes to men unbridled physical appetites, sets up a model of female duty, and displays an adherence toward male linguistic control that aligns her with the male philosophers of her day: see

Women and the Public Sphere in the Age of the French Revolution (Ithaca: Cornell University Press, 1988), pp. 129–38.

19 Wollstonecraft, *Vindication*, p. 35.

20 Wollstonecraft, *Vindication*, p. 175.

21 Wollstonecraft, *Vindication*, p. 173.

22 Wollstonecraft, *Vindication*, p. 10.

23 Edward Said, *Orientalism* (New York: Pantheon, 1978).

24 For a general discussion of the misogyny in these eighteenth-century texts, see my "The Female Monster in August Satire," *Signs* 3 (1977), pp. 380–94.

25 Ironically, then tragically, Wollstonecraft's detractors exploited precisely the images she shared with her philosophical opponents. She was depicted as one of the "phi-losophizing serpents in our bosom," a "hyena in petticoats," lampooned in *The Unsex'd Females: A Poem* as a "Poor maniac," ridiculed in a review in the *European Magazine* as a "philosophical wanton," and mocked in *The Shade of Alexander Pope on the Banks of the Thames* as "passion's slave." Similarly, her *Memoirs and Posthumous Works* was judged to be "A Convenient Manual of speculative debauchery" and in 1801 the author of "The Vision of Liberty" intoned, "Lucky the maid that on her volume pores / A scripture, archly fram'd, for propagating w——s": see Ralph M. Wardle, *Mary Wollstonecraft: A Critical Biography* (Lawrence: University of Kansas Press, 1951), p. 318, p. 321, p. 322 as well as Janet Todd, "Introduction," in *A Wollstonecraft Anthology*, ed. Janet Todd (New York: Columbia University Press, 1990), pp. 16–19.

26 Besides Poovey's and Landes's studies, see Mary Jacobus, "The Difference of View," *Women Writing and Writing about Women*, ed. Mary Jacobus (London: Croom Helm, 1979), pp. 16–17, as well as Cora Kaplan, "Pandora's Box: Subjectivity, Class and Sexuality in Socialist Feminist Criticism," *Making a Difference: Feminist Literary Criticism*, ed. Gayle Greene and Coppélia Kahn (London: Methuen, 1985), pp. 157–60. Janet Todd reviews all these critics in *Feminist Literary History* (New York: Routledge, 1988), pp. 103–10. On Wollstonecraft's making "genius a machismo male," see also Christine Battersby, *Gender and Genius: Towards a Feminist Aesthetics* (London: Women's Press, 1989), p. 98.

27 Cora Kaplan, "Wild Nights: Pleasure/Sexuality/Feminism," *Formations of Pleasure* (London: Routledge, 1983), p. 29.

28 Moira Ferguson, "Mary Wollstonecraft and the Problematic of Slavery," *Feminist Review* 42 (1992), p. 97.

29 Sandra M. Gilbert and Susan Gubar, *The War of the Words*, vol. 1 of *No Man's Land: The Place of the Woman Writer in the Twentieth Century* (New Haven: Yale University Press, 1988), chpt. 4.

30 Emma Goldman, "Mary Wollstonecraft: Her Tragic Life and Her Passionate Struggle for Freedom," Wollstonecraft, *Vindication*, pp. 254–55.

31 Virginia Woolf, "Mary Wollstonecraft," in Wollstonecraft, *Vindication*, pp. 269–70.

32 I am relying here on a term proposed by Hélène Cixous in "The Laugh of the Medusa," tr. Keith Cohen and Paula Cohen, *Signs* 1 (1976), p. 878.

33 Mary Wollstonecraft, *Maria: or, The Wrongs of Women* (1798; rpt. New York: Norton, 1975), p. 27.

34 Mary Wollstonecraft, *Mary, A Fiction* (1788; rpt. New York: Schocken, 1977), p. 102.

35 Wollstonecraft, *Maria*, p. 51.

36 Adrienne Rich, "Compulsory Heterosexuality and Lesbian Existence," *Women: Sex and Sexuality*, ed. Catharine R. Stimpson and Ethel Spector Person (Chicago: University of Chicago Press, 1980), pp. 60–91. On Wollstonecraft, see Jeannette Foster, *Sex Variant Women in Literature* (1956; rpt. Baltimore: Diana Press, 1976), pp. 56–60 and Lillian Faderman, "Who Hid Lesbian History?," *Lesbian Studies: Present and Future*, ed. Margaret Cruikshank (Old Westbury, N.Y.: Feminist Press, 1982), p. 117. Interesting in this regard is the misogyny in lesbian literature that can be traced back to Radclyffe Hall's portraits of "feminine" women in *The Well of Loneliness*, many of whom strike her mannish Stephen Gordon as manipulative, materialistic, and frivolous ("Grossly familiar": Wollstonecraft, *Vindication*, p. 127).

37 Wollstonecraft, *Vindication*, p. 128.

38 Mary Wollstonecraft, *Collected Letters of Mary Wollstonecraft*, ed. Ralph M. Wardle (Ithaca: Cornell University Press, 1979), pp. 202–3.

39 Elizabeth Barrett Browning, *The Letters of Elizabeth Barrett Browning*, ed. Frederic G. Kenyon, 2 vols (New York: Macmillan, 1897), 1, pp. 231–32. In *The War of the Words*, Sandra Gilbert and I discuss the woman writer's "turn toward the father": pp. 171–81. The two female precursors Wollstonecraft admires are Hester Mulso Chapone and Catharine Sawbridge Macaulay Graham, both discussed quite briefly in *A Vindication*, pp. 105–6, p. 137.

40 Patricia Yaeger, "Writing as Action: *A Vindication of the Rights of Woman*," *Minnesota Review* 29 (1987), pp. 74–75; and Wollstonecraft, *Vindication*, p. 77.

41 Judith Butler, *Gender Trouble*, p. 2.

42 Olive Schreiner, *Woman and Labour* (1911; rpt. London: Virago, 1978), p. 272, p. 282. The long, slow death of the New Womanly Lyndall in *The Story of an African Farm* (1883) contrasts throughout the novel with the obesity, stupidity, voracity, racism, and cruelty of the traditional woman Tant' Sannie. Like Wollstonecraft, too, Schreiner publicly protested against female dependency on men but suffered repeated thralldom to men in her private life.

43 Schreiner, *Woman and Labour*, p. 82.

44 On Schreiner's plans to produce an introduction to *A Vindication* and on *Woman and Labour* as a "Bible," see Joyce Avrech Berkman, *Olive Schreiner: Feminism on the Frontier* (St. Alban's, Vt.: Eden Women's Publications, 1979), p. 7, p. 10, and p. 2.

Schreiner's discussion of the "parasite woman on her couch" appears in *Woman and Labour*, pp. 132–33.

45 Schreiner, *Woman and Labour*, pp. 129–30.

46 Ann Douglas, *The Feminization of American Culture* (New York: Knopf, 1977), p. 6, p. 12, and p. 8.

47 Douglas, *The Feminization of American Culture*, p. 11.

48 In a recent essay, Sandra M. Gilbert explains her own attraction to D.H. Lawrence's works and that of women readers from Katherine Mansfield and H.D. to Anais Nin by envisioning Lawrence as "a proto French feminist" (Gilbert, *Acts of Attention: The Poems of D.H. Lawrence* [2nd ed., rpt. Ithaca: Cornell University Press, 1990), p. xix]. It is interesting in this regard that Rachel Blau DuPlessis' often reprinted essay "For the Etruscans" evokes D.H. Lawrence's *Etruscan Places* (*The Pink Guitar: Writing as Feminist Practice* [New York: Routledge, 1990], pp, 1–19),

49 M.M. Bakhtin, "Discourse in the Novel," *The Dialogic Imagination*, tr. Caryl Emerson and Michael Holquist, ed. Michael Holquist (Austin: University of Texas Press, 1981), pp. 293–94.

50 According to Barbara Johnson, in a subtle analysis of the impact of racial stereotypes on racial identity, "questions of difference and identity are always a function of a specific interlocutionary situation—and the answers a matter of strategy rather than truth" ("Thresholds of Difference: Structures of Address in Zora Neale Hurston," *Critical Inquiry* 12 [1985]), p. 285.

51 On "fembot," see Mary Daly, *Pure Lust: Elemental Feminist Philosophy* (Boston: Beacon Press, 1984), p. 93.

52 Germaine Greer, *The Female Eunuch* (New York: Bantam, 1971), p. 335, p. 12, and p. 157.

53 Germaine Greer, *Sex and Destiny: The Politics of Human Fertility* (New York: Harper and Row, 1984), p. 248.

54 Andrea Dworkin, *Intercourse* (New York: Free Press, 1987), p. 63.

55 Andrea Dworkin, *Ice and Fire* (New York: Weidenfeld and Nicolson, 1986), p. 72, pp. 54–55, and p. 101.

56 Dworkin, *Ice and Fire*, p. 101 and pp. 104–5.

57 Nancy Cott, "Feminist Theory and Feminist Movements: The Past Before Us," *What Is Feminism?*, ed. Juliet Mitchell and Ann Oakley (New York: Pantheon, 1986), p. 49.

58 Jane Gallop, *Around 1981: Academic Feminist Literary Theory* (New York: Routledge, 1992), p. 138.

59 For background on such debates, see Joan Scott, "Deconstructing Equality-Versus-Difference" and Theresa de Lauretis, "Upping the Anti (sic) in Feminist Theory," both in Marianne Hirsch and Evelyn Fox Keller ed., *Conflicts in Feminism*, pp. 134–48 and pp. 255–70.

60 Toril Moi, *Sexual/Textual Politics: Feminist Literary Theory* (London: Methuen, 1985), pp. 62–63 and p. 163. Later, Moi stated that her book was "written from a feminist perspective, or, in other words, from a perspective of political solidarity with the feminist aims of the critics and theorists I write about." In addition, she claimed that after "the reactionary backlash of the eighties," she found it "far more difficult to be sanguine about one's feminist position" and "would now emphasize much more the risks of being a feminist": see Moi, *Feminist Theory and Simone de Beauvoir* (Oxford: Basil Blackwell, 1990), p. 95 and p. 102.

61 Quoted in *Songs of Peace, Freedom, and Protest*, ed. Tom Glazer (New York: McKay Press, 1970), pp. 217–18. Here, as always and elsewhere, I am grateful for the help of Marah Gubar.

62 Katie Roiphe, *The Morning After: Sex, Fear, and Feminism on Campus* (Boston: Little, Brown and Company, 1993), p. 85. Significantly, Roiphe also aligns herself with John Irving and David Mamet: p. 35 and p. 107. Yet in the opening of the book, she describes her own brand of feminism which she inherited from her mother. On *Reckless Eyeballing* and Alice Walker, see Ishmael Reed, "Steven Spielberg Plays Howard Beach," *Writin' Is Fightin'* (New York: Atheneum, 1988), pp. 145–60.

63 Diana Fuss, *Essentially Speaking: Feminism, Nature and Difference* (New York: Routledge, 1989), p. 20. See also Claire Goldberg Moses, "'Equality' and 'Difference' in Historical Perspective: A Comparative Examination of the Feminisms of French Revolutionaries and Utopian Socialists," *Rebel Daughters: Women and the French Revolution*, ed. Sara E. Meltzer and Leslie W. Rabine (New York: Oxford University Press, 1992), p. 248, in which Goldberg Moses points out that "The argument that feminist discourses of 'equality' and 'difference' are neither right nor wrong but relate to historically specific concerns or opportunities is further strenghened by noting the instability of these categories."

64 Jane Gallop, *Around 1981*, p. 139.

In our reasoning...we should take account...of the puzzle about whether the dead share in any good or evil.... [For s]urely...it would be an absurd result if the dead person's condition changed along with the fortunes of his descendants.... But it would also be absurd if the condition of descendants did not affect their ancestors at all for any length of time.

—Aristotle,
Nichomachean Ethics,
(1101a33–35; 1100a29–31)

7

"MORAL DEVIANCY" AND CONTEMPORARY FEMINISM

The Judgment of Gertrude Stein

Karin Cope

...the difficulty which even the ablest men seem to experience in analysing character and the heats of a political conflict.

—Gertrude Stein,
Notes[1]

Several years ago an MLA Special Session was advertised with the following explicit mission: to figure out "what to do" with those problematic early twentieth century women writers—Gertrude Stein was a case in point—who might have been, but for fatal moral or political flaws, appropriate "foremothers" to contemporary feminism. The call for papers read as follows:

Critiquing Feminist Icons: H.D. and Gertrude Stein. Modernists H. D. and Gertrude Stein exoticized and appropriated "the other." What happens when feminist literary heroines fall short of our ideals? How do we celebrate but not exonerate them?[2]

It is no doubt important to note that although this announcement makes use of overtly politicized rhetoric, the feminist critical task mandated by the panel is neither terribly ambitious nor politically activist or challenging. Indeed, the panel suggests that the task of feminist criticism is simply evaluative and must be carefully balanced: A feminist critic must fail neither to praise nor to blame those "literary heroines" who, for one reason or the other, "fall short of our ideals." And although the call for papers announces its two-fold mandate in terms of questions, those questions are not open, for the responses to them are forecast by certain programmatic formulations within the announcement. Such a procedure is not unique to this panel; calls for papers do not ordinarily consist of open questions; generally they call for certain kinds of responses. Consequently, I am not interested in bringing the announcement to trial on charges having to do with its genre. Rather, I'm more concerned to investigate the specific and highly ambivalent program that it lays out for the grounds of a properly feminist critique.

Setting itself against the inappropriate "appropriations" made by Stein and H. D., the announcement attempts to make such misuses of "the other" available for reflection and critique. At the same time, however, the statement itself begs aspects of the very questions it faults Stein and H. D. for failing to address or understand. Who is this feminist "we"? One thing is certain; this "we" knows exactly what is indicated by the claim that "H. D. and Gertrude Stein exoticized and appropriated 'the other' "; it thus apparently and implicitly passes a suitably condemning sentence. More precisely, although this "we," along with "our ideals," means to be attentive and not "appropriative," nevertheless, it sets itself up vis-à-vis a rather monolithic and unspecified "other." Indeed the "we" of the call for papers announces itself as "not-other" and seems quite unhesitant to use "the other" for its purposes—the ostensibly laudable condemnation of the abuse of "the other" by Stein and H.D.

Such uncritical criticism is a consequence not of simple confusion, but might well be taken to be the panel's explicit program: "we" will blame H.D. and Stein in order to forestall critique *by* "the other" (which may in this case be some other part of "us") and thereby salvage (celebrate) H.D. and Stein. While at the heart of the call for papers is a profound and quite serious ethical dilemma, the effect of its particular articulation calls for critique on the one hand, and proscribes it altogether on the other. In short, it substitutes evaluation for analysis. Criticism is thus not the active component of this feminist evaluation, but a negative moment "we" must recognize and pass through in order to achieve the wholeness and "sisterhood" at the "true" heart of feminism.[3] Judgment has been passed before any hearing will have been given—either to the question of judgment or to this particular case.

Such a point might seem hyperbolic and rather too easy to make on the basis of such a short and inconsequential text; indeed it would be, if making it were simply my point here. But it is not. For I want to take very seriously the stated ethical dilemma that animates the panel (and of course, not simply this panel), to trace the rhetoric of this dilemma—claim or repudiate—in relation to Stein, and, ultimately, by way of contrast (more properly, critique) to sketch the contours of Stein's own response to some ethically "problematic" material. I have suggested above that the panel proposal's statement of its ethical dilemma forestalls certain kinds of analyses. In particular, one analysis that it forestalls (in part, by giving the *pretense* of inviting it) involves the intersection of questions of race and gender—specifically the irresolutions or non-transcendental, non-unifying notions of community and politics that questions of race and gender seem to introduce into certain treasured particulars' blithe claims to universality—the "we" of the panel, for example.

Decidedly not part of the "feminist icons," the "other" of the MLA announcement has no given name nor any feature, but might be, in the case of Stein, any of the following: Alice B. Toklas, Melanctha, any or all African-Americans, servants, "Orientals" (Stein's word), other lesbians, other Jews, other women, Stein's older sister Bertha, immigrants to the U.S., black men and women Stein encountered upon her return to the U.S. in 1934, the black cast of "Four Saints in Three Acts," or "Trac the Indo-Chinaman." One might deduce from this list of probable "others" that "the other" is sure to involve some question of race or gender (generally both), and that most of the time, although not always, "the other" has no name, or not enough of a name.[4]

Within the terms of the panel, then, the problem with Stein is that she is both overly estranged from *and* overly controlling in the relationships that she takes to any possible representatives of "the other." Put differently the charge might run thus: Gertrude Stein does not really know how to think about race or gender— or at least, she does not know how to think as "we" do. This is doubtless true, and yet it seems to me that the "we" who makes these claims does not yet know how to think as she would like "us" to either.[5] For as I have indicated, the excessive estrangement and familiarity vis-à-vis "the other," identified by the panel as the blameworthy problems of Stein and H.D., are the panel's problems as well, problems exacerbated by the brevity and extraordinary, if unavoidable generality of the MLA announcement.

I have discussed the "Critiquing Feminist Icons" announcement at such length not simply because it is, itself, logically faulty or confused, but because it is symptomatic and exemplary of a certain dilemma that faces many feminists, particularly those interested in constructing some sort of positive (and as such highly nationalized and racialized) inheritance from "feminist icons" such as

H.D. or Stein.[6] In short, animating the rather hyperbolic question proposed by this exemplary panel—what shall "we" do when certain of "our foremothers" (especially those who were or might have been lesbians, a peculiar presumption of "purity") are compromised by less than radical, "masculinist," or even "collaborationist" associations?—is this anxious ethical question: in work set against the universalization of certain particular values (the old humanism which celebrated Anglo/European fathers and sons), how is one to find values universal enough for particular evaluations? In the critical, skeptical circles of feminist poststructuralism, how is one to avoid the new charge of "moral deviancy" that has landed on other poststructuralists' heads: moral relativism? The defensive posture raised by "Critiquing Feminist Icons" ("how do we celebrate but not exonerate?"), in effect the *cordon sanitaire* drawn around certain rather troublesome "aunts," indicates that a deflection or purgation of some order is taking place, that certain questions will be foreclosed, cut off from the field of discussion, ruled out of bounds. Ironically, of course, the overt moral concern with the consequences of inattention to Stein's politics virtually dictates the sort of reading that may take place on the panel: There will be no textual analysis here, nor will there be any inquiry into the racialized genealogical presumptions of feminist "iconity," for such work could not promise to result in "balance." Consequently, the only possible task the panel could pursue would be to find the right measure of praise and blame for its "icons"—not a particularly clear disciplinary or deliberative activity.

The moral concern of the panel is quite serious, then, for what the appeal to morality masks is, in fact, a lack of serious interest in thinking about ethical questions. Put another way, the question of *value* in the panel is posed more or less as a problem of choice (we should not choose Stein if she is wrong, or choose the wrong things about her), when it is not or cannot be at all. Indeed, I will go so far as to assert that what is at stake in the questions of value directed at those "icons" who "fall short of our ideals" is not so much right thinking or doing, not so much ethical action or criticism, as the question of the right and "purity" of an extremely particular Anglo-American feminist inheritance.[7] Who shall "our" foremothers be, such that they may be vestals appropriate to bear the truths necessary to feminist icons? A number of irresolutions and difficulties are covered (if not settled) by an appeal made in the name of "we feminists." Questions of choice, of ancestry, of community, nationality, belonging, appropriateness, right, enter unasked (for they are already there) into the concern over the "fall" of "feminist icons" from the high shelf of "our ideals" and produce, not an inquiry into the discursive status of the icons (who are they; who are "we;" why did they fall here?), but a dilemma which, however profound and well-felt, serves to divert these questions, more or less permanently. In short, the consequence of this form of the crisis of judgment is no judgment at all.

PASSING JUDGMENT—TRUTH, LIE AND THE LESBIAN RULE

Let us articulate this *new demand*: we need a *critique* of moral values, *the value of these values themselves must first be called in question.*
—Nietzsche, *On the Genealogy of Morals*[8]

What would it mean to read Stein ethically, or *not* to divert the question of judgment? Upon what basis could the judgment of Stein proceed? One must recall, of course, that what the constituents of "Stein" might be is in itself a troubling question. I have indicated the fact that the emergence of a call for a new feminist evaluation of Stein—whether mine, the panel's, or other critics named and unnamed—on the heels of a dilemma about her values is no accident in the present moment. Indeed, such a call produces important and necessary sites of and for critique, both of Stein and feminism. In what follows, as an overture to a reading of *The Making of Americans*, I will examine some of the complexities of a particular piece of Stein criticism and suggest a reorientation of its modes of judgment—that is, the terms within which the problem of the judgment of Stein is put.

Certainly, Stein acquitted herself and her writing in a number of ways that have come under increasing academic scrutiny: she wrote a good deal about genealogy, sexuality, and identity; she displaced writing about deviant sexuality into writing about race (thus the plot of her 1903 lesbian novella *Q.E.D.* is reworked in her 1906 novella about black life in Bridgepoint [Baltimore], *Melanctha*)[9]; she progressively separated her writing about "other" less-privileged immigrants and her writing about assimilating German-Jewish immigrant families like her family over the course of her work on *The Making of Americans*; she wrote and spoke of herself as "a man of genius," a "husband" "pleased" with "my pretty wife" "who is all my life" Alice B. Toklas; and she was never as feminist as feminists would like writing, in *The Autobiography of Alice B. Toklas* that "she [Gertrude Stein] does not at all mind the cause of women or any other cause but it does not happen to be her business."[10] But, as Justine Ridgely writes, "although Stein claims that women's issues are not her business, her business may in fact be connected to women's issues."[11] One could thus argue that Stein both is and is not a feminist. Such a double sense of Stein's business not only undergirds but overtly structures many ambivalent feminist accounts of her. Claim is laid to Stein, but with an accompanying suspicion that it perhaps ought not be. This then is one of the reasons that such contemporary feminism might seem, after an initial period of "ancestor-acquisition" and its critique, to be engaged in an admittedly troublesome and peculiar process of revaluation; having acquired and praised enough feminist ancestors, one may now ask: is *she* one of "our" sort? Or even worse, but somehow more acutely familial: am I related to her? What would it mean to be related to her? Which of her sins will be visited upon *me*? If I claim her as an ancestor will I be engaged in the production or reproduction of a myth or a politics for which I don't want the responsibility—indeed, with which I am at odds? Can I *avoid* claiming her in some fashion? Can I avoid her claim on me?

Catharine Stimpson lays out and plays both sides of such feminist-ancestor ambivalence in a humorously diagnostic piece, "Gertrude Stein and the Lesbian Lie," which is at once celebratory and critical. Stimpson suggests that as Stein's reputation grew, "it divided against itself." Then to prove her point, she also divides Stein into two, writing of the "Good Stein" "whom the public liked," author of that "jeu d'esprit, *The Autobiography of Alice B. Toklas*," and the "'Bad Stein,' whom the public hated and ridiculed."[12] Stimpson goes on to argue that contemporary modes of evaluation have reversed the charges on the two "sides" of Stein. Thus, if initially, "the Bad Stein was guilty of a double transgression"—the "[subversion of] generic and linguistic codes" as well as the "[subversion of] sexual codes...[s]ince the 1970s, a mélange of audiences has inverted Stein's reputations. The Old Good Stein is the New Bad Stein: she is too obedient to convention. The Old Bad Stein is the New Good Stein: her transgressions are exemplary deeds."[13]

While I am not entirely in accord with Stimpson's periodizations of readerly apprehensions of Stein, it does seem to me that her point is an important one: Feminism, and no doubt poststructualism, have resulted in a revaluation of values in the evaluation of Stein; they have effected quite a substantial change in her fortunes. Thus, it seems to me that Stimpson is largely right when she suggests that formal, linguistic "disobedience" or deviancy, as well as a certain sexual perverseness, are reconfigured more and more overtly in recent criticism, not as dissolute, nonsensical, incomprehensible, tragic, or stupid attributes (all early characterizations of Stein), but as positive, progressive, "exemplary," "subversive" "*deeds*."

But what Stimpson does not analyze—although it must be said that she notes it—is that this (by her account) post-70s revaluation of values has produced not one but *two* shifts of or in value. The first, which she identifies and discusses, consists of the inversion of the terms of analysis ("bad" has become "good"). The second, however, is marked in Stimpson's text, although not commented upon by her, and might be said to consist of the transformation of character or attribute into deed. This second transformation—anything but a simple inver-

sion—is a rather hidden revaluation. In addition, if this second shift is characteristic, not simply of Stimpson's work, but of a particular feminist project, it
has indeed quite serious politico-ethical implications.

Indeed, assessment of character on the basis of deeds is, without the subversive
undertones, the appropriate site of judgment according to Aristotle's "political
philosophy," *The Nichomachean Ethics.* In Aristotle's account, virtue, the best
measure of good in human affairs, is of two kinds: one acquires virtue of thought
by teaching and virtue of character [ethos] by habit [ethos]—"hence [the] name
[of this latter] 'ethical.'" Habit of character is not natural but acculturated; further
"what is natural cannot be changed by habituation" (1103a15–18). Stimpson
seems then, in her "ambivalent account," to have presented a paradigmatically
ethical theory, or rather, to have set herself the task, not only of judging Stein's
ethics but of making ethical judgments—indeed, of making judgments that suggest that the system of evaluation in force, both before and after 1970 is the
same. But is it? What happens to Aristotelian ethics when "transgression"
becomes a virtue? Is judgment transgressed as well? Is it revalued, or is it offered
and then suspended?

In the case of Stein, Stimpson's discussion of her lesbianism as publically unacknowledged, and therefore a deed unfulfilled, seems not only false but also
morally and philosophically peculiar.[14] What then is going on in Stimpson's text?
For in exemplary fashion, in "Gertrude Stein and the Lesbian Lie," Stimpson
has redescribed accounts of Stein in order to analyze them, to question their
presumptions, and to think about her own rather ambivalent investment in what
she calls the second, post-70s version of Stein. However, it seems that with the
conversion of "transgression" into "deed" (the move that accompanies the conversion of the "Old Bad Stein" into the "New Good Stein"), Stimpson tips the
balance of her account; it ceases, at that moment, to be simply descriptive and
seems to mark instead some symptomatic quality, to show, in effect, its own
ambivalent hand. This is no doubt part of the point, for Stimpson is clearly skeptical both of the "badness" of the Old Stein and the "goodness" of the New
Stein, as well as the division of Stein into two morally unambiguous halves.
Indeed, what Stimpson offers in her article is a model of ambivalent procedure,
a sense of the need for judgment and an accompanying uncertainty about
whether any "rule" may be found to apply to Stein. Thus, as I will show in
greater detail below, in order to execute her "ambivalent" evaluation of Stein, to
avoid "denouncing the lie while exculpating the liar" (while, nevertheless appre-
ciating the resourcefulness and "courage" of Stein's "lies") Stimpson makes use of
a radically intentionalist, ideal, and more or less theological understanding of the
relations between being, language, and doing, an understanding that she also
wants to call into question or suspend.

One might call such equipoise Stimpson's own lie: the playing of both sides of a difficult question which puts in the balance, as well, the problem of producing a "properly" feminist ambivalence toward Stein. On one side then, Stimpson argues that Stein's authorship of *The Autobiography of Alice B. Toklas* produces a "text...[that] cuts against strongly felt feminist notions of a female identity that an author can present and valorize."[15] Elsewhere she cites Stein's own argument in *Everybody's Autobiography*: "That is really the trouble with autobiography you do not of course you do not really believe yourself why should you, you know so well so very well that it is not yourself."[16] The point here is to argue that Stein's "lying" writing "erases" and distorts certain truths, for in effect, Stein never seems to write or act who she is.

On the other hand, against such arguments about the clarity and divisibility of truth and lie, Stimpson counterposes a reading of the significance of what she calls Stein's "lesbian lie" in *The Autobiography of Alice B. Toklas*:

In a complex act of deception, confession, and assertion, a misunderstood, under-published author is giving the public what she calculates it can take. Her gift demands that she handle a subgenre we insufficiently understand: the lesbian lie.[17]

Thus the "lesbian lie," "a subgenre we insufficiently understand," is canny and productive. It is what "authors" Stein's coming-out story: the narrative of Stein's domestic partnership and the testimony to her intimacy with Toklas's voice and will, *The Autobiography of Alice B. Toklas*. But, Stimpson insists—now playing the other side—such a productive lie may not be a sufficient basis for celebration; its implications might, indeed, call for a certain measure of con-demnation. The grounds for this condemnation are dual and imbricated in a direct causal relation: Stein lies about herself (this implies an intention to be deceptive), and these lies lead her to be insensitive to others. In Stimpson's ("truthful") words, "Stein's public evasions of her sexual marginality and oth-erness help to distort her perceptions of other marginalized groups."[18] In short, in support of the "truth" at all costs "side" of the argument, Stimpson suggests that speech that does not lie about identity suggests that its author has the capacity to recognize other identities; such "truthful" speech is better because it is more "aware" than lying speech. All of this leaves aside, of course, the question of how, in the terms of such "truth," Stein could have not lied. What indeed would it mean to or for her writing (or any writing for that matter) for "truth", which would not be lie, to be utterable? "Awareness," then, as a subset of articulation, may not rest on the side of "truth" as *opposed* to "lie."

No doubt, the inadequacy of such a model of truth (particularly when judging writing) is why, towards the end of her article, Stimpson goes on to address this question of truth, and particularly truth and language in some measure:

> I am passing a judgment, at once sympathetic and truculent, on Stein's passing. The
> ambivalence of my judgment is related to larger, unresolved problems in feminist
> theory to which I can only point now. One problem is the shape of a feminist
> response to the lesbian lie. So far, the most influential voices have denounced the lie
> while exculpating the liar.... Adrienne Rich writes eloquently of the destructive
> consequences of the lie, for lesbians and for all women: amnesia, "the silence of the
> unconscious"; madness; the erasure of trust among women.... Yet the lesbian lie
> ("No lesbians here") has also been a source of a courageous, jaunty, often outra-
> geous style.[19]

As Stimpson indicates, what is bothersome about Stein (particularly vis-à-vis
Rich's argument that feminist language ought to be forthright and truthful) is
that Stein problematizes "our ability to draw, finally, reliable distinctions
between true and false, between language in the service of truth and language
in the service of fraud."[20] Indeed, when Stein writes, things are not as they
appear—Toklas is not the author of *The Autobiography of Alice B. Toklas*,
although, of course, there have been some feminists who have argued that she
is—and truth (Gertrude Stein is a lesbian) comes disguised in the most elaborate of lies—language.

It seems, then, that the balance has been irretrievably tipped, for Stimpson is
careful to suggest that in the domain of language lie and truth are not simple
oppositions; indeed she argues, against the side of simple "truth," that there is as
yet no adequate "feminist response" to the textual difficulty that Stein presents.
In the end this leads her to pass judgment and, also, in effect, to suspend it—to
reiterate an ambivalence about the significance of Stein's "lies" which is, nevertheless, just a little bit partisan in its own "lies"—in effect, to leave the question
of judgment largely to her reader, as well as Stein's:

> Like language, the lesbian lies. Neither vicious nor exploitative, she still knows more
> than she overtly lets on or out. Is the Old Bad Stein inventing the Old Good Stein a
> paranoid story about language in operation? If so, how paranoid should we be?[21]

Stimpson counts on the fact that for some readers the answer to this question
must be very paranoid, and for others, not at all—it depends whether you think
that lesbians, in lying, might be telling the truth (and not simply about lesbians,
but about the *truth*), and whether such a lie is frightening or dangerous. For "the
truth" of Gertrude Stein's lesbianism is certainly not disguised in any way other
than in language, so if the manifestations of her sexuality look *like* language, this

should not be surprising. One might argue that Stein writes out her sexuality, again and again celebrating and commemorating her relationship with Toklas, to cite just one instance of her apparent unwillingness to lie in the manner in which simple truth tellers might imagine. Stein makes no claims for herself on the order of a paradigmatically "honest" statement of identity like: "I am an upper middle-class highly educated American Jewish lesbian living in Paris on the proceeds of a trust fund established by my older brother Michael. When we are not living in Paris my lover Alice and our two dogs and our servants and I live in the country, at all times surrounded by Great Art." The absence of such a pronouncement does not mean, however, that she lies about or hides any of these biographical details. In fact, she makes much use of them. If Stein passes, then, it is not a function of her writing but of the readings of her writings.

I suspect that I need not (and cannot) labor this case much more, however exemplary and diagnostic of contemporary feminist accounts of Stein Stimpson's article may be. What should be clear from both the panel announcement and Stimpson's article is that in some accounts of (and accountings for) Stein, Stein's feminist ancestral status is put in question because she is a writer and as such, she lies. Such questioning (and the judgments that follow from it) is not without some merit. However, what Stein also reveals is the need for some other form of questioning and judgment, a judgment that takes into account the risks of judging a character when neither that character nor the judger (let alone the judgment) may be stable—when, in fact all appear or take place in language. Aristotle, of course, has his answers to these problems of the "lesbian lie" in what he calls (by way of an extraordinary and fortuitous homonymy) the "Lesbian rule." Not everything may be governed by law, he writes, "for on some matters legislation is impossible. For the standard applied to what is indefinite is itself indefinite, as the lead standard is in Lesbian building, where it is not fixed, but adapts itself to the shape of the stone" (1137b29–32).

Let us then examine the shape of our lying lesbian stone as it may be measured in Stein's 925-page genealogical "masterpiece," *The Making of Americans.* In effect, there, Stein shows that genealogy proceeds by way of a sort of lesbian rule—that is, it follows, not a prescriptive logic, but a descriptive one. Thus, Stein's mode of writing, in which "description is explanation," is, as Nietzsche will describe genealogy, "gray, patient and meticulous," ruminative, linguistic, and thus, "endlessly the same and endlessly different."[22] Impossibly annoying for some, impossibly boring for others, Stein's great book of genealogy inaugurates a new ethics, or habit, of reading and writing; it is the reader's task to discover its mean. The proof of this claim would be quite lengthy; I can only hope to sketch some of the contours of such an ethics, and indicate some of its virtues here.

DRAGGING FATHERS—BEING A HISTORY OF A DECENT FAMILY'S PROGRESS [23]

The Making of Americans seems to begin simply, even narratively with the following epigraph:

> Once an angry man dragged his father along the ground through his own orchard.
> "Stop!" cried the groaning old man at last, "Stop! I did not drag my own father
> beyond this tree."[24]

Framing this first paragraph and first narrative are the title, *The Making of Americans: Being the History of A Family's Progress*, and a second paragraph which glosses the first:

> It is hard living down the tempers we are born with. We all begin well, for in our
> youth there is nothing we are more intolerant of than our own sins writ large in
> others and we fight them fiercely in ourselves; but we grow old and we see that
> these our sins are of all sins the really harmless ones to own, nay, that they give a
> charm to any character, and so our struggle with them dies away.[25]

There is then a space, and *The Making of Americans*, proper, seems to begin:

> It has always seemed to me a rare privilege, this, of being an American, a real
> American, one whose tradition it has taken scarcely sixty years to create. We need
> only to realise our parents, remember our grandparents and know ourselves and our
> history is complete.[26]

None of this seems too startling or difficult. Unexceptional, even slightly antique prose, marked by an overbearing and moralizing authorial voice, the opening of *The Making of Americans* might seem patriotic, overstudied, and sophomoric—as if its author has been reading too many novels of manners. And yet, precisely because this style is not sustained throughout the novel, but undergoes a number of profound changes; because the novel begins again and again and meditates upon the processes of beginning and repeating, a reader is not simply justified in beginning at the beginning again, she is remiss if she does not. "Now again to begin."[27]

What if, for example, the novel began, as it does in a way, with the story of the angry man who drags his father along the ground? This is a simple story, one that is not at all unique, but typological in its very narrative: that is, it contains the account of its own repetition within itself. This brief narrative—which might be some cross between a moral, a joke, and an example—suggests that forceful acts, blows against one's fathers, may themselves be the most traditional or repetitive of acts, the very gesture that ties one to a generational structure and genealogical tradition: "Stop! Stop! I did not drag my father beyond this tree." The oddness of Stein's little story becomes even more marked when one considers that it is a mis-citation of Aristotle, that philosophical ur-father and apparent parent of "important things written": what a strange way to begin a new book that claims to be history and a new sort of book; how odd to begin here with an old account of an even older problem. Clearly, "the history of a family's progress" is ironized by this Aristotelian story, for such progress appears anything but historical: It is nothing but a loop, a well-worn track through the orchard. This beginning of the novel then (if it is the beginning, for it may be the beginning before the beginning, the epigraph) comments upon and revises what stands before it, its title: *The Making of Americans: Being the History of A Family's Progress.* Is it possible to write the history of a family's progress if one only tells what happens, if what happens is simply blind repetition? Beginning again, and attending to the frame of family "progress," Stein might in fact be able to write "a history" of *The Making of Americans*, a history of the process of reading and writing her book as well as the history of the process of the repetition of family life. Beginning again, then, seems to make some difference, indeed to be the condition of the possibility of the *difference* of this work.

I will consider one example of such difference in the question of Stein's beginning, that is, Stein's citation of Aristotle. When Stein cites Aristotle, she cites from Book VII of the *Nichomachean Ethics*. This book, a discussion of how one ought to judge *akrasia* or weakness of will (this is also sometimes translated as incontinence), argues that *akrasia* of emotion (say, anger) is less shameful than *akrasia* of appetite or desire (that is, excessive indulgence in eating or sex).[28] "For if someone is incontinent about emotion, he is overcome by reason in a way; but if he is incontinent about appetite, he is overcome by appetite, not by reason" (1149b3–5). Further, Aristotle argues:

> [I]t is more pardonable to follow natural desires, since it is more pardonable to follow those natural appetites that are shared by everyone and to the extent that they are shared. Now emotion and irritability are more natural than the excessive and unnecessary appetites. It is just as the son said in his defence for beating his father: "Yes, and he beat his father and his father beat *his* father before that; and pointing to his young son, he said, "And he will beat me when he becomes a man; it runs in our family." Similarly, the father being dragged by his son kept urging him to stop at the front door since that was as far as he had dragged his own father (1149b4–13).

"To begin then again," it will be clear that Stein has not simply cited Aristotle, but revised him.[29] She drags out the battle between father and son; it moves beyond the front door and into the orchard.[30] And her gloss of the significance of the battle between father and son, as a figure for one's battle with oneself, one's ambitions, and emotions, looks quite a bit different from Aristotle's. And yet, the claim that one begins by being intolerant of one's "sins writ large in others" and then, as one grows old, "our sins" appear "of all sins the really harmless ones to own" is not really at odds with Aristotle's suggestions that inability to master one's emotions is not an indefensible sin. On the contrary, it may at times be excused because it is customary, repeated from generation to generation, and as such, not particularly harmful, inhuman, or at odds with communal structure (indeed, Aristotle argues that *akrasia* of emotion may at times be a good, healthy, and right response to a particular situation; it may, in fact, be what he calls "decent").

What, then, is the point of Stein's beginning with this revisionary citation, with its more or less faithfully Aristotelian gloss? What sort of strategy might be involved in this affirmation of generational claims and classical ethical philosophy for a new young writer whose ambition was to make herself a reputation as a genius, the most important American writer, as the most important woman writer, the one who made twentieth-century writing what it is in the making of this novel? And what sort of epigraph is her Aristotelean moment to the project of *The Making of Americans*?

I can only offer brief and summary answers to these questions, for I am not here suggesting a comprehensive reading of the novel, or even of Stein's writing or career, but only the beginning of a reading of her beginning again. I have underlined Stein's gesture of beginning and beginning again because it seems to me that by beginning with a repetition, a citation, by in effect, refusing to begin where one might predict a new (rebellious, revolutionary) writing ought to begin, Stein avoids the reactive, Oedipal traps that mark much of what claims to be new.[31]

By beginning as she does, in an exergue, with Aristotle (cannily dragging him only far enough to make it clear that she hasn't taken him beyond his tree), Stein announces, as the topic of her novel, not simply generational struggle, but an investigation into those things that each generation will claim for itself: a new beginning, memory, self-knowledge, history, identity. What initially seems patriotic and descriptively, narratively simple is, by the end of the novel, shown to be possible only in its impossibility. For as Stein discusses in "The Gradual Making of *The Making of Americans*," reading and writing such a novel requires a kind of ethical—that is, habitual and shifting—discrimination, on the order of constructing or diagraming a sentence. Once you know how to diagram or construct a sentence, you may diagram or construct any sentence, and yet each sentence requires a unique sort of discrimination and work, for how and where it does what it does will be, in each case, paradigmatic and yet different.[32] There is, then, no rule to or from her work—unless that rule is a lesbian rule. Stein does not simply "take a stand" which may be taken up and repeated, rather, she calls for her readers to do their own work. She is not without strong opinions and principles, as her careful deliberations (and political mistakes) attest, but how and where these moments attach to her readers it is their task, in every moment, to determine—and in this, they too may make miscalculations and mistakes. As Stein's writing in *The Making of Americans* suggests, when researching ancestors, one must also think about the genres within and for which one searches. To return to Stimpson's trouble with Stein's lie, or the panel's censure of Stein's life, the search for feminist ancestors most certainly involves a question of ethics, but that question ought more properly to be directed toward *us* (a term I use rather advisedly) rather than those who are already dead. Put another way, the fact that your mother didn't hit her mother is not what will prevent you from hitting your own mother, your daughter, or someone else's mother or daughter for that matter. On the basis of Stein's example, I would say that what is unavoidable for a feminist ethics, particularly in its anti-racist anti-homophobic projects, is a genealogy: an account of how it accounts for where it may be understood "to begin."

Let us then begin again, and reconsider the relation of feminism to genealogy, this time in different voices, which no doubt will turn out to have been much the same.

BEGINNING AGAIN: A DIALOGUE

The liar uses the valid designations, the words, to make the unreal appear as real; she says, for example, "I am rich," when the word "poor" would be the correct designation of her situation. She abuses the fixed conventions by arbitrary changes or even by reversals of names. When she does this in a self-serving ways damaging to others, then society will no longer trust her but exclude her. Thereby people do not flee from being deceived so much as from being damaged by deception: what they hate at this stage is basically not the deception but the bad, hostile consequences of certain kinds of deceptions. In a similarly limited way people want the truth: they desire the agreable life preserving consequences of truth, but are indifferent to pure knowledge, which has no consequences; they are even hostile to possibly damaging and destructive truths. And, moreover, what about these conventions of language? Are they really products of knowledge, of the sense of truth? Do the designations and the things coincide? Is language the adequate expression of all realities?

—Nietzsche, "On Truth and Lie in the Extra-Moral Sense"[33]

Q: You have asserted several times that the crisis of value which consideration of Stein seems to have provoked in certain feminist critical circles has something to do with the attempt to establish and assess a proper—or "pure"—feminist inheritance. Could you explain what, if anything, such an inheritance has to do with your interest in and call for a feminist genealogy? What do you mean by genealogy, and how do you understand it to be a critique of notions of or claims to inheritance?

A: I borrow my particular use of the term "genealogy" from Nietzsche and from Foucault, although the critical practices that the two of them associate with genealogy are not entirely foreign to feminism—in fact, one could argue that genealogical thinking is at the root of feminism. I'll be happy to make such an argument later on, but for now I'll try to answer your first question.

In particular, I have found provocative and useful Nietzsche's suggestion that any given assertion of value or values (as, for example those given in the MLA panel) calls for an investigation. For contrary to some very cherished beliefs about values (beliefs that one might even call religious), values are not inherent, self-evident, or transcendental, and each particular expression of or call for particular values (including my own here) may be traced historically, logically, and rhetorically. As Nietzsche describes the task: "the value of these values must first be called into question—and for that there is needed a knowledge of the conditions and circumstances in which they grew, under which they evolved and changed (morality as consequence, as symptom, as mask, as *tartufferie*, as illness, as misunderstanding; but also morality as cause, as remedy, as stimulant, as restraint, as poison)..."[34] In effect, Nietzsche argues that a genealogy is a special kind of history, a mode of reading that allows one to reflect critically upon modes of evaluation and this is where the techniques of literary interpretation, of rhetoric, logical entailment, and exegesis come to have great importance.

It is this sort of critical reflection upon the terms of family, progress, history, and American that I mean to argue *The Making of Americans* performs. Stein is thus Nietzschean without, as we say, "knowing" Nietzsche (such an assertion can, of course, only complicate the question of her ethics). And like Nietzsche she is incompletely genealogical. Her texts have moments in them that must be called out, called to task; even if her racism is systematic, the mode of analysis that her texts deploy also carries with it the material with which to read and critique her systemic blindness, her racism and so forth. What this suggests is that a genealogy is not once and for all, but an expanding, palimpsestic sort of work. It is text-based; it is "gray," Nietzsche says, the color of musty documents—"the entire long hieroglyphic record...of the moral past of mankind," and not blue, the color of cerulean speculation.[35] This text is thus an expansive text: whatever may be additively read, reread, and, interpreted. It is not simply written words and traditions of interpretation, but entire socio-cultural situations. Such a notion of "text" is, of course, now rather widely accepted; indeed, Stein may only be tried for her "fall" from feminist ideals on the basis of such an expansive notion of text.

In Foucault's commentary on Nietzsche, "Nietzsche, Genealogy, History," which is also, in part, an explanation of some aspects of his own modes of procedure, he begins with the textual or exegetical aspects of genealogy. Indeed, these aspects are what give genealogical thinking its value, he suggests. For genealogical inquiry is "gray, meticulous, and patiently documentary"; it is loyal to what it finds and not to the mythologies that have sent it looking through the "entangled and confused parchments" it researches.[36] His implication is that ancestry is never as illustrious or pure as the claims made on its basis; indeed, Foucault argues that the knowledge that comes of genealogical inquiry "emphatically excludes the 'rediscovery of ourselves.'"[37] This is because, with its meticulous attention to detail,

> [g]enealogy does not pretend to go back in time to restore an unbroken continuity that operates beyond the dispersion of forgotten things…. [It] does not resemble the evolution of a species and does not map the destiny of a people. On the contrary, to follow the complex course of descent is to maintain passing events in their proper dispersion; it is to identify the accidents, the minute deviations—or conversely, the complete reversals—the errors, the false appraisals, and the faulty calculations that gave birth to those things that continue to exist for us; it is to discover that truth or being does not lie at the root of what we know and what we are, but the exteriority of accidents.[38]

Genealogical method, as Foucault understands it then, is not about the discovery or consolidation of an identity or identities, but an inquiry into how and why such consolidations are made when they are. It involves, as well, a dispersion of what might be called inheritance, rather than its accumulation—proof of the impossibility rather than the necessity of any "pure" ancestry. Such a critique runs against the currents of familial and disciplinary constitution; genealogy, in the sense that Foucault and Nietzsche use the term, is designed to read across treasured institutional boundaries rather than buttress them. Genealogical critique is thus often interpreted as negative, destructive, even valueless by those institutions it reads ("if you are not for us you are against us"). However, I do not think that criticism implies demolition or valuelessness. Neither Foucault nor Nietzsche exempt themselves from critique. The comic, mocking tone of *On the Genealogy of Morals* ought to be enough to indicate this on Nietzsche's part at least. Neither Nietzsche nor Foucault stopped revising their philosophical/historical claims. Neither did Stein. It is her fundamentally *comic* routine which, as with Nietzsche's, is given so little play (perhaps because the consequences are so serious) that interests me here.

But before I launch into a new topic, let me first respond to your last question: what do I mean by "genealogy"? By "genealogy" I mean an inquiry that does not restrict itself to questions of intellectual and topical inheritance, questions such as: is or was Gertrude Stein a feminist? Rather, by calling for genealogical critique, I am interested in drawing and expanding upon the strength of what feminism already does in its critiques of the changing gender bases and biases of certain governing ideas or coherencies—"man," for example, or "activities proper to a sex." In sum, I am interested in making use of the *suspiciousness* with which feminism has regarded those claims to paternal inheritance that have so frequently and for so long been used, in one way or another, against women.

Q: Can you say more about what genealogy has to do with feminism? Why have you taken genealogy as the pivotal point of your analysis? Do you consider your use of genealogy to be feminist?

A: I'll answer your last question first: yes. The reason for my answer will serve to respond to your first two questions as well. Yes, genealogy is or can be feminist because genealogical critique is not new to feminism; arguably feminism is, at its most critical, a more or less genealogical mode of inquiry. Funny then, that there should be a question about whether Stein is a feminist! However, perhaps because genealogy is so critical it has been both a mode of investigation and a site of anxiety for feminism: while genealogy has produced extensive insight into the bases of those ostensibly neutral designations "man," "family," and "normal," feminism has also been rather reluctant to apply such incisive criticism to some of its own "ideals" and treasured topoi. Thus, while for feminism, what we may call "genealogical criticism" has provided extensive analyses of the modes of "imprinting" of bodies by gender, and to a lesser extent by race, and while it has done a good deal to call attention to the white male bodies animating and described by the heretofore "bodiless" discourses of the "humanities" and "sciences of man," when it comes to producing genealogical criticism of its "own" peculiar characters—like Gertrude Stein—feminist criticism has all too often foreclosed its own questions and produced a crisis of split values, prior to, rather than upon the heels of its investigations.

Q: You indicated earlier that genealogy has to do with race. Could you explain this? What does this particular question have to do with Stein?

A: In the United States, certainly, *any* attempt to construct or consolidate a particular and/or *pure* ancestry cannot but partake of racist rhetoric even if it does not mean to. Thus the panel's question, "What happens when feminist literary heroines fall short of our ideals," in its positing of a set untainted "feminist ideals" from which it is possible to fall, and that some group of feminists ("we") knows, shares, and presumably reaches, points to, and more importantly polices who and what feminists are. These are, to borrow Foucault's words, modes of consolidation, rather than dispersion. By focusing upon feminist values, and whether or not Stein measures up to them, the "we" of the panel situates itself solidly inside of the bounds of its "ideals," and from that vantage point measures the distance that Stein has fallen—or the distance that keeps the panelists (that "we" who are sensitive to "the other" without necessarily understanding themselves to be "other") from being like "her." This is not a strategy designed to produce readings of what Stein writes, or even any serious consideration of "others" or otherness; indeed, it is a mode of analysis that only ostensibly pays any attention to Stein or those "others" that it makes the gesture of safeguarding. For, as I argued earlier, "Stein" only initially becomes the name for that which is not like "us"; later, after she has been roundly criticized, she may enter the pantheon of "feminist literary heroines" because, it turns out, she is probably more like those who criticize her than not. For both moments, the critique of Stein's moral deviancy vis-à-vis "the other," and her subsequent admission to the hall of feminist ancestors, proceed in the name of "the other" (who otherwise has no name) in order to forestall any specific appearances that might call into question the entire enterprise of constructing an unassailable ancestral home for "we" feminists. The panel is designed—*structurally*, for I do not believe it is intentionally—to hold off, at all costs, "the other" for whom "we" have such manifest sympathy.

Now, I argued that such a maneuver is necessarily or paradigmatically racist in the United States, for the other of which ancestry seeks to purify itself is, initially, the separation of black from white, on the part of whites—and the language of the panel cannot really be read outside of this frame or paradigm in which "otherness" means "not-white." In a country in which a "one-drop rule," by custom and by law, has established race—that is, in the United States black has been and is "any person with any known African ancestry"—any attempt on the part of whites to attest to the purity or propriety of their lineage, even if this attempt does not look like it is designed to separate white from black takes its departure from such narrow "genealogical" procedures.[39]

The argument I want to make here is relatively simple: genealogical critique is not invested in the construction or preservation of particular lineages; rather, its strength is that it opens up the procedures of claims to inheritance, and makes their mechanisms, racist and otherwise, visible. Had the MLA panel been concerned with analyzing the values that it attributed to Stein, rather than simply passing judgment on them, it would have been better able to critique them, rather than simply to repeat them. In effect, it seems to me, by formulating the problem as it did, it gave up an opportunity (which is also a necessity) to think seriously about her racism. Secondly, while there is little doubt that Stein was racist, and it is certain that she wrote racist things in her texts, her modes of writing (unlike the panel's call to values) were and are not modes of border patrol. This does not dismiss the problem of the question of race as it appears in Stein's writings, but opens the question of reading race to the depth and complexity it deserves. It's not really an either/or good or bad question—to treat it as such shortchanges the reading and analysis of race at least as much as it shortchanges Stein. Clearly, I must take up this question of Stein and race elsewhere, for this essay only sketches the contours of the problems of the judgment of Stein, it does not, indeed, deliberate on a number of important themes and sites in her work.

As I have been suggesting, because Stein's writing is exemplary of genealogical critique in the Nietzschean sense, it is writing that must be read and reread. Stein's writing "ruminates" and calls for rumination—the practice of the slow art of reading—as does any serious problem. To cite Nietzsche more directly: "[writing] has not been 'deciphered' when it has simply been read; rather one has then to begin its *exegesis*."[40] In the space of an essay such as this, I cannot even hope to begin such an exegesis, but rather, point to the direction that it might take...

Q: One last question before you go on. Haven't you just conducted something rather like a police sweep of certain kinds of feminism? In other words, hasn't your goal been to forestall things like the panel you've analyzed (to death!), to set up a new and higher rule for feminism?

A: I have two answers to this question—which by the way I think is a good, fair, and important question. First, is my critique a police action itself? I don't think so. At least, that isn't my goal—I have after all, given substantial space to the feminist inquiries I have analyzed. I am aware that some may feel that this analysis was condemnation, but if that is the case then any analysis worthy of the word is condemnation (and I do not really think this is so). Certainly, my interest has not been in denouncing the feminist projects I discussed, but rather, directed toward *recovering* the most critical strengths of feminism—that is, skepticism about the deployments of "oughts and shoulds." This is not to say that feminism does not or should not answer certain imperatives, or pass judgment against or denounce certain injustices. On the contrary, I think the concern about Stein's values could contribute to a sharpening of Stein criticism, as well as a sharpening of feminist theory by recourse to what we might call Stein's genealogical or "lesbian" criticisms. This is what I hope at least, for my own work.

Q: Didn't you say you had two answers?

A: Oh, yes. The second is more or less allegorical and involves a recitation that by now will be familiar to you:

Once an angry man dragged his father along the ground through his own orchard. "Stop!" cried the groaning old man at last, "Stop! I did not drag my father beyond this tree."

Q: Yes?

A: I just want to suggest that it is, of course, always possible that I am, here, simply engaging in a time-honored and repetitious generational war, and dragging my "mothers" along the ground through the feminist orchard.... Doubtless, such a scenario is part of what is going on in my essay, in this anthology, although (for reasons I hope are by now clear) I think that such generational rivalry does not suffice to explain the full force of my critique or other forms of critique. For in my case, what if Nietzsche has been my mother?

Q: Or even Aristotle. Not to mention Stein.

A: Oh yes, certainly Stein, that should be clear here—even Aristotle— although I think in Stein's case (and no doubt my own) he's pretty clearly a father. There are of course others as well, near contemporaries even, no doubt legible in the interstices and drift of my argument, Derrida, and a certain reading of Du Bois for example.

Q: Wait. Does this mean you've been *choosing* your ancestors?

A: I'm not sure. Perhaps as children are, I was "chosen" by these philosophical forebears.... Not elected exactly, but somehow I have gotten where I am, in some odd way, owing to them. I work on Stein, but I'm never sure if I chose to work on her, or if her working on me forced my "choice." Does she read me or I her? This is not, as my first epigraph from Aristotle indicates, a question that is as absurd as it might seem. Indeed, in the last twenty-five pages of *The Making of Americans*, Stein considers the question of death and family survivals. She writes, "Any family living is existing if there are some more being living when very many have come to be dead ones.... Any one can be certain that some can remember such a thing."[41] Of course, what one remembers and how—because of course "you cannot remember right"—is, all along, what we have been struggling over. If feminism thinks that it can remember right, the strength of that stance is to its peril. For we would be making an error to make an unconditional rule or account, to polish or purge all of what is difficult, painful, disgusting, contradictory or just plain bad from our pasts. There is no way to escape being touched and implicated by these things; it only makes it worse to try to wipe them from the record. This is why Stein's model or "lesbian rule" is so important—and precisely not a rule. It is an embrace of change and deviation, not in and for themselves—and certainly not as "improvements," but because her exploration of the ethics of reading and writing requires it.

NOTES |

I thank Kristin Bergen for her constant support and critical insightfulness; our ongoing discussions of Aristotle and Stein are the condition of possibility for this work. I am also indebted to John Vincent for his generous and critical reading of an earlier draft of this essay, and to Diane Elam and Robyn Wiegman for providing the impetus and forum for "Moral Deviancy"; above all, however, I am grateful for their editorial patience and generosity.

1 Small gray notebook 14, p. 10, Stein archives, Yale Collection of American Literature, Beinecke Rare Book and Manuscript Library. I owe Leon Katz a debt of gratitude for his transcription of Stein's notebooks, and thank the Beinecke Library at Yale for permission to publish this fragment. I have used the following edition of the Ethics: Aristotle, Nichomachean Ethics, tr. Terence Irwin (Indianapolis: Hackett, 1985). All references to Aristotle will be given in the text in standard form.

2 MLA Newsletter January 1991. This call for papers was intended for the 1991 meetings in San Francisco, although the session seems never to have taken place. I want to thank Luke Carson for sending me a copy of the announcement.

3 For an account of some of the tropes and traps of feminist invocations of "sisterhood," see Helena Michie, Sororophobia: Differences Among Women in Literature and Culture (New York: Oxford University Press, 1992).

4 Toklas is a clear exception to this rule—given that she is entitled both to a first and last name—and the "problem" of her apparently "subordinate" or "wifely" relation to Stein has generated a number of reconsiderations of Stein as an exemplary candidate for the role of lesbian-feminist foremother. No doubt much of this work stands in the background of "Critiquing Feminist Icons." The most important and influential of such critiques may be found in Catharine R.Stimpson, "Gertrice/Altrude: Stein, Toklas, and the Paradox of the Happy Marriage," Mothering the Mind: Twelve Studies of Writers and Their Silent Partners, ed. Ruth Perry and Martine Watson Brownley (New York: Holmes and Meier, 1984), pp. 122–39; Shari Benstock, "Gertrude Stein and Alice B. Toklas," Women of the Left Bank: Paris 1900–1940 (Austin: University of Texas Press, 1986), pp. 146–52; Sandra Gilbert and Susan Gubar, No Man's Land: The Place of the Woman Writer in the Twentieth Century, Vol. II, Sexchanges (New Haven: Yale University Press, 1988). For their contribution to my understanding of the issues at stake in such readings, I thank Tamara Bekefi and Mariana DiQuinzio for their very funny, informative, and pointed performance of various accounts of the Stein-Toklas relationship, including excerpts and pastiches of most of the texts above (Seminar Presentation, McGill University, Fall 1993).

5 N.B. This is not a critique from which I exempt my own work.

6 Sonia Saldívar-Hull gives a scathing dual indictment of both Stein's racism and the

racialization of the project in order to construct a feminist canon in her "Wrestling Your Ally: Stein, Racism, and Feminist Critical Practice," *Women's Writing in Exile*, ed. Mary Lynn Broe and Angela Ingram (Chapel Hill: University of North Carolina Press, 1989). Saldívar-Hull writes: "I propose we use...feminist and deconstructive methodologies in the study of Gertrude Stein...to dismantle and work out the extreme 'marital' alienation between liberal, white feminists and feminists of color whose literary and critical discourses have been exiled by their allies" (pp. 185–6).

7 For insight into aspects of the ideologically overdetermined relations between inheritance and choice in the American context, I am indebted to Werner Sollors, *Beyond Ethnicity: Consent and Descent in American Culture* (New York: Oxford University Press, 1986).

8 Friedrich Nietzsche, *On the Genealogy of Morals*, ed. and tr. Walter Kaufmann (New York: Vintage Books, 1967), p. 20.

9 This, of course, raises questions about the way in which "blackness" emerges in American thought and letters (and not simply for "blacks" and "whites") as the figure for a limit to social intercourse, and as the ultimate repository of all otherness, sexual and otherwise. Stein's shift or translation of an account of "deviant" sexuality into an account of "characteristic" racialized behavior—"Melanctha Herbert was a graceful, pale yellow, intelligent, attractive negress"—is the move most strongly criticized by Saldívar-Hall. Indeed, the fact that such a racializing move is possible—that a sexual dynamic may be reconfigured into racial stereotypes, and as such, become one of Stein's bestsellers—implicates not simply Stein but her readers in racist practice, or in a racist response to a set of genealogical questions and concerns touched upon, but not totalized by the terms of sexuality and inheritance.

10 Gertrude Stein, *The Autobiography of Alice B. Toklas*, *Selected Writings of Gertrude Stein*, ed. Carl Van Vechten (New York: Vintage Books, 1990), p. 78. I thank Sheri Weinstein for her work on and insights into Stein's "ethnic writing;" her work provoked and stimulated my thinking about the questions of Stein's situation as an "invisibly ethnic" feminist ancestor.

11 Justine Ridgely, "Stein and the 'Woman Question'—A Connection Full of Questions." Unpublished seminar paper, McGill University, Fall 1993.

12 Catharine Stimpson, "Gertrude Stein and the Lesbian Lie," *American Women's Autobiography: Fea(s)ts of Memory*, ed. Margo Culley (Madison: The University of Wisconsin Press, 1992), p. 152.

13 Stimpson, "Gertrude Stein and the Lesbian Lie," *American Women's Autobiography*, p. 152.

14 On this question of whether Stein speaks aloud about her sexuality, see my "'Publicity Is Our Pride': The Passionate Grammar of Gertrude Stein," *Pre/Text* 13, 3–4 (Fall–Winter 1992) pp. 123–36.

15 Stimpson, "Gertrude Stein," *American Women's Autobiography*, p. 164 n10.

16 Gertrude Stein, *Everybody's Autobiography* (Cambridge: Exact Change, 1993), p. 70. Quoted in Stimpson, "Gertrude Stein," *American Women's Autobiography*, p. 157.

17 Stimpson, "Gertrude Stein," *American Women's Autobiography*, pp. 152–3.

18 Stimpson, "Gertrude Stein," *American Women's Autobiography*, p. 162.

19 Stimpson, "Gertrude Stein," *American Women's Autobiography*, pp. 162–3.

20 Stimpson, "Gertrude Stein," *American Women's Autobiography*, p. 163.

21 Stimpson, "Gertrude Stein," *American Women's Autobiography*, p. 163.

22 Gertrude Stein, "The Gradual Making of the *Making of Americans*," *"Look At Me Now and Here I Am": Writings and Lectures, 1909–1945*, ed. Patricia Meyerowitz (Baltimore: Penguin, 1971), p. 86.

23 "Being A History of a Decent Family's Progress" is the subtitle of Stein's first draft of *The Making of Americans* (1903). See Leon Katz, "Introduction" to Stein's *Fernhurst, Q.E.D. and Other Early Writings* (New York: Liveright, 1971) and Donald Gallup's "Appendix" to the same volume for an account of the history of composition of *The Making of Americans*.

24 Gertrude Stein, *The Making of Americans* (London: Peter Owen, 1968), p. 3. Although it may not be very widely read, and has often and long been out of print, Stein considered *The Making of Americans* her masterpiece, the very touchstone of her writing. Indeed, I would agree that it is only by really reading *The Making of Americans* that one can learn to read Stein.

25 Stein, *The Making of Americans*, p. 3.

26 Stein, *The Making of Americans*, p. 3.

27 Stein, *The Making of Americans*, p. 299.

28 It is important to emphasize that Aristotle does not here argue against desire, but rather, obsessive, excessive desires, those desires that cause people to act contrary to their better knowledge and reason. His then is not an argument against certain actions so much as a brief for the maximization of health, sense, knowledge, and reason or deliberative ability.

29 Stein, *The Making of Americans*, p. 582.

30 Traversing long distances is no incidental detail in *The Making of Americans*, but one of the factors that Stein repeatedly claims makes Americans American—not only do most of them come, willingly or not, from abroad, but once in the U.S., they move around a good deal.

31 One of the chief signs of one's participation in such an Oedipal narrative is that one does not know the script—figuratively speaking, one is blind to one's genealogy, self, and inheritance. It comes as a surprise then, to learn that your story is more or less everyone's story, that your father dragged his father in this same way.

32 See Stein's discussion of the "question of grammar" in "The Gradual Making," pp. 89–90.

33 Friedrich Nietzsche, "On Truth and Lie in an Extra-Moral Sense" (1873), *The Portable Nietzsche*, ed. and tr. Walter Kaufmann (New York: Penguin Books, 1982), pp. 44–5. The changes in the gender and number of most of the personal pronouns, and the substitution of "people" for "man" are, of course, mine. This is not because I think that Nietzsche should have written so inclusively (it is probably quite important that he did not) but because I am deliberately mis-citing his words, to make them more appropriate to my uses.

34 Nietzsche, *On the Genealogy of Morals*, p. 20.

35 Nietzsche, *On the Genealogy of Morals*, p. 21.

36 Michel Foucault, "Nietzsche, Genealogy, History," *The Foucault Reader*, ed. Paul Rabinow (New York: Pantheon, 1984), p. 76.

37 Foucault, "Nietzsche, Genealogy, History," p. 88.

38 Foucault, "Nietzsche, Genealogy, History," p. 81.

39 F. James Davis, *Who Is Black? One Nation's Definition* (University Park: The Pennsylvania State University Press, 1991), p. 5. The exceptional character of the "one-drop rule" as the basis for racial classification is also discussed in Gunner Myrdal's report on race relations in the United States: *An American Dilemma* (New York: Harper and Brothers, 1944), and more recently in Joel Williamson, *New People: Miscegenation and Mulattoes in the United States* (New York: The Free Press, 1980), and sharply satirized in George Schuyler's 1931 comedy of race relations in the United States, *Black No More* (Boston: Northeastern University Press, 1989). There are, of course, many other discussions of this issue; the works I have listed analyze and in some measure contest the logics of recent and current racial classifications in the U.S.

40 Nietzsche, *On the Genealogy of Morals*, p. 23.

41 Stein, *The Making of Americans*, p. 925.

8

THE SINGULARITY OF MULTIPLICITY

Feminism and the Pitfalls of Valorization

Cyraina Johnson-Roullier

The writing of this essay marks the end of an eight-year period in my professional life of moving cautiously around feminists and feminism/feminist theory,[1] but never actually engaging with them or it. This doesn't mean, however, that the political and intellectual issues involved hold no concern for me—quite the contrary. I became intimately concerned with them one evening at the age of ten, when the Sunday-night bath ritual established in my family by my mother—which I shared, one after the other, with my two older brothers—was suddenly transformed from a pleasant family routine into a horror. I emerged forever and irrevocably changed, knowing that I would never recover. Our habit was usually to stand for a few moments in the hallway leading from the living room of our house, with our large, comfortable bath towels wrapped snugly about our waists, while my mother made sure that nails were clean and teeth had been brushed, before we were sent upstairs to get ready for bed.

On this specific evening, however, my mother looked at me far longer than usual. In fact, what was different about that look was that she was not really looking at me. She was looking at my body, at my just barely forming breasts far above the edge of my towel. She was looking at the coming of my woman-body, of which I was as yet unaware. I remember that her look made me uncomfortable, it being a look full of knowledge, of her knowing something about me that I didn't know about myself, a look that had not so much to do with *me* really, as it had to do with the body I inhabited. Her looking at me in this way seemed to last a thousand years. It cast me in a prison that was my body, and then she locked the door of my escape: she told me to raise my bath towel until it covered my chest. In a torment of shame, I did so, looking surreptitiously at my brothers who still stood with their bath towels proudly about their waists. Eyeing their towels, I was gripped by the mixed longing and loss with which one watches a beloved home fade into the distance while one departs into the future, never to return, as I secured my own towel beneath my armpits. For the first time during our childhood, I faced an aloneness made more pronounced by their togetherness, a togetherness I had shared until my body overtly betrayed my difference.

This look, which I first felt under my mother's knowing eyes, is one that has followed me ever since. It is the look that men, young and old, gave my blossoming sexuality, the look that has made me know what the body of a woman means, the risk of it, the danger of it. It was this look on the faces of others that taught me this meaning early on, and made me, through the first years of puberty—in secret shame-sharing with my best friend—wear (as she did) a jacket all day at school to hide the breasts that seemed to grow larger and more voluptuous each day.

I was passionately involved with feminist issues by 1977, when I was 17. I was, at that time, largely a product of ideas that had been propagated by the second wave of feminism in the United States, in which a new-fangled optimism with regard to women's life possibilities had created the romantic and exciting image of the career girl, and attested to the superwoman's certainty of success in both private and public domains.

"I don't have to cook, clean or do laundry," I told my grandmother, a housewife of forty years and mother of two, who had never worked a day outside her married home.

"You have to do that—you're supposed to!"

"I do not, and I won't!"

"You'll never get married then!"

"Fine, I guess I won't get married—in fact, I don't want to get married if that's what it means!"

My grandmother had no reply. It was beyond the range of her understanding of life's drama as being necessarily played out in terms of traditional, and therefore unchangeable, masculine and feminine adult roles.

I have described these experiences to highlight my underlying motivation for writing this essay: that is, that while I have had an almost lifelong association with what could be termed feminist politics in my personal life, my relationship to feminist theory in my professional life has been practically nonexistent. The question that must be asked in view of this is straightforward: How is it that a woman so committed to feminist politics could find herself more or less divorced from feminism, both as a movement and as a theoretical practice? When accused of feminism in my beliefs, I have staunchly proclaimed, "But I'm not a feminist!" How is it possible for a woman to live according to a feminist politics while at the same time, separating such beliefs from the activities of the movement itself? Doesn't this imply a very serious internal inconsistency in a movement designed to liberate "all women" from the vagaries of sexual oppression?

It is with precisely this internal inconsistency that this essay is concerned. The fact that such division is not only possible, but actually exists, is one of the most pressing problems in contemporary feminism. My problematic relationship to the movement—whether inside or outside the university—ensures that my task, in writing about it, is not an easy one. I cannot say that I am writing as a "feminist" in the traditional sense, because that term has until quite recently been articulated in a way that excludes a number of my concerns. Rather, I take my vantage point from the juncture of this dichotomy: between my lived experience, which might be termed "feminist," and my reluctance to call myself a feminist; or between my personal experience with feminist issues and the concerns of contemporary feminism and feminist theory.

My reluctance to call myself a feminist is engendered by the fact that while I have always recognized that I share with mainstream feminists a desire to outlaw the oppressive practices perpetrated by others in response to sexual difference, I have not often found many of these same feminists sympathetic to other concerns, such as race and/or ethnicity, that are subject to equally oppressive practices.[2] As an African-American woman, I find it impossible to focus whatever experience of oppression I have had on my sex alone. For me, as for other women of color, the experience of oppression has a complex of causes, and its forms are also, as a result, multifaceted.[3] This objection is by now a critical commonplace in feminist theory,[4] but I have not raised it simply to advance once more the oft-made observation that feminism and feminist theory share a long history of neglect with regard to such concerns. Rather, I have put it forward as the only starting point from which it is possible to begin to articulate the deeper significance of the theoretical problem of internal division itself with regard to this issue.[5] And through such articulation, I hope to open up the space for dialogue that could ultimately bring about the beginnings of visible change.

The seriousness of the problem is evidenced by the contours of the debate, which, beginning with the objections to mainstream feminists' manner of articulating feminism and feminist movement and theory made by women of color during the early 1980s, soon moved on to focus on the issue of identity and how it relates to feminism's conception of itself as a movement.[6] The sense of alienation described by women of color with regard to their understanding of feminist identity, as it was then elaborated, problematized one of the most important tenets of feminist movement—that of unity. As Rosalind Delmar notes in a recent collection of essays, entitled *What is Feminism?*:

> Unity based on identity has turned out to be a very fragile thing.... Over the past twenty years, a paradox has developed at the heart of the modern women's movement: on the one hand there is the generality of its categorical appeal to all women, as potential participants in a movement; on the other hand there is the exclusivism of its current internal practice, with its emphasis on difference and division.[7]

Delmar refers to the unity on which the second wave of feminism was constituted—the idea that feminism spoke for all women, that all women were oppressed by sexual difference from men, that all women's experience of such oppression was much the same, and that therefore the remedies would be much the same for all women as well. With the entrance of the dissenting voices of women of color, however, this powerful bond of unity was seriously threatened. If feminism did not speak for all women, for whom *did* it speak? And if it spoke for only a small segment of the female population of the world, how was this to be reconciled with the enormity of its utopic vision?

What these dissenting voices introduced into feminist theory was a further complication of the original problem of difference, which feminism had articulated as that of *sexual* difference. In feminist theory, the problem of difference had always been one that remained outside its confines. Within feminism existed the warmth and acceptance generated by sisterhood and unity; only outside of feminism were the cold enemies of division and oppression. The effect of the articulation of the objections of women of color on feminist theory, then, was to foster, as Teresa de Lauretis suggests, the realization within feminist circles that "sisterhood is powerful but difficult," that perhaps the achievement of true sisterhood would prove just as daunting a task as the eradication of sexual oppression and the obliteration of the social practices founded upon it.[8]

As it stands today, the women's movement is tortured by internal conflicts, which, when examined in detail, reveal at its heart something that may be described more generally as an opposition between singularity and multiplicity. The voice of singularity is that of the idea of unity in feminism, a utopic ideal toward which feminism has striven and yet strives; in contrast, the voice of multiplicity is that of the actual and various material reality of women, who together constitute one-half of the world's population. The inherent threat of this opposition is so great that while on the one hand, feminist theory recognizes the significance of multiplicity, it also cannot accept the reality of what it means and yet remain a coherent theoretical and political force, at least not within the terms by which it has thus far articulated itself. As a result, its acknowledgement of multiplicity remains just that—an acknowledgement—while often its central premises remain the same. We can see just such an occurrence in Delmar's elaboration of the impact of multiplicity on feminism:

> The fragmentation of contemporary feminism bears ample witness to the impossibility of constructing modern feminism as a simple unity in the present or of arriving at a shared feminist definition of feminism. Such differing explanations, such a variety of emphases in practical campaigns, such widely varying interpretations of their results have emerged, that it now makes more sense to speak of a plurality of feminisms than of one.... Could it not still be that what unites feminists is greater than what divides?[9]

In this passage, Delmar gives voice to the problematic nature of multiplicity in contemporary feminist theory. But instead of confronting the significance of this, she retreats into the desire to continue the movement (as well as the development of theories with regard to it) as it is and has been: a movement based on the eradication of inequalities produced by *sexual* difference.

Yet what exactly is it that, as Delmar writes, "unites feminists?" Is it the fact of womanhood? But what is womanhood? How can womanhood serve to unite feminists, if all women do not experience it in the same way? While Delmar tries to accommodate the problem of multiplicity in feminism by moving from a singular conception of feminism (based on the assumption of unity) to a plural one (which would admit that the multiplicity of female voices precludes any simple assertion of unity), she does not sustain this movement on a conceptual level. In seeking a solution to the problem of multiplicity in that which "unites feminists," something about which she is also not at all clear, Delmar continues to imply that there is an underlying singularity of mission in feminism, the importance of which should transcend "petty" and distracting internal differences.

In this instance, the problem with Delmar's concentration on the issue of unity is that it prevents her from recognizing how a full acknowledgement of the multiplicitous nature of women's differences could influence feminism's understanding of such unity. In fact, it is precisely the implications of such influence that Delmar seeks to avoid, because it soon becomes evident that there can be no unity, at least no unity as it was defined in the initial stages of the second wave of feminism, if differences among women are brought to bear upon the significance of the movement as a whole.

The difficulty with this is that once these subtle operations within feminism are recognized, the problem of singularity takes on a very different and far more incriminating character. In seeking to protect itself against the import of the onslaught of difference (one that is not just theoretical, but social and political as well), feminism simultaneously reinscribes itself as a dominant discourse that produces and reproduces itself in much the same way as does the discourse against which it has traditionally pitted itself: that of patriarchy.

These concerns were expressed in a 1974 interview in *Tel Quel*, between the French avant-garde intellectual group *Politique et psychanalyse* and Julia Kristeva. In response to *Psych et Po's* difficulties with what it perceives as the tenuous relationships between feminism and revolutionary and/or class struggle and anti-imperialism, which, in its estimation, produce the "risk of creating within feminism an enclosed ideology parallel to the ideology of the dominant class,"[10] Kristeva's identification of the potential problem underlying feminism's reaction to the issue of multiplicity has clear and telling implications for feminism:

> In the twentieth century, after suffering through fascism and revisionism, we should have learned that there can be no socio-political transformation without a transformation of subjects: in other words, in our relationship to social constraints, to pleasure, and more deeply, to language.... In every political apparatus, whether on the Right, or the Left, the movement, by its negativity, indicates what is otherwise repressed: that "class consciousness" for example, is not unrelated to the unconscious of the sexed speaker. The trap that is set for this demystifying force, a force that the women's movement can be, is that we will identify with the power principle that we think we are fighting: the hysterical saint plays her pleasure against social order, but in the name of God. The question is: "Who plays God in present-day feminism?" Man? Or Woman—his substitute? As long as any libertarian movement, feminism included, does not analyze its own relationship to power and does not renounce belief in its own identity, it remains capable of being coopted both by power and an overtly religious or lay spiritualism.... The solution is infinite, since what is at stake is to move from a patriarchal society, of class and of religion, in other words from pre-history, toward—Who knows? In any event, this process involves going through what is repressed in discourse, in reproductive and productive relationships. Call it "woman" or the "oppressed social class": it's the same struggle, and you never have one without the other. It seems to me that the movement's most urgent task is to make the ideological and political machines understand this complicity. But this implies that we change our style, that we get out a bit from "among women," from among ourselves, that each one of us in our respective fields fights against social and cultural archaisms.[11]

The key phrase here with regard to feminism is "renounce belief in its own identity." For Kristeva, feminism's concentration on its own singular identity does not allow it to move beyond the parameters established by patriarchal society, because it cannot transcend such parameters itself. Rather, it risks engendering only a repetition of the problems that it identitifes as part and parcel of patriarchal society and discourse, and against which it fights. While it avails itself of different terminology, feminism still makes use of the same overall structure.

Feminism's concentration on identity is the juncture at which this problem, that of its similarity to patriarchal discourse, is most evident. Its traditionally singular conception of identity possesses the perfect form by which it is possible to establish a hierarchical relationship between itself and what I will call the "discourse of the Other," whatever is "not-itself"—the same kind of hierarchical relationship that exists between feminism itself and the discourse of patriarchy.[12] The end result is the reproduction within feminism of the same system of power relations that its philosophy condemns—this time internally, in the relationship between the discourse of mainstream feminist theory and the discourse of those whose voices do not conform to it.

Arguing against what she identifies as Julia Kristeva's plan for negative struggle, Linda Alcoff writes, "you cannot mobilize a movement that is only and always against: you must have a positive alternative, a vision of a better future that can motivate people to sacrifice their time and energy toward its realization."[13] Just as the history of the women's movement shows that it was originally conceived of in terms of sexual difference, or a binary opposition in which the idea of "woman" was pitted against the idea of "man," so in feminist theory, deep within the women's movement, the concerns of women of color and poor women are being pitted against those of mainstream feminists, most often depicted as bourgeois, white and/or middle-class. In fact, the *only* moments at which such feminists are defined as bourgeois, white and/or middle-class is when they are described in relation to such "other" women. At all other times in the discourse of feminism, these feminists assume the status of the universal, similar in many ways to what feminism identifies as the inimical universal status of "man."

The inclusion of non-mainstream feminist voices is, however, at least as it was articulated during the 1980s, a struggle that is largely "against," to use Alcoff's terminology. On the issue of offering a "positive alternative," both mainstream and non-mainstream feminists are, for the most part, silent, seeing, perhaps, the problem as too large and kaleidoscopic to suggest a reasonable hope of solution, or viewing solution as simply a withdrawal from confrontation into the protective stance of "identity politics."[14]

The end result of this has been that what I have identified as the opposition between singularity and multiplicity has created a central disunity within the movement so disturbing as to produce an almost insurmountable paralysis with regard to this issue. As Teresa de Lauretis points out, this "focus on division" produces a "crisis *over* identity, a metacritical doubt and a dispute among feminists as to the notion of identity, …[and] also a crisis *of* identity, of self-definition, implying a theoretical impasse for feminism as a whole."[15] But it is the refusal to acknowledge not just the role that the issue of multiplicity plays in this "identity crisis," but the *significance* of that role, that has created in feminism what appears to be a "theoretical impasse."[16] In view of this, then, it is imperative to analyze the significance of the role of multiplicity in feminism in greater detail.

It has been established that the primary difficulty represented for feminism by the problem of multiplicity is that it violently disturbs the concept of unity, the foundational concept from which much feminist activism and theorizing are derived. If all women do not agree on what and who women are, then the philosophical and theoretical basis of feminism is revealed as vitally flawed—that is if feminism is to be understood as based upon a concept of united sisterhood, a unified identity of women engaged in the battle to end sexist oppression. In such a situation, change cannot be easy to achieve. But if change is indeed to be brought about, feminists must first identify and describe the flaw, then work to accommodate that which it represents. The question becomes, then, what exactly *is* the threat posed by multiplicity, beyond its disruption of the concept of unity?

If the idea of multiplicity in feminism may be defined as encompassing "a more plural understanding of 'women' and a notion of 'situational identities' determined by the exigencies of the social field,"[17] then it is clear that what is at stake is the foundational premise of feminism: that all women are oppressed because of their sex, and are therefore interested in destroying the power that sexual oppression may have over their lives. But while this may be true, it is also a rather simplistic articulation which conceals a more insidious premise at its heart, as Delmar elaborates:

> Feminism's fascination with women is also the condition of the easy slippage from "feminist" to "woman" and back: the feminist becomes the representative of "woman," just as "feminist history" becomes the same as "women's history"…this intensification of the use of concepts already in circulation has produced not so much a continuity of feminisms as a set of crises. It is, for example, one of women's liberation's paradoxes that although it started on the terrain of sexual antagonism between men and women, it moved quickly to a state in which relations between women caused the most internal stress. Women, in a sense, are feminism's greatest problem.[18]

Thus, at the heart of feminism's dispute over identity is the issue of the category "woman" and how it should be defined. Within the dispute over "woman" lies the answer to the "theoretical impasse" by which contemporary feminism finds itself constrained. Women are, as Delmar points out, its "greatest problem" because they themselves are *different*, and this difference causes them to experience not only different oppressions, but also to experience sexual oppression itself in many different ways. If experiences of oppression themselves are different, so then must the remedies to the problems and difficulties caused by it be different. A feminism that does not recognize the multiplicity of difference as more than just a problematic area encompassed within its own dominant discourse of sexual oppression becomes guilty of the crime it denounces: it marginalizes the oppositional discourse because it does not follow the party line.

Such marginalization keeps the menace of multiplicity safely contained. From this perspective, it may be theorized about, questioned, described, discussed, but never quite addressed in terms that would actually change the discursive parameters of feminism. To do so would dramatically alter the terms of the debate, a conclusion that a number of feminists draw, yet which only a few wish quite openly to confront.[19] But confrontation and, beyond that, acceptance of new parameters must take place if feminism is to accomplish any of its original goals. Judith Butler's understanding of the problem suggests the direction toward which feminism must move in grappling with this dilemma and, potentially, in seeking a solution to it:

> does feminist theory need to rely on a notion of what is fundamentally or distinctively to be a woman?.... When the category is understood as representing a set of values or dispositions, it becomes normative in character and hence, exclusionary in principle. This move has created a problem...that a variety of women from various cultural positions have refused to recognize themselves as "women" in the terms articulated by feminist theory with the result that these women fall outside the category and are left to conclude that (1) either they are not women...or (2) the category reflects the restricted location of its theoreticians and hence, fails to recognize the intersection of gender with race, class, ethnicity, age, sexuality, and other currents which contribute to the formation of cultural (non)identity. In response to the radical exclusion of the category of women from hegemonic cultural formations on the one hand and the internal critique of the exclusionary effects of the category from within feminist discourse on the other, feminist theorists are now confronted with the problem of either redefining and expanding the category of women itself to become more inclusive...or to challenge the place of the category as a part of a feminist normative discourse.[20]

While to some degree Butler repeats what is now well-known in feminism, she also offers something new—the articulation of a direction in which to move, without which further progression is impossible. In Butler's view, the central difficulty with regard to the issue of multiplicity in contemporary feminism is the category of "woman," something that brings up, in quite a glaring way, the debate on essentialism/anti-essentialism.[21] Simply put, essentialist feminists hold that what is important in the articulation of feminism is a specifically female culture, and a valorization of what is distinctly feminine—that which is feminine being derived at its most fundamental level from a determination of sexual difference based on essential biological difference, or the body. Such valorization is designed to counteract the centuries of marginalization, obliteration, devalorization and other neglect to which women and the cultural productions and contributions of women have been subjected. Anti-essentialist feminists, on the other hand, deny the existence of the distinctly feminine, particularly a femininity derived from biologically determined sexual difference. For anti-essentialist feminists, the body and gender roles, categories and behaviors are separate, as the category of gender is socially produced and therefore cannot be tied to an essential biologically determined sexual difference.[22]

But if the implications of multiplicity in feminism are to be confronted in any way that will bring about change, the debate must go far beyond such a mere description of its parameters. Questions with regard to this issue must probe deeper, so that answers may fall closer to the truth. Why is it that the debate seems to have stalled around this specific issue? What is it about essentialism in particular that causes such difficulty? Butler suggests that this has occurred because the category "woman" is normative and thus, exclusionary. However, it is also important to ask: in *what way* is it exclusionary?

If feminism is ultimately to move beyond this difficulty, it must accept that the implications of multiplicity in this regard are serious, and that they represent the necessity of a drastic re-elaboration of the movement itself. As Alice Jardine asks in her essay "Prelude: The Future of Difference," "do we want to continue reorganizing the relationship of difference to sameness through a dialectics of valorization, or is there a way to break down the overdetermined metaphors which continue to organize our perceptions of reality?"[23] If it is true, as Nancy Miller points out, that "the apparently neutral distinction [women are not men] is anything but innocent, in that Western culture has proven to be incapable of thinking not-the-same-as without assigning one of the terms a positive value and the other, a negative…,"[24] then the same system may be seen as operative within feminism with regard to the position of non-mainstream feminist voices. The problem of the category "woman," then, becomes not so much an issue of historical neglect in terms of the problem of sexual difference, but an issue of valorization: feminism's valorization of an essential *sexual* difference at the expense of all other kinds of differences. Because of this, the discourse of sexual difference becomes a totalizing force within feminism that encompasses and subsumes other kinds of differences. Although contemporary feminism hints that such change might be in order, it does not wholeheartedly seek to determine the actual ways in which it must alter itself to accommodate the fact that the concerns of those oppressed by sexual difference cannot be divorced from those oppressed by sexual difference *and* other differences subject to oppressive social practices. To do so produces a serious and unavoidable flaw in the credibility of the movement as a whole.

The valorization of sexual difference, at the expense of other kinds of difference subject to oppressive social practices, creates a hierarchical relationship between differences within feminism, with sexual difference at the top of the pyramid. This also creates a situation in which certain women are more privileged than others within the movement itself. It is to refuse to create a movement in which, as Cixous describes, the "class-struggle" is embraced so that it becomes possible to "split it open, spread it out, push it forward, fill it with the fundamental struggle so as to prevent [it], or any other struggle for the liberation of a class or people, from operating as a form of repression, pretext for postponing the inevitable, the staggering alteration in power relations and in the production of individualities."[25] To refuse to embrace this certainty is to ensure that feminism will always be crippled in any effort to move beyond the purely theoretical in terms of its social mission.

I am reminded in this regard of a conversation I had with one of my classmates, who was also a feminist, when I was a graduate student at the State University of New York at Buffalo a number of years ago. I was, for the duration of my studies there, the only African-American in my department (student or professor), and, once it was determined that I was interested in discussing many intellectual issues beyond those concerned solely with African-American literature and criticism, I was summarily isolated by the other students. I was, one day, just passing by the office of this student/colleague (whom I had approached several times on a casual social level), and she called me in to tell me of her attempts to teach Toni Morrison's *Beloved* in her class.

"They just sat there," she said, speaking of her students. "I was really frustrated, and I tried really hard, but they just didn't get it! They're so lily-white in all of their ideas, they just couldn't relate to Sethe's hardships."

I said something noncommittal, and she went on.

"But I'm just going to keep trying," she said, in a hard, determined voice. "I think they should make the effort to understand this book, and I'm just going to keep teaching it until they do!"

I still didn't have much of a response, beyond "Oh, really?" What could I say? I remember thinking how useless her effort seemed and how false her determination. What was the point of trying to effect change in her students with a book, when she herself drew the line within its confines? When she herself, by her actions, showed that it was okay to deal with non-mainstream experiences in the form of a book, but not in the form of a person? How did she expect her students to understand what she could not understand herself?

As a feminist, my student/colleague was deeply committed to the eradication of the oppression she felt as a result of sexual difference. Yet as a white person, she was unable to see a strong relationship between this commitment and her own personal attitudes, and how these attitudes might themselves be oppressive toward those different from herself. A feminist politics that admits the immediacy of its own struggle without recognizing its link to other seemingly different struggles risks condemning itself by refusing to acknowledge what it might mean for feminism to confront the fact that the desire to end oppressive practices is not exclusive to one group alone, but an aspiration of many different groups, that these oppressive practices are different, and that feminism might engage in them itself through its valorization of sexual difference as *the primary cause* of oppression.

Such valorization serves as a protective shield against what is really at stake in this conundrum: how feminism's explorations into the nature and causes of oppression can operate in the material world to radically and entirely change our social lives—not just to change power relations between men and women. If sexual difference is continually perceived as the most important cause of oppression, the discourse that valorizes it can then pertain only to a select few, and this is something that is in direct contradiction to what feminism professes to be about. The significance of this dichotomy is that while feminism appears to have an interest in supplying a universal solution to the problem of sexual oppression, this "universal" frequently conceals a limited range, as Barbara Christian comments:

> So often I have read books on feminist literary theory that restrict the definition of what *feminist* means and overgeneralize about so much of the world that most women as well as men are excluded. And seldom do feminist theorists take into account the complexity of life—that women are of many races and ethnic backgrounds with different histories and cultures and that as a rule women belong to different classes that have different concerns. Seldom do they note these distinctions, because if they did they could not articulate a theory. Often as a way of clearing themselves they do acknowledge that women of color, for example, do

exist, then go on to do what they were going to do anyway, which is to invent a theory that has little relevance for us.[26]

If such theory has "little or no relevance" for large numbers of women, including women of color, it is because it is a theory that often constrains itself to words on paper, separated, for the most part, from involvement on the level of actual life experience with women who might be considered "other," whether that be "otherness" of race, ethnicity, religion, class or nationality. A theory informed by involvement in terms of actual life experience with members of disparate groups cannot remain impervious to their concerns. As long as feminism continues to restrict itself to the discussion of a singular idea of oppression derived from the perception of sexual difference as the primary cause of oppression, it will run the risk of marking itself as a discourse of the privileged few, and, thus, also remain fatally flawed.

When de Lauretis writes that the "image...of a homogeneous, monolithic Feminism—whether white or black or Third World, whether mainstream or separatist, academic or activist—is something that must be resisted,"[27] her words speak to the difficulty posed by such a singular notion of the movement. But these words cannot be taken as simply a theoretical injunction: they must be carried through from the university to the realm of political activism and on into our intimate social worlds. They must be expanded beyond the call to resist the creation of a monolithic ideal in many separate forms, to an embrace of all of these forms as constituting one ideal in the fight against oppression, whatever form or forms such oppression may take. Then, and only then, will feminism begin to transform itself into what it should have been from the beginning: "a movement for social justice."[28]

NOTES |

1 Any exploration into the history of the feminist movement will reveal that it is many-sided, beginning with the practical aspect of activism and work with and on the part of actual women, developing later into an academic, theoretical, and intellectual endeavor. To emphasize that what is being referred to here is the movement in its entirety I am using the term "feminism/feminist." Even though throughout this essay I will simply make reference to "feminism" it should be read as "feminism/feminist."

2 In commenting here on oppressive practices, I do not mean to create a rather simplistic understanding of oppression by setting it up in a relation of binary opposition to the idea of freedom, by which I would also imply that all oppressions are equal.

In her essay "Hard Ground: Jewish Identity, Racism, and Anti-Semitism," in *Yours In Struggle: Three Feminist Perspectives on Anti-Semitism and Racism* (New York: Long Haul Press, 1984), p. 107, Elly Bulkin cautions against precisely this handling of oppression when she writes about "the danger of leveling oppressions, of failing to recognize the specificity of each." She goes on to emphasize the importance of "distinguishing between oppressions...not treating [them]...as if they operated in exactly the same way within each geographical and historical setting" (p. 107). What I mean here by "equally oppressive practices" is not to suggest, as Bulkin writes, that "the degree of oppressiveness is equal regardless of its form" (p. 111), but rather to assert what Bulkin later states as the ideal, that "we should all be actively opposed to every oppression..." (p. 141). See also bell hooks, *Feminist Theory: From Margin to Center* (Boston: South End Press, 1984) for a more complete discussion of how the relationship between feminism and oppression should be articulated with regard to these concerns.

3 See Linda Alcoff, "Cultural Feminism vs. Post-Structuralism: The Identity Crisis in Feminist Theory," *Signs* 13, 3 (Summer 1988), p. 412. Alcoff identifies the experience of poor women and women of color as one which embraces a "simultaneity of oppressions" that are the result of "a complex network of relations." See also Jill Lewis, "Sexual Division of Power: Motivations of the Women's Liberation Movement," *Common Differences: Conflicts in Black and White Feminist Perspectives*, ed. Gloria I. Joseph and Jill Lewis (Boston: South End Press, 1986), p. 43. Lewis bases her analysis of the complex of oppressions on capitalist society, which organizes people "into separate and competing groups and classes" so that "no one segment of the women's movement represents all the interests and concerns of all women. Even among white women, different groups confront different social and economic experiences and encounter oppression and injustice in different ways. All of these oppressions need to be recognized as valid oppressions to be struggled against. Just as racism manifests itself in a multiplicity of ways, so sexism, too, has its range of manifestations..." (pp. 43–71).

4 See Cherrie Moraga and Gloria Anzaldua, *This Bridge Called My Back: Writings by Radical Women of Color* (New York: Kitchen Table, Women of Color Press, 1981); *Home Girls: A Black Feminist Anthology*, ed. Barbara Smith (New York: Kitchen Table, Women of Color Press, 1983); bell hooks, *Ain't I a Woman: Black Women and Feminism* (Boston: South End Press, 1981); bell hooks, *Feminist Theory: From Margin to Center*; and Audre Lorde, "An Open Letter to Mary Daly," in *Sister Outsider: Essays and Speeches by Audre Lorde* (Freedom, CA: The Crossing Press, 1984), pp. 66–71.

5 The division to which I am referring here, that between mainstream feminism and feminists and women of color, is by far not the only source of internal division in contemporary feminist theory. For discussions of debates on other sites of division,

such as essentialism/anti-essentialism, culturalism/biologism, feminism/decon-struction, equality/difference, and the gay/straight split, see Marianne Hirsch and Evelyn Fox Keller, *Conflicts in Feminism* (New York: Routledge, 1990); see also *Feminist Studies* 14, 1 (Spring 1988) for further discussion of the relationship between feminism and deconstruction; and *differences* 1, 2 (Summer 1989) for further discussion of essentialism/anti-essentialism.

6 See Note 3 for a bibliography of writings discussing these concerns.

7 Rosalind Delmar, "What Is Feminism?," *What Is Feminism? A Re-Examination*, ed. Juliet Mitchell and Ann Oakley (New York: Pantheon, 1986), p. 11.

8 Teresa de Lauretis, "Feminist Studies/Critical Studies: Issues, Terms, and Contexts," *Feminist Studies/Critical Studies*, ed. Teresa de Lauretis (Bloomington: Indiana University Press, 1986), p. 7.

9 Delmar, "What Is Feminism?," *What Is Feminism?*, p. 9. See also Carol S. Vance and Ann Barr Snitow, "Toward a Conversation about Sex in Feminism: A Modest Proposal," *Signs* 10, 1 (Autumn 1984), p. 130; Teresa de Lauretis, "The Essence of the Triangle or, Taking the Risk of Essentialism Seriously: Feminist Theory in Italy, the U.S., and Britain," *differences* 1, 2 (Summer 1989), p. 3, p. 11, p. 32 and "Feminist Studies/Critical Studies," *Feminist Studies/Critical Studies*, p. 14; Alcoff, "Cultural Feminism vs. Post-Structuralism," *Signs*, p. 405, p. 419; Juliet Mitchell and Ann Oakley, "Introduction," in *What Is Feminism?*, p. 2; Judith Butler, "Gender Trouble, Feminist Theory, and Psychoanalytic Discourse," in *Feminism/Postmodernism*, ed. Linda J. Nicholson (New York: Routledge, 1990), p. 325; and Ellen Rooney, "In a Word: Interview with Ellen Rooney and Gayatri Spivak," *differences* 1, 2 (Summer 1989), p. 125.

10 "An Interview with *Politique et psychanalyse* and Julia Kristeva," tr. Marilyn A. August, *New French Feminisms*, ed. Elaine Marks and Isabelle de Courtivron (New York: Schocken, 1981), p. 140.

11 "An Interview with *Politique et psychanalyse*," *New French Feminisms*, p. 141.

12 See Mary Poovey, "Feminism and Deconstruction," *Feminist Studies* 14, 1 (Spring 1988), p. 58. This entire issue is dedicated to the relationship between feminism and deconstruction. Asserting the usefulness of deconstruction to feminist theory, Poovey writes that the "contribution deconstruction can make is to challenge hierarchical and oppositional logic. Because the practice of deconstruction transforms binary oppositions into an economy in which terms circulate rather than remain fixed, it could...mobilize another ordering system in which the construction of false unities instrinsic to binary oppositions would not prevail...in its demystifying mode, deconstruction does not simply offer an alternative hierarchy of binary oppositions; it problematizes and opens to scrutiny the very nature of identity and oppositional logic and therefore makes visible the artifice necessary to establish, legislate, and maintain hierarchical thinking.... By deconstructing the term

"woman" into a set of independent variables, this strategy can show how consolidating all women into a falsely unified 'woman' has helped mask the operations of power that actually divide women's interest as much as unite them."

13 Alcoff, "Cultural Feminism vs. Post-Structuralism," *Signs*, p. 419.

14 See Bulkin, "Hard Ground," *Yours In Struggle*, p. 141. Bulkin writes that the ideal, which would entail somewhat of a solution, is often very hard, if not impossible, to achieve. But the previously cited *Yours In Struggle* is one text which attempts to transcend the distance created by the struggle "against," in that it attempts to achieve a dialogue between women of very different backgrounds; see also Gloria I. Joseph and Jill Lewis, *Common Differences*; for a discussion of the withdrawal from confrontation into "identity politics," see Combahee River Collective, "Combahee River Collective Statement," *Home Girls*, pp. 272–82.

15 See Teresa de Lauretis, "The Essence of the Triangle," *differences*, p. 10.

16 For other discussions regarding this issue, see Teresa de Lauretis, "Feminist Studies/Critical Studies," p. 2; Diana Fuss, *Essentially Speaking* (New York: Routledge, 1989), p. 2; Alcoff, "Cultural Feminism vs. Post-Structuralism," *Signs*, p. 405; Sheila Radford-Hill, "Considering Feminism as a Model for Social Change," *Feminist Studies/Critical Studies*, p. 162.

17 Elizabeth Weed, "Introduction: Terms of Reference," *Coming to Terms: Feminism, Theory, Politics* (New York: Routledge, 1989), p. xvi. The idea of multiplicity may, however, also encompass the range of feminist thought now being explored by French feminists Hélène Cixous and Luce Irigaray and to a lesser degree, Julia Kristeva. See Hélène Cixous, "The Laugh of the Medusa," *New French Feminisms*, ed. Elaine Marks and Isabelle de Courtivron, tr. Keith Cohen and Paula Cohen (Amherst: University of Massachusetts Press, 1980), pp. 245–64; Luce Irigaray, *Speculum of the Other Woman*, tr. Gillian C. Gill (1974; Ithaca: Cornell University Press, 1985) and *This Sex Which Is Not One*, tr. Catherine Porter and Carolyn Burke (1977; Ithaca: Cornell University Press, 1985). These feminists identify multiplicity as representative of the female body, which as Cixous writes in "The Laugh of the Medusa," "articulate[s] the profusion of meanings that run through it in every direction." Their goal, then, is to force language to mean in what they define as a distinctly female way, in terms of what they perceive as the multiplicity of the female genitalia, represented through the proliferation of meanings, semantic indeterminacy, digressive stops and starts and non-linear progression.

18 Delmar, "What Is Feminism?," *What Is Feminism?*, pp. 27–28.

19 See Vance and Snitow, "Toward a Conversation about Sex," *Signs*, p. 130; in "The Essence of the Triangle," de Lauretis confronts the problem that multiplicity presents by arguing for a differently defined essentialism, one which does not, however, substantially change the terms of the debate (p. 11, p. 32); See also: Tania Modleski, *Feminism Without Women: Culture and Criticism in a "Postfeminist" Age*

(New York: Routledge, 1991); Poovey, "Feminism and Deconstruction," *Feminist Studies*, p.51, p. 62; and Delmar, "What Is Feminism?," *What Is Feminism?*, p. 8, p. 10.; In "Cultural Feminism vs. Post-Structuralism," Alcoff argues for a "third-course" feminism, one which sidesteps the difficulties posed by both post-structuralism's critique of the subject and cultural feminism's reliance on essentialism (*Signs*, p. 405, p. 414, p. 419, p. 421); Modleski's "postfeminism" is another example of "third-course feminism."

20 Butler, "Gender Trouble," *Feminism/Postmodernism*, pp. 324–25.

21 In "The Essence of the Triangle," *differences*, Teresa de Lauretis focuses on essentialism ; see also Diana Fuss, *Essentially Speaking*; Chris Weedon, *Feminist Practice and Poststructuralist Theory* (Oxford: Basil Blackwell, 1987). For discussions of anti-essentialism, see the British journal *m/f*, 5 and 6 (1981) in which the journal's editors (Parveen Adams, Beverley Brown and Elizabeth Cowie) explain their anti-essentialist position (pp. 1–4); in the following issue (*m/f* 7 [1982], pp. 87–89), their position is critiqued in a reply by Michèle Barrett and Rosalind Coward.

22 On this subject, Mary Poovey writes in "Feminism and Deconstruction": "'woman' is *only* a social construct that has no basis in nature, that 'woman'…is a term whose definition depends upon the context in which it is being discussed and not upon some set of sexual organs or social experiences." She goes on to say that from "the perspective of…[deconstruction] a feminism that bases its epistemology and practice on women's experience is simply another deluded humanism, complicit with the patriarchal institutions it claims to oppose. To argue that women's biological nature grounds a set of experiences and feelings is obviously to fall into this humanistic trap, but even to maintain that all women necessarily occupy the position of "other" to man and that their social oppression follows from this binary split is to risk reducing position to essence…" (p. 52). Thus, the poststructuralist perspective in feminism becomes an indispensable aid in the attempt to problematize the issue of sexual difference, a necessary evil in seeking to provide meaningful answers to the problem of multiplicity with regard to the position of non-mainstream feminists within the discourse of feminism.

23 Alice Jardine, "Prelude: The Future of Difference," *The Future of Difference*, ed. Hester Eisenstein and Alice Jardine (Boston: G. K. Hall, 1980), p. xxvi.

24 Quoted by Alice Jardine in "Prelude," p. xxv. Jardine quotes one of Nancy Miller's position papers which contributed to the formulation of the conference from which the book was published: "The Scholar and The Feminist VI: The Future of Difference," sponsored by the Barnard College Women's Center, New York City, April 29, 1979.

25 Cixous, "The Laugh of the Medusa," *New French Feminisms*, p. 253.

26 Barbara Christian, "The Race for Theory," *Feminist Studies* 14, 1 (Spring 1988), p. 75.

27 de Lauretis, "Feminist Studies/Critical Studies," *Feminist Studies/Critical Studies*, p. 15.

28 See Radford-Hill, "Considering Feminism," *Feminist Studies/Critical Studies*, p. 162; Radford-Hill argues here for a separatist black feminist movement as a result of frustration with what she identifies as black feminists' struggle "to help white feminists transcend their socialization," something which forced them to urge others to "join a movement that they openly attacked as racist." While I am not advocating a separatist movement because I feel it doesn't do anything to change the existing system of power relations, it must be recognized that the necessity many black feminists feel to do exactly this is a disappointing example of feminism's refusal to satisfactorily confront the challenge of multiplicity. See also bell hooks, *Feminist Theory: From Margin to Center.*

9

AUTHENTICITY IS
SUCH A DRAG!

Sabina Sawhney

On being asked the question: "What is a hijra?" by cultural anthropologist Serena Nanda, the hijras offered a double narrative in response. While some of them tried to explain their being via a recourse to various legends and tales from Hindu religion and culture, the rest attempted to demonstrate their existence by revealing their private parts. As Nanda recounts, "In some cases, a hijra I was talking with would jump to her feet, lift up her skirt, and, displaying her altered genitals, would say, 'See, we are neither men nor women!'"[1] The two responses may be categorized, using Homi Bhabha's terminology, as the pedagogical and the performative.[2] The first response attempts to construct an identity through a myth of origins that grants the identity an authority based on divine intercession. The second response, however, constructs the hijras as subjects of signification: the readable signs produced through a performance—a deliberate inscription on the material body.

The causes of being, variously attributed to divine or human intervention, seem to lie in uneasy proximity with each other: one not quite negating or superseding the other, and neither quite adequate to the task of clarification. These two hypotheses seem analogous to the most frequently expressed feeling of the hijras about themselves—"neither here nor there." Various explanations offered by the experts suffer a similar fate. Attempts to categorize the hijras—as transvestites or transsexuals, as eunuchs or castrated men, or even as providing institutionalized support for homosexuality—all seem either inappropriate or incomplete.[3] The very existence of hijras seems to be built around a number of disjunctions and paradoxes, all of which defy any simple or singular understanding.

The term, "hijra," does not offer any easy resolutions. Derived from the Arabic, "ijara," which refers to eunuches or castrated men, hijra in common Indian parlance is an umbrella name referring to eunuchs or men who have emasculated themselves, intersexed people, men and women with genital malfunction, hermaphrodites, persons with indeterminate sexual organs, impotent men, male homosexuals, and even effeminate men who are hijra imposters. The only common feature among them is their mode of dressing: they all adopt feminine costumes and apparel. They live in communes ranging from five to fifteen people and traditionally earn their living by collecting alms and receiving payment for performances at weddings, births, and festivals. A large number of hijras also supplement their income through "homosexual" prostitution. "Homosexual" is placed between quotation marks because an unqualified acceptance of this term is problematic. The difficulty lies in the application of the conventionally understood definition of homosexuality to the hijras. On the one hand, we have the authority of some anthropologists and ethnologists who have described sexual activity involving the hijras as "homosexual" and we also have a personal narrative to support this definition:

> See, we are all men, born as men, but when we look at women, we don't have any desire for them. When we see men, we like them, we feel shy, we feel some excitement. We want to live and die as women. We have the same feelings you have, Serena, just as you women fall in love and are ready to sacrifice your life for a man, so we are also like that. Just like you, whenever a man touches us, we get an excitement out of it.[4]

This is Kamladevi recounting her experience to Serena Nanda, and the context of this statement makes it clear that Kamladevi is not the only hijra who feels this way. On the other hand, however, we do know that the hijra herself deviates from the biological norm of maleness, and hence it is difficult to categorize the hijra as a homosexual, if homosexuality is understood as an expression of desire for the same sex. Furthermore, in cases where the partner is not a hijra, he is never considered a homosexual within Indian society; the hijras' customer is seen merely as a garden variety john. In effect, there is a certain amount of overlapping between the categories of the homosexuals and the hijras such that, again, the hijras are "neither here nor there." The category of the hijra and the category of the homosexual cannot be simply collapsed into each other. In fact, due to their indeterminate genders, the hijras unsettle our accepted modes of categorization and identification.

The apparently insurmountable problems that confront us as we try to categorize the hijras in some ways bear a remarkable similarity to the predicaments posed by the issue of *identity within feminism*: women and hijras have more than just their dress in common. The group called "hijras" and the group named "women" are analogous in being impossible to categorize. Just as it is not practical to determine who, or even what, exactly constitutes the "hijras"— impossible to label them in terms of their gender, their sexual orientation, or profession—similarly, the people collected under the title of "women" are inaccesible to any single, overarching identity. And herein lies the problem for feminism. The impetus propelling the feminist movement has been the desire to see a greater representation of women in a wide-ranging spectrum of discourses ranging from the political to the legal to the socio-cultural as well as the academic. This motivating force, however, has foundered precisely due to the difficulty of categorizing women, of defining or discovering their identity. That is to say, the demand for greater representation must, after all, emerge in concert with a definition of the subject on whose behalf this demand is being expressed. But it is this foundational premise of definition, of a pure and simple categorization, one that will enable us to recognize that the signifier "woman" has an explicit, unambiguous, transparent, and precise signified, that has always eluded feminists.

The fact that there can be no single identity to which we can attach the "woman" label poses a serious obstacle to feminism. If we accept that feminism as such is always defined in relation to women, then feminism leads us into very puzzling situations. Because the basis of feminism's self-definition—the category of woman—is inherently unstable and protean in its manifestations, feminism has to engage in some tricky acrobatics in order to maintain itself and not fall flat on its face. One could, perhaps, designate feminism simply as a movement on behalf of women with the added rider that the term "women" includes within it all the various differences and diversities found within this group. This, however, presupposes that women have a common identity that overrides their differences. Just as some hijras seem to think that their authentic identity will be exposed once the camouflaging costume is discarded, feminism seems to be relying similarly on the notion that the authentic identity of woman would be revealed once the drag is removed. That is to say, when her various "clothes"— racial, ethnic, hetero/homosexual, class-textured—are removed, the real, the genuine woman would appear and her identity would pose no puzzles. But surely that is a dangerous assumption, for it not only prioritizes certain forms of identity-formation over others but also essentializes a sexual *or* gendered identity as already known in advance. We not only need to interrogate the way in which the concept of woman functions in the discourse of feminism, but also review the two coordinates—sex and gender—that formulate this concept.

My essay addresses these issues through the example of the hijras. The argument that I shall be pursuing may be roughly divided into three parts. The first part considers the problem of feminism if it retains its primary attachment to the contested notion of woman. The example of hijras, in this part of the argument, functions as a metaphoric instance. That is to say, while I use the hijras in order to interrogate the culturally determined identity of woman, a similar effect could have been accomplished through a use of any other category that has been added after the fact in the discourse of white, American feminism. In other words, the function that the hijras perform could have been accomplished by the invocation of the category of the African-American woman, the lesbian, or the postcolonial woman. However, I must insist on a cautionary qualification: while any of these categories could be used interchangeably to pose a challenge and contest the discourse of American feminism in the last few decades, the trajectory of their questionings would be vastly different. The specificity of each category suggests a multifarious set of challenges, and it may perhaps be wise not to assume the end-result in advance.

Hence, parts two and three of my argument consider the hijras in their material, cultural, and historical specificity, and the ramifications of that knowledge on Western feminism. I do this not only to protect myself from the accusation of flirting with the exotic other, but also to indicate the ways in which an informed understanding of the categories, initially ignored by American feminism, forces us to reconsider the foundations of feminism's conceptualization. That is to say, if the hijras as *a metaphoric concept* suggest ways of destabilizing the gendered category of woman, such that the ideological constructs that inscribe "woman" become suspect, educating ourselves about the *material realities* of the hijras indicate that the biological norms that determine femaleness might be equally suspect. The two moves are linked together in their questioning of feminism's real. By bringing both "woman" and "female" under scrutiny, the hijras enable us to examine the role and necessity of feminism. We need to reconsider whether the oppositional strategies and the revisionist re-readings of culture that feminism has produced must be necessarily tethered to either gender or sexual determinations, or whether such an association fosters a monolithic vision of feminism that must maintain itself through repression. In other words, the desire to articulate a genuine feminism for authentic women may itself be implicated along with those questionable practices within feminism that marginalized the concerns relating to race, class, nationality or sexual preference.

I.

Only the Shallow Know Themselves.

—Oscar Wilde[5]

The realization that "woman" does not allude to a common identity, that a complex and intersecting matrix of race, ethnicity, class, sexual preference, national affiliations, and genders constitutes any subject does seem to present formidable obstacles to the task of feminists. To add to the difficulty, once the term "women-subjects" is put under scrutiny, the term "feminists" no longer seems to possess any obvious clarity. Who are the feminists? What women are they representing? On whose behalf are they making demands? The urgency of these questions became apparent as more and more women began charging the feminist movement with ignoring the concerns of all but middle-class, heterosexual, white, American, and European women. Audre Lorde, for instance, demanded to know: "[i]f white american feminism need not deal with the differences between us, and the resulting difference in our oppressions, then how do you deal with the fact that the women who clean your houses and tend your children while you attend conferences on feminist theory are, for the most part, poor women and women of Color? What is the theory behind racist feminism?"[6] This was, in fact, the same accusation that white feminists had laid against the dominant, male culture: the conflation of maleness with humanness, and the relegation of femaleness to the position of also-rans; the margins that needed to prove their fitness in order to be considered a legitimate part of the human race.

For the most part, the feminist movement responded swiftly to the complaints of those who felt that the movement had not made adequate efforts to include all women; it acknowledged that a change was necessary in order to extend the condition of humanness beyond the category of men and white, middle-class women. The proferred solution was one that attempted to seek out marginalized or hitherto excluded communities of women in order to provide all with a place in the sun, so to speak. That is to say, a number of feminists made determined efforts to make the category of "woman" as wide as they possibly could, a sort of inclusive universalization in which all diversities could be comfortably accomodated. This solution followed quite logically from the initial aims and strategies of the movement. Because the first order of business had been the demand that the category of universal personhood must not exclude women, that women (as a group) must be added as an essential component within that framework, it seemed quite right to assume that a similar demand must be met with precisely the response that the feminist movement had desired from the dominant culture.

To a certain extent, both demands—the one made by the feminist movement

on the dominant culture and the one made by women on the feminist movement—suffer from what may be termed the "Jericho syndrome." It isn't easy
to discard the belief that the mere sound of the trumpets (or the assertion of the
demands) will bring tumbling down the walls that are obtruding our progress
towards legitimate representation.[7] The problem with this approach is not only
that the walls generally prove to be notoriously rockhearted to the appeal of the
trumpets, but more significantly, that the demands themselves are based on a
radical misunderstanding of the issues involved. On the surface, the demands
may seem simple enough—"Extend the boundaries! Let us in"—assuming as
they do a reply that adheres to the basic norms of civility: "Oh sorry, we didn't
notice you out there! Please do come in." This scenario, however, does not take
into account the fact that any extension of the boundaries radically alters the
basic framework and that any inclusion mandates a re-evaluation of the original categories. After all, the courtesies extended to a guest are based on the
assumption that the guest will eventually leave and not become a co-owner. In
the latter case, the concept of ownership and the boundaries of living space have
to be redefined.

Surprisingly enough, the response of the feminist movement to the voices of
women, who asserted their differences from the aims and direction of the movement as it had been originally conceived, was an excess of civility. Or perhaps it
wasn't quite so surprising, considering that girls have always been told to be
nice. As I've mentioned, the feminist movement made a wholehearted effort to
specify various categories: African-American women, Latina women, Native
American women, working-class women, postcolonial women, lesbians, lesbian
women of color.... The motives underlying the creation of this seemingly
never-ending list are certainly admirable. And taking these imperatives into
account, the hijras may certainly assert their rights to be considered as subjects for
feminist inquiry, considering that they do define themselves as women. In addition, the very marginality of the hijras within the community of women
becomes a justification for their inclusion; we may happily invoke the notion
of political correctness. And indubitably the hijras fit the bill of political correctness admirably. Not only are they marginalized within the North Atlantic
culture, but they also belong to a different race and culture. What's more, most
of them live in poverty. As ethnic exotics, the hijras can scarcely be bettered.
Hence, if we follow the logic that mandates a representation of those who are
marginalized or forgotten within a discourse dominated by the concerns of the
North Atlantic culture, then we must grant the hijras a self-evident right to be
considered as legitimate subjects of interest and inquiry within feminist studies.

However, there exists a number of problems with this approach. One, the
mere listing of categories may become an end in itself. That is to say, in a situa-

tion where specifying a group (especially those historically ignored or victimized) means to affirm the existence of the said group, this naming may displace the efforts needed to explore the cause for such affirmation. As Edward Said explains in "The Politics of Knowledge," "Just the names do not provide you with a program, a process, or a vision."[8]

Two, a simple addition to the repertoire of items that must be studied within any specific discipline, without interrogating the reasons for such inclusion, does a disservice, both to the discipline as well as to the subjects that constitute it.[9] After all, additional subjects do not merely extend the reach of the discipline leaving its basic structure intact; it is precisely the very concept of the discipline that undergoes a major transformation. For instance, if instead of just relying on the accounts of self-defined historians, the discipline of history included within it the personal letters and diaries of various ordinary individuals as well, the basis of historiography itself would need to be analyzed and questioned.

One needs to make a similar argument about the discipline of feminist studies and the subject of hijras. The hijras do not meekly join the proliferating lists but question brazenly the fundamental structures of such a discipline and its lists. That is to say, the marginality of the status of the hijras gives us an example of the way in which they interrogate the formation of disciplinary structures. It is at the margins of discursive configurations that one must test the assumptions that sustain the structural integrity of such configurations. The methodological approach towards the framing of a discipline needs to be analyzed through the perspective of those at the margins. Do the hijras possess a natural right within the discipline of feminism, or do they need to get a temporary visa in order to cross the boundaries? Is there a strict identity criteria that needs to be fulfilled before a subject can be deemed worthy of inclusion? And if yes, how is that identity to be determined? Will a mere expression of interest in feminism suffice, or must one demonstrate feminism in action? In either case, how is feminism to be defined, and who makes such definitions? To understand the manner in which the specific question of hijras poses a problem to the disciplinary integrity of feminism, it is necessary to study the hijra role in the Indian society at some length.

But before I do that, I want to explain a third problem: the presumed universality of feminism. The vision of a strong feminist movement—across disciplines, politics and nations—mobilizing its troops in order to take on the patriarchy is decidedly an appealing one. Snags arise, however, when we try to translate this stuff of daydreams into reality. Neither patriarchy nor feminism is available as monolithic structures that can be set to fight with each other. Hence, while Susan Bordo's desire for "gender coherencies across cultural differences" may be understandable, it is certainly not realistic.[10] In fact, the very desire for a unity across cultural boundaries based on gender betrays an ignorance of the meaning of cultural differences. Not only is gender articulated differently across cultures, but gender is also only one of the many axes along which a woman's identity is constituted. Assuming an abstract notion of gender identity would invariably lead to a form of cultural tourism practiced by first-world feminists as they try to engage with the issues confronting women in the rest of the world. In other words, the concept of a universal feminism that takes the different issues of the various categories into serious consideration would have to put both "feminism" and "universal" on hold: they would become concepts that have to be perpetually negotiated.[11] To risk repeating myself, it is not only the list that can generate itself endlessly but also the concerns related to each name within the list that are equally limitless. One way out of this difficulty would be to cease searching for a single vision or for a unified agenda, and instead deal with the diversities of feminisms as and when they arise. So, rather than having "A Feminism" responsive to different and occasionally opposing concerns, one has varieties of feminisms, each creating its own strategies and negotiating the diverse issues that face it. Feminism would then be the composite picture of many feminisms beside one another.

The problem, however, does not admit such a simple solution; the concerns related to identity remain unresolved. Diverse and divergent feminisms concentrating on issues dealing with, for instance, African-American women, or postcolonial women, or bisexual women, would still be granting ethnic, racial, or sexual identity a substantive or ontological basis, such that the constitution of such identities is left uninterrogated. National, ethnic, racial, or economic origins may go part of the way in explaining our differences, but they must not be reified in terms of a natural phenomena. The construction of these origins through various institutions, and the manner in which these origins operate as alibis or attacks, must continue to remain the subject of inquiry.[12]

The preceeding discussion has been based on the assumption that we know a woman when we see one. That is, whether we talk of one feminism or many, or whether we talk of different issues relating to different women, the debate has been based on the postulations that a) we know what is a woman, and b) that women are the authentic subject for feminism. But neither of the two suppositions can be held as absolute. If gender is a cultural determination, then "woman" must remain questionable. Let's look at the problem of feminism from another angle. Whose concerns will feminism/s *not* address? Well, the answer, obviously, is: men's. However, how do we define men? After all, a number of studies have established that within the structures of a patriarchal society one method of asserting hegemonic control by a particular group is through the feminization of the rest of the population.[13] The arbitrary division of human qualities as being either masculine or feminine, and the prioritizing of the former over the latter, leads to the frequent assertions of the dominant groups that the subjugated peoples possess feminine qualities that require rule and control.[14] That is, if one is not born but made a woman, then men can be women just as easily. This cultural feminization, as opposed to biological determination, puts a new wrinkle in our considerations of the manifold subjects of feminisms. But a recourse to culture and a denial of nature still does not satisfactorily answer all my questions. To understand this fully, we must return to the hijras.

But before we finally do this, it is necessary to remind ourselves that the hijras do not function as an example of the authentic "other." The purpose of this essay is not to add another item to the list of all "others"—all finally to be incorporated into some version of a global McSisterhood. Nor am I engaging in the task of detailing a catalog of past injustices, sifting out the victims and the victimizers—although that task is certainly important. The rationale behind my choice of the hijras is to point to the problems and pitfalls that lie in an unmediated acceptance of the "other." The politics of representation are not resolved through gestures of simple humanism—despite the goodwill and generosity of those making such gestures. As I have indicated, we are not all the same once we remove our clothes; the hijras force us to re-examine not only our clothes and our selves but also the way in which we distinguish between the two.

II.

A nice face and a gown of gold brocade
A haw of rose, aloes, paint and scent
All these a woman's beauty aid,
But man, his testicles are his real ornament.[15]

To study the hijra role in Indian society, it is necessary to first recognize the variety and significance of alternative gender roles and gender transformations in Indian mythology and traditional culture. The numerous references to various types of hermaphroditism are undoubtedly significant to the success of the hijra role. As a symbolic reference point, which imparts crucial meaning to the lives of the many different kinds of people who make up the hijra community, this role provides an alternative to the "absolute" or "virile" masculinity by providing an escape from oppressive gender roles. As Judith Still and Michael Worton point out, Hindu culture "simultaneously upholds notions of "warrior" virility (with all the anxieties of potency that these entail) and offers psychologically determining texts and images which foreground ambivalence and gender ambiguity."[16] In other words, like the gender of the hijras, the culture inscribes considerations of masculinity and manhood into an irresolvable dialectic.

This indeterminacy also marks the society's response to the figure of the hijra. The Indian community's attitude is equally difficult to categorize: the hijras are both respected and ridiculed. On the one hand, Hindu religious myths and legends extol the qualities associated with *klibatva*: the harmonious intermingling, in equal parts, of the feminine and masculine principles within one body. According to some forms of Hindu belief, the Supreme Being itself manifests the qualities associated with hermaphroditism, possessing both female and male principles. Shiva, one of the three major gods of the Hindu pantheon, is frequently depicted as "Ardhanariswara," i.e., half man-half woman. According to the legend, the "ardhanariswara" form of Shiva results from his union with his consort, Parvati. Thus, in painting and sculpture, Shiva is frequently represented as a hermaphrodite with female characteristics on her left side and male on his right.[17] There are also many legends in which the male gods take on female form (I have not been able to uncover any goddesses who engage in similar activities, although there do exist myths about women transforming themselves into men). Vishnu, another of the three major gods, became an enchanting beauty known as Mohini—one who attracts—in order to settle a dispute among the gods and demons. Shiva was so enticed by the charms of Mohini that he begged Vishnu to revert to this form again. When Vishnu obliged, the two gods engaged in intercourse, giving birth to Harihara, a hermaphrodite deity and one of the ruling deities of the hijras. The repressed homosexual content of this myth needs no comment.

Given this tradition, the respect evoked by the hijras in the conservative elements of the Hindu society should not come as a particular surprise. Their presence is required at certain rituals and ceremonies, specifically those dealing with issues of fertility. Hence it is a common practice to have hijras sing and dance at the wedding or birth of a son. They are requested to bless the groom and the new-born son in order to confer prosperity and fertility. This may seem questionable, considering the fact that the hijras, due to self-inflicted or natural causes, are unable to procreate, but another legend about Shiva provides the answer. This legend, often referred to as a myth of origins for the hijras, has as its subject the self-castration that Lord Shiva endured to people the earth. This myth holds a very significant place in the hearts of devout Hindus who customarily worship the Shiva-lingam. The Shiva-lingam, ordinarily translated as the divine phallus, is actually a replica of the mutilated penis of Shiva—a penis thrown off in the act of castration. The lingam, thus, becomes a source of universal fertility as soon as it has ceased to be a source of individual fertility. This bears directly on the position of the hijras whose refusal to appropriate the penis for purposes of individual procreation grants them, analogous to the god Shiva, the ability to confer fertility on others. So although the hijras may be intersexed, impotent, and unable to reproduce, they can, through emasculation, transform their perceived liabilities into a source of creative power. It is the Hindu theme of creative asceticism that provides an explanation of the positive role given the hijra in the Indian society.

Furthermore, this approbation extends to the hijra practice of dressing like women; in the Hindu culture this is not a particularly aberrant eccentricity. There exist numerous narratives of saints and gods who attempt to reach *klibatva* through meditation and practice. In fact, two of the more well-known reformers of Hinduism in the nineteenth and the twentieth centuries—Chaitanya and Ramakrishna—both dressed as women and adopted feminine habits and mannerisms in order to combine the two principles more effectively. In this regard, one may consider Gandhi's desire "to be God's eunuch" as part of a long tradition of Hindu religious beliefs. Male cross-dressing is often encouraged in certain sects in Hinduism. Despite their androgyny, the major gods are still very much identified as male figures, so the believers often seek to achieve union with the gods by becoming their "wives." Male followers of these sects dress like women and affect the behaviors, habits, and movements of women, including the imitation of menstruation, during which they abstain from worship. In the past, many of them used to emasculate themselves, and all were supposed to play the role of women during sexual intercourse—that is, to allow themselves to be penetrated as an act of devotion.[18] The term, hijra, is also applied to these men.

Furthermore, when individuals join a hijra community, they take female names and use female kinship terms, such as "sister," "aunt," or "grandmother" for each other. In public transport or other public accommodations, hijras request the "ladies only" seating, and periodically demand to be counted among the females in the census. Despite all this, however, the hijras evince no interest in "passing," as do many Western transsexuals or transvestites. That is to say there is no attempt to seriously imitate or to be considered indistinguishable from the "normal" woman in Indian society. In fact, it is not at all uncommon to see hijras wearing saris and sporting beards of several days' growth. Their gestures and dress burlesque feminine behavior, and their performances and mannerisms are exaggerated to the point of caricature. They also use sexually explicit language and gestures in opposition to the Indian ideal of demure and restrained femininity. The hijras seem to engage in a deliberate parodic rendition of a culturally validated model of feminine behavior.

The disjunction between their stated gender identity and their performance of that identity is perhaps one of the reasons why the hijras are mocked and derided. All the positive instances and stories, and the recourse to religion and mythological beliefs that I have recounted at some length, do not impinge upon the material conditions of the hijras in contemporary India. Neither alms nor payment for performances enables them to exist comfortably. Most of them live in poverty and are ridiculed as they go about their daily work. This scorn and abuse derive from a number of sources. Many Indians no longer believe in the religious sanctions that authorize a special, sacred role for the hijras. But perhaps, even more significantly, the hijras existing in the margins of Indian society are subject to the contempt reserved for those who are perceptually different from the accepted norm. The impossibility of categorizing the hijras in terms of their sex *or* gender does not render them invisible. Actually, the effect is quite the opposite, considering the normally quite loud and brazen behavior as well as the flashy clothes indulged in by the hijras. While it is impossible to ignore them, the type of attention that the hijras get is more often than not derogatory and malicious. Straddling the boundaries between male and female, as well as between masculinity and femininity, the hijras present an obvious threat to any society based on these binary divisions. The hijras, in fact, call into question the basic social categories of gender on which Indian society is built.

III.

"Women is easy to understand," Jake said, "they're just like men, more or less, almost, an' sometimes."[19]

The more we learn from the hijras the harder it is for us to accept feminism the way it has hitherto been defined. For the hijras insistently call into question the parameters that delimit feminism and its scope. Probably the most restricting romance in which feminism has unquestioningly engaged has been its coupling with "woman"—both in its gendered and sexed manifestation. The confining aspects of the relationship between the two are brought into relief once the hijras join the affair. In fact, by refusing to accede to demands that they announce their identity in terms of a binary, the hijras create a wedge between the signifier (feminism) and its signified (woman). The sign no longer functions as significant. The very idea of feminism, when allied to women assumes the existence of a binary opposition between men and women. We have already seen how that opposition cannot be maintained in terms of a gender divide. The hijras, however, tell us that it cannot be maintained even in terms of a sexual divide.

It is by now a veritable commonplace of cultural criticism that sex and gender do not have a natural or innate bond. In other words, the old argument about nature and culture is replayed in terms of a biological sex and a culturally inscribed notion of gender.[20] What this means for most of us is that while biology or anatomy may be destiny, gender (or how we deal with that biology) lies within the realm of free will.[21] On the one hand, the hijras certainly seem to validate the truth of this formulation. By parodying and exaggerating feminine gestures, the hijras demonstrate the manner in which a female body is culturally constructed to articulate its gender. By splitting the sex from its gender, they seem to deconstruct the way in which culture inscribes the relationship between sex and gender as natural. On the other hand, for most of the hijras (and trans-sexuals) gender is destiny, while anatomy may be subject to change. That is to say, the hijras actually indicate a basic flaw in this formulation, which seems to regard biology as being somehow outside the domain of culture. It is not only one's gender that belongs in the domain of culture but also one's sex.

I want to clarify that I am not denying that the linkage between sex and gender is artificial and culturally constructed. What I want to emphasize is that the division between the two is equally artificial: not that gender necessarily follows from sex but that both are *unnaturally* constructed. In other words, while most of us are perfectly willing to accept Beauvoir's formulation: "One is not born, but rather becomes, a woman,"[22] I want to insist that one is not born but rather becomes a female as well. Sex and gender are both products of culture. There can be no biological sex that exists in isolation (as a *tabula rasa* so to speak) from the gendered determinations of culture.[23] The very sexing of the body is a response to cultural genderisms. Or to slightly misquote Dr. Anne Fausto-Sterling: "How small does a penis have to be before we can call it a clitoris?"[24]

However, the adjudication or doctoring of a sexed identity through medicine is not the only reason to radically question the sex/gender opposition in terms of its alliance with the nature/culture divide.[25] The example presented by the hijras leads to a re-working of the whole nature/culture dichotomy. The demarcation between the two, such that both "nature" and "culture" exist as two identifiable and distinct spheres (though overlapping occasionally), is not authorized by any transcendent principle. The operation of the antithesis between nature and culture facilitates an understanding of the structural determinations of society. But this understanding is based on a false dichotomy: that we can identify what is natural and hence not formulated through human agency, and what is cultural and hence available for immediate access and intervention.

But the opposition between the two, the drawing of the divisions, is itself a human act—an act performed from within the constraints of culture. Take for instance, the way in which a wilderness is situated against a cultivated garden. One seems to belong to the category of nature and the other of culture. But the mere fact of creating such a distinction between the two, of situating the wilderness within the sphere of nature, is itself a cultural act. The wilderness is set up as a realm against which the cultivated garden is made to signify the workings of culture. In effect, the determination of one—the wilderness—as "not-culture" is a cultural necessity, performed in order to make viable and intelligible the workings of culture in the other—the cultivated garden. Thus, it is not only the gendered notions of masculinity and femininity, but also the biological sexual determinations that are brought to a crisis by the hijras. The cultural effect of the hijras is to destabilize all such binary divisions, including sex and gender. Thus, the concepts of either an authentic woman or an authentic female are exploded.

A couple of questions remain: do the hijras, through their ambiguous gender and sexual identity, provide a liberatory strategy for breaking with dominant ideologies? Does the explosion of the concept of authenticity provide a smooth highway along which feminism can proceed with impunity? Is the "gender-fuck," represented by the hijras, a wonderful chance for us to thumb our noses at the tenacity of cultural mandates? The answers unfortunately, are "no." In order to understand and emphasize that the hijra role does *not* offer a utopian escape from the dominance of culture, a move beyond the prison of gender into a realm of free and happy sexing, I think it is important to reconsider the ambivalent attitudes displayed towards the hijras. Of course, some of their personal narratives are an adequate testimony opposing such easy resolutions. For instance, Nanda recounts that most of the hijras seemed to alternate between viewing their lives as having an authentic ritual validity and as being merely "a convenient niche for gender 'misfits.'"[26] According to Meera, being a hijra is "God's answer. He made us this way, because we have to make a living; he made people like us so we can earn."[27] Salina disclosed that her "parents were sad when I was born, 'neither here nor there.' The doctors all said, 'No, it [the organ] won't grow, your child is not a man, and not a woman.'"[28] These accounts certainly do not encourage consideration of the hijra role as one of unrelieved freedom from societal and cultural constraints.

But perhaps, even more significantly, their positions as being both inside and outside of society (inside insofar as the hijra role has a sacred significance and is validated by religious sanctions, and outside in that they are the butt of jokes and abuses directed to those who are considered to be outside the pale of normalcy) is merely a misapprehension. While they may seem to inhabit a space of contradictions, on closer inspection, the contradictions seem to vanish. In fact, both these positions—of respect and scorn—are authorized by the dominant culture. There isn't any outside of culture that is available to the hijras; the framing of society that allows a marginal space to them is configured by the same culture that deems them important for its religious rituals. The two opposing responses do not allow for a subversion of society; their simultaneous effect is one of complementarity. The religious sanctions undercut any effective rebellion from the margins, and the marginal position defies any attempt to gain a dominant status based on divine authority. In effect, the role of the hijras is structured so as to perpetuate the authority of the hegemonic culture.[29]

What then is the purpose of learning about the hijras, other than as an anthropological curiosity? The inquiry into the hijra-role may not provide us with a representation of the margins as being relatively free from the restraints of the dominant culture, but it does indicate that the binarisms between nature and culture and between the center and the margin are all culturally inscribed and institutionalized. And what, to return to the original question, does this have to do with the issue of feminism? To answer this, I must refer to the issue of ambivalence that has been foregrounded at almost every step of the analysis of the hijras in Indian society. It is this ambivalence that refuses a binary divide, a simple opposition, such that there is no singular or unitary truth of identity. This essay has not been an attempt to reveal the truth about the hijras so that the margins of feminism (along with the consciousness of feminists) may be expanded. The hijras and any of the various "others" that we may so designate make explicit those assumptions that determine the form and function of sundry disciplines.

It is not coincidental, then, that the emergence of a feminist movement within the United States gave rise to a "masculinist" movement. The men's movement came into existence as a response to feminist scholarship. The feminist questioning of masculinity as forming the horizon of generic human experience directed attention toward the study of masculinity as a specifically male experience.[30] The constructions, as distinct and separate, were based, in part, on the desire to keep distinct the genres of discourse so that they may not enter into any inter-disciplinary conflict. However, at the margins, where the divisions get blurred, we have to accept the possibility of adulteration of one discipline by another, and we have to foreground the conflicts that exist at the border of these modes of discourse and bring these to the center. The adulteration is apparent not only in the specific cases of intersexuality, but also in the many similar approaches and modes of inquiry that the two movements utilize.

The desire to keep the disciplines separate and the conflict at the margins is not merely a result of the famed timorousness of academics. The "internal" peace, bought at the price of persistent confrontation at the outskirts, is necessary for the construction and perpetuation of identity based on the essence of these modes of discipline. But what is the essence of a female identity, or of a male identity? And are we willing to concede any text, any mode of inquiry, any subject as lying outside the domain of feminist inquiry? Feminism, as theory and practice, as critical re-readings and as subversive practices, must lie, not with, but *beside* women, and yes, *beside* men. These gendered or sexed divisions, in fact, serve the purpose of containment, a strategy that would keep everything and everybody in their places, a neat little ghettoization of disciplines that would enable the perpetuation of status quo, with the added advantage of being politically correct. We simply add another item to the list, and create an orthodoxy with its own power structures. In regard to the academy, this means that while the proliferation of departments may be especially attractive to those of us struggling to find a job, it would defeat precisely the purpose of bringing the margins to the center. Just as a study of the hijras subverts any structural integrity of feminism, so must a consideration of feminism subvert any concept that authorizes insularity, both within disciplines and through the disciplining of the "margins." This is not a feminist call for arms to all the sisters under the skin. On the contrary, what I am suggesting is that we must re-evaluate the basis of our strategies of connection and division. As the hijras demonstrate the speciousness of the notion of "authentic genders," feminism must scrupulously interrogate and study the foundations of its existence.

NOTES |

1   Serena Nanda, *Neither Man nor Woman: The Hijras of India* (Belmont: California University Press, 1990), p. 15.

2   See Homi K. Bhabha's "DissemiNation," *Nation and Narration* (London: Routledge, 1990) which develops this idea in reference to the formation of a national culture and national identity.

3   See for instance G. M. Carstairs, *The Twice Born* (London: Hogarth Press, 1957), and M. Opler, "The Hijras of India and Indian National Culture," *American Anthropologist* 62 (1960), pp. 505–511.

4   Nanda, *Neither Man nor Woman*, p. 16.

5   Oscar Wilde, "Phrases and Philosophies for the Use of the Young," *The Importance of Being Earnest and Related Writings*, ed. Joseph Bristow (London: Routledge, 1992), p. 200.

6   Audre Lorde, *Sister Outsider* (Freedom, CA: The Crossing Press, 1984), p. 112.

7   To a certain extent the belief that merely bringing various injustices to light is enough to authorize a change in the system, is encouraged by the dominant groups. It serves as a necessary safety valve, and provides an excellent alibi for present injustices. Most of the important changes in the system are brought about through repeated attacks (both verbal and physical) making the continuation of the system, as it exists, unfavorable to those who had formerly profited from it. But it is in the interest of the dominant groups to take credit for these changes, to present them as responses to hitherto unrecognized grievances. Hence, the end of colonial domination in India, for instance, has been presented as occurring due to the awareness of the British that colonizing another country was an unfair practice. It was their finally awakened sense of fair play and justice that led them to give up their colonies. It is merely coincidental, according to this logic, that this 'awakening' transpired during massive revolts from the colonies.

8   Edward Said, "The Politics Of Knowledge," *Raritan* xi, 1, (Summer 1991), p. 26.

9   I wish to clarify that "discipline of feminism" does not refer exclusively to its status in the academy manifested in the feminist influence on various modes of inquiry or in the existence of Women's Studies departments. The term "discipline," in this case, pertains to the implicit and explicit rules and regulations that govern the functioning of the feminist movement, as well as its mode of analysis (internally and externally directed) both inside and outside of the university. In any case, the division between the academy and the "outside world" is not one that is accepted by a number of feminists.

10 Susan Bordo, "Feminism, Postmodernism, and Gender-Scepticism," *Feminism/ Postmodernism*, ed. Linda J. Nicholson (New York: Routledge, 1990), p. 138.

11 According to Judith Butler, "The term 'universality' would have to be left permanently open, permanently contested, permanently contingent, in order not to foreclose in advance future claims for inclusion" ("Contingent Foundations," *Feminists Theorize the Political*, ed. Judith Butler and Joan Scott [New York: Routledge, 1992], p. 8).

12 As Christina Crosby points out, "The problem is that differences are taken to be self-evident, concrete, *there*, present in history and therefore the proper ground of theory. Theory is identical with history: …[leading to] a circularity in which only what is already known—'differences,' for example—can be seen. It is impossible to ask how differences is constituted as a concept, so 'differences' become Substantive, something in themselves—race, class, and gender—as though we knew already what this incommensurate triumvirate means!" ("Dealing with Differences," *Feminists Theorize the Political*, p.137).

13 In this context see Frantz Fanon's *Black Skin White Masks*, tr. Charles Lam Markmann (New York: Grove Weidenfeld, 1967) and Ashis Nandy's *The Intimate Enemy: Loss and Recovery of Self under Colonialism* (Delhi: Oxford University Press, 1983).

14 I am referring to the Gramscian concept stating that hegemony functions by making the subjected peoples acquiesce to their subjugation through the force of opinion and persuasion. According to Gramsci: "the supremacy of a social group manifests itself in two ways, as 'domination' and as 'intellectual and moral leadership'…. It seems clear…that there can, and indeed must be hegemonic activity even before the rise to power, and that one should not count only on the material force which power gives in order to exercise an effective leadership" (*Selections From the Prison Notebooks*, ed. Quintin Hoare and Geoffrey Nowell Smith [London: Lawrence and Wishart, 1971], p. 57).

15 Khushwant Singh, *Delhi: A Novel* (New Delhi: Penguin Books, 1990), p. 179.

16 Judith Still and Michael Worton, "Introduction," *Textuality and Sexuality: Reading Theories and Practices* (Manchester: Manchester University Press, 1993), p. 49.

17 For a more detailed study on Indian myths see Wendy O'Flaherty's *Women, Androgynes, and Other Mythical Beasts* (Chicago: University of Chicago Press, 1980).

18 I am indebted to Vern L. Bullough's and Bonnie Bullough's *Cross Dressing, Sex and Gender* (Philadelphia: University of Pennsylvania Press, 1993) for this information.

19 David Bradley, *South Street* (New York: Scribner Signature Editions, 1975), p. 174.

20 Judith Shapiro defines the relationship between sex and gender as "at once a motivated and an arbitrary one. It is motivated insofar as there must be reasons for the cross-culturally universal use of sex as a principle in systems of social differentiation; it is arbitrary, or conventional, insofar as gender differences are not directly derivative of natural, biological facts, but rather vary from one culture to another in a way in which they order experience and action. In any society the meaning of gender is constituted in the context of variety of domains—political, economic, etc.—that extend beyond what we think of gender per se" ("Transsexualism: Reflections on the Persistence of Gender and the Mutability of Sex," *Body Guards: The Cultural Politics of Gender Ambiguity*, ed. Julia Epstein and Kristina Straub [New York: Routledge, 1991], p. 271).

21 Free will in this context is merely used in opposition to biological or anatomical determinations. I do not mean to imply that choosing a gender is covered by, say, the Freedom of Choice Act. Currently, biology seems, for the most part, inaccessible to human intervention, determining whether we are born with a vagina or a penis. But what we do with these organs is, to a limited extent, up to us. What the possession of these organs means is determined by culture; the only "free will" we possess is in nuancing those meanings slightly, not in overthrowing the bounds of gender.

22 "No biological, psychological, or economic fate determines the figure that the human female presents in society; it is civilization as a whole that produces this creature" (*The Second Sex*, tr. H. M. Parshley [New York: Vintage Books, 1974], p. 301).

23 Judith Butler makes the same argument in *Bodies That Matter* (New York: Routledge, 1993) when she writes about the "construal of 'sex' no longer as a bodily given on which the construct of gender is artificially imposed, but as a cultural norm which governs the materialization of bodies" (p. 3).

24 Anne Fausto-Sterling, *Myths of Gender: Biological Theories About Women and Men* (New York: Basic Books, 1985), pp. 84–85. The interpellation of a subject as male or female may be most visible in medical practices, but is not specific to them. If we accept that sex and sexuality are determined by cultural constraints, then the way in which we articulate our sex depends on our adoption of norms which makes such articulation comprehensible. In other words, the subject assumes a sex and then depicts that sex through the various rules and regulations which govern its performance.

25 The management of sex through medical intervention is a lot more common in the West than in India. As Suzanne J. Kessler reports in "The Medical Construction of Gender: Case Management of Intersexed Infants," physicians determine the sex of intersexed babies, basing their deliberations on "such factors as the 'correct' length of the penis and the capacity of the vagina" (*Signs* 16, 1 [Autumn 1990], p. 3).

26 Serena Nanda, "The Hijras of India: Cultural and Individual Dimensions of an Institutionalized Third Gender Role," *Journal of Homosexuality* 11, 3/4 (1985), p. 45.

27 Nanda, *Neither Man nor Woman*, p. 75.

28 Nanda, *Neither Man nor Woman*, p. 99.

29 Judith Butler makes a somewhat similar point in her discussion of Herculine's ambiguous sexuality: "Whether 'before' the law as a multiplicitous sexuality, or 'outside' the law as an unnatural transgression, these positionings are invariably 'inside' a discourse which produces sexuality and then conceals that production through a configuring of a courageous and rebellious sexuality 'outside' of the text itself" (*Gender Trouble: Feminism and the Subversion of Identity* [New York: Routledge, 1990], p. 99).

30 In this connection see Harry Brod's "A Case for Men's Studies," *Changing Men*, ed. Michael S. Kimmel (New Delhi: Sage Publications, 1987), pp. 263–277. While Brod argues most comprehensively for support of men's studies in terms of its connection to women's studies, most of the popular works on the men's movement prefer to ignore this connection. For instance, Robert Bly's *Iron John* (New York: Addison-Wesley Publishing Co., 1990), while adopting the principles of consciousness-raising from the women's movement, resolutely demarcates the techniques and the results of such exercises. The book, thus, turns out to be a rather defensive guide, couched in mythic langage, on how to be "manly men."

Could the room without a name be evidence of a growing desire to provide a framework within which the members of a family will be better equipped to enjoy each other on the basis of mutual respect and affection? Might it thus indicate a deep-seated urge to reassert the validity of the family by providing a better design for living? We should very much like to think so, and if there is any truth in this assumption, our search for a name is ended—we should simply call it the "family room…"

—George Nelson and Henry Wright,
*Tomorrow's House: A Complete Guide for
the Home-Builder*

If I am right, the problem that has no name stirring in the minds of so many American women today is not a matter of loss of femininity or too much education, or the demands of domesticity. It is far more important than anyone recognizes. It is the key to these other new and old problems which have been torturing women and their husbands and children, and puzzling their doctors and educators for years. It may well be the key to our future as a nation and a culture.

—Betty Friedan, *The Feminine Mystique*

My name is Ruth.
—Marilynne Robinson, *Housekeeping*[1]

10

HOUSEBREAKING HISTORY

Feminism's Troubled Romance with the Domestic Sphere

Dana Heller

SPACES, WOMEN, HISTORY

I begin this essay with side by side passages from three vastly different post-World War II texts to emphasize feminist historiography's status as a field of competing discourses, each struggling to establish woman's prop-

er place through an act of naming.[2] On the American home front, in the years
following the Second World War, this competition intensified. In 1946, George
Nelson and Henry Wright dubbed a new household terrain in accordance with
the postwar imperatives of domesticity and family unity. Behind their call for
"mutual respect and affection" was undoubtedly a degree of concern about
woman's changing role in the public sphere and its impact on employment
opportunities for returning G.I.s. However, Nelson's and Wright's "new design
for living" is more than a precautionary move against anticipated economic
shifts. It suggests a need to unify and spatially recodify the female subject. Woven
into the manifesto-style rhetoric is a concern with containing that network of
relations and sentiments associated with the feminine. While the passage avoids
any direct expression of gender-specificity, it implies a turn away from Rosie
the Riveter as representative of culture's feminine ideal. Waiting in the wings
to take Rosie's place were Donna Stone and June Cleaver, television moms who
gracefully embodied the values of "the room without a name" in their visibly
wholesale commitment to the domestic sphere.

In 1950, when the popular women's magazine *Better Homes and Gardens*
renamed the "room without a name" the "family-television room," it was a
sign that efforts to unify the post-war family romance were under siege by the
very exigencies of its mass-marketability.[3] The marriage of the intimately
sequestered nuclear family and its correlative cultural ideal, the television set,
indicated that the terms of woman's centrality within the private sphere were
far less stable than they might have appeared on *Make Room For Daddy*. These
terms were, in fact, conditioned by a moral obligation to consume the new technologies that vied with one another to rename "woman's sphere." Accordingly,
advertising strategies were developed to equate the value of household gadgetry
with *both* women's responsiveness to family needs and their own needs for self-
empowerment.

Thirteen years later, in 1963, Betty Friedan sought to evaluate the impact that
contradictions such as these were having on women's lives. In *The Feminine
Mystique*, Friedan asked readers to look deeply into the recesses of the room that
has no name in order to recognize "a problem that has no name." The fami-
ly/television room was redubbed a prison house in which hundreds of thousands
of American women struggled with inarticulate longings. *The Feminine Mystique*
thus proceeded to reject the name that had architecturally circumscribed middle-
class American women in an effort to raise awareness of their subordination to
patriarchy's romance with the family.

Undoubtedly, *The Feminine Mystique* contributed significantly to a new pop-
ularization of feminist consciousness raising, primarily among women who could
claim the social and economic status necessary to pursue the goals Friedan

encouraged; higher education and professional credentials. However, the terms of the second wave's leading banner, "the personal is political," were organized around a spatial problematic inherited from the nineteenth-century women's suffrage movement. This movement cleverly appropriated the late Victorian concept of "the angel in the house" to assure skeptics that by granting women the right to vote, the virtues of domesticity would be brought outward into the public sphere, to the moral benefit of all. In the mid-1960s, this challenge to an ideology of separate spheres found expression not in the promise of moral betterment, but in the revisionary logic of a motto suggesting that history was not—and had never been—a discourse of consensus, but a field of opposition where oedipus and ideology, femininity and masculinity, private family and public marketplace, criss-crossed and mutually constructed one another.

A serious theoretical oversight of pioneering feminists like Friedan was the failure to acknowledge the same oppositions and contradictions in feminism's own evolving critique of the domestic sphere. As the quotations placed at the outset of this essay are intended to demonstrate, this evolving critique may be read—and perhaps should be read—as romance, or as multiple redescriptions of the controversial and illusive sub-genre known as family romance. In this regard, the three quotations may be read as a kind of narrative, a story built upon a convergence of discursive trajectories driven by American feminism's anxieties about its historical relationship to the ideology of separate social spheres, the family romance of classical psychoanalysis, and the semiotics of popular culture's focus on the domestic. In the following pages, I will to examine this convergence for the purpose of understanding feminism's resistance to its own history, a resistance founded on a rejection of a structurally unified domestic sphere, or a consensual family romance.

Over the more than a century of development of feminism as a political movement and, more recently, an academic institution, the genre of family romance has served feminist historiographers in inconsistent and contradictory ways. However, since the end of World War II, these contradictions have increasingly become the object of focus for feminists rather than obstructions on the path toward a unified analysis of woman's oppression. In some instances, this has led to a rejection of domestic tropes and matrifocal theories as alternative paradigms for representing the female subject. In a recent narrative account of the history of feminist literary criticism, a story told through an examination of critical anthologies, Jane Gallop concludes that while history is in some ways like mother, it is also "not like mother." "I am beginning to realize," Gallop admits, at the end of a text that itself amounts to a lengthy meditation on the maternal, "that feminists need to stop reading everything through the family romance."[4]

But *whose* family romance is this anyway? Gallop suggests that feminists have relied too much on Oedipal themes and familial metaphors that have limited their engagements with culture to a self-perpetuating reiteration of the "Mommy Dearest" motif. In its place, she recommends that feminist critics see themselves as "pros," outlaw agents of a public sphere which Gallop privileges over the worn-out domestic spaces of earlier feminist centralization. But as Bonnie Zimmerman demonstrates in a discussion of recent lesbian criticism, there is an equally long history of radical feminist self-fashioning that relies on images of female "outlaws, and transgressors against Man's law."[5] The question I pose in this essay concerns feminism's efforts to disentangle itself from this dualistic dilemma. Does representing feminist history in a postfeminist age really come down to the choice Gallop seems to offer, a choice between naming ourselves as insiders or outsiders to the family romance? How is feminism's anti-romance with the family related to current debates over the usefulness of separate sphere ideology as a means of identifying the origin of women's oppression? And how do recent reconfigurations of narrative genre embody these debates so as to suggest the necessity of placing feminism against itself?

Zimmerman broadly addresses these questions when she suggests that feminist critical strategies have changed over the course of the last several years, thus displacing the very terms of Gallop's distinction. "This shift…is reflected in the tropes we now use…. Metaphors of position and space now dominate in the way those of sight did a decade ago."[6] Indeed, the spatial concerns that underwrite postmodernism's vocabulary of textual and social production suggest a complete rethinking of the meanings of those spaces that have historically represented women. The condition of postmodernity rejects, or at least questions those conceptual boundaries used to maintain divisions between works of high culture and works of popular culture, social institutions and individuals, fictional and non-fictional modes of writing.

A corresponding feminist spatial problematic is pre-figured in contemporary feminism's self-acknowledged over-investment in the historical validity of the separation of public and private spheres as the source of women's oppression. And while some feminist/gender theorists applaud this commitment to the partial, the plural, and the local as a movement away from essentialism, others worry that the emphasis on a "politics of location" delimits the potential viability of a feminist movement.

For this reason, I think it worthwhile to study the cultural roots of feminism's changing relation to family romance as history and history as family romance. And in addition, I propose that the realignment of spatial subjectivity, which feminism has undertaken throughout the course of the twentieth-century and in the various refashionings of its history, is most powerfully, albeit ironically, inscribed in contemporary fictional narratives that make use of the traditional themes and dynamics of classical family romance precisely in order to redescribe those dynamics in light of recent skepticism concerning the usefulness of categories such as "identity," "family," and "genre." This skepticism implies a shift from an idealization of coherence, linearity, and origin to a preoccupation with representational systems themselves—i.e. texts and various semiotic networks—as constitutive of what the familially situated subject takes to be her "self." However, what I offer by way of defining a post-family romance is speculative and partial. My hope, for the purposes of this essay, is to lay some of the groundwork that such a definition might require.[7]

MASTERS, HOUSES, TOOLS

Isn't storytelling always a way of searching for one's origin, speaking one's conflicts with the Law, entering into the dialectic of tenderness and hatred?
—Roland Barthes, *The Pleasure of the Text* [8]

Romance has long been theorized by feminists and non-feminists alike as a limit-breaking genre, a genre of excess. However, the sub-genre known as family romance has often been misrepresented by feminist critics as a tool of patriarchal ideology, a genre that enforces rather than exceeds limits. Obviously, any reading of the romance can promote its purely formalistic values, in which case family romance is about the impending threats and ultimate restorations of spatial boundaries that organize historical narrative: the boundaries of public and private, of older and younger generations, of social class, race, and gender. In this regard, Tony Tanner's classic study of the bourgeois European novel, *Adultery in the Novel*, still provides one of the more comprehensive and compelling analyses of the genre's history.[9] Here, he specifies the figure of the adulterous woman as symbolizing a disruption to the boundaries of inside/outside and a threat to patriarchal authority in both the public and private sphere. Indeed, these boundaries have remained to a significant degree mutually constitutive of properly gendered subjectivity and legible narrative acts. Nevertheless, while the efficacy of social hegemonies and cultural representations has historically depended on maintaining a sense of certain categorical oppositions as stable, contemporary feminism (like Tanner's adulterous woman) has become the trope of a fundamentally decentered historical consciousness. In the dissolving master narratives of family romance, female subjects are produced as flashpoints of dualistic instability and historical contingency.[10] And while the conventional generic function of family romance has been to resolve woman's destabilizing potential for the constitution of the masculine subject—a function reified in the Freudian formulation of subjectivity—it appears that more recent family romances differ in their willingness, in effect, to foreground the dissolution, or to put the female subject to work in highly productive and contradictory ways that challenge traditional accounts of personal and public history.

But how personal is the political? Where do we experience most powerfully the overlaps and stress points of the personal and the political? These questions have become the source of deep debate within feminist criticism. The terms of this debate stem from the genealogy of separate sphere ideology, a gender-specific system of belief that has long organized feminism's thinking about the institutional structuring of modern Western society. More importantly, the doctrine of separate spheres has been a powerful influence on feminism's thinking about itself and its own origin. By seeming to satisfy Western feminism's wish to legitimate and unify its own purposes by naming a singular source of women's social and economic oppression, the private/public separation has fueled the construction of a totalizing narrative, the result of which has been the erasure of differences within and among women. However, as Linda Nicholson points out in *Gender and History: Social Theory in the Age of the Family*, there exists within contemporary feminism an increasing recognition "that the divisions between...spheres are not as rigid as we are led to believe and that conceiving them in such a manner obscures the realities of women's lives."[11]

Nicholson explains that early feminists inherited the terms of this separation from eighteenth and nineteenth century discourses such as psychoanalysis, liberalism, and Marxism. As industrialization and newly emergent social institutions engendered a growing separation of the family, the state, and the economy, these social theories were all attempts at producing new political alignments of the private and the public. However, these theories also tended to universalize their claims on history, suggesting that all cultures organize themselves according to the same categories and principles that Western culture has fashioned for itself. According to Nicholson, early feminist thinkers also relied on these categories, which necessarily limit historical analysis by reifying dualisms (such as public/private) and by privileging the notion of unified origin.

Thus, from the nineteenth-century establishment of feminism as a significant public discourse, feminist historiography has tended to construct the domestic sphere as an arena of female consensus in opposition to increasingly multiple and contradictory public spheres. And while this is still the logic many feminists use in their analyses of history, more and more critics are abandoning these terms, and abandoning as well the search for a universal source or origin of women's oppression. Contemporary feminism's focus on the family emphasizes its status as a social rather than natural formation. By recognizing the family's complex interconnections with the rest of society, feminists "have begun to develop the means for becoming self-conscious about the very historical forces which have brought modern feminism into being."[12] For this reason, Nicholson argues, contemporary feminism offers the best position from which to theorize the relations of private and public as historically contingent.

Contemporary feminism has indeed become far more self-conscious about the need to acknowledge historical contingencies and fluidity as a feature of all narrative, including its own master-narratives. However, what Nicholson overlooks, in her otherwise comprehensive analysis, is the extent to which this fluidity is built into the very discourses in opposition to which feminism has defined itself—discourses that intersect with and help shape feminist historiography. In other words, the fluidity of public and private spheres is no more the unique revelation of a discrete feminist perspective than essentialism is the unique product of a discrete psychoanalytic, liberal, or Marxist tradition. And while my own spatial constraints prohibit me from providing a theory-by-theory proof of this claim, I want to turn briefly to Freud's essay on "Family Romances" in order to show how contemporary feminism's redescription of public/private limits rehearses a poetics of resistance similar to that which is utilized by the genre of romance *and* by psychoanalytic theories of familially-situated subjectivity.

In "Family Romances," Sigmund Freud describes a "specific form of imaginative activity," a fantasy that structurally unifies normative subjectivity and social consensus, while providing a bridge between the terrain of the bourgeois private sphere and the industrialized public sphere.[13] "Family Romances" thus proceeds to define the fantasy-that-has-no-name in terms of the culmination of the Oedipal drama, the "latter stage in the development of the neurotic's estrangement from his parents" through which the son struggles to accept the social privilege that is his birthright—paternal authority, or classical phallic masculinity.[14] By imaginatively reinventing the father, Freud suggests that the child imaginatively rewrites the history of modernity and by so doing constitutes a more secure basis upon which to articulate a coherent masculine self. The phallus becomes a lightening rod for those creative and intellectual forces which ultimately liberate the child from his guilty role within the family—defined as a reenactment of historical trauma—and insert him instead into his guilty role within history is defined as a reenactment of familial crisis and resolution.

However, Freud's family romance does more than consolidate the power of the phallus. Indeed, if anything it stresses the extent to which fantasy may be more "real" than reality in the formation of social privileges and sexual hegemony. By elaborating the stages of familial disentanglement, Freud laid the groundwork for theorizing that the family, like the romance which constitutes it, is poesy—which is to say that it is constructed through a collaboration of ego and history and made accessible to consciousness through the interpretive process.

Indeed, as Stephen Heath has suggested, it was Freud's essential vision of psychoanalysis to articulate a critical apparatus for an understanding of the family as the cultural catalyst for the relations of private fantasy and public belief. These relations remain for Freud generally formative of "subject coherence," and so, to the extent that such notions as "origin" and "subjectivity" have remained more or less unproblematized, family romance has remained the predominant paradigm of all narrative activity concerning "the provision and maintenance of fictions of the individual."[15] For Freud, as for the majority of European intellectuals at the turn of the century, subjective coherence was directly commensurate with the father, the locus of origin. However, Freud's privileging of origin suggests a more significant link between the paternal function and historical structures of representation, the collective fantasies that confer value upon ideological reality. In "Family Romances," origin does not denote a reality principle so much as a relation to specific narrative occasions. And indeed, what recent feminist re-readings of Freud invite us to consider are the implicit representational strategies by which the family, as private experience, comes into alignment with romance, or historical fantasy.

By challenging Freud's Oedipal terrain, feminism has developed some of its more forceful challenges to the universality of family romance. And coextensively, by challenging the family romance, feminism has engendered the rewriting of its own history. This new historicizing strategy often takes early feminist readings of Freud to task for assuming that he privileged inside over outside, or instinct over culture. Noting that Freudian theory plays ambiguously at the borderline of nature and culture, some "postmodern" feminists view the work of feminist essentialists and constructivists as naive in its insistence on locating Freud's theoretical commitment to the family either inside or outside of the house.[16] More recent critics such as Kaja Silverman and Jane Flax argue that Freud was uniquely successful in articulating the important connections between psychic and social spaces, ego and ideology.[17] Why, they implicitly ask, has it been so difficult for feminists to acknowledge that irresolution, contradiction, and incongruence are the compelling features of Freud's work? For Flax, the crucial move towards a more historically informed feminist theory would involve, on the contrary, an acceptance of the existence of antinomies and an investigation of "why Freud could neither recognize nor reconcile them."[18]

Nevertheless, it should also be noted that despite the recent accommodation of Freudian contexts to theoretical models that exteriorize consciousness, some commentators have usefully emphasized Freud's compulsion to return to the patriarchal family romance as the origin of human experience, an investment suggesting that psychoanalytic theory itself constitutes a sort of meta-romance.[19] Socialist feminists have rightly pointed out that Freud's preoccupation with formative fantasies involving the attainment of class rank serve as reminders that

Freud's thinking was the product of a particular historical moment that was witnessing the end of a consensual public sphere. However, what has not been sufficiently explored is the extent to which this development signaled the end of a consensual *private* sphere and a centralized definition of woman's role within the family.

Freud's "Family Romances" attempts to formally appropriate the genre of romance as an expression of a mutually productive subversion and ultimate recuperation of the patriarchal bourgeois family with its organizing metaphor of the phallus. Freud's identification of the fantasy-that-has-no-name suggests that there is no given or stable commensurablity between romance, as a narrative mode, and patriarchy, as a collection of mutually supportive institutions and beliefs that require narrative structures for their communication and credibility. Thus, to speak of "family romance" is perhaps to evoke a contradiction in terms, for while "the family" has been variously deployed throughout the discourses of Enlightenment rationalism to signify unity, consensus, nature, origin, privacy, nurturance, property, labor, and universality, "romance" troubles all of these concepts and asks us repeatedly to question the terms of their use. What Freud's essay shows, possibly in spite of itself, is that there is nothing inherently romantic about the family or, for that matter, familial about romance. Also suggested is the extent to which patriarchal logic has, throughout history, enacted certain distortions on romance, on the one hand appropriating it for its interests, on the other discrediting it as crudely popular, or mere "women's writing" when it claims to have no use for it.

Nevertheless, the ambiguities and slippages of Freud's essay on romance raise the possibility that, contrary to some critical claims, Freud was not romanticizing the family so much as familializing the romance, or rethinking the elusive inevitability of the romance across domestic boundaries. This transgression is established as the inevitable pre-condition of subjectivity, and in this regard the Freudian romance anticipates the border-disruptive aspects of feminist theory in subtle, albeit inconsistent ways. Indeed, for Freud, feminism and the family romance would seem mutually to establish one another as legitimate narratives precisely at the moment when they can no longer be contained within the respective limits of a consensual domestic sphere.

POSTCULTURE, POSTMODERNISM, POST-FAMILY ROMANCE

Even the illusion of perimeters fails when families are separated.
—Marilynne Robinson, *Housekeeping* [20]

One of the most influential figures for feminist reconstitutions of the family romance has been the French psychoanalyst Jacques Lacan. The Lacanian shift from an understanding of identity in terms of substance to identity in terms of lack, and the shift from a discrete and expressive human subject to a discrete and expressive symbolic order, has provided feminist theorists with important tools for intervention into the Freudian paradigm. For Freud, the family romance is wholly reliant on the power of the phallus; for Lacan the phallus is wholly reliant on the powers of language, or on the extrinsic operations of a linguistic romance that inevitably intrudes upon and splits the human subject. For Freud, identity is founded on the consolidation of the phallus; in the broadest sense, this is true of Lacan's rewriting of the romance as well; however, Lacan focuses far more critically than Freud on the extent to which the phallus, as universal signifier and agent of cultural disenfranchisement, remains always a symbol of lack.[21]

Lacan's work has helped make it possible for feminists to conceptualize the domestic sphere as first and foremost a symbolic system founded on the operations of language. However, critics of Lacan have pointed out that his work tends to enact a simplistic substitution whereby the universal structure of the bourgeois family is replaced with a far more totalizing universal structure of language. Critics also stress Lacan's association of the female with "otherness," an aberrant trope of resistance that compels the consolidation of dominant signifiers. This association is reiterated in aesthetic terms by Andreas Huyssen's claim that woman has historically represented high art's "other."[22] She remains, in this sense, the discursive mark of the low, of a popular aesthetic in contradistinction to which high art defines itself through exclusion. Indeed, modernism has been generally characterized by its self-distancing from, and strong distaste for, the mutually contaminating forces of the popular and the feminine. In the United States, women's association with a mass culture aesthetic has remained historically contingent, albeit pervasive and suspect, from Nathaniel Hawthorne's condemnation of the "damned, scribbling mob" of popular women writers of sentimental domestic fiction, to moralistic attacks against the postfeminist pop icon and multi-million dollar image manufacturer, Madonna.[23]

Throughout this evolution, family romance has represented another sort of "low" cultural engagement for women writers, an engagement that nevertheless affirms patriarchy's conceptual isolation of women within the domestic space. Such irony is compounded by the recognition that a reification of the American literary tradition has occurred, in this century, largely in accord with a critical tendency—most impressively demonstrated by Eric Sundquist's *Home As Found*, Richard Chase's *The American Novel and Its Tradition*, and Leslie Fiedler's *Love and Death in the American Novel*—to concentrate on the male American writer's ambiguous, yet powerfully romantic attachments to this domestic space and the concept of origin.[24]

However, just as contemporary feminism has changed woman's historical relationship to language and high culture, so has it changed our perception of woman's relationship to mass culture. Some recent theorists, taking issue with the Frankfurt School's equation of mass culture with fascism and user-passivity, are attending more thoughtfully to the user, to the agency of fans and audiences who, many conclude, *do* have some say.[25] Janice Radway's research on the dialectical relationship of female readers to romance fiction has been instructive in this sense, laying the basis for understanding that romance and social change are not necessarily exclusive to one another.

Radway's claim is that the romance form, while commonly acknowledged as eliciting readers' complicity with the status quo, also allows for resistance and subversion, if only in the act of reading itself. Thus, there may be, in the representation of family and in the organizing logic of romance, niches of feminist recuperation and resistance. Radway successfully questions the assumption that romance allows only for passive consumerism in its largely female readership. It is difficult to disagree with her insistence that to see readers as totally helpless and passive, and to see texts as totally dominating, is to "petrify the human act of signification."[26] Furthermore, Radway invites us to see that while "the ideological power of contemporary cultural forms is enormous, indeed sometimes even frightening...interstices still exist within the social fabric where opposition is carried on by people who are not satisfied by their place within it or by the restricted material and emotional rewards that accompany it."[27]

To a surprising degree, Radway's research served as a kind of cultural wake-up call, a reminder that woman's relation to mass culture forms and modes of production has become in many respects more conflictual than at any previous time in American cultural history. As feminist discourse has helped establish the politicization of the private sphere, the reading and writing of family romance has taken on new significance for women who feel themselves drawn to spaces where fantasy and reality overlap, or where their private yearnings and their public obligations as mothers, daughters, and lovers appear to merge. In other words, in the material and situational act of reading, fantasy begins to transgress its domestic barriers to establish the generic principle of historical excess, which Diane Elam identifies as characteristic of both romance *and* the postmodern.[28] To this extent, feminism and postmodernism would seem to have similar objectives in mind, objectives that become manifest in what I have provisionally termed post-family romance. Elam's study suggests that romance, and by association, the figure of woman, is identifiable as "the signature of postmodernism." However, Elam's argument works primarily to recuperate the meanings associated with the feminine for the canons of high theory, as her selection of textual examples would appear to indicate. Here, again, we see how feminism, in its determination to rescue woman from denigrating entanglements with the popular, is driven to sustain the traditional hierarchy of high culture/low culture divisions even as it celebrates the border tensions of contemporary theory.

According to Linda Hutcheon, such border tensions are primary features of postmodern expression. However, Hutcheon maintains the categorical division and structural hierarchy of high culture/low culture far more programmatically than Elam. This is particularly evident when she takes aim at Jean Baudrillard's description of television as the ultimate postmodern medium, insisting that television's "*unproblematized* reliance on realist narrative and transparent representational conventions" produce "pure commodified complicity, without the critique needed to define the postmodern paradox."[29] While such an argument may be perfectly valid, it would certainly appear to give little credit to the actual users of television, while assuming a culturally elitist perspective that patrols the very borders Hutcheon would otherwise praise postmodernism for disrupting.

Postmodernism's problematic challenge to the validity of high culture vs. popular culture distinctions is paralleled by its challenge to the dual-gender system, a movement that has precipitated a shift from the study of women to the study of "gender" as a historically situated, socially constructed, and largely discursive system. However, as gender theory and postmodernism explore (and in some cases explode) the limits of masculine and feminine subjectivity, and public and private spheres, they are creating new spaces in and across which new forms of writing may be engendered. As feminists proceed to theorize about the possibility of a post-family romance, we may expect to see, on the one hand, a celebration of such boundary-bashing, and on the other hand, a reactionary tendency to strengthen and police those borders. The private sphere has long served patriarchy as a symbol of confidence in the stability and shared value of the institutional structures of signification that organize society.

However, as semiotic systems of gender inscription have come increasingly under attack in the wake of feminism and post-structuralism, it stands to reason that the family romance, one of modernity's founding fictions, should come under attack as well. What social critics have been gloomily referring to over the course of the last several decades as the "crisis" of the American family might indicate more about the extent to which familial *images*, rather than realities, are experiencing something similar to what Silverman terms "ideological fatigue," or historical trauma, in relation to male subjectivity.[30] Perhaps we have not lost faith in the family itself, but in the efficacy of its representation, its symbolic logic. Indeed, there can no longer be, it seems, an image of the family that is not at the same time a parody of that institution, and there can be no family romance that does not at the same time cast a sidelong suspicious glance at its own generic conventions and history.

The cultural task at hand is thus a redescription of family romance from a master narrative whose structure is no longer viable to a narrative that decenters history and establishes the family romance as fundamentally ex-centric. In "Burning Down the House? Domestic Space and Feminine Subjectivity in Marilynne Robinson's *Housekeeping*," Paula E. Geyh enters upon the possibility of such a critique.[31] Geyh locates at the intersection of postmodernist and feminist theory a challenge to the "centrality of the space of the house in the construction of feminine subjectivity," a rethinking of the female subject across the boundaries of home as symbol.[32] In its validation of a transient feminine subjectivity, *Housekeeping*, Geyh argues, counters traditional narratives of male flight by situating some of its conventions beyond the limits of patriarchal institutions.[33]

Indeed, Robinson's novel has been much praised by feminist critics for its poetic transformations of conceptual dualisms such as private and public, self and other, inside and outside.[34] What is less observed is the novel's complex meditations on family romance in relation to history and domestic space. *Housekeeping* announces itself to be a post-family, feminist romance in its opening statement, an act of self-naming as ideologically charged as Wright and Nelson's designation of the "family room" or Friedan's identification of the nameless "problem" that afflicts women. "My name is Ruth," the narrative begins, thus wresting authority from the masculinist tradition of Melville's Ishmael. From here, the adolescent narrator, Ruth, proceeds to redescribe, from a uniquely transient perspective, those spaces from which female subjectivity has been historically positioned to speak.

In her efforts to comprehend the paradox that women don't keep house as much as houses keep women, Ruth is initiated by her Aunt Sylvie, a dedicated drifter whose unconventional sense of domestic maintenance requires no resistance to the forces of nature, weather, the outdoors. Dead leaves, pools of water, and decaying animal carcasses collect in the living room as Ruth observes that "Sylvie in a house was more or less like a mermaid in a ship's cabin. She preferred it sunk in the very element it was meant to exclude."[35] In this way, Sylvie transpositions houses, narrative, and family, indicating that these structures—like language itself—need to be viewed as symbolic attempts to fix women, events, and identity itself, to hold them in place against the inevitable disruptions that history will enact against all ideological notions of essence and coherence.

The climax of the novel occurs when the sheriff and townspeople move to separate Ruth and Sylvie out of concern for the latter's well-being. Before their daring escape across an elevated railroad bridge that symbolically separates the ordinary world of domesticity from the extraordinary world of female transience, Sylvie and Ruth attempt to set fire to the house that they have been living in, the house that Ruth's ancestors have lived in for generations. However, the fire dwindles before destroying the house. Reluctantly, they leave the structure still standing, as they will later observe from passing train windows. "For families will not be broken," Ruth narrates, "Curse and expel them, send their children wandering, drown them in floods and fires, and old women will make songs out of all these sorrows and sit in the porches and sing them on mild evenings. Every sorrow suggests a thousand songs, and every song recalls a thousand sorrows, and so they are infinite in number, and all the same."[36]

These images powerfully evoke the historical specificity *and* the desire for essence that connects women as authors and storytellers with family romance and popular narrative modes. In a manner that is both inventive and sensitive to past traditions, this passage suggests what I have been arguing throughout this essay. Robinson's *Housekeeping*, like so many epistemological projects at this time, is a narrative shaped by a paradigm shift that requires no less than a complete reevaluation of the spatial metaphors and historical narratives with which feminism has organized accounts of its own origins.

To be sure, recent controversy over disintegrating family structures is related to concern over disintegrating master narratives, social topographies, and identity categories. The historical significance of these concerns, however, is traceable to a larger picture of which feminist family-bashing is just a part. That picture *is* the historical process of American social transformation, a process that has led from images of a separately reified public and private sphere to an explosion of takeable, breakable spaces, a plurality of "publics" and "privates," each one different and historically situated. Nevertheless, the continued feminist interest in deconstructing and reconstructing family romance as a transpositional genre and as a metaphor for the radical blurring of historically situated dualisms, the mutually productive interactions of fantasy and ideology, the personal and the political, indicates that the symbolic structures in which family romance thrives continue to be regarded by contemporary feminists as a tool for rewriting and reconnecting with feminist history.

NOTES |

1 George Nelson and Henry Wright, "Tomorrow's House: A Complete Guide for the Home-builder," in Lynn Spigel, *Make Room For TV: Television and the Family Ideal in Postwar America* (Chicago: University of Chicago Press, 1992), p. 39; Betty Friedan, *The Feminine Mystique* (New York: W.W. Norton, 1963), p. 32; Marilynne Robinson, *Housekeeping* (1980; rpt. New York: Bantam Books, 1982), p. 3.

2 This definition of feminist historiography reflects the "discourse-sensitive" nature of the current debates concerning the representation of culture. See Jim Collins,

Uncommon Cultures: Popular Culture and Post-Modernism (New York: Routledge, 1989) for a comprehensive and insightful analysis of this shift.

3 Spigel, *Make Room For TV*, p. 40.

4 Jane Gallop, *Around 1981: Academic Feminist Literary Theory* (New York: Routledge, 1992), p. 239.

5 Bonnie Zimmerman, "Lesbians Like This and That: Some Notes on Lesbian Criticism for the Nineties," *New Lesbian Criticism: Literary and Cultural Readings*, ed. Sally Munt (New York: Columbia University Press, 1992), p. 4.

6 Zimmerman, "Lesbians Like This," *New Lesbian Criticism*, p. 3.

7 These imbrications of feminist history, the ideology of separate spheres, and popular romance, are given in-depth exploration in my forthcoming book, *Family Plots: The De-Oedipalization of Popular Culture* (University of Pennsylvania Press, forthcoming). This essay provides a realignment of the book's central concerns in accordance with a focus on feminism's self-fashioning of its history.

8 Roland Barthes, *The Pleasure of the Text*, tr. Richard Miller (New York: Hill and Wang, 1975), p. 47.

9 Tony Tanner, *Adultery in the Novel: Contract and Transgression* (Baltimore: Johns Hopkins University Press, 1979).

10 For example, Toni Morrison's protagonist Sethe in *Beloved*, and Sarah Connor, the muscle-toned "mother of the future," played by Linda Hamilton in the popular film *Terminator 2: Judgment Day*.

11 Linda J. Nicholson, *Gender and History: The Limits of Social Theory in the Age of the Family* (New York: Columbia University Press, 1986), p. 11.

12 Nicholson, *Gender and History*, p. 4.

13 Sigmund Freud, "Family Romances," *Collected Papers*, vol. 5, ed. James Strachey (1909; rpt. London: The Hogarth Press and the Institute of Psycho-analysis, 1952), pp. 74–78.

14 Sigmund Freud, "Family Romances," *Collected Papers*, p. 75.

15 Stephen Heath, *Questions of Cinema* (Bloomington: Indiana University Press, 1981), p. 125.

16 Nancy Chodorow bases much of her work in feminist object-relations theory on the opinion that Freud's instinctual determinism partially blinded him to the socio-cultural reproduction of mothering. Juliet Mitchell's *Psychoanalysis and Feminism* (New York: Pantheon Books, 1974), one of the most influential revisionist treatments of Freudian psychoanalysis, suggests that Freud's account of the family romance has its origin not in biology but in patriarchal relations of domination. In other words, there is nothing essential in Freud's view about the family or relations between men and women. More recently, in *Male Subjectivity at the Margins* (New York: Routledge, 1992), Kaja Silverman corroborates this point via Jean Laplanche's radicalizations of Freudian texts, citing numerous instances of Freud's

separation of sexual drives and their ideological aims.

17 Silverman, *Male Subjectivity at the Margins*, pp. 17–19.

18 Jane Flax, *Thinking Fragments: Psychoanalysis, Feminism, and Postmodernism in the Contemporary West* (Berkeley: University of California Press, 1990), p. 16. Undoubtedly, this is an important task, although I think an equally important task would be an investigation of why feminism itself has just recently begun to acknowledge these paradoxical elements of Freud's texts and insists on readings that place him within *this* historically specific frame.

19 See Peter Stallybrass and Allon White, *The Poetics and Politics of Transgression* (Ithaca: Cornell University Press, 1986), p. 153. Stallybrass and White have been particularly attentive to this tendency, pointing out that for Freud, events and influences outside the domestic scene exist ultimately and primarily as symbols of the original parental situation. Persons, places, and situations outside the family are valuable to the extent that they lead back inside to the romance, thus ironically allowing Freud to conceptualize the "splitting of the subject" across ideological lines only so long as he "proceeds to suppress the social terrain through which that split is articulated."

20 Robinson, *Housekeeping*, p. 198.

21 See especially, Lacan, "The Signification of the Phallus," and "The Agency of the Letter in the Unconscious, or Reason Since Freud," *Écrits: A Selection*, tr. Alan Sheridan (New York: Norton, 1977).

22 Andreas Huyssen, *After the Great Divide: Modernism, Mass Culture, Postmodernism* (Bloomington: Indiana University Press, 1986).

23 See Susan Trausch, "Proof we all live in a material world," *Virginia-Pilot/Ledger-Star* (May 3, 1993). Trausch, a columnist for the *Boston Globe* criticizes Madonna's 60 million dollar deal with Time-Warner Inc., noting that there is something very wrong "in our world when so much money gets plunked down for so little." In addition to lamenting the fact that Madonna's money could be raised for homeless shelters and food for the poor, Trausch compares Madonna to Ella Fitzgerald, a far more talented female vocalist in Trausch's view, who never commanded such enormous bargaining power. Notwithstanding the existence of racism within the music industry, Trausch represents this scandal as the disruption of cultural hierarchies traditionally oppressive to women and non-whites—oppositions of low culture/high culture, female nurturance and male self-interest. The pop singer (Madonna) is less deserving of reward than the essential artist. Similarly, the female celebrity (Madonna) is held to standards of generosity and moral obligation considerably higher than the multi-million dollar male celebrities and sports figures whom Trausch does not mention.

24 See Eric Sundquist, *Home As Found: Authority and Genealogy in Nineteenth-Century American literature* (Baltimore: John Hopkins University Press, 1979); Richard Volney Chase, *The American Novel and Its Tradition* (Garden City, New York:

Doubleday, 1957); and Leslie A. Fiedler, *Love and Death in the American Novel* (New York: Stein and Day, 1966).

25 In some instances, this "say" extends so far as actually reconstructing popular texts. See Henry Jenkins, *Textual Poachers: Television Fans & Participatory Culture* (New York: Routledge, 1992) for a fascinating account of this process.

26 Janice A. Radway, *Reading the Romance: Women, Patriarchy, and Fiction* (Chapel Hill: University of North Carolina Press, 1984), p. 7.

27 Radway, *Reading the Romance*, p. 222.

28 Diane Elam, *Romancing the Postmodern* (London: Routledge, 1992), pp. 2–3, 12–13.

29 See Linda Hutcheon, *The Politics of Postmodernism* (London: Routledge, 1989), p. 10. Hutcheon fails to take into account the meanings produced by the very material conditions of television's introduction into post-war American culture, the extent to which the marketing of the television set itself—let alone the majority of it programming content—suggests a historical dissolution of the boundaries of domestic privacy and consumerism as a public activity. For an outstanding analysis of television's historical function in this regard, see Lynn Spigel, *Make Room For TV*.

30 Silverman argues that classical male subjectivity has remained wholly reliant on the ideological commensurability of penis (the male organ) with phallus (transcendental signifier). At those historical junctures when this equation falters, masculine identity flounders, a condition which becomes discernible in cultural texts that either directly or indirectly expose the illusion of transcendent masculine authority.

31 Paula E. Geyh, "Burning Down the House? Domestic Space and Feminine Subjectivity in Marilynne Robinson's *Housekeeping*," *Contemporary Literature* 34 (Spring 1993), pp. 103–122.

32 Geyh, "Burning Down the House?," *Contemporary Literature*, p. 104.

33 See Nicholson, *Gender and History*, p. 55. Nicholson indirectly refers to this new kind of transient subjectivity when she usefully distinguishes nineteenth century feminism from the twentieth-century second-wave feminist movement by citing a "concept which was central to the latter: the concept of a 'role.' This concept implies a solitary being who can *move* among different activities, taking on different norms appropriate to the activity in question" (emphasis mine).

34 See Thomas Foster, "History, Critical Theory, and Women's Social Practices: 'Women's Time' and *Housekeeping*," *Signs* 14, 1 (1988), pp. 73–99; Dana A. Heller, "'Happily at ease in the dark,'" *The Feminization of Quest-Romance: Radical Departures* (Austin: University of Texas Press, 1990), pp. 93–104; Elizabeth A. Meese, "A World of Women: Marilynne Robinson's *Housekeeping*," *Crossing the Double-Cross: The Practice of Feminist Criticism* (Chapel Hill: University of North Carolina Press, 1986), pp. 57–87.

35 Robinson, *Housekeeping*, p. 99.

36 Robinson, *Housekeeping*, p. 194.

III

BESIDES...

11

PERSONAL CRITICISM

Dialogue of Differences

Christie McDonald

When Gertrude Stein threw her autobiographical voice like a ventriloquist to Alice B. Toklas, she marked out a problem for female identity: rather than centered, female autobiography was to be mediated through otherness. This was more than a mere literary technique. It was a problem located in the lack of a model within the literary tradition for the expression of a female identity. By the early 1990s, work centering on women's identity, along with re-readings of the Western tradition from that perspective, had been logged into publishing in significant ways in a number of fields: a focus on women's stories and on women's lives, the uncovering of archives and publication of unpublished works by women, as well as a good deal of theorizing about the place of women in literature and society. Recently, a new genre has been developing called "personal criticism."

Personal criticism is the expression of neither private nor public life; it is a complex interweaving of the two. It no longer simply opposes the women's world of the home and domestic life to the world of men in the public arena, as was the case traditionally. Rather, in personal criticism, what has been conceived of as a protected, private area suddenly finds itself the center of public concern: whether it be in the realm of politics, where the lives of politicians often are the undoing of the public figure, or in the realm of reproductive rights where a woman's right to abortion, for example, is pitted against the government's right to intervene in a person's intimate life.

The implication of the individual's voice, what I call the "personal" here, has altered the critical landscape in a number of ways. For instance, in addressing the problem of change and transition in Western culture, Jane Flax deliberately brings together political science, psychoanalysis, and feminism to address the philosophical questions of postmodernism. She suggests that "An integral and especially important aspect of postmodernist approaches is a refusal to avoid conflict and irresolvable differences or to synthesize these differences into a unitary, univocal whole."[1] She goes on:

> These transformations have deeply disrupted many philosophers' self-understanding and sense of certainty. One of the paradoxical consequences of this breakdown is that the more the fault lines in previously unproblematic ground become apparent, the more frightening it appears to be without ground, the more we want to have some ways of understanding what is happening, and the less satisfactory the existing ways of thinking about experience become. All this results in a most uncomfortable form of intellectual vertigo to which appropriate responses are not clear. It is increasingly difficult even to begin to know how to comprehend what we are thinking and experiencing.[2]

Flax remarks that as voice and meaning in individual stories become more important, and local truths more available, the possibility of reconciling these voices seems to wane. The question is: Where does the feminist who may be an intellectual, philosopher, or artist find a place, and how does one bring together these many voices? My rather heuristic solution is to look to examples and cases, individual or singular events, that, while they do not necessarily illustrate principles—as the part that would be encompassed within the whole—nevertheless suggest the possibility for linking discourses and voices.

I will concentrate briefly on several episodes involving biography and autobiography (real and fictional) because these are privileged genres in which the line between fiction and fact, and the relationship to otherness, is, if not blurred, often at best tenuous. I am interested in determining how the individual is subsumed into a discourse of singularity whose force goes beyond the individual's voice or position. My premise is that narration of personal episodes and stories accompanies political and philosophical thought, often revealing the impasses and contradictions of rational discourse. Because change occurs between the singular event or text and inherited schemata of thought, such narratives help to bring out a theoretical problem that cannot be approached by theory alone:

the way in which fictions of life, however fragmentary, engage values transmitted from the past and transform them.

I will argue that analysis of these bio-fictions can help us understand the epistemological shifts at work in critical times: by marking turning points in thinking that demand a re-evaluation of the theoretical models at work within their respective traditions; by showing how the theoretical thinking at work in each one carries with it the necessity for examining areas of resistance to a systematizing or generalizing theory. What is at stake is a re-reading of the question of origins: of the human being, of language, of society. What is also at issue is the way in which facts, events, and values are resisted or are subsumed into inherited patterns of thought and how one passes from individual discourse, in conflicting value systems, to a discourse on the self as subject that raises the problem of ethics in narrative. Recently, these questions have taken on renewed urgency, first, because questions left unanswered during the structuralist period and its aftermath required development and refinement, and second, because the humanities today find themselves caught in a newly developing relationship between the academic world and the world at large—or the world out there, as we say.[3] As the end of the twentieth century approaches, the humanities face a crisis in definition: both in its ways of thinking as well as in its disciplinary boundaries.

Second wave American feminism began with so-called subjective experience, the authority of experience as a means of criticism. As feminism and feminist studies became more accepted, their institutionalisation had an impact on at least two levels: a depersonalized kind of exploratory work (through archives, critical work and retrieval of women's writing across the disciplines) and alongside that more experimental work in criticism, in autobiographical or personal writing which has become increasingly polemical and explicitly political. These are voices situated in and developed from strategies that posit and position a plurality of sites and choices.

Such ideas give rise to a major concern: how are ideas, which the tradition has not prepared us for, to be handled or legitimated? This lack of preparation means that they have not fully emerged in either a concrete demonstration or complete theoretical articulation, and that an anxiety is created by the lack of closure. Jane Flax maintains that it is important to stay with the anxiety, to maintain the contradictions and partial answers without leaping at the prospect of a new system or general theory—which would only repeat past schemata. In this regard, admission of imperfection or lack of mastery could allow for imperfect metaphors or a lack of polish, acknowledgment that this is a time of change and exploration of new values and scenarios for them. There have been experiments with a kind of feminist teaching in which the emergence of questions finds no definitive response and the process remains open-ended.[4] Furthermore, more and more personal stories that account for women's lives have emerged.[5]

One insistent question repeatedly asked within contemporary literary and political debates is: in whose name does one speak? If the answer is solely that the "I" speaks always from a defined position, "*AS A...*,"[6] then there is no place for commonality or consensus. Some middle ground is needed here. Because there is always a reciprocity between facts and fiction, writing, as Henry Louis Gates suggests, is a cultural event.[7] To speak in the name of someone who is herself a member of a group or of a number of groups, to speak *AS AN...*, is to decide what is the dominant mark in a complex network of elements: is one a woman first? a writer? is writing universal? and is ethnic or gender identity contingent? To innovate, it is important not to limit categories too much within these identities. Negotiation, a kind of flexibility, is necessary. There has to be an effort to work between the personal and the positional in order to avoid falling back into inherited schemata of thought.

Is all this another way of conjuring up the issue of political correctness? Is it a form of giving in to extreme, polarized positions and losing what seems to me to be one of the most precious aspects of the privilege of university life: the power of a kind of analysis that is at once nuanced and reflective? These questions should not be answered too quickly, because the debates are ongoing—if rough and often contentious—and the outcome still open. This does not mean that I am opposed to making decisions or to acting when it is required. It does mean that I do not believe that analysis should collapse under the pressure of radicalizing positions.

This piece will deal with the way in which feminist criticism, in focusing on local and contextual voices with specific histories rather than on universal principles or truths, has developed a performative discourse. This discourse works at the limits between the public and private spheres, fiction and reality, high theory and practical instantiation. It aims to question and unsettle, to refocus issues with a view to change. I will touch briefly on the work of Nancy Miller in her book, *Getting Personal*, Patricia Williams in *The Alchemy of Race and Rights: Diary of a Law Professor*, and the remarkable exchange between Vice President Dan Quayle and TV character Murphy Brown. In literary criticism (Miller), legal theory (Williams) and prime time TV (Murphy Brown), "personal" stories provoke a re-assessment of the definitions of gender and racial identity, as well as of the role of the family in politics.

All of these texts deal with the problem of otherness in relation to the self, questions of fact and fiction, of proximity and distance. The idea is that pooling individual stories permits local or partial solutions for complex problems in a world that no longer claims the consensus of any social, political or religious totality. Thus, personal criticism as a form does not seek to resolve conflicts; it marks out and takes stock of the space in which those conflicts occur. In reclaiming the voice of identity, personal criticism does not stop at the questions it asks about the foundation or validation of its own voice, the question Gertrude Stein so admirably avoided. It acts in the name of an identity, however constructed, to engage and even provoke others to make of controversy a locus of dialogue.

I precede these discussions with a brief look at the *Confessions* of Jean-Jacques Rousseau. This may seem a surprise because Rousseau is not noted as much of a precursor to feminism. Quite the contrary. And Rousseau is certainly not the founder of feminist personal criticism. But he did in fact lay the groundwork for arguments concerning the uniqueness of the individual relative to the conventional similarity of all human beings, and he thus provides insight into contemporary dilemmas about the limits of a discourse attempting to speak in the name of truth and yet account for difference. The problem of storytelling in Rousseau is precisely the problem of how the personal and the political converge, a problem that is situated between the poles of intimate confession and abstract theory.

ME, MYSELF, AND THE SOCIAL OTHER

In Book I of the *Confessions*, Rousseau recounts a scene in which he shows himself to have passed through the same stages as the hypothetical society he described in his anthropological works: the secularized fall from nature into society. The scene is entitled "The Comb Episode" ("*l'épisode du peigne*"). With his mother dead since his birth and his father in self-exile from Geneva, Rousseau had begun to live in a world lacking in maternal love and paternal authority. Under the guardianship of his uncle, Bernard, he and his cousin were sent to board with the Minister Lambercier in the ideal rural world of Bossey, ideal that is until the day when he is accused of a crime: breaking the teeth of a comb that had been left out to dry. Rousseau, who had been studying in the room next door, is accused circumstantially by the adults. The crime is serious:

> Who was to blame for the damage? No one except myself had entered the room. On being questioned, I denied that I had touched the comb. M. and Mademoiselle Lambercier both began to admonish, to press, and to threaten me; I obstinately persisted in my denial; but the evidence was too strong, and outweighed all my protestations, although it was the first time that I had been found to lie so boldly. The matter was regarded as serious, as in fact it deserved to be. The mischievousness, the falsehood, the obstinacy appeared equally deserving of punishment.... My cousin was accused of another equally grave offence; we were involved in the same punishment. It was terrible.[8]

[A qui s'en prendre de ce dégat? personne autre que moi n'étoit entré dans la chambre. On m'interroge; je nie d'avoir touché le peigne. M. et Mlle Lambercier se réunissent, m'exhortent, me pressent, me menacent; je persiste avec opiniâtreté; mais la conviction étoit trop forte, elle l'emporta sur toutes mes protestations, quoique ce fut la prémière fois qu'on m'eut trouvé tant d'audace à mentir. La chose fut prise au serieux; elle méritoit de l'être. La méchanceté, le mensonge, l'obstination, parurent également dignes de punition (...) Mon pauvre Cousin étoit chargé d'un autre délit non moins grave: nous fumes enveloppés dans la même execution. Elle fut terrible.][9]

Recalling this event at age 50, Rousseau declares himself innocent and feels within himself the same moral rage at the thought of what happened as he did at the time. It is the injustice of being falsely accused and punished that so inflames him still. Yet, as time goes by, the feelings immediately associated with himself and his own experience wane, and the force of those feelings, first associated with this event, become attached to the actions and lives of others:

> That first feeling of violence and injustice has remained so deeply graven on my soul, that all the ideas connected with it bring back to me my first emotion; and this feeling, which, in its origin, had reference only to myself, has become so strong in itself and so completely detached from all personal interest, that, when I see or hear of any act of injustice—whoever is the victim of it, and wherever it is committed—my heart kindles with rage, as if the effect of it recoiled upon myself. When I read of the cruelties of a ferocious tyrant, the crafty atrocities of a rascally priest, I would gladly set out to plunge a dagger into the heart of such wretches, although I had to die for it a hundred times. I have often put myself in a perspiration, pursing or stoning a cock, a cow, a dog, or any animal which I saw tormenting another merely because it felt the stronger.[10]
>
> *[Et ce sentiment, relatif à moi dans son origine, a pris une telle consistance en lui-même, et s'est tellement détaché de tout interest personnel, que mon coeur s'enflamme au spectacle ou au récit de toute action injuste, quel qu'en soit l'objet et en quelque lieu qu'elle se commette, comme si l'effet en retomboit sur moi. Quand je lis les cruautés d'un tyran féroce, les subtiles noirceurs d'un fourbe de prêtre, je partirois volontiers pour aller poignarder ces misérables, dussai-je cent fois y périr. Je me suis souvent mis en nage, à poursuivre à la course ou à coups de pierre un coq, une vache, un chien, un animal que j'en voyois tourmenter un autre, uniquement parce qu'il se sentoit le plus fort.]*[11]

The episode thus puts an end to his childhood serenity. Childhood in fact ends right there, he says.

We remained a few months longer at Bossey. We were there, as the first man is represented to us—still in the earthly paradise, but we no longer enjoyed it; in appearance our condition was the same, in reality it was quite a different manner of existence.[12]

[*Nous restames encore à Bossey quelque mois. Nous y fumes comme on nous réprésente le prémier homme encore dans le paradis terrestre, mais ayant cessé d'en joüir.*][13]

Thus his own secularized "fall" from paradisaical nature is accompanied by the acute consciousness of social injustice: first that which befell him, and then, through sympathy (what he calls pity), that which befell others. That he remembers this episode as inaugural, as determining, serves to point up the displacement of the symbolic imagery: the comb (a woman's instrument for primping) displaces the biblical apple that appears parodically only a few pages later, in a repetition of St. Augustine's scene of stealing pears. And, from then on, the young Rousseau participates fully in the post-lapsarian society around him, doing as many bad things as possible. Now this so-called "unique" incident repeats paradoxically at the ontogenetic level what Rousseau had described in phylogenesis: the emergence of society through a fall from nature to culture, both unprovoked and undesired by mankind—exempt thereby from original sin. In Rousseau's case, it happens in the midst of a world where relations are defined by an idyllic harmony. When injustice and discord irrupt into the life of the child Rousseau, they seem to come from outside the confines of this ideal world of the extended family. Coming at the end of his life, the autobiography underscores two aspects of Rousseau's social thought that are important here: first, the relationship of uniqueness to an other, here his cousin; and second, the end of an ethic of care and the beginning of injustice. For the lesson is that social justice will have to be established by convention and right.

In a remarkable sequence of fragments from the "*Ébauche des Confessions,*" Rousseau gives a series of arguments about the necessity of incorporating otherness within the autobiographical project. First, he makes this assertion, well-known since Freud, about the determining influence which the smallest events of childhood often have on men's deepest character traits [*"la force qu'ont souvent les moindres faits de l'enfance pour marquer les plus grands traits du caractére des hommes"*[14]]. Then, he states that it is necessary to know at least one other person in order to judge one's placement in what he calls the moral order (*"l'ordre moral"*), that one must know, besides oneself, at least one fellow man in order to distinguish in one's heart what belongs to the species from what belongs to the individual [*"Il faudroit connoitre outre soi du moins un de ses semblables, afin de démeler dans son propre coeur ce qui est de l'espéce et ce qui est de l'individu"*[15]]. The problem is that many people think they know others, but he asserts, they are wrong; that is what he observes in the judgment of others about him. None of the judgments *of him*, he knows through his conscience (the infallible inner feeling that constitutes existence), are either correct or true.[16] One judges others by one-self. So, he writes, the rule is that to know oneself one must know at least one other than oneself, and this leads to the following clever division: he will himself serve as other to himself, writing *in the present* about *another past self*. Thus, Rousseau serves as other to himself.[17] Now, the kind of proof of veracity demanded here blocks Rousseau's desire for complete uniqueness. It brings him back to the necessity for a society based on the principle of pity and identification with others, according to which human beings were related in primitive times through commiseration rather than hostility: this principle was to establish grounds for a pacific society.

That each of Rousseau's stories contains only men as subject (Rousseau and his cousin; Rousseau in relation to himself) is not surprising. For while Rousseau's social theory was highly developed with regard to the abstract question of social equality, his own relationship to women and to paternity were woefully lacking (his discussions of Sophie's difference from Emile in *Emile*, both in her capacities and her education, as well as the abandonment of Rousseau's own five children testify to that). However, to condemn the whole of his thought for the part that one might judge today to be regressive, or judge even to be symptomatic of his time, is to miss the importance of what was gained. In his autobiographical as well as his anthropological and socio-political works, Rousseau articulated the passage from natural inequality to a concept of conventional equality that became particularly important for the Enlightenment: the move from rights based on unequal social and economic *status* (rank, heredity, family) to the redistribution of those rights through a social *contract*. The personal was then, as it is now, not only political but also theoretical, as Nancy Miller has pointed out.[18] For Rousseau, the passage from one to the other was to be found in the move between individual value and collective legislation. Put another way, Rousseau's social theory grounded the kind of claims for equality that Simone de Beauvoir would begin to make as of 1949, in her sociological, historical and theoretical analysis in *The Second Sex*, before working into a personal engagement with feminism only many years later.

My point here is to show that autobiography depends upon a view not only of the self but of the other as well, thereby implying ethical, social, and political relations. The extraordinary quality of the *Confessions* resides not only in the exhibitionism for which Rousseau continues to be known, but also in the establishment of the underpinnings for his political theory—in the general Will—by returning to a notion of the self as subject inscribed both in a personal and social history. The general Will was to establish an indivisible relationship between the individual and the social order.

Because the "facts" of history "compromised the ideal" (in Rousseau's terms mankind had become degenerate), he had formulated the abstract concept of the people against the notion of change or progress and apart from practical action.[19] "Since the will always tends toward the good of the being who wills, since the private Will always has as its object private interest and the general Will common interest, it follows that this last alone is or ought to be the true motivation of the social body."[20] Paradoxically, then, for Rousseau individual rights were born with the state.[21] Yet the spectacularly attractive side of the *Confessions* comes also with the admission of human weakness and failing, something for which the *Social Contract* could not account.

That this very concept became one that generated change is in itself an interesting paradox; for as the subsequent history would show, although the general Will became one of the guiding principles of the French Revolution, no consensus could be maintained long enough to stabilize the society it was designed to guarantee. Rousseau's real test for the newborn values of society came in the fictions of life. In his narratives of himself and others, the narratives rather than abstract theory tend to create truth: that is, to show the way in which facts and rights would merge. Rousseau did not have what Richard Rorty has dreamed of for the theorist: a narrative of ideas rather than people.[22] Rousseau's more literary account or narrative of people (*The Nouvelle Héloïse*) did not merely flesh out but it actually countered the conclusions of his more conceptually formulated social, philosophical, and political ideas. It was this aspect of his thought that brought out what Rorty asks for in the present day context of solidarity: identification through different human experiences. It is perhaps in the inability of this discourse to prove its veracity, other than through identification, that it comes closest to certain postmodern attempts at personal criticism.

It may seem a paradox to juxtapose two contemporary feminist writers with Rousseau's statement of the importance of autobiography. If he is chronically cited as the founder of modern autobiography, it is decidedly male autobiography (though St. Augustine and Montaigne certainly served as at least partial models for him). Rousseau insures that his "marginal" life recapitulates the development of society through the hypothetical history of his early anthropological works (*The First and Second Discourses* and the *Essay on the Origin of Languages*), marking the "he-ness" of this history. The models for female autobiography and biography are only now in the process of being hewn, as Carolyn Heilbrun has eloquently shown.[23]

PERSONAL CRITICISM

I am going to sketch rapidly the way in which Nancy Miller articulates a notion of personal criticism that has grown out of French critical theory, but has begun to blossom in an interesting hybrid in the United States. Miller's central idea, in her book *Getting Personal*, has to do with autobiography as a performative genre of criticism. That is, personal criticism involves a "self-narrative woven into critical argument" that avoids the confessional model in which Rousseau locates himself.[24] The idea is to transmit not so much the truth of a self as the personal or aubiographical effects of a discourse. At stake are the foundation of authority, of an authoritative voice, and the production of theory. Miller thus posits a representation of the self as both a critical and political act: asking who is represented by whom and how?

For the generation of academics brought up on, and in some sense formed by, structuralism on the North American continent, this may seem an anomaly. After all, criticism as personal narrative is the very opposite of generalizing and systematic theory; it may even seem like a rejection of theory. However, that is not necessarily the case, and certainly not with Miller. While this kind of criticism turns away from the general and systematic focus of structuralism as being a part that took itself for the whole, personal criticism brings up local issues, contextual positions, anecdotes that point to differences, not to sameness. This is a criticism born of the focus on margins that contests the notion of a truth-centered tradition that might be called logocentric or phallogocentric, a criticism that goes beyond the level of structural or semiotic analysis. By privileging the informal testimonial as a locus of social revision, personal criticism meets ethical and social issues as they emerge in individual stories—stories that signal infinitesimal changes, like the anarchic consciousness-raising groups of the late 1960s in North America. It is an understanding and privileging of a different kind of theory from that developed in France from the 1960s to the 1980s in which readings of Rousseau curiously played a crucial role.[25]

To explore this other kind of theory, Miller repeats a classic gesture of deconstruction by questioning the opposition between the public arena (as the domain of men) and the private space (given over to women). That is, she focuses on the less privileged term, the private space she then transforms. When, for example, one speaks "personally" in a public place (like the university, for example), she asks, who is embarrassed? The speaker? The public? And what is at stake? Particularly when it is a question of the body?

The inscription of the body in academic discourse marks a difference from abstract language, the kind of language by which women have been made invisible and from which they have been excluded. The visibility of the body, the expression of the body as differentiated and concrete, disturbs the quest for a universalizing theory removed from tangible experience. Miller cites an example from Jane Tompkins, who mixes thoughts about epistemology within the seemingly incongruous context of going to the bathroom, and she dwells upon the conventional effects of the kind of authority insured by a neutral discourse in an academic setting.[26]

Miller shows the importance of French critical theory for the development of a certain strain of American academic criticism. During the structuralist and post-structuralist periods, that is during the last thirty years, theory was filtered through questions of language, discourse, system, network, and machine—all suggesting something extremely impersonal, beyond the realm of the individual.[27] But who, she asks, is the *WE* or the *ONE* used in impersonal discourse? And Miller is not alone in asking this question. What's more: What are the effects of the use of impersonal discourse? Are individuals forced to engage in a kind of involuntary complicity as they employ one or the other of these pronouns?

Such a concern was certainly part of the reason for changing the convention of the impersonal pronoun "he" standing for humanity to the range of solutions: he/she, she, etc. The re-marking of generally accepted conventions or traditions, in names as well as pronouns, meant that the particular could no longer simply be taken for the general—and not recognized as such; it forced all speakers to scrutinize their relationship to gender (if only linguistically) and to authority, in and through language. If the reaction can be, "oh how awkward these forms are," each person is nevertheless forced into confronting the differences that separate speakers rather than the forms that homogenize them. The move from the first person singular (I) to the first person plural (we) is not easy, especially if one is determined to maintain differences in the translation. Various national and ethnic groups have adopted an individualizing group stance that repeats at a social level the pronominal question posed in personal criticism. But the use of the first person exacts from theory, criticism, and writing that which a neutral or impersonal discourse allows to be too easily effaced in its universalizing stance.

One important reference point for Miller in tracking this itinerary in criticism is the second period of Roland Barthes's writing, when he abandoned his strictly semiotic work and opted for an equivocal kind of rhetoric between autobiography and biography. (Think of the book *Roland Barthes par roland barthes,* which parodies autobiography through the semiological disappropriation of the subject in signs.[28]) For Miller, the follow-up to this rhetoric is a negotiation of oppositions previously considered to be non-negotiable: between the body and the mind, theory and process (experience), poststructuralism and feminism.

Feminism has led to a questioning of the way in which knowledge emerges from a context—and that context can be very local and material indeed: a room, a state of the body. It has led to a questioning of models and the tradition in which they were formed. Miller suggests managing the double jeopardy of being a woman and a feminist as a survival strategy for academic women, by choosing a strong critical identity from the panoply of current theories (although, as Lévi-Strauss pointed out, this does not mean believing in the truth value of such a theory) and operating according to the well known strategy of subversion from within the system. Yet personal criticism necessarily goes beyond the opposition of a centralized voice of power to those voices external to it. Between the proclaimed death of the author on one side, and the revision of the canon on the other, personal criticism offers neither a disembodied function of a signifying system nor an original voice of authority. The author is somewhere in between, in a necessarily complex rip-tide of theoretical and social currents that find expression in the current interest in cultural practices.

In *The Alchemy of Race and Rights: Diary of A Law Professor*, Patricia Williams deals with questions of race and rights through narratives of personal experience.[29] This new genre is a hybrid between autobiography, legal theory, the editorial, and allegory. In reflecting upon complex questions within contemporary society, she enlarges our sense of what is pertinent to an argument. In her analysis of the law the positioning of the self is everything, she asserts. Her field is constitutional and contractual law, African-American history, feminist jurisprudence, political science, and rhetoric. Traditionally, "Legal writing presumes a methodology that is highly stylized, precedential, and based on deductive reasoning."[30] Her own method, however, differs quite radically from this: She relies upon an experiential model that parodies the analyses of systems in order to bring alive complex social problems. This involves the transfer of critical theory to legal studies where psychology, sociology, history, and philosophy become relevant by turns. Her aim is to write in the spaces left blank, the gaps in traditional legal writing: the spaces in which intersubjective legal constructions force the reader to participate in the making of meaning. Because she wants to render the process itself evident, her writing includes poetry, fables, and more. She seeks connection in order to realize her belief that the "theoretical legal understanding" in Anglo-American jurisprudence need not be opposed to social transformation.

Williams defines three principles that underlie Anglo-American jurisprudence. First, the hypostatization of categories and polarities that appear to be clear and distinct: rights/need (care), moral/immoral, public/private, black/white. Second, the belief that legal truths are transcendent, universal, based on pure procedures, not subject to context. Third, the sense that unmediated voices channel universal truths: judges, lawyers, logicians, "practitioners of empirical methodologies."[31] Here idealized images of "real people" experiencing "real" lives are "corroborated" by implicit models of legitimation.

In her writing, Williams seeks to shake the sense that clarity inheres in such principles. She presents complex examples that disturb neat binaries by questioning the notion of universality whenever choice in personal experience and the opacity of differing voices are presented. I will give one example from the chapter entitled, "Crimes without Passion." The anecdote comes from an experience that Williams had with a student who did not contest a grade, but who contested a question in an examination by arguing that the question itself was racist—whereupon the student was accused by a school administrator of being an activist. The question was on Shakespeare's *Othello,* in which Othello is described as a "black militaristic African leader" who marries a "young white Desdemona" whom he then kills out of sexual rage. The students were asked to imagine a murder trial and to identify the elements of the murder. "The model answer g[ave] points for the ability to 'individualize the test' of provocation by recognizing that 'a rough untutored Moor might understandably be deceived by the wiles of a more sophisticated European.'"[32]

Here are some of the dilemmas Williams raises:

Dilemma 1: Responding to a question formulated in the above way supposes agreement with its presupposition to order to find the "right" answer.

Dilemma 2: The professor thought he was respecting minorities and women when he raised the question of race, class, and gender explicitly within the course curriculum.

Dilemma 3: How can teachers discuss disturbing problems by highlighting or accenting the questions that underlie them, rather than by reproducing or repeating—gratuitously and without pedagogical purpose—the inherited stereotypes of a culture?

Dilemma 4: How can one give value to elements important in "personal" life that have no traditionally recognized legal pertinence for a given trial—race, class, and gender are explicitly rendered irrelevant when, in fact, they often remain an integral part of the problem?

Dilemma 5: Is it better to stay with impersonal discourse?

Dilemma 6: How can one change thought through criticism without censoring or infringing on individual speech?

These dilemmas are at the heart of a number of ethical problems faced within the academy and outside it, and they form a constellation on a vast canvas brushed by Williams through a singular and personal design. In this particular example, she studies examinations on a wide variety of subjects from many universities. She then reproduces a long memo written to her colleagues about the necessity for professors of law to scrutinize the power that they assume as teachers—about the importance she accords to refusing to legitimate or authorize perspectives that are blind to their own racist or sexist premises, but that are presented as models of universal and impartial justice. As a teacher, Williams shows there is an implicit contract made between teachers and students, and that teachers have a *duty* to play by certain rules. In order to work through the kind of dilemmas just mentioned, it is necessary to understand that there is a "real" relationship of power between teacher and student.

What interests her is the resistance of her colleagues to her memo: 1) her colleagues were hurt; 2) she was perceived as preaching, as censoring them, and as doing so in an indirect way because she did not name the people in question. So her own dilemma became: how to raise questions of principle in an interpersonal situation without implicating particular individuals and destroying relationships. Yet she staunchly maintains that to pretend that access to power is without personal implication is a ruse—because the call for neutral or universal understanding is always staged in a context, located in a specific place. And the price for desiring neutrality is power without connection.

As for Miller, "getting personal" for Williams is a form of cultural criticism, as well as a specifically literary or legal form. Williams defines her sense of "the personal" by writing in detail about issues that trouble her, mulling over problems that she has encountered in specific situations. Her method entails a kind of personal reflection destined to help cut through these difficult dilemmas. Both Miller and Williams seek connections beyond the inadequacies of impersonal discourse without falling back into the kind of universalizing to which Rousseau ultimately appealed. For Williams, the personal is not private life; it is not confession; "the personal is often merely the highly particular."[33]

DIALOGUES OF DIFFERENCE

The notion of the highly particular in the cases of both Miller and Williams cuts across the opposition between public and private life. Nowhere has such line-crossing been brought so directly into the political arena and shown its potential explosiveness than around the prime time television sitcom *Murphy Brown*. Murphy is a character played by Candice Bergen. Much of the program is devoted to the "off-screen" personal lives of the character Murphy and her colleagues, who form a kind of family of friends. Murphy is a blond media anchor-superstar; she's also a smart-aleck[34] who is intelligent, articulate, "opinionated,"[35] and so much a perfectionist professionally that she often compromises herself personally. The show was very popular, running for several years with high ratings. But in 1992–1993 it went off the scoreboard for popularity when Murphy became the center of a national debate in the United States around "family values." That season was dominated by Murphy's decision to exercise choice, her political persuasion concerning abortion, and to keep a pregnancy as a single mother.

In a now famous speech made in San Francisco on May 19, 1992, then Vice President of the United States, Dan Quayle, attacked the fictional character during a talk on poverty and the ills of society, thereby triggering a "national event."[36] "I believe," he said, "the lawless social anarchy which we saw [referring to the LA riots] is directedly related to the breakdown of family structure, personal responsibility and social order in too many areas of our society."[37] He went on to suggest that "marriage is a moral issue that requires cultural consensus, and the use of social sanctions."[38] And then he dropped the sentence that ignited the controversy: "It doesn't help matters when prime time TV has Murphy Brown—a character who supposedly epitomizes today's intelligent, highly paid, professional woman—mocking the importance of fathers, by bearing a child alone, and calling it just another 'life-style choice.'"[39]

Quayle acted as point man opening the debate on family values for an electoral campaign that the Republican Party carried through the Republican Convention later in the summer. But his message was definitely mixed, and it confused the White House for several weeks. The then Republican administration had endorsed a pro-life position, and therefore should logically have been in favor of Murphy's keeping the baby. The "real" executive producer of the program, Diane English, shot back her answer unequivocally: "If the Vice President thinks it's disgraceful for an unmarried woman to bear a child, and he believes that a woman cannot adequately raise a child without a father, then he'd better make sure abortion remains safe and legal."[40] She even challenged the Vice President to a debate, although she said that neither Candice Bergen nor she felt "comfortable operating on a national political level."[41]

Quayle confused the issues, which led the "real" media journalists to ask a number of personal questions to both Quayle and Bush: what would Quayle do if his thirteen year old daughter became pregnant, and Bush, what about one of his grandchildren? What ensued was a debate in the media and among politicians concerning the definition of the family (must a family be constituted out of a traditional nuclear group headed by a father and mother, or can it be opened up to include many possible choices: single parent families, homosexual parents, etc.?). The debate was heated on all sides. By mid-summer no one could define what family values were, and by the election it became a dead issue. But in the interim the controversy was high melodrama.

As the fictional executive producer of the program FYI puts it, "we're one big happy family." And indeed, the group of friends provides a remarkable crossover of gender roles. Two of the men, Frank (another journalist) and Elden (Murphy's somewhat hippy live-in house painter who is an artist at heart and becomes the 'spiritual guide'—read male nanny—for Murphy's baby) display maternal instincts, while Murphy seems completely devoid of them. Her friends fear that pregnancy will cause her to change and become less good at her job— less, as it were 'virile.' This locates the debate on defining "woman" and "man" (a debate on the table since Simone de Beauvoir's *Second Sex*) on the side of cultural construction rather than biology.

For me, because I was already working on some of these issues in the tradition of French literature and philosophy, what was extraordinary about the event and its follow-up was that a dialogue had been engaged between a politician (no—*more* than a politician—a distinguished representative of a country) and a fictional character grappling with her personal life (her pregnancy and the changes that she was undergoing because of it) in the very public world of prime time TV. That is, the then Vice President of the United States placed a personal story smack in the middle of the public arena. Personal matters, in particular abortion, were already high on the agenda of public debate. But here was a story curiously worthy of attack.

Among those opinions vigorously sought-after during the controversy were those of the actress, Candice Bergen. She refused comment most of the time, breaking her silence once when she received an Emmy Award for her role in the program *Murphy Brown* and on a few other rare occasions. Her "personal" response was to come from the character Murphy Brown only at the beginning of the new season in September, after the monumental miscalculation of the Republican Convention in its insistence on family values during a major recession. I will come to this response in a moment.

Time came dangerously close to pre-empting literary criticism in a rather good article entitled "Folklore in a Box."[42] The author, Lance Morrow, speaks of the new "electronic metaphysics" of TV and video, and the explosive stories they tell: from the Rodney King tape and its effect on the burning of LA, to the Murphy Brown affair. What he suggests is that there is a war of "American myths, a struggle of contending stories. And pop culture, often television, is the arena in which it is being fought. Stories are precious, indispensable. Everyone must have his history, her narrative. You do not know who you are until you possess the imaginative version of yourself. You almost do not exist without it...."[43] He argues that the family needed a new "folklore," and analyzed the way in which "myth is embedded in oddments of visual memory...and a few national epics like the story of the Kennedys...." I agree with Morrow that "people invent stories to explore their own behavior and to imagine their own possibilities." I also agree that "especially when venturing into new territory where mere habit will no longer suffice, people require the stabilizing, consoling, instructing influence of other human tales."[44] But I would go further and say that without these, there may no longer be any guiding buoys in a turbulent sea of change.

Morrow contends that when an individual story like Murphy Brown's is channelled through prime time TV, it takes on a curiously universalizing quality. "Television is almost always unsettling and amazing when one thinks about it. It imposes upon America a strange simultaneity, if not a unity...."[45] While individual stories express the plurality of a society like the United States or Canada, "television acts often as a universalizing, mediating influence." Morrow focuses on the positive influence of television, seeing in it a counteraction to fanaticism, when it even risks becoming a "shaming agent" for tolerance of choices in such diverse societies. He even sees it, "in a bizarre way," as a "form of representational democracy—or symbolic democracy anyway."[46] Now Quayle accused the Murphy-makers of being from the cultural elite, and he attacked that elite without flinching. Yet Morrow's argument stresses that what counters any universalizing tendancy here is the necessary market-appeal to many points of view for prime time TV.

With respect to the notion of the elite, Quayle divided the USA into two cultures: "the cultural elite and the rest of USA."[47] "The cultural elites respect neither tradition nor standards," he said. "They believe that moral truths are relative and all 'life styles' are equal. They seem to think the family is an arbitary arrangement of people who decide to live under the same roof, that fathers are dispensable and that parents need not be married or even of opposite sexes. They are wrong."[48] He then accused the elite of being politically correct when dismissing "those who speak of moral values." The idea here is that the culture being wrought from these attitudes is "guilt free," "avoids responsibility" and flees "consequences." In breaking culture into two camps, Quayle created a notion of a majority "we" and a minority "they" with the result that he can speak in the name of a consensus (which ultimately proved wrong at the election). The reaction among those targeted (single parents, women, blacks, homosexuals, and the poor) was that the push for re-election was, in effect, scape-goating certain segments of society in the name of a tradition that had in fact always excluded them. Quayle came under attack for veiling his own racism in his criticisms of a middle class, white, TV character.

The line between fiction and reality became one of the major points of fascination in this case—a line frequently crossed within the program itself. Throughout the many segments, the journalists make periodic jabs at "real" well-known television journalists.[49] American congressmembers themselves have appeared in fictionalized dreams, even before Clinton's election campaign attacked, with regularity, the American right-wing from a fairly well-defined liberal position.

But the national melodrama of Quayle and Murphy Brown, like the Anita Hill-Clarence Thomas hearings (labelled the "genderquake" by Naomi Wolf[50]), drew record numbers of spectators to the opening night of the 1992 fall season, when Murphy responded to Quayle. It followed by about a month the Republican convention during which two women's voices were intended to deliver rather different "personal" messages: Marilyn Quayle and Barbara Bush. In preparation for this moment, the "real" Vice President sent the fictive baby boy (born of and on television in the spring) a stuffed elephant, symbol of the Republican party, and a note written by hand from the then Vice President: "Dear Baby Brown, I want to be one of the first to welcome you into the world. You may not realize it yet, but you've helped start an important discussion on ways to strengthen our traditional values. President Bush and I will do everything possible to make sure you and all children—no matter what their family situation—have the opportunity to grow up in prosperity."[51] The Vice President, having been accused of insensitivity to the problems of the poor, went on that fateful night to a poor section of Washington in order to watch the program with several real families.

Murphy's ineptitudes are personal and private; her true competence is in the public arena, where she decides to respond to Quayle on the news broadcast, FYI. Her report is on family values, and it constitutes her answer to his attack. Taking the high road, she reproaches Quayle's political tactics in the scape-goating of an individual (a fictive one, remember) on personal grounds: "These are difficult times for our country. And in searching for the causes of our social ills we could choose to blame the media, or the Congress or an administration that has been in for 12 years. Or we could blame *ME*."

American feminism, nourished as it has often been on French critical theory, has also been accused of being elitist, removed from the everyday problems of "real" women: poor women, women of color, and ethnic minorities. "Fictive anchor person" Murphy Brown invoked "real" single parent families whom she introduced to the public. This lesson was meant to show that Murphy's example did not offer a univocal model, but rather one choice or possibility among many. That, unlike the Vice President's rigid demand for a single family model (a mother, father, and child), contemporary changes in family structure demand multiple solutions. Curiously, here was a Republican politician, from a party traditionally against state intervention, inviting sanctions against women, and a "fictive" liberal (traditionally for more state programs) fighting for individual liberty. All the lines were crossed: between the political and the personal, between the state and the individual, between social issues and the fictions that hover around them.

The program—like personal criticism—presented a radically singular situation (pregnancy) for which there is no one general law, signifying system, or overarching theory. The ability to generalize and theorize depends upon the contextualizing of one character in relation to others. It is almost as though the Western tradition were being reforged from performative anthropology: not from scrutinizing other cultures to better understand one's own, but from looking within through a process of distancing and individuation—through the personal narrative as a form of criticism. Not only is the personal political, but the well-known feminist adage has been turned around: the political is also personal, as Gloria Steinem has suggested.[52]

For Miller, Williams, and the writers of *Murphy Brown*, a constant emerges that is radically different from Rousseau's vision. Woman has become the controversial and paradoxical referent.[53] Perhaps Rousseau was right when he wagered that, when truth is inaccessible by observation or analysis, it is necessary to create the fictions that will invent it. Rousseau wanted to prove man a sentient being. Miller, Williams, and Murphy Brown do not deny the need for connection but want to prove woman a social agent as well.

Yet the spectator or reader must still deal with the ambivalence emerging from individual and often conflicting stories. As Flax has suggested:

> ambivalence is an appropriate response to an inherently conflictual situation. [And] the problem lies not in the ambivalence, but in the premature attempts to resolve or deny conflicts. The lack of coherence or closure in a situation and the existence of contradictory wishes or ideas too often generate anxiety so intense that aspects of the ambivalence and its source are repressed.[54]

Flax is saying that it is necessary to stay with the anxiety that individual stories create, whether through conflict or the kind of singularity that puts them outside traditional categories or models; it is necessary, that is, to resist the desire to leap into or grasp at any new metanarratives.

In the effort to be self-reflective, Nancy Miller, Patricia Williams, and the writers of *Murphy Brown*—at least briefly—have called attention to personal observation and engagement, and especially to the memory that enfolds individual experience. They do not propose a new metanarrative, but they do implicitly call on individual memory and the context in which the individual finds himself or herself to deal with the kind of social principles, of equality and justice that Rousseau evoked through his social and political writings. And the fiction of Murphy Brown's pregnancy ended up in a broad dialogue of differences—albeit confused—concerning the family and society as a whole.

Because I don't want this to be only a theoretical piece that observes and criticizes from afar the efforts of personal criticism to effect change, I will end by evoking my own work in progress, for which these analyses have served as fodder. It is a manuscript about Anne Eisner (1911–1967). When she left New York City to live in Africa in 1946, she was a dedicated artist. When she came back in 1954, she was a writer and ethnographer as well. She was the first woman and the third Westerner to live among the Pygmies (only P. Schebesta and her husband, Patrick Tracy Lowell Putnam, preceded her). From 1947 through 1954, she lived and worked in the Ituri forest of Zaïre (the ex-Belgian Congo) in close proximity to thirty-five Pygmy families. Although she wrote a highly successful book, *Madami* (1954), and documented a return stay between 1957 and 1958 in an article for *The National Geographic Magazine* (1960), an important part of Anne Eisner's experience and work in Africa still remains untapped in the letters and personal papers, as well as the drawings and paintings of Africa, that she left.

I have joined my voice to hers in writing her "personal" story. Perhaps the most important ingredients in my selection of material comes from the forty years in which feminism has intervened, creating a sensibility for what is personal and particular to women's perceptions and experience of places, reserved in the past largely for men. If you add to this the consciousness that post-colonialism has raised about the difficulty of putting cultures together and coming up with harmony or consensus, Anne and I are linked by a cultural memory that goes beyond either of us. And we are linked by something else that is important as well: I am her niece.

This is a family romance in the new order. My memory comes not only from the experience of having known her; it comes from her writing and her art: Anne's letters, journals, and notes, her paintings, watercolors, and hundreds of drawings of everyday life. Add to this the memory of her contemporaries that I have interviewed and with whom I have corresponded. It took six years of research and organization of the material to develop this "memory." This will not be a book about Anne's life as she lived it. It will be about Anne's life as I rewrite it from the period 1950 to 1956 in a first person narrative. The "I" is not simply hers; it is not simply mine. It is not even simply ours. It is a weaving of the two that attempts to find a non-foundational identity through otherness and to learn to tell the story in between one and the other of us: her voice with mine, my voice with hers. In the process both Anne and I have been changed. She never could have written this book, because she didn't benefit from the understanding that feminism has given to women because she died in 1967. I never lived through what she did, so I can only understand what is common to us through difference. Yet the discovery of our link, in the reconstruction of her life, has changed me forever. Gertrude Stein put her voice beside herself to make her own identity in writing; I join mine to another's to forge a life of Anne through our dialogue of difference as we can only know it now. Is that not what personal criticism is about? To teach us, from the perspective of the very particular, that something that has spun us apart historically, culturally, even personally, nonetheless connects us in writing.

NOTES |

1 Jane Flax, *Thinking Fragments: Psychoanalysis, Feminism, and Postmodernism in the Contemporary West* (Berkeley: University of California Press, 1990), p. 4.

2 Flax, *Thinking Fragments*, p.6.

3 See Lindsay Waters, "Review of David Lehman's *Signs of the Times*: Deconstruction and the Fall of Paul de Man," *Contention: Debates in Society, Culture, and Science* 1, 2 (Winter, 1992), pp. 24–46.

4 Nancy Miller, *Subject to Change* (New York: Columbia University Press, 1988), p.35.

5 There is an ongoing seminar at the New York Institute for the Humanities on Women Writing Women's Lives in which biographers present and discuss their material. See Carolyn Heilbrun's book *Writing A Woman's Life* (New York: Ballantine Books, 1988). As for the transformation of academic theoretical writing into personal reflection, see Susan Suleiman's *Encounters with Contemporary Art and Literature* (Cambridge, MA: Harvard University Press, 1994).

6 This is Nancy Miller's way of indicating that one only has to fill in the rest: as a woman, man, heterosexual, homosexual, black, white, etc.

7 Henry Louis Gates Jr., "'Authenticity,' or the Lesson of the Little Tree," *New York Times Book Review* (November 24, 1991).

8 Jean-Jacques Rousseau, *The Confessions of Jean-Jacques Rousseau* (New York: Random House, 1945), p. 17.

9 Jean-Jacques Rousseau, *Confessions, Oeuvres complètes*, 1 (Paris: Bibliothèque de la Pléiade, 1959), p. 19.

10 Rousseau, *The Confessions of Jean-Jacques Rousseau*, p. 19.

11 Rousseau, *Confessions*, p. 20.

12 Rousseau, *The Confessions of Jean-Jacques Rousseau*, p. 19.

13 Rousseau, *Confessions*, p. 20.

14 Rousseau, *Confessions*, p. 1157. Translation mine.

15 Rousseau, *Fragment 2, Confessions*, p. 1158. Translation mine.

16 Rousseau, *Fragment 3, Confessions*, pp. 1157–59.

17 Rousseau, *Fragment 5, Confessions*, pp. 1157–59.

18 Nancy Miller, *Getting Personal* (New York: Routledge, 1991), p. 21.

19 See Thomas Kavanagh, *Writing the Truth: Authority and Desire* (Berkeley: University of California Press, 1987), p. 158.

20 Jean-Jacques Rousseau, "Geneva Manuscript," *On the Social Contract*, ed. Roger D. Masters, tr. Judith R. Masters (New York: St. Martin's Press, 1978), p. 167.

21 Kavanagh, *Writing the Truth*, p. 142.

22 Richard Rorty, *Contingency, Irony and Solidarity* (Cambridge: Cambridge University Press, 1989), p. 107.

23 See Heilbrun, *Writing A Woman's Life*.

24 Miller, *Getting Personal*, p. 2.

25 See Jacques Derrida, *Of Grammatology*, tr. Gayatri Chakravorty Spivak (Baltimore: The Johns Hopkins University Press, 1974); Paul de Man, *Blindness and Insight* (New York: Oxford University Press, 1971) and *Allegories of Reading* (New Haven: Yale University Press, 1979).

26 Jane Tompkins, "Me and My Shadow," *Gender and Theory: Dialogues on Feminist Criticism*, ed. Linda Kauffman (New York: Basil Blackwell, 1989).

27 Miller, *Getting Personal*, p. 13.

28 Roland Barthes, *Roland Barthes*, tr. Richard Howard (New York: Hill and Wang, 1977); *Roland Barthes par roland barthes* (Paris: Éditions du Seuil, 1975).

29 Patricia Williams, *The Alchemy of Race and Rights: Diary of a Law Professor* (Cambridge, MA: Harvard University Press, 1991).

30 Williams, *The Alchemy of Race and Rights*, p. 7.

31 Williams, *The Alchemy of Race and Rights*, p. 7.

32 Williams, *The Alchemy of Race and Rights*, p. 80.

33 Williams, *The Alchemy of Race and Rights*, p. 93.

34 *Time* (June 1, 1992).

35 Richard Corliss, "Having It All," *Time* (September 21, 1992), p. 76.

36 *New York Times* (September 21, 1992).

37 Prepared remarks by the Vice President, Commonwealth Club of California, Office of the Press Secretary, San Francisco, CA, May 19, 1992.

38 Vice President, p. 6.

39 Vice President, p. 6.

40 *Time* (June 1, 1992).

41 *New York Times* (September 21, 1992).

42 Lance Morrow, "Folklore in a Box," *Time* (September 21, 1992), p. 78.

43 Morrow, "Folklore in a Box," p. 78.

44 Morrow, "Folklore in a Box," p. 79.

45 Morrow, "Folklore in a Box," p. 79.

46 Morrow, "Folklore in a Box," p. 79.

47 *New York Times* (June 10, 1992).

48 *New York Times* (June 10, 1992).

49 See Rebecca L. Walkowitz, "Reproducing Reality: Murphy Brown and Illegitimate Politics," *Media Spectacles* (New York: Routledge, 1993), pp. 40–57. With many similar concerns in mind, Walkowitz shows how Murphy Brown replays issues that have been publicized around the public and personal lives of contemporary women journalists.

50 Naomi Wolf, *Fire with Fire: The New Female Power and How It Will Change the 21st Century* (New York: Random House, 1993).

51 *The Gazette* (September 22, 1992).

52 Gloria Steinem, *Revolution From Within* (Boston: Little Brown and Co., 1992), p. 17.

53 Reference to a talk by Claudia Brodsky at the 100th Celebration of the Admission of Women to the Graduate School at Yale University.

54 Flax, *Thinking Fragments*, p. 11.

12

PERVERTS
BY CHOICE

Towards an Ethics
of Choosing

Elspeth Probyn

There are times when the thought of having to choose can cause waves of indecision to come over me. Thankfully, I am not alone in my choice-induced hesitation. As Judith Butler recalls, "I almost always read the signs on bathroom doors marked 'men' and 'women' as offering normative and anxiety-producing choices, delivering a demand to conform to the gender they indicate."[1] To this, I would add that my anxiety is increased when establishments pander to the sexes by "cutsifying" the symbols on the doors (one restaurant in Montréal uses budgerigars versus cockatoos). Beyond toilet doors, however, it is the current "celebration" of women and choice in popular culture that fuels my choice-panic. As I look around, I am struck by examples of choice. Caught up in the rush of images, I nonetheless want to catch these examples in their singularity. Simply put, the argument I trace out here about choice must, of necessity, run through "found" fragments, examples, singularities and differences.

In other words, I will not be building towards a totalized comprehension of the general signification of choice; rather, it seems to me that images of choice compel an alternative theoretical model, a model of thinking through fragments. In turn, as Gilles Deleuze and Félix Guattari put it, the question is "how to think about fragments whose sole relationship is sheer difference—fragments that are related to one another only in that each of them is different—without having recourse to any sort of original totality...or to a subsequent totality that may not yet have come about."[2] Thus, rather than thinking of choice in the terms of either an original or an emergent totality, I shall analyze current examples of choice for the ways in which they may move us towards an ethics of choosing that is neither individualist nor universal.

Thus forewarned, now notice flashes of advertising pronouncements: Nike telling us that "It's never too late to have a life and never too late to change one"—to "Just do it"; *Good Housekeeping* taunting us to choose the home over career; Cybil Shepherd seductively revamping hair dye slogans from "only your hairdresser knows for sure" into "because I deserve it." All these choices and so little time. And it's an odd thing, this choice thing. For instance, in the August 1993 issue of *Vanity Fair* (the one with k.d. lang and Cindy Crawford on the cover playing with sexual choice), Connie Chung is asked if she were to die, what she thought she would come back as. To which she responds "a man." Yet when asked what she would *choose* to come back as, her answer is: "a woman."[3] Thus, when it is a question of simple reincarnation (where one presumably isn't allowed to have preferences as to one's future form), Connie comes back as a man, but if she were allowed to *choose*, it would be as a woman.[4]

There is no doubt that, in popular culture, "choice and women" has become an item. Moreover, binding women and choice together gives a construction of women as thinking about choice but unable to choose. Thus one of the Nike ads aimed at women is an eight page teleological text showing how, as girls, we are constitutionally indecisive but that given the chance, and the right product, as women, we can finally "choose ourselves." The corporate strategy behind this particular selling of choice to women turns on Nike's idea of "self-empowerment." It is reported that "Nike people have to go on about women being 'more introspective athletes' than men."[5] When it comes to choosing, Nike portrays women as less swayed by external forces, as better individuals than men (this is, of course, despite the fact that "for years at Nike the only female of prominence was Nike herself—the winged goddess of victory"[6]).

However, just when I think that maybe all this proliferation of choice and women might be a victory of sorts, just when I think that I can make up my mind, I remember the dark side of choice: in the wars of nationalism, women's bodies become one of the key grounds upon which "national choices" are played out—be it in the rapes used to mark out national territories in the former Yugoslavia or in the more benign battles for sovereignty in Québec. And in journalistic representations, women and children serve to humanize these issues, just as the case of individual children aggrandize the so-called benevolence shown in British Prime Minister John Major's drawn-out decision to finally take in one victim.[7]

More obviously, choice hits women in every aspect of reproduction as it does in the continuing contestation of affirmative action programs within economic production in the workplace. And while k.d. and Cindy look good, sexual choice flip flops from being in the hands of lesbians to being a weapon against us: The respected ethicist Margaret Sommerville states that in regard to sexual choice "we treat people differently when we think that their actions are based on biological chance rather choice." What is a girl to do? Or more to the point, what is a feminist to do?

The popular selling of choice to and for women is a tricky subject for feminists. For a start, it's hard to complain too loudly in that the commercialization of choice and women is arguably one of the most evident signs of an incorporation of feminism into popular culture. It is, of course, more of an "echo-effect of feminism"[8] than a straightforward sell, but, nonetheless, there is a certain sense of "well, you wanted choice, you've got it." Thus the advertising executives behind the *Good Housekeeping* campaign selling the idea of women happily choosing to return to the home could nearly convincingly argue that "It was never an issue except among feminists who felt that we were telling women to stay home and have babies. We're saying that's okay. But that's not all we're saying. We're saying they have a choice. It's a tough world out there."[9]

In this tough world, choice seems like a safe issue, and for a long while the issue of choice was fairly clear within feminism. Couched in terms of access to equality and connected to our right to choose what to do with our bodies, the issue of choice was fairly straightforward: women did not have enough of it, and feminism was there to help us to move towards a society wherein women would choose as freely as men. Thus ultimately, women might hope to reach what Robert Bly describes as the essence of masculinity: a "joyful decisiveness."[10] Recently, however, some feminists wonder about the tone and the reach of choice in feminism. For instance, Andrea Stuart sums up the 1980s feminist line: "Being a feminist had come to say more about what you didn't do—eat meat, fuck men, wear make-up—than what you did do."[11]

When I first read Stuart's article, I thought that she was being a bit harsh in her judgment. Thinking back on it now, she may have a point. Certainly in the late seventies and the early eighties, it was hard to be an eater of meat, fucker of men, and painted woman. Having since, by choice, given up the first two, I'm still rather amazed at how within correct circles you can now wear either eyeliner or bright red lip-stick. But doing both seems to cancel out the feminist effect.[12] This type of dividing line is also expressed for me in the example of two buttons that I possess. One, bought in the local gay, lesbian, feminist bookstore, proclaims: "Redheads for choice." When I purchased it, I thought that the idea was kind of cute. From the button basket, you also had the choice of being Blond-, Brunette- or Grey-haired-For Choice. I've since become rather wary as to what articulation of choice I had bought into. On a very simple and literal level, these buttons express what I have come to think of as a representational model of choice. In other words, the button depicts, or represents, me as being for a larger project that metonymically represents choice *as* feminism. It represents me as one red-headed individual who stands in for all red-headed feminists who are all univocally for this abstract choice project. And like all universalist representations, wherein the one stands in for the whole, it commits racism by omission. In other words, it seems to me that the choices on offer here proceed from an assumption of whiteness, implicitly privileging Northern European stock as dominant.

I've stopped wearing that button and replaced it with one which a bi-queer friend gave me.[13] It simply announces: "Perverts By Choice." Here choice is understood as a more down-to-earth type of thing; it is choice as "becoming" to use Deleuze's terms. It fits in quite perfectly with the logic of an idea that I've been playing around with recently. Inspired by Deleuze and Foucault, and fed up with the epistemological assumptions as well as the tenor of "identity politics," I want to use the idea of "be-longing" as a theoretical basis for rethinking identity. Rather than conceiving of identity as a stable and evident projection of a personal possession, I prefer the notion of be-longing as a loose *"combinatoire"* of being and longing, becoming and nostalgia, as composed of lines of desire that run along the singularities of sexualities, bodies, spaces and places. A theoretical project of being "by choice" thus can focus on and lubricate the relations of sheer difference that connect singular instances of choice.[14]

Given this project and given my general, but sometimes joyful, indecisiveness, I obviously cannot offer an unequivocal reading of choice. What I do want to argue in this essay is that as a pressing problematic for our times, the question of choosing articulates and rearranges some rather persistent concepts within feminism: notably, the status of the individual, the personal, agency, community, and the political. Taking up the term *"choiceoisie,"* I propose that we consider current discourses of choice as an emerging "dispositif" (apparatus) that redeploys the old standbys of liberal humanism at the same time that it offers other, more interesting possibilities.[15] This is to regard choice outside of any normative evaluation and, despite itself, choice seems no longer to offer discrete normative options. That is, at least, outside of feminism, where in popular culture, bits of choice are so pervasive and present that they dispel any attempt to marshall choice into one normative line. In this sense, one could call *"choiceoisie"* epidemic: "it has lost its discreteness and specificity and become a condition, no longer of knowledge, but a contemporary epistemic condition of articulation."[16]

Bluntly put, the contemporary episteme of *choiceoisie* turns on images of "*choice by*," whereas, in the main, within feminism, it is still a logic of "*for choice*" that rules. This is a very delicate distinction, one that I hope not to belabor beyond its breaking point. However, my point is that the idea of "being by choice" presents and confronts the materiality of discursive positivity. In other words, "by choice" functions in a productive way, multiplying choice to the point at which discourses of choice fold upon themselves. By contrast, "for choice" operates within and reproduces a normative delimitation of choice, whereby in the end all choices must be made to signify the same thing. Here choice is constantly weighed to see if it's good or bad, the measure of the balance being an impossible ideal of good for all women at all times.

Both of these senses, and others, are at work within *choiceoisie* as epidemic, choice as the "contemporary condition of articulation." For instance, *choiceoisie* englobes current articulations of a political identity crisis which turns on renewed divisions of "us" versus "them." Indeed, the tenor of much of what passes as identity politics seeks to delineate new lines of who belongs to "us" or to "them." What is interesting or new about these discourses is that the onus is on the individual to invest in an "us" that is not a collective but rather a grouping of like-minded individuals. In line with this logic, the discourses of *choiceoisie* work at the affective level of individual investment. Here again we can feel the pull of be-longing: a desire to become mixed in with the nostalgia of longing, longing for simpler times, for the lost possibility of community.

As an example of these tensions, another Nike advertisement plays on the lines that connect and separate being and longing. Entitled "Falling in Love in Six Acts: A Passion Play," the ad presents what happens to "us" women when we (or rather in the individualized terms of Nike, it's "*you*") "fall down that long well of passion over a person, a place, a sport, a game, a belief, and your heart goes boom and your mind leaves town." The text plays perfectly with the longing to become, arguing that "Lust isn't a sin, it's a necessity, for with lust as our guide we imagine our bodies moving the way our bodies were meant to move." In "Act VI: The Finale," passion gives way to love, and we learn the lesson: "So this is love, as demanding and difficult as it can be, and as strong and wise as it makes you become." The final punch is that "There is something to be gained from commitment. There are rewards for staying when you would rather leave.... Just do it."

Personally, I think that this is a rather brilliant advertisement. It manages to combine hope and loss, being and longing in a totally seamless manner. It also makes me wonder what the ad boys and girls are currently reading; they seem to have graduated from Thomas Sebeok and gone straight to Deleuze. From Deleuze and from Elizabeth Grosz's use of Deleuze, *the* ad text seems to incorporate Grosz's argument that we should "look at lesbian relations and, if possible, all social relations in terms of bodies, energies, movements, inscriptions rather than in terms of ideologies, the inculcation of ideas, the transmission of systems of belief or representations...."[17] And indeed, in the ad, love and passion are depicted as precisely fuelling bodies and energies in such a way that they surpass heterosexuality. It is supremely easy to read the ad as figuring women and women on women; a veritable orgy of female homo-sociality. Of course, it helps that these scrumptious and sometimes androgynous women in the ad are offered to "me" in terms of their energies and bodies, encouraging me to renew mine.

At the same time that I revel in these images, I also find this ad to be an expression of deep loneliness: the loneliness of an individual facing abstract choices where the only idea is to commit oneself to something, to anything, to a person or to a belief. The structure of feeling discernable here is that of a pervasive and sexed "alone-ness." The tone of the text plays on this as it both congratulates and commiserates with women: yes, we've come a long way but where are we? Nike thus starts from an assumption that women have "advanced" in the world, but that we've reached a sort of plateau in our achievements, that now we need encouragement to break through the barrier. In other terms, we need to give it one more shot, to "just do it." And by "just doing it," we may perhaps displace loneliness. There is here an articulation of women stranded, of an individual alone in front of her own choices, and fuelled by the wish to be-long somewhere, anywhere, she invests in choice. It is choice for its own sake, commitment for the sake of committing. It is the perfect picture of a confused individual enjoined to become part of an aggregate of individuals who have put aside their indecisiveness and are "doing it." As it pushes fear and longing to fever-pitch, it also shows that decision and choice have no qualities in this scenario except for their enactment; the only thing that remains is the individual act of choosing.

GENERATIONS BESIDE THEMSELVES

These images send choice spiralling in several directions. To paraphrase the text, choice makes me "feel funny inside, funny outside." Choice is both the point of euphoria and (to quote the ad again), it "is where the doubt begins, where the mind comes back from shopping, yells at the heart, binds and gags it to a nice lounge chair and allows guilt, failure, and remembrance of things past to sit in for a nice game of bridge." Nike takes up feminism and deploys woman as an individual for choice; it also revamps that feminist individual by showing her in the throws of indecision brought on by choosing.

While Nike brings us choice by reworking the tropes of feminism, within feminism itself, individuals and choice are being used to trope the history of feminism. This is particularly evident in the current boom in feminist anthologies documenting the state of feminism. An exemplar of this trend is the recent collection edited by Gayle Greene and Coppélia Kahn, *Changing Subjects: The Making of Feminist Literary Criticism.*[18] As the editors state in their introduction, the book takes as its premise that "Over the past twenty years, a generation of feminist scholars has come of age…. We are now in a position to assess this movement and to see ourselves as part of a historical process."[19] While no doubt a worthwhile project, reading the essays in this book I am struck by two tendencies. The first is, for me, the rather annoying way in which American feminist literary criticism tends to see itself as feminist theory *tout court*.[20] Given that I am both non-American and non-lit, this causes me some concern. But there are larger stakes at hand that are expressed in the second tendency evident in this particular book. To wit, having constructed themselves self-consciously as *the* generation, as occupying a position from which to assess "a historical process," the authors tend to conflate their choices with choice in feminism. Alongside this move, "history" comes to be abridged through the figure of the individual, feminist, literary scholar.

These observations should not be misunderstood as an attack on the fine essays individually presented here. For instance, two articles that particularly sum up the tendencies described are both enjoyable and instructive. In "Decades," Nancy Miller describes her experiences through the heuristic device of decades, equating them with the changes in feminist literary theory and along the way makes me yearn to have been born earlier.[21] As unrealistic as my mother's wish to have been a *précieuse* of the Parisian *salons littéraires*, I longed to have flâned as a wealthy American woman in the smoky bars of Paris in the early sixties. When I "did" France, things were rather different; for a start, in principle I was at the Université de Nice (*donc, dans les provinces n'est-ce pas*), and in practice I was broke and spent more of my time working in a gay bar outside of Nice than listening to "*les grands hommes*." However, it is not Miller's time in Paris that I begrudge but rather the way it stands in for a larger story: a story told in the assured terms of those who need not acknowledge the material singularity of their situation.

In Bonnie Zimmerman's article, "In academia, and out: the experience of a lesbian literary critic," the romanticizing tone of Miller's essay that turns individual choices into history is replaced with one of destiny. While Zimmerman vacillates on the independent nature of her choice, choice nonetheless serves as an articulation of personal decision and feminist determinism: "I don't know to what extent I freely chose to be a lesbian and to what extent the women's movement simply allowed me to claim an identity already 'planted' in my soul: I suppose for me the process involved both inclination and opportunity."[22]

Given this emphasis on choice, it is strange to note that, in Zimmerman's account of her experiences, feminism is posed as ineluctable: "Because I had always respected ideas—because I still believe that if a theory makes sense, one should seriously consider living by it—once introduced to the basic concepts of the second wave of feminism, I had no choice but to redefine and redirect my life."[23] While I agree with the spirit of Zimmerman's idea about living theory, I am struck by the way in which she places her sexual choice as somehow outside of her control. In line with her abstraction of choice, Zimmerman's position seems to halt history: history as product rather than process. History, and moreover, the present history of feminism becomes a hermetic and finished text. As she puts it, "Everything we have written since ['roughly 1968 through 1972'] has been a refinement, development, refutation or reconfiguration of the concepts developed in that pioneering literature." And make no mistake about who was responsible: "The generation of women who produced these texts— 'my' generation—were pioneers."[24]

It would be churlish to denounce the right of these women to reminisce, and it would be wrong to deny the importance of "their" generation. However, in turn, it seems a bit petty for them to condemn others, a move not limited to these two writers but nonetheless clear in their judgements about the state of other generations. Both announce that the energy that marked their generation is lost: Miller takes up Marianne Hirsch's and Evelyn Fox Keller's lament that their generation's conviction that there is "important work to be done" is gone.[25] In Zimmerman's terms, "the more recent generation of feminists cannot have this edenic (and apocalyptic) consciousness. What my generation learned through consciousness-raising, they can learn in the classroom."[26]

These are, I think, moot points. For me and for others of my age, consciousness-raising came wrapped up in hippy touchy-feeliness. Preferring disco to Holly Near, I had my consciousness raised in the dance clubs of the 70s. I do not, however, want to place "my" generation against that of the authors in *Changing Subjects*. For a start, "we" occupy a rather slippery demographic and institutional position. In Québec at least, those from 18 to 35 are considered as "*la génération manquée*," the lost generation, post-baby boom. I am thus on the cusp of a baby boom that is rather strangely defined in terms of actual age rather than date of birth. Neither in nor out of that historic divide, as a tenured academic, I have a very "boomer" kind of job. Thus, rather than exposing the petty angst of my own socio-demographic position (like what will happen on my 36th birthday), I want to turn to another book that I read alongside *Changing Subjects* in order to let two clearly defined generations rub up against each other.

The rather unwieldy subtitle of *Feminist Fatale* effectively delineates a distinct generation: *Voices From the "Twentysomething" Generation Explore the Future of the "Women's Movement."* In it, Paula Kamen (a graduate of the Journalism Department at the University of Illinois who is presumably in her twenties), interviews various and numerous American "twentysomething" types about feminism and the women's movement. Perhaps not surprisingly, choice immediately comes to the fore as being synonymous with feminism. Moreover, choice is articulated both as a critique of older generations of feminists and as central to the very definition of feminism. For instance, Kamen quotes one of her interviewees from Rutgers University as saying, "Now that some women have fought for a bigger slice of the pie, it's time to change the recipe."[27] She then extends this point to argue that this "means looking carefully at choice, and who still does not have enough of it."[28] If this places choice in the hands of older and more privileged feminists, it remains key to the younger generation's understanding of feminism. Kamen reports how she finally "took the risk and actually talked with a bonafide [twenty-four year old] feminist.... When I simply asked her to describe the typical feminist or rank the most important feminist issue, she said that the whole idea of feminism wasn't to have a typical feminist—you were supposed to make the choices best for you."[29]

Definitions abound given that Kamen's book has the double objective of reporting what the twentysomething generation thinks of feminism, as well as educating them about feminism. From one side of the age divide, feminism is variously defined by young women and men in the following ways: "[F]eminism was commonly perceived as meaning one thing: equality"; "Feminism is a belief that we should all have the same rights and that what you do with those rights is up to you"; "Feminism is the ability to make choices. To define who you are, not to have someone tell you who you are"; "Feminism is the struggle to keep choices open to women and the struggle against the oppression of all people."[30] When asked to name the major issues for women now, the consensus seems to be: "to fight violence against women, secure abortion rights and achieve equal pay for equal work." Moreover, "the family was a major issue throughout conversations that called for more tolerance of women's choices and a higher valuation and more support for motherhood."[31]

Some rather evident points emerge from this non-encounter across the ages. Obviously choice is seen to be the linchpin of feminism when viewed from the position of the twentysomethings. And for the fortysomethings, choice has become integrated into their sense of feminism's (read, their own) history. In the words of those interviewed by Kamen, choice opens into equality, rights and individual values. As one young feminist put it, we live in a society that reveres "'masculine' tendencies above the female tendencies so that we make decisions based on profit, expediency and aggressiveness—and lack of importance of individual needs."[32] Given that Barbara Ehrenreich is Kamen's older feminist of choice, it is coincidental that Ehrenreich and Deirdre English argue in *For Her Own Good* that "feminism seems to become ever more determined about its undeterminedness, more nervously defensive of 'choice' for its own sake, less and less prone to ask how these came to be choices in the first place."[33] While attacking choice, Ehrenreich and English uphold as corrective "the 'womanly' values of community and caring [that] must rise to the center as the only *human* values."[34]

From all sides then, choice is conflated with visions of the individual. From my own theoretical choices, I want to take this articulation of choice and the individual through some recent debates in feminist theory. In part, this choice is motivated by the ways in which these debates highlight a certain (mis)understanding of the status of the individual. In the United States, these debates foreground a deep anxiety about the right choice of theory. The agony of the ampersand can be felt in countless articles entitled "Feminism & _____" (fill in the blank: feminism & postmodernism; feminism & Foucault, etc.). This use of "and" tends to be misleading in that it is more often a case of opposing feminism to _____ (fill in the blank). Here the "and" more often translates as an opposition of the two terms and betrays a logic that turns on the seeming impossibility of the arrangement. This return of the ampersand is even more intriguing given the now fashionable calls for the deconstruction of all binaries. Without joining the chorus, it seems to me that choice raises the stakes as it complicates what it means to be beside the binary.

For a start, what comes across in these debates is that one has to choose one thing as opposed to another thing, i.e., that choice always entails thinking and acting in terms of the one or the other. As expressed in Kamen's interviews, choice is interpreted as a zero-sum game wherein the choices of some detract from the possibility of others having choices. While this view is quite understandable, it installs a logic of "either-or" at the expense of raising the exigency of analyzing and changing the material conditions that severely limit the ability to choose, as well as the range of choices possible. In turn, this emphasis on a binary system of opposing terms plays out in feminism as an immensely difficult moral conundrum. Thus, on the one hand we find an insistence (both implicit and explicit) to go with politically sanctioned choices, and on the other, there is the idea that the fall-out of my choice will directly (and harmfully) effect other women. There is a sense here that the wish of the one becomes the general (and oppressive) rule.

An instance of this interrelated type of thinking for me is raised by the quite astounding amount of emotional energy that was spent on the question of lesbianism. Without denying the homophobia that continues to circulate in certain forms of feminism,[35] it strikes me as both insane and sad that some heterosexual feminists continue to feel guilty about their presumably chosen sexuality: sad in that it seems to be a waste of affective energy; insane in that it places sexual choice at the level of the same zero-sum logic. I am also astonished that within some queer circles, it seems that one has to have been born queer in order to qualify as a bonafide dyke. Having finally come out at a relatively advanced age, it appears that my choice is written off by some as a mere thing of the moment, a passing fad. Apart from the amazing presumption that one can judge the motives of others, this type of move effectively effaces the intricate and long materiality of coming out; the continual engagement at social, political and affective levels that requires one to come out again and again (as a tee-shirt puts it, "this is not a phase"). At the risk of simplifying matters, the problem is that seeing choice in these terms reifies some choices, while it personalizes the question of choice. In other words, choice is abstracted from the material and discursive conditions in which one chooses, and it is grounded in the figure of the individual woman who must face up to choice. Cut off from the questions of the time, manner and place of the operations of choosing, choice becomes ahistorical. This then reinforces the power of the individual as it reduces ethical questions to seemingly straightforward, individualized matters of moralism.

IN BETWEEN THE POSTS

In another anthology that marks itself self-consciously as seriously monumental (how else can one take a title like *American Feminist Thought at Century's End*?), Linda Kauffman gathers together a collection of milestone feminist articles. In her own article (which is also published in *Changing Subjects*), Kauffman takes on "personal criticism" which seems to encapsulate everything that Kauffman finds wrong with feminism at the moment. Her critique centers on the ways in which "personal testimony" turns on a conception of "the individual—removed from history, economics, and *even from the unconscious*—[who] is depicted as someone who always has choices, and whose choices are always 'free.'"[36] Kauffman thus wants to counter the implosion of personal choices and feminist history that marks *Changing Subjects*. But, even as I agree with her attack on individualism, her understanding of "the individual" seems to me to be rather limited. For instance, Kauffman argues that Jane Tompkins' stance is pure individualist ideology.[37] She thus argues that "to be a subject (to recognize oneself as a free and unique being) is itself an effect of subjection to ideology."[38] At another point, Kauffman articulates the moral of Margaret Atwood's *The Handmaid's Tale* as providing a timely warning to feminism: "apocalypse is inevitable if we continue to be sunk in subjectivity."[39]

What emerges here is a rather basic poststructuralist critique of individualism, and more exactly, it is constructed and conducted along the lines of Althusser's theory of ideology. As such, it condenses a number of problematics that have been separated and reworked since the 1970s moment of "high theory." Thus, for Kauffman, as for the Althusser of "Ideology and State Apparatuses," the construction of the individual is the *raison d'être* of ideology. As we all remember, ideology works by "always-already" interpellating individuals as subjects.[40] In the Lacanian-influenced second part of the essay, Althusser elaborates the doubled nature of this specular, or mirrored, representational arrangement which in turn is constitutive of ideology and allows for its functioning.

In this Althusserian mode, which Kauffman implicitly reproduces, ideology constitutes a totalized system of representation whose task is to produce the subject who misrecognizes herself as an individual. As Teresa de Lauretis succinctly argues in reformulating Althusser, it is very clear that part of the ideological working of gender is precisely to blur the distinction between class and individual: "so gender represents not an individual but a relation, and a social relation; in other words, it represents an individual for a class."[41] This is also a fundamental a priori for materialist feminists.[42] What de Lauretis allows us to see is that women as historical subjects are caught up within the workings of at least two systems of representation. As I read de Lauretis's argument, the "subject of feminism" is precisely that slippage between the self-representation that individual women form and the representation of woman qua woman. In Kauffman's argument, however, we are back within a *mono*lithic system of representation wherein the subject is an effect of subjection to ideology. In this line of argument, the "choices" that are expressed in "personal criticism" would seem to be but instances of Althusser's imaginary forms through which individuals live their relation to their real conditions of existence. The problem is that Kauffman's critique of the ideological subjection of the individual does not allow her to consider the possibility of distinguishing the individual from individuation, subjection from subjectification. Thus, Kauffman wants to deconstruct the individual within feminism but, paradoxically, she does this by focusing her critique on individual writers and not on the wider material bases that allow for individualism within feminism. Moreover, there is no room within her critique for a consideration of the various ways in which women do individuate themselves.

Choice, therefore, can be formulated as entailing a constant movement between these two systems of representation. While clearly the liberal figure of the Individual is not the base from which to formulate feminist politics for the "century's end," we cannot afford to ignore the affect and desire expressed in the movement declenched by examples of choice. Rather than seeing these examples as always-already ideological, as pernicious enticements to subjection, I suggest that we need another model of thinking about how, where, and why

individual women choose. In taking seriously the idea that we are all continually caught up in choosing, we move away from an Althusserian model of the
individual relentlessly interpellated by state apparatuses. Perhaps more importantly, it allows us to consider the place of a politics of subjectification within
feminism where choices are not always weighed down by impossible ideals,
products of a single system of representation. In turn, this allows us to begin to
conceptualize an ethics of choosing where choice is figured as relational.

Concretely, this reformulation of choice plays out in two ways. First, choice
can no longer be thought of as representing a coherent political project in the
sense that feminism is always "for choice." Second, in foregrounding the relations between representation and self-representation involved in choice, we may
undermine the ideology of the individual within feminism. In the place of individual choices being conflated as choice in feminism, a logic of being by choice
forces us to consider choice as a mode of subjectification. Here the emphasis is
no longer on the subjection of women, subjection (*assujetissement*) being understood as either the result of domination or as a celebration of the individual in all
her glory. Rather, subjectification (*subjectivation*) entails a material analysis of the
conditions of possibility that are rendered visible in the process of choosing.
Choice as a closed project of representation is thus rejected in favor of choice as
production: being by choice as a mode of multiplying choices. Or as Deleuze
puts it, "there is no more representation, there is only action, action of theory,
action of practice in relations of relays or networks."[43] To catch these relays in
action, let me turn to a consideration of how multiple and multiplying examples
of choice might be made to work.

CHOICE EXAMPLES

Recalling my earlier examples of the plethora of choice, I now want to emphasize the work of the example in deconstructing choice as representation. In her
consideration of postmodernism, Butler questions how a quotation can "serve as
an 'example' of postmodernism, symptomatic of the whole?" As she argues, "if I
understand part of the project of postmodernism, it is to call into question the
ways in which such 'examples' and 'paradigms' serve to subordinate and erase
that which they seek to explain."[44] Here the example can be seen as a "trickster,"
in that it actually undoes the representational work it purports to do. In other
words, the example seems to be standing in for larger statements, it pretends to
be symptomatic of something, but in actual fact it is already beside that which it
seems to express. As Giorgio Agamben argues, the example refuses to stand in for
whatsoever; as he states, it is "a concept that escapes the antinomy of the universal and the particular."[45] In other words, the example must be used not as a
sample or representative of a larger instance, but as that which is "defined by

the absence of property."[46] Indeed, translating from the Greek *"para-deigma,"* the example is "that which appears beside."[47] The example throws us away from any affirmation about the essence of the thing it qualifies; it breaks up direct lines of equivalence. It is non-representational and throws us outside of the reach of both senses of representation. For me, this concept of the example renders operational Butler's argument about the risk of foundationalism within feminism. As she states, "To establish a normative foundation for settling the question of what ought properly to be included in the description of women would be only and always to produce a new site of political contest.... This is not to say that there is no foundation, but rather, that whenever there is one, there will also be a foundering, a contestation."[48]

Extending Butler's argument, the concept of the example allows me to consider more closely the everyday working of this movement between the utterance of foundations and its necessary and concomitant foundering. Simply put, examples of choice no longer coalesce into representational statements of being "for choice." I apprehend these quotidian images and examples of choice first and foremost in their singularity, and not as an ensemble belonging to one or another foundational premise. In other words, the relations of difference among examples of being "by choice" emphasizes the foundering, the confusion of any normative project—be it inside feminism or out.

From this fairly abstract point, I plunge with hesitancy into full confusion. One of the most obvious and difficult uses of choice is, of course, in the abortion debates. It is perhaps one of the remaining sites within feminism where foundational principles rarely meet with foundering, where universalist statements go undeconstructed. For me, and for others, the right to abortion is such a fundamental issue that one is nearly compelled to put aside any intellectual quandaries. Concomitantly, the feminist voices that have contested the seeming evident and universal nature of the right to abortion have been extremely rare. Given this apparent consensus, it was with some courage that Valerie Amos and Pratibha Parmar argued in 1981 that "in asking for abortion on demand, white women are failing to recognize what contraception and abortion *mean* to black women."[49] And given the somewhat righteous tone of feminism on this subject, it must have taken guts for them to argue, "Having a child is sometimes the only way in which a black girl can show that she has some control over herself. It may be the only thing she *wants* that she can *have*."[50] In their argument, Amos and Parmar refuse the romanticization of either the maternal or abortion. Here abortion is figured in material terms and as such it becomes a question of abortion by choice, choice being allowed or disavowed by the conjunctural articulations of material circumstances and affective investments. Apart from these isolated feminist articulations of abortion as a contextual question, the overwhelming train of thought on abortion has tended to run smoothly along the lines of what Mary Poovey calls "the basic tenets of liberal individualism—choice, privacy, and rights."[51]

Indeed, Poovey's article is itself still fairly rare in that she tries, through an intelligent and motivated use of poststructuralism, to question the feminist abortion position in terms of the ways in which such ideals are implicitly circulated. The cogency of her argument is due, in part, to the fact that she primarily draws on feminist legal theorists and not literary critics, and that the problematics of abortion and of poststructuralism are brought together at a concrete level. In critiquing the postulates of both the Roe decision and that of Webster, Poovey shows how choice, be it in relation to the "privacy defense,"[52] the "equality defense,"[53] or in anti-abortion rhetoric, plays into "the metaphysics of substance." In simple terms, the metaphysics of substance refers to the ideal of a common and reasoning "core" which guarantees "personhood" and the concomitant claim to rights. That this is an abstraction that never truly remains indifferent to the body (its color or sex) that houses the "core" is fairly obvious. It is precisely Poovey's point that this core needs to be demasked and rid of its ideal status. As she argues, "As long as we engage in what is essentially a metaphysical debate about abstract rights, choices, and privacy, we will remain blind to the fact that metaphysics can be used to reify and rationalize a set of social practices that prohibit access to concrete rights, choices, and privacy."[54] In her discussion of the logic motivating the Webster decision, Poovey makes it clear that the logic of "for choice" may be better suited as a strategy for right-leaning judges rather than as a tactic in pro-abortion arguments. At least the Rehnquist court seems to understand the usefully ambiguous nature of "for choice" when they ruled that "Curtailing public funds…left a pregnant woman with the same choices as if the state had chosen not to operate any hospitals at all."[55]

From Poovey's argument, we can begin to understand abortion as a relational matter. Abortion by choice sets in motion the relays of the necessary relations between abortion, funded day-care, pre- and post-natal care, etc. In her introduction to the posthumously published writings of Linda Singer, Butler raises similar issues when she speaks of Singer's reaction to the choices proffered in the treatment of her cancer: "What she reflected on in those final months was the 'absurdity' (her word) of making a choice for which no definitive justifications could be found and no certain consequences could be predicted."[56] Akin to Poovey's conclusion that "once the concept of individual choice is granted, it is very difficult to decide what choices will be declared legitimate,"[57] this is to realize the deep anxiety of choice. From their different points of departure, both Butler and Poovey concur about the necessity of recognizing, on the one hand, that "choice cannot remain abstract,"[58] and on the other, that it compels an analysis of "the discursive production that the demand for a decision incited and sustained."[59]

BECOMING CHOICES

From these arguments, I now tentatively reformulate the problematic of choice: Choice takes place in a discursive field, it produces and is produced through individual pain, death and pleasure as it displaces the individual into the collective processes of individuation and subjectification. While we are very alone in choosing, at the same time, and of necessity, we place ourselves through our choosing into relations with others. While there is no guarantee of where these relations and relays will go, for me, the singularities expressed in examples of choosing raise nothing less than questions about how we wish to live our lives, about who we are becoming. These examples, and the women caught up within them, also forcefully compel feminism to recognize the limitations of posing choice as a moral project. Putting our proclivities for judgement aside, we may realize that the very productive and multiple relays set in motion by choice preclude any single moral line. Indeed, the relations between choices means that morality becomes impossible, at the same time that it renders possible an ethics of choosing. Following Foucault, Deleuze argues that ethics opposes morality, and that morality kills the possibility of ethics: "morality presents itself as a set of restrictive rules of a special type, which consist of judging actions and intentions in terms of transcendental values (this is good, this is bad...); ethics is a set of optional rules by which to evaluate what we are doing, what we are saying in regards to the mode of existence that they imply."[60] This mode of thinking and living opens into questions of style, "a style of life, not in the least anything personal, but the invention of a possibility of life, of a mode of existence."[61]

For me, this is the challenge that being by choice offers. It acknowledges that choice is always situational, that it is never a mere abstract issue that can be deadened and arranged on one side of a moral line. Be it in matters of life or death, of pleasure or pain, being by choice returns us to an ethics wherein we ask alongside our actions, our words, our choices, what is implicated here? And this question is couched not in moral and transcendental terms but in very concrete ways. Thus, to take two very different examples, abortion must always be by choice; coming out and becoming a lesbian is by choice: These are examples of choices that cannot be conducted in the name of an abstract principle. In simple terms, being by choice focuses us on practices not principles, practices that take their meaning in relations with others. My individual choices conjoin me with others as they re-enact relations to myself. This doubled line, this folding of choice upon itself and upon me is thus a process of individuation, of subjectification.

At the beginning of this essay I spoke rather derisively of my indecision. While not always fun to live with, this indecision is productive. For a start, it mocks the idea, central to certain forms of feminism, of a coherent individual fearlessly facing up to her choices. Rather, indecision catches me up in the very processes of choosing, it foregrounds the singularities of different choices. As Foucault argued of curiosity, indecisiveness and choosing must be understood as evoking "the care one takes for what exists and could exist; a readiness to find strange and singular what surrounds us…a fervour to grasp what is happening and what passes; a casualness in regard to the traditional hierarchies of the important and the essential."[62] For in the end, choice doesn't meet up at one point, rather it fractures and sends us off in different directions; haphazard or not, we bump into others and are in turn caught up in their choices. Simply put, and at the risk of sounding like a Nike ad, an ethics of choice reminds us that it is in the process of choosing that we invent ourselves—over and over and over again.

NOTES |

My research was funded by the Social Sciences and Humanities Research Council of Canada and les Fonds pour la Formation de Chercheurs et l'Aide à la Recherche (FCAR). My thanks to the organizers of the "Bring a Plate: Feminist Cultural Studies" Conference, University of Melbourne, for inviting me to present a version of this paper.

1 Judith Butler, "Editor's Introduction," Linda Singer, *Erotic Welfare: Sexual Theory and Politics in the Age of Epidemic* (New York and London: Routledge, 1993), p. 10.

2 Deleuze Gilles et Guattari Félix, *Anti-Oedipus: Capitalism and Psychoanalysis*, tr. Robert Hurley, Mark Seem and Helen R. Lane (New York: Viking Press, 1977), p. 42.

3 Connie Chung, "Social Studies," *Vanity Fair* (August 1993), p. 174.

4 Reincarnation has shown up in several recent Hollywood films. For instance, in Blake Edward's *Switch* the hero comes back as a woman and has to deal with his (now, her) girlfriend.

5 Frank Deford, "Running Man," *Vanity Fair* (August 1993), p. 54.

6 Deford, "Running Man," p. 54.

7 For those for whom this reference will already be long gone, in the summer of 1993, much was made of the fact that John Majors "rescued" a young girl from Bosnia in order to hospitalize her in England. For those who do not live in areas caught up in the difficulties of choosing national allegiances, I merely wish to raise the ways in which "national choices" are gendered and racialized. Without making any equivalence between the state of civil war in the former Yugoslavia and the continually impending separation of Québec, it is nonetheless instructive that

women have been blamed for the failure of Québec's sovereignty referendum as were Native Canadians for the failure on the part of the Canadian populace to chose the "Meech Lake" constitutional accords. Elsewhere, I develop an argument about the articulation of sexual and sexed choices and national ones (Probyn, forthcoming).

8 Judith Mayne, "*LA Law* and Prime Time Feminism," *Discourse* 10, 2 (1988), pp. 30–47.

9 Cited in Leslie Savan, "Op Ad," *Village Voice* (1989), p. 49.

10 Joe Dolce, "The Warrior, the Wound and Woman-hate: The Politics of Softfear," *Changing Men: Issues in Gender, Sex and Politics* 26 (Summer/Fall 1993), p. 8.

11 Andrea Stuart, "Feminism: Dead or Alive?," *Identity, Community, Culture, Difference*, ed. Jonathan Rutherford (London: Lawrence and Wishart, 1990), p. 32.

12 See Inge Blackman and Kathryn Perry, "Skirting the Issue: Lesbian Fashion for the 1990s," *Feminist Review* 34 (1990), pp. 67–78. For a summary of the lesbian style wars see Joan Nestle's wonderful collection of essays on butch-femme styles and desires, *The Persistant Desire: A Butch-Femme Reader*, ed. Joan Nestle (Boston: Alyson Press, 1992). In Montréal dyke circles, sorting out the make-up lines becomes even more complicated due to stylistic and linguistic differences. Thus, on top of the generational distinctions, the butch-femme questions, and the theoretical and political splits, dress codes also operate to indicate whether one is francophone or anglophone.

13 My thanks to ki namaste for the button and for reminding me of the crucial distinction between "being by choice" and "being for choice." For a compelling socio-semiotic analysis of other choices, see ki namaste, *Deconstructive Que(e)ries: Identity, Social Semiotics, and Queer-Punk Culture*, Thèse de doctorat en sémiologie (Montréal, Québec: Université du Québec à Montréal, 1994).

14 In a different context but in a similar theoretical spirit, Kimberley Anne Sawchuk argues that contemporary advertising discourses act to "lubricate the customer along transactional marketing highways." See "Semiotics Cybernetics and the Ecstacy of Marketing Communications," *Baudrillard: A Critical Reader*, ed. Douglas Kellner (Oxford: Blackwell, 1994).

15 The term "choiceoisie" was coined by Leslie Savan in her "Op Ad" column in the *Village Voice*. Taking up her argument that advertisers increasingly portray women as happily returning to (choosing) the home, I have appropriated the term in order to consider the discursive operations of choice. Thus, for me, "choiceoisie" designates the production of discursive relations between distinct sites of choice.

16 It must be emphasized that Butler is here taking up the terms of Linda Singer's argument about illness and AIDS as epidemic, where "epidemic" has lost its definite or indefinite article. In arguing that choice seems to operate along epidemic lines, I hope not to do violence either to the singularity of AIDS nor to the specificity of

Singer's argument and Butler's contextualization of that argument, see Butler, "Editor's Introduction," *Erotic Welfare*, p. 11.

17 Elizabeth Grosz, "Refiguring Lesbian Desire," Paper presented at McGill University (Montréal, Québec: 1992).

18 *Changing Subjects: The Making of Feminist Literary Criticism*, eds. Gayle Greene and Coppélia Kahn (London and New York: Routledge, 1993).

19 *Changing Subjects*, p. 1.

20 Of course, this is not a new development. Jacqueline Rose among others, has documented the way in which feminism in the United States became institutionalized primarily in English or Literature departments. See Jacqueline Rose, "The State of the Subject (II): The Institutionalisation of Feminism," *Critical Quarterly* 29, 4 (1987), pp. 8–15. One could make similar arguments about the institutionalization of Cultural Studies (which, of course, was originally developed mainly in sociology departments in the U.K.) or about the actual departmentalization of gay and lesbian studies into Queer Theory, again in literature departments.

21 Nancy K. Miller, "Decades," *Changing Subjects: The Making of Feminist Literary Criticism*, ed. Gayle Green and Coppélia Kahn (London and New York: Routledge,1993).

22 Bonnie Zimmerman, "In academia, and out: the experience of a lesbian feminist literary critic," *Changing Subjects*, pp. 114–5.

23 Zimmerman, "In academia, and out," *Changing Subjects*, p. 114.

24 Zimmerman, "In academia, and out," *Changing Subjects*, p. 115.

25 Miller, "Decades", *Changing Subjects*, p. 42.

26 Zimmerman, "In academia, and out," *Changing Subjects*, p. 116.

27 Paula Kamen, *Feminist Fatale: Voices From the "Twentysomething" Generation Explore the Future of the "Women's Movement"* (New York: Donald I. Fine, 1991), p. 7.

28 Kamen, *Feminist Fatale*, p. 7.

29 Kamen, *Feminist Fatale*, p. 10.

30 Cited in Kamen, *Feminist Fatale*, pp. 24–25.

31 Cited in Kamen, *Feminist Fatale*, p. 30.

32 Kamen, *Feminist Fatale*, p. 11.

33 Barbara Ehrenreich and Deidre English, *For Her Own Good* (New York: Doubleday, 1978), p. 323.

34 Ehrenreich and English, *For Her Own Good*, p. 324.

35 Given the current boom in Queer Theory in the United States, it may be difficult for some readers to acknowledge that this issue isn't dead. Given that I (sort of) thought it was dead indeed, I was brought up short when, following a brief that some friends and myself presented at the Québec Human Rights Commission into Violence and Discrimination Against Gays and Lesbians, a feminist group retaliated against us. It was reported as stating that to give "homosexual couples the same

rights as heterosexuals [would be]...against nature." See *La Presse* (November 19, 1993).

36 Linda Kauffman, "The Long Goodbye: Against Personal Criticism, or An Infant Grifter Grows Up," ed. Linda Kauffman, *American Feminist Thought At Century's End: A Reader* (Oxford: Blackwell, 1993), p. 269.

37 See Jane Tompkins, "Me and my Shadow," *The Ultimate Critique: Autobiographical Literary Criticism*, ed. Diane P. Freedman, Olivia Frey and Frances Murphy Zauhar (Durham: Duke University Press, 1993). I also find Tompkins' use of her self to be a bit much. In fact, at times it becomes a caricature of a theoretical position. However, in taking Tompkins as the measure of "personal criticism," Kauffman reduces the fairly complex and variant uses of the self to the level of caricature. For other readings and theories of using the self in feminist criticism, see Martin Biddy, "Lesbian Identity and Autobiographical Difference(s)," ed. Brodski and C. Schenck, *Life/Lines: Theorizing Women's Autobiography* (Ithaca: Cornell University Press,1988) as well as Elspeth Probyn, *Sexing the Self: Gendered Positions in Cultural Studies* (London and New York: Routledge, 1993).

38 Kauffman, "The Long Goodbye," *American Feminist Thought*, p. 269.

39 Kauffman, "The Long Goodbye," *American Feminist Thought*, p. 265.

40 Louis Althusser, "Ideology and Ideological State Apparatus (Notes toward an Investigation)," *Lenin and Philosophy, and Other Essays*, tr. Ben Brewster (London: New Left Books, 1971).

41 Teresa de Lauretis, *Technologies of Gender* (Bloomington: Indiana University Press, 1987), p. 5.

42 Colette Guillaumin, "Pratique de pouvoir et idée de nature (II). Le discours de la nature," *Questions féministes* 3 (1978), pp. 5–28.

43 Gilles Deleuze, *Pourparlers* (Paris: Les Éditions de Minuit, 1990), p. 4. Translation my own.

44 Judith Butler, "Contingent Foundationalism: Feminism and the Question of Postmodernism," ed. Judith Butler and Joan Scott, *Feminists Theorize the Political* (New York and London: Routledge, 1992), p. 4.

45 Giorgio Agamben, *La communauté qui vient. Théorie de la singularité quelconque* (Paris: Seuil, 1990), p. 16.

46 Agamben, *La communauté qui vient*, p. 17.

47 Agamben, *La communauté qui vient*, p. 16.

48 Butler, "Contingent Foundationalism," *Feminists Theorize the Political*, p. 16.

49 Valerie Amos and Pratibha Parmar, "Resistances and Responses: The Experiences of Black Girls in Britain," ed. Angela McRobbie and Trisha McCabe, *Feminism for Girls: An Adventure Story* (London: Routledge, Kegan & Paul, 1981), p. 147.

50 Amos and Parmar, "Resistances and Responses," *Feminism for Girls*, p. 147.

51 Mary Poovey, "The Abortion Question and the Death of Man," *Feminists Theorize*

the Political, p. 239.

52 As Poovey explains, "As the Supreme Court has interpreted the due-process clause, individuals have been granted the right 'to decide for themselves ethical and personal issues arising from marriage and procreation'" ("The Abortion Question," *Feminists Theorize the Political*, p. 239).

53 "[A]dvocates argue [that due to the 'gender dimension' of the abortion issue] antiabortion laws violate the equal-protection clause of the Fourteenth Amendment because they impose upon women burdens that men do not have to bear" (Poovey "The Abortion Question," *Feminists Theorize the Political*, pp. 239–240). Interestingly, in Canada, the arguments for equality stemmed more from geographical differences: the abortion law was struck down as unconstitutional, because women could not obtain abortions equally across the country.

54 Poovey, "The Abortion Question," *Feminists Theorize the Political*, p. 251.

55 In the Supreme Court ruling of January 24, 1994, which holds that federal anti-racketeering laws may be used to sue militant protestors who block abortion clinics, Rehnquist seems to recognize that the relations between anti-abortion strategies do effectively prevent a woman from choosing to have an abortion. Cited in Poovey, "The Abortion Question," *Feminists Theorize the Political*, p. 249.

56 Butler, "Editor's Introduction," *Erotic Welfare*, p. 3.

57 Poovey, "The Abortion Question," *Feminists Theorize the Political*, p. 250.

58 Poovey, "The Abortion Question," *Feminists Theorize the Political*, p. 250.

59 Butler, "Editor's Introduction," *Erotic Welfare*, p. 3.

60 Gilles Deleuze, *Pourparlers*, p. 137. Translation my own.

61 Deleuze, *Pourparlers*, p. 138. Translation my own.

62 Michel Foucault, "Foucault Live (Interviews, 1966–84)," *Semiotext(e) Foreign Agents Series*, tr. John Johnston, ed. Sylvère Lotringer and Chris Kraus (New York: Semiotext(e), 1989), pp. 198–9.

13

WRITING NAWAL EL SAADAWI

Fedwa Malti-Douglas

Sparks flew when the leading Arab feminist, the Egyptian physician and writer Nawal El Saadawi,[1] ran into the distinguished scholar and Palestinian leftist activist, Edward Said, at a conference in London in 1992. "Why do you attack me?" Dr. El Saadawi asked Said, referring to an article Said wrote in *The Nation* in which he called her "overexposed (and overcited)."[2] "I am more of a feminist than you are," Said replied.[3] Said's answer evaded El Saadawi's question. He could have easily replied that his position was by no means unusual; it represents, as we shall see, one of the negative consensus positions on the Egyptian feminist. But in doing so, he would have entered into a dialogue with El Saadawi on the merits and demerits of this assessment and, perhaps, on the entire nature of Arab feminism.

In the many years I have spent as an Arab woman writing a book on Nawal El Saadawi,[4] my own intellectual adventure has brought me into contact with audiences for whom the notion of Arab feminism is anathema, and for whom Nawal El Saadawi is not simply "overcited" but is someone who should be silenced. Well-meaning friends and colleagues have sometimes gently, and sometimes not so gently, sought to discourage this obsession of mine of treating El Saadawi as a writer worth investigating. At a prominent conference on women in the Middle East (whose location and date are con-

cealed to protect the guilty), I was shocked and dismayed by the nervous giggles
of an audience of supposed feminists during a discussion of El Saadawi's work.
Most recently, a female friend, after a public lecture I delivered on Nawal El
Saadawi's *Fall of the Imam*, confessed to me that she would give the novelist
another chance.[5] But, be warned, my friend added, she was not going to let me
"convert" her. I confess that I found the evocation of religion here interesting.
Did that make me a believer? And, if so, in what? I did not ask. But I suspect that
it was the "f" word. Another friend, a prominent Palestinian woman poet, reacted to the gift of my *Woman's Body, Woman's Word*, with the following: "Why did
you have to write two chapters on Nawal El Saadawi?" I did not respond.[6]
These incidents are, unfortunately, not isolated.[7]

Why is the reaction to Nawal El Saadawi so vehement? Her anti-patriarchal
discourses, as we shall see, are perceived as fanning the fires of Western anti-Arab
attitudes. That on the one hand. On the other, Nawal El Saadawi has been an
inspiration to many Western readers fascinated with the Arab woman. Her study,
The Hidden Face of Eve (a work we shall meet again below), is by now a classic
in the West.[8] Her novel, *Woman at Point Zero* (Imra'a ᶜind Nuqtat al-Sifr), boasts
perhaps more readers in the West than any other work of contemporary Arabic
letters.[9] With her discussions of genital mutilation, El Saadawi also touches a
chord with African-American writers. For instance, in *Possessing the Secret of Joy*,
Alice Walker thanks El Saadawi for her work on clitoridectomy.[10]

At the same time, the first book written about El Saadawi in her native Arabic
(and still the only one) is not a book *about* her. It is a book *against* her: a
Freudian-based argument that her writings are in contradiction with true womanhood. Its Arabic title, *Unthâ Didd al-Unûtha* (A Female Against Femininity),
accurately reflects its politics. In its English translation as *Woman Against Her Sex*,
the book is the only extended work *on* El Saadawi in an European language.[11]
This is most extraordinary for a Middle Eastern intellectual.

But this consistent presence and its corollary of being a household word in
Middle Eastern studies is a double-edged sword. There is perhaps no other writer
about whom so many mistakes and errors have been propagated by critics, some
of whom might otherwise consider themselves favorably disposed to the
Egyptian feminist.[12]

To err is human, of course, but that is not the point. This controversial figure
seems to have accumulated more than her share of such errors and the mistakes
more often than not tend towards a reinterpretation that has the effect of marginalizing the Egyptian writer. It is almost as if critics feel the need to create an
alternate biography of Dr. El Saadawi. From her birth to her medical vocation
to her writings: false data is cavalierly presented to the uninformed reader. Her
year of birth has been changed.[13] Her medical concentration has been trans-

formed into the one that is most closely attached to women's bodies and befits the physician's gender: gynecology. This speciality is then used to explain some of her work on sexuality, gender, etc.[14] Oddly enough, this is a specialty that El Saadawi never practiced. The translation of the feminist's works has been misattributed.[15] And finally, her own relationship to Egyptian publishing history, a not insignificant fact in the life of an Arab intellectual, has been misrepresented. The publication of her prison memoirs, for instance, was transposed from Cairo to Beirut, a fact that casts an undue shadow of censorship (and foreignness) over the publishing circumstances of the work by the well-known Egyptian Nasserite, Muhammad Fâ'iq, and his Cairo publishing house, Dâr al-Mustaqbal al-ᶜArabî.[16]

Nawal El Saadawi was born in 1931 in the village of Kafr Tahla in the Egyptian Delta, and "grew up in a large family of nine brothers and sisters."[17] She attended public schools before going on to study at the Faculty of Medicine at the University of Cairo. This was not a field El Saadawi chose. Rather, "the Faculty of Medicine takes the best students, those with the highest grades."[18] As a physician, she practiced in the areas of thoracic medicine and psychiatry. She was briefly Egypt's national Public Health Director, a position she lost in 1972 due to her frank writings on sexuality, specifically in *Woman and Sex*.[19]

But the dangers that El Saadawi risked because of her uncompromising views became more dramatic. She was imprisoned in 1981 by Anwar Sadat, along with many other Egyptian intellectuals. This period, though quite brief, had a powerful artistic impact on the Egyptian feminist. The novel she wrote, which is so heavily inspired by the Sadat regime, *The Fall of the Imam*, placed her name on the death list circulated by conservative Islamist groups.

It was also after this imprisonment, in 1982, that Nawal El Saadawi founded the Arab Women's Solidarity Association. In 1985, the Association was granted "consultative status with the Economic and Social Council of the United Nations as an Arab non-governmental organization."[20] On June 15, 1991, the Egyptian government closed down the Arab Women's Solidarity Association and diverted its funds to a religious women's organization. El Saadawi, with her usual energy and convictions, took the Egyptian government to court, but to no avail. The Association's magazine, *Nûn*, has also disappeared from public life.[21]

It was not Nawal El Saadawi's activism, however, that caused the strong negative reaction in her detractors. It was a much more dangerous activity: her writing. At age thirteen, in 1944, she had already penned a novel, *Mudhakkirât Tifla Ismuhâ Suᶜâd* (Memoirs of a Female Child Named Suᶜâd).[22] Half a century of writing has brought forth an impressive array of fictional and non-fictional texts. No other Arab woman writer (and few Arab men) approaches El Saadawi in the breadth of her writing. The Egyptian feminist has also never shied away from subjects others might not even consider speaking about. Male-female relations, gender boundaries, sexuality, medicine, the body: These are issues that inhabit El Saadawi's works and help to mould a powerful discourse that unveils universal patriarchy in its social, political, and religious guises.

If medicine is less a major player than art and writing in El Saadawi's life, the roles of all three are nevertheless played out against the backdrop of politics. Even as a student, she was actively involved in politics. Yet despite this and despite her strong and unswerving allegiances to political causes (such as that of the Palestinians) Nawal El Saadawi never joined a political party.[23] At a public forum at which I was the speaker, a male member of the audience refused to accept the idea that this distancing from a strict political allegiance was possible. For him, El Saadawi had to be linked ideologically and concretely to political parties and male political leaders.

This listener's reaction is perhaps excusable. For a Middle Eastern intellectual, an absence of overt political allegiance might seem inconsistent. But, in fact, this position simply foregrounds the complicated relationship between politics and women's liberation in a non-Western and a non-dominant cultural context.[24] In a seminal work by now almost twenty years old, Fatima Mernissi argued that because women's liberation in the contemporary Middle East is associated with Westernization, the entire issue of feminism becomes entangled in political and cultural debates.[25] Scholars have investigated the complex role of women and nationalism in El Saadawi's home country.[26] The Egyptian feminist has even gotten into the fray herself.[27]

For most Arab intellectuals (both those of the Middle East and of North Africa), to be a leftist or a Marxist means to be politically (though not necessarily culturally) anti-Western and, specifically, anti-American. And while leftist politics in a third-world context normally imply support for the general idea of women's equality, such politics are nevertheless frequently compatible with hostility to movements that advocate equality for women. Cultural critics are by now familiar with the story of women's active roles in the Algerian War against French occupation. It is also clear by now that the expulsion of the foreigner freed Algerian women to move from the battlefield to the kitchen, and this under a leftist, modernizing, anti-imperialist FLN government. Similar gender dynamics have appeared in the Palestinian struggle, which was, until recently, a consensus issue among Arabs worldwide. Liana Badr, a prominent Palestinian woman writer, eloquently lays out what she perceives to have been the weaknesses of the Palestine Liberation Organization vis-à-vis women's issues. Her conclusion?: "Like all Arab regimes, the PLO has a cautious, perhaps reactionary attitude towards women."[28]

Hence, in the Middle East, to be a supporter of liberation causes does not necessarily indicate effective support for women's liberation. In many a situation, Nawal El Saadawi has been questioned about political priorities. Should not the political struggle of oppressed and occupied peoples, like the Palestinians, take precedence over women's issues? After the expulsion of the foreigner, or after the revolution (or, for some, after the creation of the Islamic society), we will be able to sit down among ourselves and work out these vestigial problems. Dr. El Saadawi's opposition to imperialism and the Western powers has been consistent throughout her career, most recently represented by her condemnation of the Gulf War as Western oil-inspired imperialism.[29] Indeed, her forthright position created rifts with some ostensibly radical American feminists. Yet her replies to these questions and their putative optimism on the gender issue have been just as consistent and categorical: women's oppression must be fought in the context, and as an integral part, of all other struggles for human liberation in the region, and indeed worldwide. Here, she differs from many. To quote Liana Badr again: "However deeply I empathize with the women's issue, I can't give it priority in a society which is rife with social and political problems."[30]

But, it is not just that El Saadawi's refusal to adjourn women's issues to some future time is pragmatically essential in a region with no dearth of national, social, and political claims. The Egyptian writer's understanding of the interrelationship of gender with class and other forms of oppression (a relationship clearly reflected in her writing) reverses the political priorities.[31] Without an attack on gender oppression, no durable blows can be delivered against the citadels of injustice. Nawal El Saadawi does not accept the either/or argument of women versus society as a whole. Neither should we. In a way, these nationalist-based arguments against the urgency of women's concerns are local variants of a more general challenge, elegantly refuted by Mary Daly in her *Beyond God the Father*. For Daly, this tactic of asking: "'But isn't the real problem *human* liberation?'" is simply a way to "make the problem [of women's liberation] disappear by *universalization*."[32]

Mary Daly has not imagined, however, all the ways in which an Arab feminist, like Nawal El Saadawi, can be dismissed.[33] Her detractors are made uncomfortable by her writings because they threaten many of the existing discourses on women in the Middle East. Discourses on Arab women both in the Middle East and the West are privileged (and this is not necessarily a positive factor!) by being imbricated in many other discourses, ranging from Orientalism, imperialism, and post-colonialism to world feminism and postfeminism.[34] To discuss the situation of Arab women today is to be dragged willy nilly into these debates. The potentially fiery nature of many of these discussions is rendered even more explosive by other political and religious developments in the region, like the rise of the Islamist movement. El Saadawi, by inserting religion into many of her recent textual creations, has plunged herself into the heart of this debate.[35]

What all these issues have in common is a concern with the problem of the West: as oppressor of the region, as purveyor of negative stereotypes (seen as linked to the first), and more specifically as the origin of a foreign movement, called feminism, which, because of its foreignness is either inapplicable or detrimental to Arab-Islamic culture and society. El Saadawi then becomes, in this view, despite her opposition to Western imperialism (an opposition that her critics usually manage to avoid recalling), a tool of Western imperialism. At the least, she can be labelled an outsider. How convenient it is to symbolically expel from the tribe the person you do not wish to hear! And how ironic, because what is most devastating about the arrows shot by this daughter of the Egyptian countryside is that their points are sharpened by an insider's knowledge.

Thus, many object that El Saadawi's work is giving the Arabs a bad name (read: in the West). Even the critic who discusses the Saadawian corpus is guilty here, because he or she gives credence, or at least exposure, to her positions. It is difficult for me to count the number of times that these objections have been directed at me. I am repeatedly told that the Arabs have a far from favorable press in the West and discussing the likes of Nawal El Saadawi is simply feeding that negative fire.[36] I cannot argue with the first part of this proposition (the negative image of Arabs) but I certainly object to the second (the resulting imposed silence).

These arguments seek to force the discussion of Arab women into a rigid and politically loaded binarism: on the one hand, positive appreciations that easily turn into apologetics, and on the other hand, critical assessments that are characterized as attacks. A pernicious label has even begun to become attached to some of these critical positions: Orientalist feminism.[37] To begin, we can point out that a defensive apologetic slides too easily into a defense of those in power, when not a particular form of cultural arrogance that holds that the Arabs cannot survive a frank discussion of their social problems. Dr. El Saadawi has more confidence in the cultural and intellectual vitality of her people than that. And we, Arabs and non-Arabs alike, should share that confidence.

Of course, the implication behind these arguments levelled at El Saadawi is a simple one: feminists like El Saadawi should be silenced lest they reveal to non-Arab readers dark secrets about the Arab world. I have talked elsewhere about the implications of this silencing that is nothing short of censorship.[38] Suffice it to say here that this silencing takes place when questions of gender are at stake, but is rarely deemed necessary when questions of class or other oppression are raised. No one accuses the leftist writer who denounces the upper classes or political despotism of giving the Arabs a bad name. And, of course, none of this is meant to imply that El Saadawi skirts issues of class. Far from it. Class perspectives are always integrated into her gender analyses. Simply, gender problematics are treated in her writing with a directness that is rare, not only in Arabic letters but in mainstream media throughout the world. It is this that makes her so threatening. The image-of-the-Arabs-in-the-West is a smokescreen. It is the attack on values long cherished (and not only in the Middle East) that is the real problem.

But this accusation of stoking anti-Arab fires almost always carries other related charges in its wake. Is not Nawal El Saadawi writing for a Western audience? Does this not make her then a "Western" feminist? An Arab-American woman declared to me after a public lecture in which I exposed Nawal El Saadawi's subversive rewritings of the classical Arabo-Islamic tradition: "I still think she is a Western feminist." The "still" tells it all, seeking to negate any evidence that might prove the assertion wrong. It follows then, from this Western allegiance, that El Saadawi's writings do not provide their reader with an "authentic" vision of Arab women and the Arab world.

Any reasonable discussion of the issue of the Western nature of an intellectual and political ideology and its applicability in a non-Western context must be expanded to include not only feminism but other ideologies and movements as well. The most obvious of these would be Marxism. While there are many in the Middle East, notably neo-traditionalists, who reject Marxism as foreign and irrelevant, this is not the position of the overwhelming majority of those, inside and outside the region, who question the applicability of feminism.[39] No one in the scholarly community seems uncomfortable with categories like class, imperialism, capitalism, and exploitation applied to Middle Eastern societies. Advocates of the "shouldn't be used there because not invented there" school of thought most often direct their objections not to ideologies that they themselves may harbor, but to ideologies that they find distasteful. Gender analyses seem to generate much more intellectual squeamishness than those derived from other social problematics.[40]

Gender consciousness is far from new to Middle Eastern society. Social, cultural, historical, and legal questions relating to male-female roles, equality of women, etc. have been part and parcel of Arabo-Islamic discourse for centuries.[41] This is one area where the culture had no need of a Western import.

The physician feminist and writer, Nawal El Saadawi, has locked her powerful pen on many of the gender obsessions in her own culture and has woven memorable narratives around them. Her work demonstrates that it is possible to denounce women's oppression without taking a pro-Western stance and without forgetting the reality that class differences make in the differing patterns of women's oppression. But to seek to exclude feminist perspectives (that is, the reality that as groups males dominate females across the planet) from particular geo-political zones, in this case the Arab world, the Middle East, or the world of Islam, is to automatically privilege patriarchal discourses within these zones.

Anti-imperialism can easily become a trap through which nationalism, while seeking to defend the native against the outsider, really defends those in power in the native society. A feminism that is not internationalist will find itself powerless because it will allow nationalisms to be used against the empowerment of women in each separate society.

How tempting it is for some to dismiss as Western feminism the entire intellectual and artistic venture that examines these constructs! Yet, El Saadawi's very concrete discussions, her often sociological novels based on her own observations of the lives of women in the city, in the country, in the upper classes, and in the lower classes, stand as an eloquent refutation of this position.

The problem, however, lies deeper than the sociological specificity of Dr. El Saadawi's work. It goes to the heart of the problematic notions of authenticity and East-versus-West. When, in 1991, a major university press advertised a translated novel by a Moroccan woman, it did so on the premise that this novel was "uniquely Moroccan," in contrast to the fact that: "Most novels by women of the Middle East that have been translated reflect Western views, values, and education."[42] At the time of this advertisement, the largest number of "novels by women of the Middle East" available in English translation were, indeed, those of El Saadawi. Ultimately, it is of little importance whether or not she was refered to in this highly questionable categorization of women's novels in the Middle East, because this advertising copy only articulates in writing what many voices utter in corridors or in closed gatherings: novels that present problematic images of the Middle Eastern woman "reflect Western views." The "uniquely Moroccan" in the advertisement for the translated work also implies that the reader will get a more intimate and authentic look at the lives of Middle Eastern women.

But the world in which both our Moroccan author and Nawal El Saadawi are circulating is an international one in which the East-West dichotomy is often misleading. Both our writers begin in a regional context that is linguistically defined. They do this by their decision to write in Arabic. At the same time, they are swiftly drawn, more willingly than not, into a transnational circulation of cultural products.[43] The more successful Arab writers and scholars are part of an international market in which everyone strives to have his or her text sold. There are no Arabic authors who do not wish to see their work translated and integrated into the world literary scene. Anyone who thinks this phenomenon is limited to the secularists, or to the leftists, or to the Westernized intellectual class, needs but to walk into the Islamist bookstores of Paris and London to find loving translations into the languages of the colonizers of the works of the most anti-Western Islamic neo-traditionalists. And this is to say nothing of the Middle Eastern intellectuals whose lives are spent in exile in Western countries, hence partaking of at least two cultures. It is difficult to pace through the corridors of the Institut du Monde Arabe in Paris without bumping into some of the Arab world's most beloved intellectuals and artists. And this is also to say nothing of many of the literary genres, like the novel and the short story, in which non-Western writers indulge (like our Moroccan woman writer) and which are originally Western. Universities around the globe are also zones of such cultural hybridization, but one need not belabor the obvious.

To speak of authenticity in this context is as vain as the tourist search for the authentic, unspoiled site that ceases to be authentic as soon as the tourist has set foot on it. For there is no authentic modern Arab world (or discourse) if that means one untainted by Western culture. Just as it would be equally vain to speak of an authentic medieval Arabic culture, if this means one untainted by influences from Greece to Persia. The historic greatness of Arabic culture, indeed, has been its capacity to act as the cosmopolitan vehicle for the integration of diverse civilizational strands. Modern Arab culture, from its most secular to its most religious manifestations, from its most elite to its most popular products, bears the inescapable imprint of Western cultural exports. More important, there is no contemporary intellectual figure, man or woman, the most neo-tradition-alist of Islamic revivalists, whose thought has not been powerfully affected by modern European ideas. The discourse of authenticity in this context plays two political roles within the region. The first is the attempt to discredit as foreign one's ideological opponent. The second is a plea for recognition on the part of the budding artist or intellectual who has yet to gain access to the more lucrative international markets.

When El Saadawi writes, she is not speaking for all Arab women. She realizes what a vain venture this would be. Her voice is that of one Arab woman. And it speaks of the condition of Arab women (and men, of course, in the process) in her own society. Though not all of her work is realistic in the literary sense, her texts are overwhelmingly based on her own direct knowledge and experience.

By the same token, to call attention to the transnational role played by many of El Saadawi's writings is not to deny their linguistic specificity. Nawal El Saadawi's narratives are intricately woven tapestries in which the choice of a word, like the color of a thread, becomes an important marker. The rich linguistic specificity of the Saadawian narratives runs the danger of being eliminated when her writing is transposed into another language, such as English. Mistakes creep in, sections are eliminated.[44]

Let us take, as an example, the work that made El Saadawi a celebrity on the international feminist stage: *The Hidden Face of Eve*, whose title in the Arabic original is *al-Wajh al-ᶜArî lil-Mar'a al-ᶜArabiyya*.[45] Translated literally, the title should read: *The Naked Face of the Arab Woman*. The title of the Arabic original has but one word in common with its English counterpart, *al-Wajh* (Face). But going outwards from the face, both titles manage to center on obsessions dear to their own cultures: naked face, hidden (read: covered) face.[46] For the Arab woman, El Saadawi wanted to emphasize the uncovering. For the Western reader, the translation wanted to evoke the veil and its fascination. For this reader as well, the Arab woman becomes transmuted into Eve, a more universal symbol for women. Cultural critics do not have to be reminded of the importance of book titles. But imagine my surprise when I heard one of the more serious young women scholars in Middle Eastern studies invoke and discuss the English title, *The Hidden Face of Eve*, to demonstrate the importance of Eve in the contemporary Middle East and for a feminist figure like El Saadawi. This is not to belie the importance of Eve, either for El Saadawi or for gender criticism.[47] Simply, in the title of her work, written originally in Arabic, the Egyptian feminist wished to emphasize the Arab woman and her struggle.

This game of titles reminds us that a translation is a new cultural product, one that speaks to different audiences and different cultural concerns. El Saadawi's popularity in the West should not mislead critics who are unable to deal with the texts in their original Arabic into treating the English translation as an adequate guide to the subtleties of her art.

Of course, part of this responsibility lies with the specialists in Middle Eastern literature. Rather than analyzing this feminist literature, they wish to isolate it from the mainstream of Arabic literature. A recent assessment from a Middle East specialist bears quotation:

> The Egyptian physician, polemicist and authoress [sic] Nawal al-Saadawi has several works in English translation: some of these are extended in length and partly imaginative and are therefore considered to be novels. These include *Woman at Point Zero*...; *God Dies by the Nile*...; *Two Women in One*...; *Memoirs of a Woman Doctor*...; *The Fall of the Imam*...; and *The Circling Song*. In each case these works combine autobiographical references and personal opinions with fictional representations of persons either real or imagined in a radical feminist context with heavily emotional, anti-establishmentarian and anti-Islamic overtones. They are hightly controversial in the Arab world.[48]

The implied suggestion that snippets of autobiography and polemical journalism have been spread out with some imaginative material to the length of virtual novels would be demeaning were it not methodologically naive and factually inaccurate.

But more is at issue here. Does the frankly polemical force of so much of El Saadawi's work mean that it is somehow not fully literary? The debate over art and the politically engaged writer is an old one. Dr. Nawal El Saadawi is clearly an *engagé* writer. Readers (and critics) may certainly disagree about the literary qualities of her work. But to deny its artistic status because of her engagement in the cause of women is to oppose this cause, and, in effect, to contribute to the maintenance of existing gender relations both in the Middle East and in the West.

NOTES |

1 Because Nawal El Saadawi is now teaching in America, she has, in a sense, anglicized her name. I will use this form of her name rather than a simplified direct transcription from the Arabic, except when Arabic sources are being cited.

2 Edward W. Said, "Embargoed Literature," *The Nation* (September 17, 1990), p. 280.

3 Personal Communication with Nawal El Saadawi, April 14, 1993.

4 Fedwa Malti-Douglas, *Men, Women, and God(s): Nawal El Saadawi and Arab Feminist Poetics* (Berkeley: University of California Press, forthcoming).

5 Nawâl al-Sa‘dâwî, *Suqût al-Imâm* (Cairo: Dâr al-Mustaqbal al-‘Arabî, 1987), translated by Sherif Hetata as *The Fall of the Imam* (London: Methuen, 1988). See also Malti-Douglas, *Men, Women, and God(s)*, chap. 5.

6 See Fedwa Malti-Douglas, *Woman's Body, Woman's Word: Gender and Discourse in Arabo-Islamic Writing* (Princeton: Princeton University Press, 1991), pp. 111–143.

7 I have discussed other incidents of what constitutes feminist censorship in "Dangerous Crossings: Gender and Criticism in Arabic Literary Studies," *Borderwork: Feminist Engagements with Comparative Literature*, ed. Margaret Higonnet (Ithaca: Cornell University Press, 1994), pp. 224–29.

8 *The Hidden Face of Eve: Women in the Arab World*, tr. Sherif Hetata (Boston: Beacon Press, 1982).

9 Nawâl al-Sa‘dâwî, *Imra'a ‘ind Nuqtat al-Sifr* (Beirut: Dâr al-Adâb, 1979), translated by Sherif Hetata as *Woman at Point Zero* (London: Zed Press, 1983).

10 Alice Walker, *Possessing the Secret of Joy* (New York: Harcourt Brace Jovanovich, 1992), p. 285.

11 Jûrj Tarâbîshî, *Unthâ Didd al-Unûtha* (Beirut: Dâr al-Talî‘a, 1984). This work has been partially translated by Basil Hatim and Elisabeth Orsini as *Woman Against Her Sex: A Critique of Nawal el-Saadawi* (London: Saqi Books, 1988). El Saadawi penned a reply to this criticism which was published in the same volume.

12 Many of the arguments in the following pages have been taken from the first chapter of my book, *Men, Women, and God(s)*.

13 See Miriam Cooke, "Arab Women Writers," *The Cambridge History of Arabic Literature: Modern Arabic Literature*, ed. M. M. Badawi (Cambridge: Cambridge University Press, 1992), p. 453.

14 See Emmanuel Sivan, *Radical Islam: Medieval Theology and Modern Politics* (New

Haven: Yale University Press, 1985), p. 182. The later expanded edition of this work solves the problem by eliminating all reference to Nawal El Saadawi. See Emmanuel Sivan, *Radical Islam: Medieval Theology and Modern Politics*, enlarged ed. (New Haven: Yale University Press, 1990).

15 See the short biography by Margot Badran and Miriam Cooke, "Nawal al-Saadawi," *Opening the Gates: A Century of Arab Feminist Writing*, eds. Margot Badran and Miriam Cooke (London and Bloomington: Virago and Indiana University Press, 1990), p. 203.

16 Cooke, "Arab Women Writers," p. 454. The error here is understandable and is most likely due to a misreading of the Arabic original, since the Dâr al-Mustaqbal al-^CArabî is on *Beirut* Street in Heliopolis (Misr al-Jadîda).

17 Nawal El Saadawi, "An Overview of My Life," tr. by Antoinette Tuma, *Contemporary Authors Autobiography Series*, vol. 11 (Detroit, Michigan: Gale Research Co., 1990), p. 62.

18 Allen Douglas and Fedwa Malti-Douglas, "Reflections of a Feminist: Conversation with Nawal al-Saadawi," *Opening the Gates*, p. 397.

19 El Saadawi, "Overview," p. 70. The date for the dismissal was given to me orally by El Saadawi herself. For the works on sexuality and gender, see Nawâl al-Sa^Cdâwî, *al-Mar'a wal-Jins*, third edition (Cairo: Maktabat Madbûlî, 1974); Nawâl al-Sa^Cdâwî, *al-Unthâ Hiya al-Asl* (Cairo: Maktabat Madbûlî, 1974); Nawâl al-Sa^Cdâwî, *al-Rajul wal-Jins* (Beirut: al-Mu'assasa al-^CArabiyya lil-Dirâsât wal-Nashr, 1976); and Nawâl al-Sa^Cdâwî, *al-Mar'a wal-Sirâ^C al-Nafsî* (Cairo: Maktabat Madbûlî, 1983).

20 Nawal El Saadawi discusses this Association in her "Introduction," *Women of the Arab World: The Coming Challenge*, ed. Nahid Toubia, tr. Nahed El Gamal (London: Zed Books, 1988), pp. 1–7. The volume is composed of papers presented at an AWSA conference in Cairo.

21 I am grateful to Nawal El Saadawi for many of these biographical details.

22 Nawâl al-Sa^Cdâwî, *Mudhakkirât Tifla Ismuhâ Su^Câd* (Cairo: Manshûrât Dâr Tadâmun al-Mar'a al-^CArabiyya, 1990).

23 El Saadawi, "Overview," p. 66.

24 For the complexity of these issues, see, for example, the essays in *Third World Women and the Politics of Feminism*, eds. Chandra Talpade Mohanty, Ann Russo, and Lourdes Torres (Bloomington: Indiana University Press, 1991). The linked issues of nationalism and feminism are also dealt with in Kumari Jayawardena, *Feminism and Nationalism in the Third World* (London: Zed Books, 1986).

25 See, for example, Fatima Mernissi, *Beyond the Veil: Male-Female Dynamics in a Modern Muslim Society* (Cambridge, Mass.: Schenkman Publishing Company, 1975), pp. 99–102. See also the pamphlet by Muhammad Fahmî ^CAbd al-Wahhâb, *al-Harakât al-Nisâ'iyya fî al-Sharq wa-Silatuhâ bil-Isti^Cmâr wal-Sahyûniyya al-^CAlamiyya* (Cairo: Dâr al-I^Ctisâm, 1979).

26 See, for example, Afaf Lutfi al-Sayyid Marsot, "The Revolutionary Gentlewomen in Egypt," *Women in the Muslim World*, eds. Lois Beck and Nikki Keddie (Cambridge: Harvard University Press, 1978), pp. 261–276; Thomas Philipp, "Feminism and Nationalist Politics in Egypt," *Women in the Muslim World*, eds. Beck and Keddie, pp. 277–294; and L. Ahmed, "Early Feminist Movements in Turkey and Egypt," *Muslim Women*, ed. Freda Hussain (New York: St. Martin's Press, 1984), pp. 111–123.

27 Nawal El Saadawi, "Women's Resistance in the Arab World," *Women in the Middle East: Perceptions, Realities and Struggles for Liberation*, ed. Haleh Afshar (London: The Macmillan Press Ltd., 1993), pp. 139–145.

28 See, for example, Frantz Fanon, *A Dying Colonialism*, tr. Haakon Chevalier (New York: Grove Press, 1967), pp. 35–67, pp. 99–120; and the inside cover of Kaci, *Bas les voiles* (Paris: Les Editions Rochevignes, 1984). Of course, there is nothing sociologically unique or even particularly Islamic in this development. It is well known that, after World War II in the United States, women who had entered the work force in the national emergency were eased back into more domestic roles. For a discussion of this issue in other Middle Eastern materials, see Allen Douglas and Fedwa Malti-Douglas, *Arab Comic Strips: Politics of an Emerging Mass Culture* (Bloomington: Indiana University Press, 1993), chap. 10. See, also, Bouthaina Shaaban, *Both Right and Left Handed: Arab Women Talk About Their Lives* (London: The Women's Press, 1988), pp. 158–159, and for the quote, p. 159. Issues of nationalism as they link to gender and the Middle East are also discussed in Val Moghadam, *Modernizing Women: Gender and Social Change in the Middle East* (Boulder, Co: L. Rienner, 1993); and Deniz Kandiyoti, "Identity and Its Discontents: Women and the Nation," *Millennium: Journal of International Studies*, vol. 20, 3 (1991), pp. 429–443.

29 I have been present at lectures and participated on panels with Dr. El Saadawi on many occasions at which she has enunciated these positions.

30 Shaaban, *Both Right and Left Handed*, p. 160.

31 See the analyses in Malti-Douglas, *Men, Women, and God(s)*.

32 Mary Daly, *Beyond God the Father: Toward a Philosophy of Women's Liberation* (Boston: Beacon Press, 1973), p. 5.

33 Joanna Russ, *How to Suppress Women's Writing* (Austin: University of Texas Press, 1983), discusses a variety of other tactics used against women writers.

34 For a recent attempt to link Orientalism and feminist approaches to the study of Middle Eastern women, see Edward W. Said, *Culture and Imperialism* (New York: Alfred A. Knopf, 1993), pp. xxiv–xxv. See, also, Trinh T. Minh-ha, *Woman, Native, Other: Writing Postcoloniality and Feminism* (Bloomington: Indiana University Press, 1989); and Leila Ahmed, *Women and Gender in Islam: Historical Roots of a Modern Debate* (New Haven: Yale University Press, 1992), pp. 144–168. Many of the stud-

ies in *Arab Women: Old Boundaries, New Frontiers*, ed. Judith Tucker (Bloomington: Indiana University Press, 1993), deal, on one level or another, with some of these questions.

35 See, for example, Malti-Douglas, *Men, Women, and God(s)*, chap. 5, 6, and 7.

36 The negative image of Arabs in the West has been much studied. One of the most interesting works in this regard is that of Jack G. Shaheen, *The TV Arab* (Bowling Green: Bowling Green State University Popular Press, 1984).

37 See, for example, Malika Mehdid, "A Western Invention of Arab Womanhood: The 'Oriental' Female," *Women in the Middle East*, p. 48.

38 Malti-Douglas, "Dangerous Crossings."

39 See, for example, ᶜAbd al-Wahhâb, *al-Harakât al-Nisâ'iyya*; Mustafâ Mahmûd, *al-Mârksiyya wal-Islâm*, 6th printing (Cairo: Dâr al-Maᶜârif, 1987); and Mustafâ Mahmûd, *Li-Madhâ Rafadt al-Mârksiyya?*, 3rd printing (Cairo: Dâr al-Maᶜârif, 1989).

40 See Malti-Douglas, "Dangerous Crossings."

41 See Malti-Douglas, *Woman's Body, Woman's Word*.

42 See the University of Texas Press, *Readable Books: Prose and Poetry, Literary Criticism, Linguistics, and Language* (January 1991), p. 6.

43 For a discussion of this phenomenon in much of contemporary Arab culture, see Douglas and Malti-Douglas, *Arab Comic Strips*, chap. 12.

44 For other pitfalls that can be caused by the use of translated work for analysis, see Malti-Douglas, *Men, Women, and God(s)*, especially chap. 8.

45 Nawâl al-Saᶜdâwî, *al-Wajh al-ᶜArî lil-Mar'a al-ᶜArabiyya* (Beirut: al-Mu'assasa al-ᶜArabiyya lil-Dirâsât wal-Nashr, 1977).

46 The localization of the face is not devoid of importance in contemporary Arabo-Islamic discourse. See Fedwa Malti-Douglas, "Faces of Sin: Corporal Geographies in Contemporary Islamist Discourse," *Religious Reflections on the Human Body*, ed. Jane Marie Law (Bloomington: Indiana University Press, forthcoming).

47 In fact, El Saadawi does discuss Eve in her work and in one of her recent novels, Eve makes a prominent appearance. See Nawâl al-Saᶜdâwî, *Jannât wa-Iblîs* (Beirut: Dâr al-Adâb, 1992). See, also, Malti-Douglas, *Men, Women, and God(s)*, chap. 6 and 7. Works on gender that deal with Eve are innummerable. For some recent examples, see Gerda Lerner, *The Creation of Patriarchy* (New York: Oxford University Press, 1986), p. 180ff.; and Carol Meyers, *Discovering Eve: Ancient Israelite Women in Context* (Oxford: Oxford University Press, 1988).

48 Trevor LeGassick, "The Arabic Novel in English Translation," *The Arabic Novel Since 1950*, ed. Issa Boullata, *Mundus Arabicus*, 5 (1992), p. 59, emphasis added. It is difficult to imagine anything that could be autobiographical in a novel, like *Suqût al-Imâm*, whose female hero rises repeatedly from the dead. Examples could be multiplied. But the reader is invited to see the analyses in Malti-Douglas, *Men, Women, and God(s)*.

14

'68 OR THE REVOLUTION OF LITTLE QUEERS

Lauren Berlant

ON REVOLUTION (AND ITS CONTRADICTIONS)

Revolutionary discourse is the kitsch of American national culture. It is a political claim and a patriotic promise that creates the most fervent inspiration, attachment, and embarrassment. It signifies a desired rupture between a past and all possible futures, and yet also affirms the self-identity of nationality and exerts an almost ethical pressure to bring itself into representation. As the originary motive for the American brand of practical utopian politics, it has framed and made sacred the temporalities of a thing called national culture, always promising the imminent resolution of contradictions, difficulties, and desires citizens experience in the present tense. In addition, the revolutionary proclivity that Americans take as their divine and birthright inheritance self-generates an ever-expanding archive of evidence, argument, and unassailable proof of the ongoing virtue of its power.

And yet revolution has also been cast as a claim that must be left behind as a form of aspiration, for it is often considered an unserious model for social transformation. It is too easily assimilated into a form of what Adorno calls pseudo-activity; it is too available for the production of kinds of false-consciousness, as when, in the first volume of *The History of Sexuality*, Foucault discredits a revolutionary politics articulated around sexual liberation.[1] In this negative light, revolutionary-style performance can appear as a shameful mode of distraction. It claims to have already incited foundational changes whose utopian outcomes seem always deferred; it makes it hard to think about formations of violence in the face of the good effects a politics promises; and meanwhile certain specific individuals, classes, and social movements will find themselves abandoned to continue struggling to transform the very same modes of domination that have engendered the constraints they have long suffered. It is as though the revolution existed but not for them, as though their own particular histories were irrelevant, were waste material, in the work of revolution. And if identity, the fetish of unporous selfhood, is the form of personhood made possible by the promise of universal legitimation avowed by the Enlightenment revolution, national culture is also constantly providing evidence of its own tendency to denigrate the very form its revolutionary model has generated. Marx might have called this ruse of bourgeois revolution the tragedy/ farce modality.

In other words, in modern nations and in the context of bourgeois nationalism, revolutionary discourse has been kept alive both as a utopian promise and discredited as a name for a kind of insubstantial utopian praxis and historiography. In the political public sphere, virtue tends to adhere to those who can claim an unimpeded aspiration to, and identification with, the form of identity that claims a revolutionary-national genealogy and a hardwired utopian promise. Thus, for example, the self-described "Reagan revolution," in the domains of national income concentration and federal civil rights law, took up the language of founding fatherhood to transform the logic of national politics during the 1980s; meanwhile, from '63 to '93, anti-racist, anti-misogynist, anti-homophobic marches on Washington have struggled to harness the revolutionary promise to democratize identity, to make national identity a truly utopian identification. Still, however fierce this contestation over the revolutionary privileges of polity and practical life might be, the form of national identity constantly trumps the other identities that aspire to membership in the nation's symbolic order[2]: and so revolutions and counter-revolutions, through public spheres and counterpublics, continue to engender politics by making identity into a kind of booty and by appropriating its enormous value in organizing the longing for a better political, social, cultural, and sensual life.[3]

Judith Butler's *Bodies that Matter* argues that the work of unpredictable social change that queer politics stands for will not only *necessarily* keep playing in the field of identity, but must do so, if "queer politics" is not to lose "its democratizing force."[4] By democracy she refers to the gays and lesbians who feel un- or under-described by queerness. It seems to signify a mode of distributive justice among persons named by established identities. The aspiration to abstraction

that even Butler's elastic notion of identity supports, suggests a narrow conception of what kinds of activities constitute democratic politics and a false equation
of democracy with the ideologies of inclusion, tolerance, and wishful pluralism
that have consistently distracted citizens from grasping how the identity form
of national personhood has authorized the complex violences to, among other
things, the exorbitant and noncoherent worldmaking and sexual activities of
American gays and lesbians. We have barely imagined the conditions of democracy and citizenship outside the identity form that installs an atemporalized
national fetish as the sign and the proof of legitimate identity in American national culture. To do so would require not only a rethinking of the relations between
patriotic nationalist and coercive constitutionalism, but a commitment to developing and describing the knowledges and activities these national forms egest. It
is this double task—to imagine revolution into something other than a new,
improved, but always bio-degradable identity model; and to imagine queer revolution generating a politics that risks the humiliation of being both serious and
desirable—that animates this essay. It is in this sense that this essay continues to
undertake, without finishing, the project of coming after "'68."

Elsewhere I have described some ways in which the half-muted story of practical and symbolic suffering dominated American subpopulations have experi-
enced can become mobilized on behalf of a radically agentive diva citizenship.[5]
Here I want to think about the centrality of the revolutionary claim to the
threats a virtually illegal, but absolutely vital, sex-radical culture poses in and for
the contemporary political public sphere. For the charge and the claim that contemporary sex-radical movements are indeed revolutionary has become a major
weapon in the struggle to define the terms of not-just-sexual justice in the
United States. These struggles include questions about the distribution of health
care resources, pension, immigration rights, and other privileges of citizenship.
But different kinds of fundamental terms of participation in national life are also
central to the contemporary activity of sex-radical politics in America. Let me
tell you a brief fairy tale about it: Once upon a time, "gay and lesbian" signified
to straight people a kind of sex and perhaps some styles of corporeality; now,
however, queer culture represents to straights a mode of emergent revolutionary
historicism and political identification.

The fight to decriminalize gay participation in American social life has generated a counterrevolutionary politics and aesthetics of its own, which stages its
anxiety as an anxiety over the national future. I will organize this discussion
around three genres of political imagination that have become central to the
sustained public sphere resistance to gay politics: one, a discursive mode we
might call "the hypothetical," by which I refer to a genre of supposing or sce-
nario-making that speculates about the future in order to terrorize the scenes of

contemporary politics. This form of speculative narration melds the referential objectivity of realism with the looming national future and has direct political effects both in everyday sexual discourse and official policy. My archive of sex hypotheticals is culled from the battles for and against gay and lesbian civil rights in Oregon and Colorado and from the congressional discussion of gay service in the military, in particular on a phenomenon called "the gay agenda."

The second and third genres of commentary on queer revolutionizing are mediated by a different breed of *unheimlich* narrative. My examples will be taken from Blanche McCrary Boyd's novel *The Revolution of Little Girls*. On the one hand, Boyd's narrative represents what ought to be impossible: an avant-garde populist semiotic through which sex generates a radically-improvised fictive counterhegemonic identity. On the other hand, the novel brings sexual revolution under scathing comic scrutiny. In a blaze of anxiety and elite resistance to the diverse spectacular acts and promises of American feminism in the 1970s and 1980s, the novel participates in a *Time* magazine-like cynical anti-political politics of caricature, one in which the recent history of left politics becomes recoded as evidence of lesbian-feminist shallowness. But it does not simply disavow feminist revolutionary energy. It borrows the collective, public, nation-shaking, world-making auratic of the feminist sexual revolution on behalf, finally, of a hyperprivatized discourse of self-help culture, replete with pop psychology notions of the "revolutionary" ways fantasies of consolidated identity can heal the very wounds the identity-form has helped to generate. In so doing, the novel accurately represents one aspect of what has happened to mainstream American feminism, as it has accomodated therapeutically to the family values rhetoric of conservative or heterosexually-identified women. However, the novel's imperceptive concession to inner child feminism must be understood as a bad bargain with national capitalism and the commodity form of identity; it must be read as a cautionary tale for queer politics. This conjuncture of sex genres—the hypothetical narrative, the populist avant-garde aesthetic, and the satirical antipolitical fiction—constitutes some means by which queer politics is degraded and disciplined in the political public sphere. But what homeopathy other than the currency of identity can we imagine using to counter the dialectic of revolutionary reference and future shock in these contemporary United States?

By the way, this is not an essay about '68, if by '68 we mean the transnational student uprising against the authority of nation-states, universities, patriarchal families, and people with money to govern the conditions of legitimacy which students find horrifically is their class entitlement. There is actually nothing about '68 in this essay. In the longer essay that inaugurated this project, "'68, or something," '68 stands for a whole set of things: a weapon used to ridicule activists whose modes of praxis remind '68ers of political failures they'd rather forget; a moment that has generated little piles of waste and inspiration whose steamy decay might motor other ways of thinking and describing broad-scale social change; it stands for risking political and intellectual embarrassment and even failure at a moment when public sphere experts and theorists emphasize the pragmatics of rational opinion cultures; finally, it stands for a commitment to undercooked transitional thought—about the modes of violence, domination, exploitation, and devastation that have become naturalized as the prices we, those of us who are citizens of liberal democratic cultures, are told we must pay for freedom; and thus about the possibility and politics of futurity itself.[6]

This is also an essay about the lesbian/queer challenge to the conventional sexual imaginaries of feminist and gay politics. It requires a complex dialectical language for describing not what lesbian/queer practices are but all the things they might be making possible, as we harness a motley assemblage of texts and acts that no longer equate identity with safety, safety with privacy, and freedom in a world without violence. After all, the discourse of revolution is always a discourse about violence, and the choice to participate in that kind of praxis redistributes the pains and privileges that collective life generates.[7] It considers sexuality as a thing that cannot be simply testified to in a discourse of unmediated experience, but which must function as a media-form for generating the scene in which we find ourselves acting, making narratives, arguments, displays, and history. In this light, sex (sex between women, lesbian sex) is not an example of everything, nor an object that we can historicize and give such dimension to that we can tell the whole history of the world through it. I say "lesbian/queer" here to mark a constantly-muted story of sexual performance and culture-building that has an important genealogical relation to feminist sexual revolutions and the history of civil rights; I say "lesbian/queer" to counter the ways "queer" often means merely "cool gay man from a city." But if "queer" were to come to mean a set of relations between practice, history, sex, and the imagination of change that took the risk of not giving in to the pseudo-revolutionary capitalist culture of identity exchange, if it meant re-deploying the sensations of minority—violence and envy, linguistic and corporeal displacement—toward an unpredicted way to make occluded pasts and practices into possible futures, and grounds for redescribing the unbearable contradictions of the sexual scene that we might already be experiencing, and if it no longer took the male-dominated post-Stonewall cosmopolitan club scene as its utopian form—well, then happily, I would simply use the word queer. I would argue for a radical engagement with queer sexuality as a mode of production that forces new relations of cultural commentary, revised understandings of what might constitute the work of making a history. I would suggest how transformed norms and media of evidence and argument might mean a radically shifting archival imaginary, within and outside of the academy, a queer mentality that no longer whiplashes between the falsely polarized standard great narratives of historical change and an "authentic" local culture. I mean to promote queer thinking about the costs and the prospects of being post—postmodern, postnational, post '68, post-sexual revolution, and so on—and in particular to consider what it might feel like to inhabit the no-longer state-dominated spaces of erotic proclivity after the great pain of sexual identity, and also its great protections, are stripped away.

PRIVATE FUDDPUCKER GOES TO WASHINGTON: THE HOMOSEXUAL AGENDA

In 1993, America witnessed a series of mass media be-ins against a suddenly virulent thing called "The Homosexual Agenda." It will not surprise you to hear that the homophobic film *The Gay Agenda*, distributed last year in Oregon and Colorado, rather incoherently represents gays and lesbians, but its incoherence has a logic to it. The film features gays and lesbians as spectacularly naked, leathered, dancing maniacs who put on nasty "in your face" parades to display their unnatural rhythm and immorally bad taste in fashion. Whatever eloquent liberal fantasies gays and lesbians might express in their arguments for civil rights, these raunchy images of leather queens, dancing muscular butts, and bouncing breasts become hypothetically the iconic image of post-gay civil rights America, the prophetic terroristic image archive of the homosexual public sphere to come, should civil rights privileges be extended to the animals who seek to be let out of their legal cages to live their lives anywhere they want, including close to your and, horrors, their children.

On the other hand, and crucially, in the expert testimonial talking-head voice-over of *The Gay Agenda*, gays and lesbians are not much spoken of as corporeally disgusting. Instead, queers seeking civil rights are captioned "excessively political and governmental." This is to say that the really dangerous gay agenda is to simulate competence in the register of the public sphere; public sphere drag masks dangerously the sexual perversity that constitutes the core of the homosexuality the filmmakers imagine. As the recent Bill Moyers special on Colorado attests, many straights say they don't worry about what sexual others do "in the privacy of their own bedrooms": indeed, this phrase, "in the privacy of their own bedrooms" and phrases like it are repeated so fervently they join phrases like "I love you" and "I do" as sites of a passionate national fantasy to return all sexuality to the bedroom itself, away from the public sphere which has become, in all sorts of ways, so sexually nasty for the non–diva identified population. It is when the privacy protections of the bedroom are extended to the public and informational contexts of everyday life that gayness takes on the word agenda and becomes a national menace.

Counter to the gay agenda is, I have suggested, the straight hypothetical about gays. Registering the fear that rationalized gay personhood is a kind of drag masking animal predilections, the straight hypothetical has been never so well and so narratively expressed and deployed as in the senatorial probe of gay participation in the military. We have most recently seen the hypothetical form, or the queer story problem, on the front pages of many national newspapers, in illustration of the procedural policing crisis created by the Clinton administration's revision of the meaning for military policy of sexual orientation:

> *Situation*: A servicemember witnesses an act of sodomy by two enlisted men in a barracks room and notifies his superiors. Military law enforcement agents who respond see photographs of one of the suspects engaging in sodomy with other servicemembers. Should those other members be investigated?.,,
> *Situation*: An enlisted man who sees an officer in a well-known homosexual bar and later walking with another man in a park late at night threatens to report him unless he pays $10,000. The officer says nothing but tells the M.C.I.O [Military Criminal Investigative Organization] that he has been blackmailed.[8]

These examples join other "situation noncomedies"—the female officer carrying a sign in a gay pride parade that indicates she is a lesbian, the gay officer who holds hands with a same-sex lover, the straight officer caught hugging someone of the same gender—all leading to the same punch line: "What action should the [M.C.I.O.] take?" More than simply creating scenarios for the law to imagine its future applications, and more than simply providing imaginary guidance for the military queers, these scenes and others have become the way of charting the historic meanings of sexual identity in the contemporary U.S., for gay men, especially.

What's important here is the way the hypothetical charts the future by providing a fictive but historically binding precedent of intention for military and federal court procedure. These scenes are the future of gays in the military, and elsewhere, should this policy stand. But more than this juridically marked future is at stake in the hypothetical future of American sexual subjects. I close this section with a story about senators, military men, and hypothetical violence. I witnessed this incident on the television channel, C-Span, where two senators—William Cohen of Maine, Sam Nunn of Georgia—and a Lieutenant General called Calvin Waller convened to imagine the disciplinary effects open gayness might have on the military. The importance of this episode to the everyday experience of gay civilians is in its banality. It provides for heteronational culture a whole new arsenal of rational ways to express virulent strains of homophobia. And it provides these weapons in the currency of humor, of digression, that is, in the waste languages that reveal the consensual tacit homophobia foundational to even ordinary conversation in the official public sphere.

The scene is organized by a nervous, jocular running debate between Nunn, Cohen, and Waller over how to name the hypothetical gay soldier whose sexual orientation, practice, and self-description raises the policy question. General Waller begins: "If a person then comes into me, I call him in, let's say his name is Cohen." To general laughter Cohen, offscreen, says, "Let's not say, let's not say his name is Cohen. Let's say it's Nunn." More general laughter, and a "No" from somewhere off the screen. Waller responds, "Let's say his name is Fuddpucker." After the break they shortly take, Waller makes an apology: apparently, someone shockingly heard the word "buttfucker" for Fuddpucker, and he meant to slur no-one. He comments that he has used "Fuddpucker" as a generic name for "soldier" for twenty years, as though this duration clears him of having a sexual unconscious. It is probably also relevant that "puddfucker" is a slang term for "masturbator." To Waller's apology Cohen comments, "You wouldn't have had this problem if you'd named him Nunn."

Policy was being created during this remarkable conversation. Senator Cohen notes that "we have an unusual situation in the country, where the Supreme Court declares that you can burn a flag and that is the equivalent of speech which is protected under the constitution; if you declare a sexual preference that is considered to be an act because it implies that you will take some action in the future, although it's unrealized...." Nothing in the concept of performativity has explained this to us: that in the United States to say that you are gay or lesbian means that actions are *about to* unscroll from your body, like so many pencil shavings falling away from the pencil's sharpened point. It's not just the reproduction of sex and actual future generations at stake, but the intelligible terms of national history itself, no longer assured a future by Providential or Imperial logics.

Thus the national theory of sexual identity casts the description of sexual identity as a theory of history: to say "I am gay" is to take up the imaginable space of causality, of the future, and thus of the national prospect.

We might contest this notion of the relation between sexual speech acts and their historical effects. We might, for example, believe the character in *The Revolution of Little Girls* who says, "Sex is a state...not an act. If you think it's an act, you'll miss it," thus producing in the heroine, Ellen, a state of consciousness unorganized by any grammar of sexual value we know.[9] That state of consciousness is commonly called an orgasm: I will return to this later. In any case, the mode of liberal speech that argues for minority legitimation by appropriating constitutional notions of the autonomy of citizens will be a crucial counter to the informal violence of the kinds of semi-official conversation we have here witnessed, and here identity politics might be the form our counter-punches will take. But the counterpolitics of a homosexual agenda can certainly not aspire to speak within the frames of the dominant polity, and our commitment must be to reconceive what kinds of risk a queer public sphere will take as it flakes away at the privacy protections of the hegemonic sex classes, opening up identity to history. I am especially interested in fouling the referent of national personhood, which equates the safety of a timeless superpersonal identity with the capacity to abstract oneself from the ball and chain of a history, and the material body, bodily practice, and genealogy that accompanies its degradations (the inexorable race, class, gender, sex, and ethnic violences of difference superintended by American culture). In this ongoing project, my archival material will be, among other things:

TEDDY BEARS, PEYTON PLACE, ASHRAMS, REVOLUTION

I open this section by fixing on something small, a nipple. The heroine of *The Revolution of Little Girls*, whose name is also a sentence, Ellen Burns, is looking at her friend Hutch, in the opening scene of the novel. She notes that his "nipples were tiny buttons, perfectly formed"; and contrasts these to her own, "pale and shriveled, like white raisins."[10] Ellen does not know what to do with these observations—this is the last moment before she embraces the narrative conventions of futurity that sexual identity ordinarily configures. But the pre-adolescent experience of noting and touching these public genital tissues stays with Ellen as she accrues the entirely disorganized sexual experience the novel narrates. Throughout the novel she longs for a relation of identity that refuses the claim of an already mapped-out future on what feels like a desperately ad-libbed present.

For little else in Ellen Burns's experience supports her instinct to be free, experimental, or even sexually interesting. When she leaves Duke University in 1966 for Harvard, she immediately tries to lose her virginity with a man: but she does this ambivalently, while wearing her girdle, and in the process sprains the man's finger. He brandishes his bright blue injury as a trophy, but she just wants to hide. Humiliated, she jumps at the chance when her mother calls and asks, "Why don't you fly home this weekend and get measured for your hand-sewn human-hair wig?"[11]

Ellen goes home to be fitted for the wig, a huge French twist. All the women in her family wear the wig—her mother, her sister Marie, her Aunt Doodles. Ellen loves wearing it. She says that the "wig not only changed how I looked, it changed how I felt about myself. When I got back to school, boys stopped pursuing me…I abandoned…parties, and my study habits improved."[12] The *Three Faces of Eve*-like effect of the wig was very powerful: indeed, "when I was wearing the wig I dressed like a Duke sorority girl and studied calmly, but when I was not wearing the wig a certain wildness seemed to overtake me."[13]

At length the wig gets dirty, and she has to send it to the cleaners. The absence of her wig, which we now have to see as the mental equivalent of her girdle, makes Ellen do wild things with her copy of *Peyton Place* and her teddy bear. "I read the sex scenes of *Peyton Place* and drifted into them like hypnosis, my old teddy bear clutched tight between my legs. I felt bad about my teddy bear, who was not holding up well under this assault, but as long as I didn't touch myself, I was sure I couldn't be doing anything wrong."[14] Soon after, having picked up a boy named Nicky, she has the first companionate orgasm of her life. This orgasm imitates a scene in *Peyton Place*. This scene registers the first unashamed sex the thirty-three-year-old Constance MacKenzie ever has; it comes after a long night of confessing to her lover, Michael Rossi, the shameful sexual secrets of her youth. When they make love, Rossi says to MacKenzie things like "I love this fire in you" and "Your legs are absolutely wanton, do you know it?"[15] But the lines from *Peyton Place* Ellen Burns reports in the novel are "Do it to me" and "Your nipples are as hard as diamonds,"[16] and when she comes she shouts "Diamonds!"

Ellen masturbates so fervently in the six days the wig is at the cleaners that she wears the book out, and is buying another one when she meets Nicky. Grateful for this valuable orgasm, Ellen marries Nicky and takes to becoming a bourgeois liberal, that is, a social activist by day and a vague addict to inchoate sensation at night. This splitting also has to do with the pain of her lifelong exorbitance to the disciplinary culture of the girdle and the wig, and the violent abuse of her body by an uncle who loved, she says "the fears of children."[17] The uncle, Royce, burns her body with cigars: that her proper name seems almost to invite the form of the pain Ellen experiences is one of the many quiet ways the novel has of registering the ordinary violence of the identity form.

To survive these experiences Ellen disintegrates, as well she might. Yet none of her experience is recycled, finally, into the utopian language of a transformed consciousness or a desire for a world that might support her impulses toward revolutionary practices: the politics of identity and trauma she describes having engaged in during the seventies and eighties appear here to be drag performances indeed, but camp without the diva inflection.

Ellen does comes to participate in sexual politics, recognizably the lesbian feminism of the seventies and eighties. In 1973, "I was divorced and...proclaimed myself a lesbian revolutionary in a twenty-four page letter to my mother, who was not happy with this news."[18] But she turns out to have no respect for the history of her sexual experimentation, nor the politics that supports it. The novel mercilessly parodies 1970s "revolutionary" lesbian culture. This culture is characterized in the novel by: an addiction to cultivating altered consciousness, an association with alcoholism and other forms of chemical addiction and a deployment of a lifestyle discourse that takes her from the Ashram to AA—all of these modes of self-dramatization look suspiciously to Ellen, like liberal avant-garde self-indulgence, and in retrospect she seems like an exemplary player in a sexual farce about pseudo-freedom.

Ellen affirms the shallowness of her revolutionary lesbianism by temporalizing it as a mere series of distorted analogues: first she is married; seven years later she is "the left's newest lesbian";[19] "a number of years later...[she] had exchanged being a revolutionary for being a television writer in Hollywood";[20] "a number of years" later she falls in love with an analyst named Meg,[21] and yet "later" still the inner child appears to make revolution happen.

Yet for all this parody of the sexual revolution, Ellen never parodies her orgasms. Orgasm #2 changes everything about the inevitability of repeating the racy plots her heteromaternal genealogy seems to have left her. Indeed, sex with Meg breaks apart the image/narrative archive of straight identity logic:

> I saw visions making love with Meg, dark, swimming images of boys I'd been
> attracted to, women I'd thought I'd wanted, and people I'd never seen before: a
> man staring up at me through water, androgynous children with wise faces. Once I
> saw a landscape like a desert....[22]

There is nothing thematically lesbian about the archive of reference Ellen produces here. The revolution she wonders her way into experiencing not only reorganizes her erotic imaginary, but revitalizes and transforms her relation to revolutionary experience. It banishes the model of consciousness and identity performance central to the parodic anti-conventional aesthetic of the sexual liberation movement. But it retains from this movement the animating centrality of the orgasm as figure and engine of world transformation. This orgasm, not nearly as hard as diamonds, is consequently not a sign of the body's mastery over histories of repression: more *jouissance* than climax, it is an experience of breakdown and breakthrough. It frees Ellen from using sex as at all definitional. The form of the sex act, which has so long obsessed what counts as evidence for sexual identity in America, no longer matters; the exchange of identity and value that is conventionally the effect for which sexual relations are the cause is not the point.

This event opens Ellen up to history, and to a cluster of memories and connections that transform her relation to her future in it. Additionally, the nipple, the main organ of her sexual pleasure, becomes here a vehicle not of natural analogy or romantic capital but of sublime intimate violence, the violence of hard sucking, of scratching, and one pole of a whiplash between hard and gentle sex too, another movement that disregards, perhaps even breaks down, the circuit of sex-identity-abstract personhood we have seen as peculiarly American. Yet the very dialectic of this particular revolution divides Ellen from politics, and sexual politics, forever. The very orgasm that American feminist politics has helped her name—not as world-changing in itself, but as the sensational index of her power in the world—erases the conditions of its own production. Ellen becomes emptied entirely of a desire for history outside of the exorbitant personal narrative that now saturates her. She turns into Gloria Steinem.

The need for that politics, in its ambition to replace the violences of social domination with a world organized around modalities of personal and collective pleasure and creative agency, remains as an occluded possibility, transformed into what must be read as the post-feminist title of the book: *The Revolution of Little Girls*. The novel's transformation of political/sexual revolution into inner child discourse reveals, in my view, a regressive desire to deploy revolution to achieve a synthesis of self through the dissolution of the incommensurate histories and ideologies of entitlement and domination that constitute the scene of identity in practical life: if nothing else, this state of things might well push queers to relinquish the dream of an archive that will draw a transcendent boundary between any "us" and any living "other," a boundary based on property and privacy, and on the family's domination of the scene in which history and futurity are mediated and made habitable.

However, Boyd's text here turns to an analogy between an integrated personhood, politics, sexual identity, and home. Three inner children—a femme bulemic, a girl in a Supergirl costume decorated by the American flag, and a scarred, magical girl—appear to her as the unintegrated material of her self: they vomit hamburgers in the back of her car, go to the beach with her, speak to her, and come to her therapy sessions. But then, so strongly wanting not to have need, so strongly wanting to come to terms with a past she can actually possess and thus dispossess, Ellen allows them to return her to loving her mother. And she does this by literally letting them into her body, thus reversing mother-child causality by giving birth to her and securing a logic of natural extension not only from subjectivity to identity, but also from identity to intimate practice and political consciousness, now nicely territorialized.

Revolution becomes, then, equated with the most paradoxically representational form of utopia: the utopia without need that transcends the activity of transformation. It is not surprising that the image of this return to an ersatz-revolutionary synthetic self-politics returns as well to the self-pleasuring light of self-transcendence, which we first saw in her reading orgasm at *Peyton Place*. As the book ends and she lets the little girls become absorbed into her body, "I began to shudder from so much light." Not diamonds, exactly, but the refracted light from her enlightened metaphysic. And so the novel's title comes down to this: simply letting all of the complex and contradictory histories of love and abuse, capitalism and spirituality, social movements and sensual memory dissolve into the psychological kitsch of capitalist culture and its ongoing revolutions. This is not exactly a revolution in the bourgeois, nationalist, public sphere sense, for it requires the absorption of spectacle and not its production as well as the transformation of self and self-culture without a ripple effect or dialectical pressure in the world. On the other hand, the burden of the person to contain and take pleasure in the contradictory demands of a history saturated by the pseudo-activity of identity in the public sphere is, in the end, celebrated but now under the sign of the lesbian-maternal inner child, a hypercorporealized person in a synthetically abstract "adult" casing. Meanwhile, the stuff of personal and collectively supported sexual experiment is displaced into the archive of shame, silliness, and adolescent overvaluation.

But what has happened to the desire for a collective social practice that links revolutionary thinking, feeling, working, and self-knowing to challenging the modes of domination and exploitation that have become the ordinary everyday costs of survival in consumer society? What has happened to the desire for a sustained unembarrassed lesbian-feminist analytic that would seek to explain why buttfucking, masturbation, and orgasm remain vitally disturbing matter for legitimacy politics in the national public sphere? What has happened to a desire not for the end of history but its transformation? And what has happened to the notion of a revolution without low self-esteem?

I keep thinking of a moment from Jamaica Kincaid's novel *Lucy*. Coming from the West Indies to be a nanny in America, Lucy is amazed by the evacuations of self that white, bourgeois personhood seems to require. Living in America, she understands that, for all of its addiction to revolutionary change, the nation really produces and mourns the waste its revolutionary fetish generates. She begins to think of the revolutionary force of waste. She writes her name on a blank page and erases it with tears; she takes pictures of a space after the events that bring them into being have happened—she keeps the events open; she chronicles the decay and waste of quotidian life in America.

Experiencing the difference between radical and commodity privilege-saturated art, liberal politics and real thinking, pseudo-change and violence too sublime to be contained in official testimony or personal memory, Lucy re-thinks what it means to be historical, to be in history but not at its center: this requires her constantly to draw and erase the boundaries that dominate what she can explain and desire about personal and collective life, traversing the identity, family, sexual preference, and privilege model of the good life in the United States.

History is full of great events; when the great events are said and done, there will always be someone, a little person, happy, dissatisfied, discontented, not at home in her own skin, ready to stir up a whole new set of great events again.[23]

Lucy says this to herself, walking along the street, sometime in 1968. Refusing to abjure these minor objects, refusing to banalize the violences of economy and the logic of commodity personhood, refusing to embrace expensive notions of personal uniqueness as the source of utopian community—these refusals would allow us not to leave history or identity but to refuse the inevitable privatization of their dialectic. For what we have seen, here, and in this double reading of lesbian/queer revolutionary activity in America, is that the real fear we face, as scholars and activists, is not that queers in America will have sex, but that morning, noon and night, in the streets and everywhere, queers in America will have politics.

NOTES |

This essay was written in conjunction with another, by Michael Warner, titled "'69." Thanks to Michael, Geoff Eley, and Jody Greene for talking it through.

1 See Theodor Adorno, "Commitment," *The Essential Frankfurt School Reader*, eds. Andrew Arato and Eike Gebhardt (New York: Continuum, 1982), pp. 300–318.

2 I describe the subjectification of national identity through the mechanism of the national symbolic in *The Anatomy of National Fantasy* (Chicago: University of Chicago Press, 1991). See also Lauren Berlant and Elizabeth Freeman, "Queer Nationality," *Fear of a Queer Planet*, ed. Michael Warner (Minneapolis: University of Minnesota Press, 1994), pp. 193–229.

3 For more on the need to produce a contemporary politics of left revolutionary activity, see the important title essay of Ernesto Laclau's *New Reflections on the Revolution of Our Time* (New York: Verso, 1990), pp. 3–85.

4 Judith Butler, *Bodies that Matter: On the Discursive Limits of Sex* (New York: Routledge, 1993), pp. 226–230.

5 Lauren Berlant, "The Queen of America goes to Washington City (Harriet Jacobs, Frances Harper, Anita Hill)," *American Literature* 65, 3 (September, 1993), pp. 549–594.

6 Lauren Berlant, "'68, or something," *Critical Inquiry* (Summer 1994), forthcoming.

7 The non-diegetic quality of lesbian/queer cultural self-production has been most fully theorized by Teresa de Lauretis, both in *Technologies of Gender* (Bloomington: Indiana University Press, 1987) and in *differences* 3, 2 (Summer 1991), the special

issue she edited called "Queer Theory."

8 *New York Times*, 23 December, 1993, A1.

9 Blanche McCrary Boyd, *The Revolution of Little Girls* (New York: Random House, 1991), p. 185.

10 Boyd, *The Revolution of Little Girls*, p. 5.

11 Boyd, *The Revolution of Little Girls*, p. 53.

12 Boyd, *The Revolution of Little Girls*, p. 55.

13 Boyd, *The Revolution of Little Girls*, p. 56.

14 Boyd, *The Revolution of Little Girls*, p. 56.

15 Grace Metalious, *Peyton Place* (New York: Dell, 1956), p. 385.

16 Metalious, *Peyton Place*, p. 58.

17 Boyd, *The Revolution of Little Girls*, pp. 60–63.

18 Boyd, *The Revolution of Little Girls*, p. 16.

19 Boyd, *The Revolution of Little Girls*, p. 17.

20 Boyd, *The Revolution of Little Girls*, pp. 18–19.

21 Boyd, *The Revolution of Little Girls*, p. 21.

22 Boyd, *The Revolution of Little Girls*, p. 185.

23 Jamaica Kincaid, *Lucy* (New York: Penguin, 1990), p. 147.

Whispering into the hibiscus stalks and listening to breathing, he suddenly saw himself pawing around in the dirt for a not just crazy but also dirty woman who happened to be his secret mother that Hunter once knew but who orphaned her baby rather than nurse him or coddle him or stay in the house with him. A woman who frightened children, made men sharpen knives, for whom brides left out food (might as well—otherwise she stole it). Leaving traces of her sloven unhousebroken self all over the country.[1]

15

THE WILD WOMAN AND ALL THAT JAZZ

Drucilla Cornell

At the heart of Toni Morrison's novel *Jazz* is the allegory of the Wild Woman. This allegory also remains at the heart of my essay in which I offer a re-reading of the psychical fantasy of the Wild Woman and of wildness. If there is an imaginary figure who stands in the unconscious for the Woman who is beside herself it is undoubtedly this figure. The Wild Woman is figured as beside herself in at least two senses. She is beside herself in that she refuses both the very limitations of ego identity we call a self, and challenges the ordered world of established meaning imposed by the masculine symbolic. Indeed, she is the very figure of the limit of meaning. As Other to the masculine symbolic and the ordered world of sense she is a problematic figure for a certain kind of feminist. If the psychical fantasy of Woman splits us into two kinds—good girls and bad girls—the Wild Woman clearly threatens as the archetypical "bad" Woman. A feminism that wishes to show that feminism is a sensible project committed to a safe program of reform will hardly want to embrace this figure. And yet there is undoubtedly an association between the woman writer and this figure. How could it be otherwise in a symbolic order in which creativity is symbolized as phallic and the woman who dares to claim her own creativity will be read as stealing the phallus, appropriating what cannot rightfully be hers? Can one imagine the Wild Woman as other than the ultimate phallic woman who, complete in herself, is not driven to enter the masculine symbolic? No wonder she appears as so "scary," the witch whose powers must be taken from her if "man" is to defend himself and the established order of the symbolic.

And yet she is also the promise of the ecstasy of being beside oneself, no longer limited by ego identity. The consequences of being seen as "scary" and yet infinitely desirable have obviously been devastating for women who are read as "wild." What then can a woman writer do with this figure? What is the relationship between the re-reading of Wild for what has come to be identified as writing as a woman? Can a woman writer even tell the story "true" if she narrates her story so as to pass as the "good girl" whose image demands that she "whiten" herself to the point of erasure? In Morrison's allegory, we are forced to confront the operation of the psychical fantasy of Woman on the woman writer herself. And we are forced to confront the toll of passing on creativity. If the subject is passing, should there not be the expectation of a revelation in which the writer—and now I am speaking of myself—realizes and then confesses to just how she was passing and, as she does so, passes into some other story she thinks would be better to tell, thus transforming herself by the very confession? To tantalize you, I promise that there will be both a revelation and a confession. I promise too a transformation, because it can only be "made" through the enactment of a mimetic identification in which the significance of all that jazz can finally be "known," and with that knowledge, the other story can begin as it does with the re-reading of Wild in Toni Morrison's *Jazz*.

By the "enactment" of mimetic identification, I return to the discussion of mimesis in my first book, *Beyond Accommodation*.[2] I mean enactment in the psychoanalytic sense because it performs an identification that is not just given but must, through its enactment, be brought into "being." Through this enactment, which necessarily takes place within the established gender hierarchy with its fantasies of whom Woman "is," the meaning of the fantasies and the stereotypes of the feminine change as they are affirmed rather than repudiated. As such, such a re-reading is a political act. In *Jazz*, the confession crucial to the development of the other story, takes place through the enactment of just such a mimetic identification. That other story, which must begin as it does in *Jazz* with the return of the Wild Woman, is not a liberal story and therefore is incomptabile with the liberal feminism of the "good" girl.

It is not a liberal story, at least insofar as we identify liberalism with the separation of the "messy" world of private fantasy and desire from the realm of public debate and sensible politics. Jazz is out there, in the streets, in the meeting places, in the marches, in the air, everywhere, penetrating even into those who seek to keep it out:

> She knew from sermons and editorials that it wasn't real music—just colored folks stuff: harmful, certainly: embarrassing, of course; but not real, not serious. Yet Alice Manfred swore she heard a complicated anger in it; something hostile that disguised itself as flourish and roaring seduction. But the part she hated most was its appetite. Its longing for the bash, the slit; a kind of careless hunger for a fight or a red stickpin for a tie—either would do. It faked happiness, faked welcome, but it did not make her feel generous, this juke joint, barrel hooch, tonk music. It made her hold her hand in the pocket of her apron to keep from smashing it through the glass pane to snatch the world in her fist and squeeze the life out of it for doing what it did and did and did to her and everybody else she knew of knew about. Better to close the windows and the shutters, sweat in the summer heat of a silent Clifton Place apartment than to risk a broken window or a yelping that might not know where or how to stop.[3]

Jazz is the dissonance that disrupts the liberal's purportedly calm, rational, always in the daylight, public space, a space that at least in the fantasy is separable from the nightworld in which the "dark" side reigns and haunts this "whitened" world as its Other, which is inevitably signified as "black." The threat of jazz to the narrator is precisely that it puts her, and anyone else who will listen, besides herself. Jazz is dangerous because it signals the return of the repressed "dark" side. Of course, the liberal who prides herself or himself on being open to new experiences attempts to ignore the threat of jazz so that the public and symbolic significance of jazz cannot be acknowledged, enjoying it as music as long as it is safely kept in its proper place of aesthetic interest.

But jazz, all that jazz, can never be kept in its proper place. Jazz keeps breaking in, as the tremors that shake the foundation of so-called race-neutrality, which is always only a bar that pushes into the unconscious the significance of race so that the signifiers "whiteness" and "blackness" have so congealed that that which is signified as public reality appears as colorless. It is the bar that allows the liberal to "forget" that whiteness is a signifier that colors those to whom it is attributed with a series of beneficial characteristics, goodness, seriousness, rationality, calm, as all that is other to the "dark side." The color bar remains in that forgetting which erases the phantasmatic dimension of race and thus confuses figuration with a so-called reality that denies how the imagination envisions the Other as racialized and all that jazz as threatening precisely because it is associated with what is dark.

This forgetting accounts for the failure of liberalism, as I have defined it, "to notice a disrupting darkness before its eyes"[4] and at the same time, to dismiss all that other jazz as beyond the realm of rational cognizability. To begin to heed all that jazz in its metaphorical power and, therefore, in its public meaning, involves a call to remember, to go in reverse, back through the trajectory of figuration and symbolization, to imaginatively re-collect how and why certain figures have been "blackened." And there is no "blacker" figure than the Wild Woman, no greater foe, as I have already suggested, to civilized order. She is imagined to gobble up men without a qualm, steal their most prized possession and fly away with it over the moon without even glancing back. The ultimate "dark continent," she is the scariest of all women and thus, of course, the most desirable. Like Joe in Morrison's *Jazz*, unfortunately, to have her you have to kill her first. And then, of course, you are left with nothing at all. But the Wild Woman is never really dead, just pushed under and thus fated to return in another form. So she must be killed again and again, because in the end it is never She that dies, just her latest embodiment. Men see her everywhere, because they can't see her at all.

The story of the Wild Woman, because she is only as she is imagined by men, is not her story at all but the story of the men who try endlessly to hunt her down. A tragic tale, indeed, or so it has been told before the allegory of the Wild Woman in *Jazz*. She can only be re-collected in allegory precisely because she has been everywhere and forever dismembered. In bits and pieces, she can only be put together again if she is re-imagined, given body, touched and affirmed through mimetic identification as she is by the narrator in *Jazz* who finally,through this kind of recollection of the Wild Woman, begins to tell the story true. But who is the Wild Woman in *Jazz*?

The Wild Woman enters the scene of *Jazz* when the narrator re-collects how Joe and Violet's myths of the meaning of their past and their life together are intertwined in the myth of Golden Gray passed down to Violet by her grandmother True Belle and then re-told by the narrator. For those unfamiliar with the cast of *Jazz*, Joe and Violet are a married couple come up from the South to New York many years before. Joe is also the murderer of his teenage lover, Dorcas. Violet, in her metamorphosis as her other, "Violent," is a woman who tries to slash the face of the dead Dorcas. Alice Manfred is the woman who raised Dorcas, and at least until her acceptance of Violet/Violent, had to try to keep all that jazz out there, so it could not pull her niece down into its depths.

Of course, Alice does not succeed in protecting Dorcas, because who Dorcas was marked out to become in the story made it inevitable that she would respond to exactly what her aunt didn't want her to know. But Alice couldn't "know" this at the beginning of *Jazz*, anymore than Violet and Joe could "know" the truth about their own story, because the narrator herself, the story-teller, did not understand what she was trying to say and how to tell " the truth" of the story. She has to re-tell the myth of Golden Gray and the allegory of the Wild Woman and, then, in the very act of "telling", understands for the first time what she has told before; she can "know" and in her knowledge trans-forms the story.

I will re-tell the myth in which the allegory is contained. According to True Belle, she had, prior to her daughter Rose Dear's calling her to come help her with her children (including Violet), raised a beautiful mulatto who was "col-ored" in the hue of champagne. The boy, Golden Gray, was the son of True Belle's mistress, Vera Louise, who was disowned and fled to Baltimore with True Belle when it was discovered that she was pregnant and, worse yet, that the baby had been fathered by a "black" man. When he grew to adulthood, he deter-mined to kill the man who, in spite of his golden color, had marked him as "black." On the way to carry out his patricide, he came upon the Wild Woman and so frightened her that she fell against a tree and knocked herself uncon-scious. In spite of his horror of this wild being who seemed creature-like, not human, he felt he had to bring her to shelter once he discovered that she was pregnant. The shelter he finds belongs to Hunter, Golden Gray's father who arrives just in time to help deliver the Wild's baby. Wild refuses to touch or mother the child in any way and help has to be sent for to take the baby and nurse it. In the course of this event, finding the Wild Woman and participating in the birth of the baby, Golden Gray decides not to kill his father. As the narra-tor tells us, "it must have been the girl who changed his mind."[5] In the course of coming to terms with her own ambivalence about Golden Gray's attitude toward his "black" heritage, the narrator begins to understand that she is not telling the story "true," because she is missing a more profound comprehension of this young man and his character:

> What was I thinking of? How could I have imagined him so poorly? Not noticed the hurt that was not linked to the color of his skin, or the blood that beat beneath it. But to some other thing that longed for authenticity, for a right to be in this place, effortlessly without needing to acquire a false face, a laughless grin, a talking pos-ture. I have been careless and stupid and it infuriates me to discover (again) how unreliable I am...
>
> Now I have to think this through, carefully, even though I may be doomed to

another misunderstanding. I have to do it and not break down. Not hating him is not enough; liking, loving him is not useful. I have to alter things. I have to be a shadow who wishes him well, like the smiles of the dead left over from their lives. I want to dream a nice dream for him, and another of him. Lie down next to him, a wrinkle in the sheet, and contemplate his pain and by doing so ease it, diminish it. I want to be the language that wishes him well, speaks his name, wakes him when his eyes need to be open.[6]

Wild, of course, returned to the wilds, lurking in the forest, always lurking, but never "there." Hunter's Hunter sometimes thought he should have done a better job tending her and so does the narrator. Sometimes Hunter thought she was dead, but then her presence would be felt again, in a bite that came out of nowhere, a slight movement in the grass, quiet steps that were not those of an animal.

When Joe, as a young man, started to track with Hunter's Hunter, he, like everyone else, became obsessed with the Wild Woman. Obsessed, as well, with the fantasy of killing her. But Hunter warned him away, with a special look at Joe, that men should not prey on women and that he was to remember that she was somebody's mother. Joe, who was orphaned and lived with another family, saw in that look, for the first time, the "truth" of who Wild really was, his "real" mother: the one he desired more than anyone else, the one he had to find. Once, he sat by the hibiscus stalks and begged his mother to put out her hand, he begged for a sign. He got none. Finally, he found her cave, crawled in and was dazzled by a blinding light:

> Unable to turn around inside, he pulled himself all the way out to enter head first. Immediately he was in open air the domestic smell intensified. Cooking oil reeked under stabbing sunlight. Then he saw the crevice, He went into it on his behind until a floor stopped his slide. It was like falling into the sun. Noon light followed him like lava into a stone room where somebody cooked in oil.
>
>   . . .
>
> But where was she?[7]

Oh, to be back in that wonderful cave, to crawl back in and feel completely safe in that mother's body. No wonder Joe had to keep looking. Don't we all?

Of course, the Wild Woman has to be colored "black." In his discussion of the myth of the Wild woman of the forest, the anthropologist, Michael Taussig, points out that the very idea of wildness, and particularly of the Wild woman and of witchcraft, is profoundly associated with blackness.[8] In the end, there are only "black witches." To quote Taussig:

The Inquisition claimed to have uncovered covens of female witches worshiping the devil, and even in the covens of Spanish women it was alleged that women from Africa played a crucial role. It was also said that beyond the towns of the Christians, slave and free, pagan Indians were supplying those black women sorcerers with the herbs they required.[9]

And blackness, in turn, in its association with wildness is, for Taussig, what he calls the space of the death of signification:

> Wildness challenges the unity of the symbol, the transcendent totalization, binding the image to that which he represents. Wildness pries open this unity and in its place creates slippage and a grinding articulation between signifier and signified.[10]

Wildness, for Taussig, and the sinking into it, carries both the excitement and the danger of the purportedly pre-symbolic realm of that blackest of all women, the Phallic Mother. In a sense, wildness, if understood in this way, is close to what Julia Kristeva has referred to as the semeiotic.[11]

If wildness excites Taussig, it ultimately terrifies Kristeva who, particularly in her later work, leaves no place for the subversive power of the feminine semeiotic. To risk sinking into her again is to risk insanity. For Kristeva, it is only through the identification with the paternal and the ultimate abjection of the Phallic Mother that the subject can come in to writing.

But the problem is that such a writer, who abjects that Mother and that embrace, will get the story all wrong, just like the narrator did in *Jazz* when she was determined to keep all that jazz out in the street where it "belonged," in its "proper place" away from her:

> So I missed it altogether. I was sure one would kill the other. I waited for it so I could describe it. I was so sure it would happen. That the past was an abused record with no choice but to repeat itself at the crack and no power on earth could lift the arm that held the needle. I was so sure, and they danced and walked all over me. Busy, they were, busy being original, complicated, changeable—human, I guess you'd say—while I was the predictable one, confused in my solitude into arrogance, thinking my space, my view was the only one that was or that mattered. I got so aroused while meddling, while finger-shaping, I overreached and missed the obvious. I was watching the streets, thrilled by the buildings pressing and pressed by stone; so glad to be looking out and in on things I dismissed what went on in heart-pockets closed to me.[12]

Because the "heart-pockets" were closed to her, the narrator didn't even know

Joe wasn't really looking for Dorcas and that his tears weren't just for her. She didn't realize what Joe was seeking in Dorcas Wild's "chamber of gold." She also couldn't help her character Violet understand that Joe had just been a substitute for her unconscious love-object, that beautiful golden boy who haunted her life by his absence and yet was always a presence in a myth that shaped her character and limited who she could become. Once the writer knows the power of that myth, she can help Violet discharge it and help Joe and Violet come together differently. As a result, Violet can finally remember herself as the woman she wants to be:

> Now I want to be the woman my mother didn't stay around long enough to see. That one. The one she would have liked and the one I used to like before…. My grandmother fed me stories about a little blond child. He was a boy, but I thought of him as a girl sometimes, as a brother, sometimes as a boyfriend. He lived inside my mind. Quiet as a mole. But I didn't know it till I got here. The two of us. Had to get rid of it.[13]

Only when she stops being afraid and can read the significance of her own allegory of the Wild Woman can the narrator reach into those "heart-pockets" and tell the story true.

Here, in Morrison, we have the complete rejection of Kristeva's horror of the feminine imaginary. The Wild Woman is not the death space of signification, indeed, it is through her embrace that the narrator finds the language to tell the story true. The writer finally becomes the language, as she sought to do earlier, who wishes her characters well. Kristeva's writer only writes at the expense of the story as Morrison's narrator initially did. But the narrator, unlike Kristeva, learns.

> I'd love to close myself in the peace left by the woman who lived there and scared everybody. Unseen because she knows better than to be seen. After all, who would see her, a playful woman who lived in a rock? Who could, without fright? Of her looking eyes looking back? I wouldn't mind. Why should I? She has seen me and is not afraid of me. She hugs me. Understands me. Has given me her hand. I am touched by her. Released in secret.
>
> Now I know.[14]

Me too. Or, I hope I have learned the lesson she taught me: to finally admit it in public. I know Wild too and I address her when I write. I will go one step further. I love her. How could I not? She is the language that allows me to write as me. Finally to give up the shame so that you can make yourself up again and again as the other story, the truer one, the one faithful to the characters who remain beyond you. That's what she taught me to do. Give up the shame. To stop passing, to stop pretending that Wild is out there, nothing to do with me. And then the writer can live with the danger of the secret inherent in writing that what is written remains to be known. But how does any writer share that secret? The narrator of *Jazz* leaves us with the paradox of writing the story true.

> But I can't say that aloud; I can't tell anyone that I have been waiting for this all my life and that being chosen to wait is the reason I can. If I were able to say it. Say make me, remake me. You are free to do it and I am free to let you because look, look. Look where your hands are. Now.[15]

NOTES |

1 Toni Morrison, *Jazz* (New York: Alfred A. Knopf, 1992), p. 178.

2 Drucilla Cornell, *Beyond Accommodation: Ethical Feminism, Deconstruction, and the Law* (New York and London: Routledge, 1991).

3 Morrison, *Jazz*, p. 59.

4 Toni Morrison, *Playing in the Dark: Whiteness and the Literary Imagination* (Cambridge and London: Harvard University Press, 1992), p. 91.

5 Morrison, *Jazz*, p. 173.

6 Morrison, *Jazz*, pp. 160–61.

7 Morrison, *Jazz*, pp. 183–84.

8 Michael Taussig, *Shamanism Colonialism and the Wild Man: a Study of Terror and Healing* (Chicago: University of Chicago Press, 1986), pp. 218–19.

9 Taussig, *Shamanism*, pp. 218–19.

10 Taussig, *Shamanism*, p. 219.

11 See generally, Julia Kristeva, *Black Sun: Depression and Melancholia* (New York: Colombia University Press, 1989).

12 Morrison, *Jazz*, pp. 220–21.

13 Morrison, *Jazz*, p. 208.

14 Morrison, *Jazz*, p. 221.

15 Morrison, *Jazz*, p. 229.

CONTRIBUTORS |

LAUREN BERLANT teaches English at the University of Chicago. She is the author of *The Anatomy of National Fantasy: Hawthorne, Utopia and Everyday Life* (University of Chicago Press, 1991).

RACHEL BOWLBY teaches English at Sussex University. She is the author of a number of books on topics related to consumer culture, psychoanalysis, feminism and literature: *Just Looking* (Methuen, 1985), *Virginia Woolf: Feminist Destinations* (Blackwell, 1988); *Still Crazy After All These Years: Women, Writing and Psychoanalysis* (Routledge, 1992), and *Shopping with Freud* (Routledge, 1993).

KARIN COPE teaches in the English Department at McGill University. She is at work on a book on Gertrude Stein entitled *Passionate Collaborations: The Making of Gertrude Stein* (University of Minnesota Press, forthcoming).

DRUCILLA CORNELL is Professor at Benjamin N. Cardozo School of Law, Yeshiva University. She is the author of *Transformations* (Routledge, 1993), *The Philosophy of the Limit* (1992), and *Beyond Accommodation* (1991), all published by Routledge, and *The Imaginary Domain: A New Perspective on Abortion, Pornography, and Sexual Harassment* (Routledge, forthcoming).

DIANE ELAM teaches in the English Department at Indiana University and McGill University. She is the author of *Feminism and Deconstruction: Ms. en Abyme* (1994) and *Romancing the Postmodern* (1992), both published by Routledge.

SUSAN STANFORD FRIEDMAN is Virginia Woolf Professor of English and Women's Studies at the University of Wisconsin-Madison. She is the author of *Psyche Reborn: The Emergence of H. D.* (Indiana University Press 1981) and *Penelope's Web: Gender, Modernity, H. D.'s Fiction* (Cambridge University Press, 1990); co-author of *A Woman's Guide to Therapy* (Prentice Hall, 1979); co-editor of *Signets: Reading H. D.* (University of Wisconsin Press, 1990); editor of *Joyce: The Return of the Repressed* (Cornell University Press, 1993) and guest editor of a special issue of *The Journal of Narrative Technique* (1990).

SUSAN GUBAR is Distinguished Professor of English and Women's Studies at Indiana University. She has collaborated with Sandra Gilbert on a number of critical books: *The Madwoman in the Attic* (Yale University Press, 1979), *No Man's Land: The Place of the Woman Writer in the Twentieth Century* (Vol I, *The War of the Words*; Vol. II, *Sexchanges*) (Yale University Press, 1988), and the forthcoming

Letters from the Front. Together, they are currently working on a new edition of their *Norton Anthology of Literature by Women.*

DANA HELLER is Assistant Professor of American Literature and Gender Studies at Old Dominion University. She is the author of *The Feminization of Quest-Romance: Radical Departures* (University of Texas Press, 1990) and *Family Plots: Gender, Romance, and the Private Sphere,* (University of Pennsylvania Press, forthcoming).

CYRAINA JOHNSON-ROULLIER is an Assistant Professor of English and Comparative Literatures at the University of Notre Dame. She is the author of "The Echo of Narcissus: Anxiety, Reflexivity and Language in '*Envois,*'" *International Studies in Philosophy* and "Joyce Inside the Other or, the Flip Side of the Cultural Icon"*(James Joyce Broadsheat).* She is currently working on a book on the role of "otherness" in modernism.

MARIE LESSARD is presently completing her doctoral thesis at the Department of Comparative Literature of the Université de Montréal ("Les récits autobiographiques chez Marguerite Duras et Kathy Acker: postmodernité, réécriture de la modernité ou pratique d'écriture féminine?"). She is the author of "Narración y escritura de la historia," published in *El Quebec tiene cara de mujer,* ed. Blanca Arancibia Rosario, Editorial de la Luna nueva, Argentine, 1994. Forthcoming: "Narration et écriture de l'histoire. Étude comparative de deux romans historiques canadiens" (Les Éditions Balzac, 1996).

FEDWA MALTI-DOUGLAS is Professor of Arabic, Semiotics, and Women's Studies and Chairperson of the Department of Near Eastern Languages and Cultures at Indiana University. She has published extensively in Arabic, French, and English on classical and modern Islamic studies. Her two latest books are *Woman's Body, Woman's Word: Gender and Discourse in Arabo-Islamic Writing* (Princeton University Press, 1991) and, with Allen Douglas, *Arab Comic Strips: Politics of an Emerging Mass Culture* (Indiana University Press, 1994). Her study of Nawal El Saadawi, *Men, Women, and God(s): Nawal El Saadawi and Arab Feminist Poetics* is forthcoming as a Centennial Book from the University of California Press.

CHRISTIE MCDONALD is Professor of Romance Languages and Literatures at Harvard University. She is the author of *The Dialogue of Writing* (Wilfrid Laurier University Press, 1984), *Dispositions: Quatre Essais sur les écrits de Jean-Jacques Rousseau, Stéphane Mallarmé, Marcel Proust et Jacques Derrida.* (Montréal, Hurtubise HMH, 1986) and *The Proustian Fabric* (University of Nebraska Press, 1991).

DEBORAH E. MCDOWELL is Professor of English at the University of Virginia. She is the author of *The Changing Same: Studies in Fiction by Black Women* (Indiana University Press, forthcoming), co-editor with Arnold Rampersand of *Slavery and the Literary Imagination* (John Hopkins University Press, 1989), and founding editor of the Beacon Black Women Writers Series.

ELSPETH PROBYN is an Associate Professor in the Département de sociologie, Université de Montréal, where she teaches cultural studies. She is the author of *Sexing the Self: Gendered Positions in Cultural Studies* (Routledge, 1993), co-editor with Elizabeth Grosz of *Sexy Bodies: Feminist and Queer Corporalities* (Routledge, forthcoming), and has published numerous articles on feminist theory.

JUDITH ROOF teaches at Indiana University. She is the author of *A Lure of Knowledge: Lesbian Sexuality and Theory* (Columbia University Press, 1991), and has written essays on feminist theory, film, modern drama, psychoanalysis, and law. She is also the co-editor of *Who Can Speak?* (University of Illinois Press, forthcoming) and *Feminism and Psychoanalysis* (Cornell University Press, 1989).

SABINA SAWHNEY teaches English at Daemen College and has published articles on feminism and postcolonial literature. She is currently working on *The Other Colonialists: Imperial Margins of Victorian Literature,* which deals with the impact of colonialism on the narrative structure of nineteenth-century British novels.

VALERIA WAGNER teaches English literature at the Université de Genève. She is currently working on issues of agency in literary and philosophical texts.

ROBYN WIEGMAN is Assistant Professor of Women's Studies and English at Indiana University. Her *American Anatomies: Theorizing Race and Gender* is forthcoming from Duke University Press. She has also co-edited, along with Judith Roof, *Who Can Speak?* (University of Illinois Press, forthcoming).

INDEX